RETAIL BUYING
FROM BASICS TO FASHION

SIXTH EDITION

RICHARD CLODFELTER

University of South Carolina

FAIRCHILD BOOKS

NEW YORK · LONDON · OXFORD · NEW DELHI · SYDNEY

FAIRCHILD BOOKS
Bloomsbury Publishing Inc
1385 Broadway, New York, NY, 10018, USA
50 Bedford Square, London, WC1B 3DP, UK
29 Earlsfort Terrace, Dublin 2, Ireland

FAIRCHILD BOOKS and the Fairchild Books logo are trademarks of
Bloomsbury Publishing Plc

Fourth edition published 2012
Fifth edition published 2015
This edition published 2018
Reprinted 2019 (twice), 2020, 2021

For legal purposes the Acknowledgments on p. x constitute an extension of this copyright page.

Cover design by Eleanor Rose
Cover images © Getty Images

No responsibility for loss caused to any individual or organization acting on or refraining from
action as a result of the material in this publication can be accepted by Bloomsbury Publishing Inc
or the author.

Library of Congress Cataloging-in-Publication Data

Names: Clodfelter, Richard, author.
Title: Retail buying : from basics to fashion / Richard Clodfelter, University of South Carolina.
Description: 6th edition. | New York, NY : Fairchild Books, 2018. | Includes index.
Identifiers: LCCN 2017035643 | ISBN 9781501331978 (pbk.)
Subjects: LCSH: Purchasing. | Merchandising.
Classification: LCC HF5429 .C54 2018 | DDC 658.8/700687—dc23
LC record available at https://lccn.loc.gov/2017035643

ISBN: PB: 978-1-5013-3197-8
       ePDF: 978-1-5013-3198-5
       eBook: 978-1-5013-3199-2

Typeset by Lachina
Printed and bound in the United States of America

To find out more about our authors and books visit www.fairchildbooks.com and sign up for our
newsletters.

CONTENTS

EXTENDED CONTENTS

PREFACE

The purpose of *Retail Buying* is to prepare students for merchandising careers in retailing. Throughout the text, students are introduced to basic concepts, principles, and techniques used by retail buyers as they complete their day-to-day duties and responsibilities. For example, step-by-step approaches are presented for buying tasks such as these: identifying and understanding potential customers, developing sales forecasts, preparing a six-month merchandise plan, planning merchandise assortments, preparing an assortment plan, identifying criteria for selecting vendors, preparing for a market visit, negotiating with vendors, making purchases in a foreign market, placing an order, and coordinating promotional activities. References to a wide range of merchandising careers are also found in the text.

Up-to-date information about current buying practices and techniques can be found throughout the text. Specifically, the impact of technology and social media on retail buying is emphasized. For example, understanding customers through techniques such as retail analytics, data warehousing, data mining, database marketing, RFID (radio frequency identification) technologies, and mobile marketing are highlighted. In addition, globalization concepts and the impact of foreign purchasing are also emphasized. Basic mathematical calculations performed by retail buyers are also included to review and reinforce students' retail math skills.

Features of the Text to Enhance Learning

Many special features are used in *Retail Buying* to explain buying concepts in a challenging and practical manner.

- Each chapter begins with a list of *Performance Objectives* and ends with a *Summary* of key points presented in the chapter.
- Throughout the text, tables present current data that affect many aspects of the retail buyer's job, illustrations show examples of current retail practices in actual stores or showrooms, and sample forms used by buyers are presented to illustrate the kinds of reports that buyers may encounter.

- *Vocabulary terms* related to retail buying are also highlighted in the text and listed at the end of each chapter.
- A variety of questions are included for each chapter. *Understanding What You Read* questions can be used to generate class discussion and review information presented in the chapter. *Analyzing and Applying What You Read* questions provide students with the opportunity to explore buying principles presented in the chapter in practical situations. For chapters with a heavy math focus, math exercises are provided in *Retail Buying Math Practice* sections.
- An *Internet Connection* section is included in each chapter. Suggested activities that utilize research on the internet are presented to reinforce material found in the chapter. Additionally, online videos are cited to enhance concepts in the chapter.
- To further develop concepts found in each chapter, Snapshots are included to present up-to-date highlights of current merchandising concepts, strategies, and techniques being used by actual businesses. The goals of the *Snapshots* are to spark student interest and make the material found in each chapter more relevant.
- *Trendwatch* sections are also included to enhance the material in each chapter and make it more relevant. Examples of current trends are presented related to content presented in the chapter. Remember, however, that trends by their very nature were developing as this text was being written and published. Students will want to continually monitor the marketplace to discover new trends as they begin to appear.

Retail Buying STUDIO

An online multimedia resource—*Retail Buying STUDIO*—is also included. The online *STUDIO* is specially developed to complement this book with rich media ancillaries that students can adapt to their visual learning styles to better master concepts and improve grades. For those chapters that include retail math concepts, students have the opportunity to apply those concepts by developing and using spreadsheets.

- Study smarter with self-quizzes featuring scored results and personalized study tips.
- Review concepts with flashcards of essential vocabulary and basic retail math formulas.
- Practice your skills with downloadable Excel spreadsheets to complete the end-of-chapter *Spreadsheet Skills* exercises.
- Enhance your knowledge with printable worksheets featuring step-by-step solutions to common retail buying math problems.
- Watch videos related to chapter concepts.

STUDIO access cards are offered free with new book purchases and are also sold separately through www.Fairchild Books.com.

Instructor Resources

- An instructor's guide is available with the text and presents suggested teaching ideas and a key to chapter review activities.
- A test bank of questions with an answer key is provided for each chapter.

Instructor resources may be accessed through www.Fairchild Books.com.

Chapter Highlights

In Part I, "Understanding the Retail Environment Where Buying Occurs," students will learn that to be a successful buyer, they must understand the retail environment in which buying occurs. The first three chapters introduce buying practices and procedures of various types of retail businesses. In Chapter 1, students are introduced to buying and are presented an orientation to factors that will influence many of the decisions that buyers make, such as online retailing, mobile and social media platforms, and omnichannel approaches. A discussion of trends and challenges facing retailers is also included. In Chapter 2, students examine merchandising careers in retailing. Detailed job descriptions for a buyer, assistant buyer, and merchandise manager are presented. Information is also presented on how to plan for an internship or career in retail buying. In addition, the chapter emphasizes the use of calculating quantitative measurements to evaluate a buyer's performance. In Chapter 3, students learn how the buyer's job differs in various types of retail formats. A discussion is included on how the distinction between many of these formats is blurring. Retail organizational structures are presented, and the relationship of merchandising to other departments is highlighted. The chapter also emphasizes how to mathematically measure the success of strategic decisions that buyers make.

Part II, "Getting Ready to Make Buying Decisions," discusses how, once buyers understand the marketplace, they need to develop an understanding of customers and trends affecting future sales. In Chapter 4, students examine sources of information that would be available to them when making buying decisions. Internal and external sources are described. In Chapter 5, information is presented to help buyers better understand their customers. Recent changes in the consumer markets are described, and reasons why customers buy are discussed. Targeting customers by using technology, such as database marketing, data mining, and data warehousing, is examined. In Chapter 6, students gain an understanding of what types of products customers purchase. New product trends, especially products with fashion appeal, are studied. Product life cycles and fashion adoption theories are explained.

Part III, "Planning and Controlling Merchandise Purchases," deals with making purchasing plans once retail buyers understand their customers and the retail environment in which they will be operating. In Chapter 7, the scope of forecasting is described, and students examine the steps for developing effective sales forecasts. In addition, material is presented about forecasting decisions to predict inventory needs. Emphasis is also placed on how retail analytics will impact the future of retail buying. In Chapter 8, students learn how to develop merchandise plans for fashion and basic merchandise. In Chapter 9, students plan merchandise assortments and develop an assortment plan. In Chapter 10, different inventory control plans are presented, and the mathematical calculations needed by buyers are explained. RFID is described in relation to purchase planning and merchandise control.

Part IV, "Purchasing and Pricing Merchandise," concerns how buyers who have prepared their merchandise plans are now ready to select vendors from whom to make purchases. In Chapter 11, students examine various types of vendors and learn how to identify criteria for selecting them. The development of partnerships between retailers and vendors is emphasized. In Chapter 12, steps for planning a market trip are explained in detail. Negotiation practices frequently used by buyers are presented. The focus is on developing a negotiation strategy that results in a win-win outcome. In Chapter 13, students examine a step-by-step process for using foreign sourcing to make planned purchases. Benefits and drawbacks of foreign purchasing are also discussed. In Chapter 14, terms of the sale and special buying situations are described. Procedures for placing the final order are presented. In Chapter 15, students examine the mathematical calculations needed to price incoming merchandise and make price adjustments on in-stock merchandise.

Appendix A, "Basic Retail Math Formulas," is presented as a handy reference to review the basic math used in merchandising. Appendix B, "Decision Making," outlines a step-by-step process of approaching individual and group decision making in classroom activities, as well as in retail buying careers. A glossary of over 250 terms related to retail buying is included for students to use as a quick reference of key terms found in the text.

ACKNOWLEDGMENTS

The sixth edition of *Retail Buying,* like the five previous editions, has been based on extensive research involving both secondary and primary sources. Many retail professionals have provided me with information on current buying practices that are included in this text. Representatives of Parisian, Bloomingdale's, Racke's, Rich's, Lowe's, Hartmarx Corporation, Walmart, Carolinas-Virginia Fashion Exhibitors, Belk, and Belk Store Services provided the answers to many questions as previous editions were written. In addition, many educators provided me with a wealth of comments and suggestions that have been incorporated in this text. Special thanks to J.C. Penney, where I completed a two-week professor internship with the retailer at their store in Columbia, South Carolina, and at corporate headquarters in Dallas, Texas. Special thanks also go to the Direct Marketing Association and the Direct Marketing Educational Foundation for allowing me to participate in two institutes for direct and interactive marketing.

I also appreciate the many helpful suggestions made by the reviewers of the manuscript for this edition. These experienced and creative instructors included Misha Behbehani, FIDM; Katherine Burnsed, University of South Carolina; Carol Lazich, George Brown College; Jemma Oeppen, University of South Wales; Dong Shen, California State University, Sacramento; Adele Thorley, Birmingham City University; and Carol Lazich, George Brown College.

I remain grateful to Mary McGarry, Joann Muscolo, Jaclyn Bergeron, Amy Butler, Linda Feldman, and Amanda Breccia, former editors at Fairchild, for their guidance and encouragement in previous editions. Finally, I am especially grateful to Corey Kahn, Fairchild development editor, for this revision.

The publisher wishes to gratefully acknowledge and thank the editorial team involved in the publication of this book:

Acquisitions Editor: Wendy Fuller
Development Editor: Corey Kahn
Editorial Assistant: Bridget McAvoy
Art Development Editor: Edie Weinberg
In-House Designer: Lachina
Production Manager: Claire Cooper
Project Manager: Chris Black

PART 1

UNDERSTANDING THE RETAIL ENVIRONMENT WHERE BUYING OCCURS

TODAY'S BUYING ENVIRONMENT

CHAPTER 1

Performance Objectives

- Recognize the importance of understanding the retail environment when making buying decisions.
- Describe how online retailing has changed the retail environment and its impact on decisions made by retail buyers.
- Identify mobile and social media strategies that can benefit retail buyers.
- Differentiate between multichannel and omnichannel retailing.
- Identify examples of how omnichannel strategies have been implemented by retailers.
- Identify current trends affecting retailing and buying.

Welcome to the exciting world of buying, one of many functions occurring every day in all retail businesses. By its very nature, retailing is dynamic and continuously changing. Within a single season, the merchandise assortment and market position of a retailer can be altered, and virtually overnight, pricing, promotions, and inventory levels can be changed. Within this fast-changing environment, buyers are making merchandising decisions daily.

INTRODUCTION

Retailing consists of all the business activities involved in the selling of goods and services to the ultimate consumers. Retailing, however, does not always require a store. Catalog sales, vending machines, e-commerce, and mall kiosks all fit within the scope of retailing. No matter where retailing occurs, however, someone must perform the buying function. **Buying** is the business activity that involves selecting and purchasing products to satisfy the wants and needs of consumers. Buying involves complex decision making in areas such as

- forecasting the wants and needs of consumers;
- planning merchandise assortments to satisfy consumer wants and needs;
- selecting vendors from whom to purchase merchandise;
- negotiating contracts with vendors;
- pricing merchandise;
- keeping sales and inventory records; and
- reordering merchandise.

Over the next several weeks, you will learn more about buying as well as develop skills necessary to perform these primary buying tasks. But first, some of the major forces affecting the retailing environment, such as online retailing, mobile technologies, social media, and omnichannel retailing, will be described, and their impact on retail buying will be presented. Trends that will be affecting the future of both retailing and buying will also be examined. Retailing may look quite different tomorrow from the way it looks today. Because retailing is changing, the buying function is also changing. If you are to be a successful buyer, you need to understand where customers currently make purchases and where and how they are likely to make them in the future.

E-COMMERCE AND ONLINE RETAILING

One of the key forces that is dramatically impacting traditional shopping is online retailing. Today, e-commerce and **online retailing** continue to grow and thrive worldwide, creating a customer shift from in-store to online shopping. In fact, as shown in Figure 1.1, online sales revenues are forecast to grow about 65 percent from 2015 to 2021, and with the proliferation of smartphones and tablets, that growth is expected to continue at a rapid rate. In fact, one recent consumer survey found that almost half of Americans prefer to shop online, but that percentage is much higher for younger age groups, which are most attractive to many retailers. Moreover, 56 percent of Gen Xers and 67 percent of millennials indicated they preferred to shop online rather than in the store.

What has emerged is that many of the traditional **bricks-and-mortar** retailers—those firms who, in the past, had storefronts on Main Street or in the mall—developed a **clicks-and-mortar** approach. In other words, these retailers developed an online presence in addition to their traditional storefronts. For these companies, online retailing created another **touchpoint** in the marketplace where customers could interact with retailers and make purchases. For example, even when making an online purchase, physical stores remain vital for many customers—25 percent of consumers have made an online purchase while they were in the retailer's store.

Figure 1.1

Retail E-Commerce Sales in United States from 2015–2021 (Ranked by billions of dollars). Online sales revenues are forecast to grow about 65 percent from 2015 to 2021.

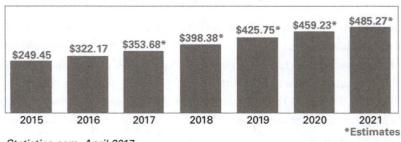

Statistica.com, April 2017

Benefits of Online Retailing

The internet is truly a global medium that allows shoppers to click from a retailer in their local community to another retailer halfway around the world—in seconds. This ease and convenience of making purchases is cited by most customers as to why they prefer making purchases online (Figure 1.2). For most shoppers, online purchasing means no waiting in long lines, especially if they have children in tow. Other online shoppers, especially young working millennials, are less and less interested in making store visits that require a major allocation of time. In contrast, the internet provides 24/7 access and allows for a leisurely shopping experience at a convenient time for them. Moreover, many consumers shop online because it allows them to find the best price for products more efficiently across many different websites, instead of having to physically visit many different stores. In addition, customers may also find a greater selection of merchandise online, particularly in sizes and colors offered.

For retailers, e-commerce sites can have benefits over a bricks-and-mortar store. Online sites usually do not require expensive storefronts; instead, more cost-effective warehouses can be used to store, hold, and distribute merchandise for online sales. This is especially true for **pure play** retailers who only operate online. Another advantage that online retailing offers is the savings generated from not having the heavy advertising and promotion budgets that bricks-and-mortar retailers typically have. Communicating with consumers online costs a lot less than communicating with them using traditional media such as print and broadcast. A digital catalog can be produced for much less than the cost of reproducing and mailing printed ones. Online promotion also offers greater flexibility, allowing retailers to make real-time adjustments to their promotional offers. In fact, an online catalog can be adjusted daily or even hourly, adapting product assortments, prices, and promotions to match changing market conditions. To acquire new customers, however, most online retailers, such as the one shown in Figure 1.3, must also use some traditional advertising.

Figure 1.2
Convenience is cited most often by customers who prefer to make purchases online.

Figure 1.3
Many online retailers must still rely on traditional advertising to attract customers.

Challenges of Online Retailing

Online retailing, however, faces some challenges. The internet offers millions of websites and a staggering volume of information. Thus, navigating the internet can be frustrating, confusing, and time-consuming for some consumers. Also, many online shoppers still worry that unscrupulous snoopers will intercept their credit card numbers and make unauthorized purchases.

Among other reasons cited for consumer resistance to making online purchases and preference for in-store shopping are the ability to see the products in person, the simplicity of making in-store returns, and the ability to ask a sales associate in the store lots of questions. Loss of privacy, however, remains a primary concern for many online customers. Additionally, one of the most important challenges facing online retailers is quick delivery. Most shoppers want their purchases immediately, yet "same day or next day delivery" is an added expense for retailers that must be passed on to the customers in some way.

Another challenge facing online retailers is that the average purchase for in-store shoppers is higher than online; in-store customers tend to make more impulse purchases. In-store merchandise displays can still influence shoppers to make an impulse purchase, and they are much harder to ignore than online ads. In fact, 40 percent of shoppers spend more than they had planned while shopping in stores, but only 25 percent of shoppers do so when shopping online. Online ads and promotions will need to be more enticing to cause shoppers to browse more of the site after they find the product they came online to purchase.

For several reasons, online has *not* turned into big business for some retailers who operate their online channel as a separate entity in the company. The reality is that far too many retailers have been lagging in their online product offerings. They have offered a wide variety of products in their stores, but their online channel featured a limited inventory that was stocked separately in dedicated online fulfillment centers.

Today, online shoppers readily purchase books, food, and clothing online, yet many of them hesitate before making purchases of high-end items such as appliances and furniture, and for more expensive purchases, online shoppers want more than the retailer just to accept a credit card. They are looking for other types of longer-term financing, which most online sites do not currently offer. Also, many customers shop as a social activity or a day to browse with friends—an experience that simply cannot be duplicated online.

Online Shopper Expectations

In an effort to keep up with ever-connected consumers' changing expectations, retailers often trade basic merchandising strategies in favor of eye-catching online experiences. Some companies have focused on driving sales growth through experiential services such as live chat, social media integration, and even virtual reality videos. But, many retailers fail to optimize baseline customer experience—a practice that provides the basic details shoppers need to make a purchasing decision. One research report indicated that 78 percent of respondents said the quality of online product content was very important when making purchase decisions, and one fourth of them had abandoned an online purchase because of poor product information.

Online shoppers also expect quick service with lightning-fast load times. A third of online shoppers will click away if they have to wait more than five seconds for a page to load. The portion of users who click away while waiting for a page to load is referred to as the **bounce rate**. However, they are willing to wait longer if they can expect a solid deal when they connect. Lost online shoppers means lost revenue for retailers, and it can be a significant loss. For example, two-thirds of retailers consider each online visitor worth a minimum of twenty dollars, and some merchants estimate their value at much more than that. So the loss of thousands of potential sales due to slow-loading pages can be a real problem.

Small conveniences can make a big difference with online sales. Pages must be optimized for smartphones and tablets, and checkout should be as simple as possible. Customers are just as frustrated online having to wait as they are waiting in a store. Customers should be offered opt-in capabilities where they can make purchases with just one click. Making it easier for shoppers to pay for purchases with fewer clicks (using Apple Pay, PayPal, credit card information on file, etc.) can pay off with greater sales. Above all, online retailers must stand out from the competition.

Future of Online Retailing

As Americans continue to do more of their shopping online, local bricks-and-mortar retailers are suffering. Yet, despite the ease of online shopping, many consumers still prefer shopping in a physical store. Even though physical stores are still formidable at selling merchandise, their share of total sales has been declining for over a decade, but more importantly, the line between in-store and online retailing has blurred.

In the future, more consumers are going to shop online, but many of them will still enter stores to interact with sales associates, learn more about the product, try it on, and experience its quality. Customers may not purchase the product in the store, but without that store interaction, it is likely that many sales would not occur. An increasing number of shoppers are **showrooming**, by visiting local bricks-and-mortar retail stores before they go online to compare prices and make a purchase. Meanwhile, a large number of customers participate in **reverse showrooming**, where they research products online before making an in-store purchase to avoid the wait to receive the merchandise and to avoid shipping charges. Companies must realize that both shopping processes are now part of the retailing landscape, and they must better integrate both in-store and online experiences for their customers.

Even the largest retailers are betting on the continued growth of online retailing. Walmart's acquisition of Jet.com, an online marketplace, is noteworthy since it shows that chain's belief that its future growth will be online. Sam's Club is also betting on the growth of online retailing; their web site now gets 16 million visits a month and offers 51,000 different items for sale. Furthermore, Sam's has also launched daily deals to spur online growth even more.

Neither is the largest online retailer resting on past success. In fact, Amazon is doing so many different things on so many different fronts that it is not surprising that other retailers are having a difficult time keeping up. The company seems to be relentlessly innovating. One of the innovations that has had immediate impact is Amazon Prime memberships, which offer free deliveries to shoppers who are members. In fact, during one five-year period, households that subscribed to Amazon Prime grew from 10 percent to 30 percent. More importantly, over two-thirds of Prime users say they tend to check Amazon before buying anything online. Additionally, Amazon already offers one-hour delivery service to Prime members in thirty metropolitan areas worldwide, and during a recent Christmas season, Amazon was responsible for 46 percent of online sales in the United States. The next closest competitors were Best Buy, Walmart, and Target, at less than 5 percent each. For a list of the ten most popular online sites, based on unique online visitors, examine Figure 1.4. Amazon.com was a clear number one. Both Amazon's breadth of assortments and efficiencies built into the ordering process resonated with shoppers.

Many traditional retailers are struggling as online shopping continues to accelerate. But, they are also faced with other problems such as declining mall traffic, time-strapped consumers, and more price-conscious shoppers. Online has changed the retailing environment very quickly, and to remain competitive, retailers will need to try lots of new and innovative ideas.

Figure 1.4

Most Popular Retail Websites in the United States (Ranked by millions of visitors). Amazon is clearly the most popular online site based on unique visitors.

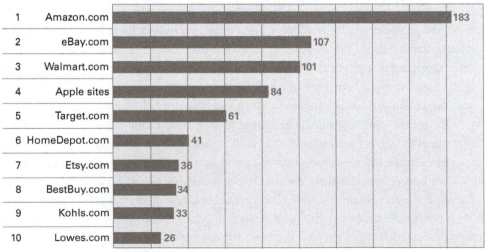

Statistica.com, July 2016. Numbers are in millions

MOBILE TECHNOLOGIES AND SOCIAL MEDIA

For years, retail had been neatly divided into two categories—online and bricks-and-mortar. But, the arrival of technologies such as smartphones and tablets created a new retail environment melding the digital and physical worlds. In fact, engaging consumers on their smartphones is one of the biggest opportunities for retailers in that they provide them with unprecedented opportunities for interaction with consumers (Figure 1.5). For many of these consumers, smartphones have become an extension of themselves—they cannot leave home without relying on them every day, from getting directions to obtaining product reviews to making purchases. Furthermore, facilitated by the convenience of constant access through smartphones, many consumers go online over 100 times a day. In addition, millions of consumers regularly frequent online **social media** platforms, which provide another means by which retailers can reach and influence consumers.

Social media as a communication tool has the ability to build relationships and communities between individuals who share common interests, and for many of them, shopping is a common interest. The sheer number of individuals already accessing sites such as Facebook, Pinterest, Twitter, YouTube, Google+, or LinkedIn cannot be ignored by retailers. In fact, recent estimates indicate that social media users *influenced* more than $1 trillion in total purchases in the United States.

Impact of Social Media

Over the last several years, consumers have shifted from being passive recipients of pushed information, such as direct mail and advertising, to being active, informed shoppers. For most retailers, this means that traditional marketing efforts alone will no longer be as effective as they once were. Social media has allowed consumers to wield more power and influence than ever, and retailers that listen and engage with consumers on those platforms can find opportunities for business growth. In fact, over

Figure 1.5
Engaging consumers on their smartphones is one of the biggest opportunities for retailers.

90 percent of retailers have begun investing in social media marketing to some degree. These retailers are increasing their online merchandising budgets, a portion of which is clearly earmarked for social media activities that engage consumers to promote two-way interaction.

Yet, promotion through social media should not be approached haphazardly; it must be a planned strategy. When implementing social media as an element of the promotional mix, retailers should choose a few critical social media platforms that are most relevant to the company's target market. Then, the social media platforms selected should be used to conduct meaningful dialogues with users that are both relevant and engaging.

Social media is not going to replace a retailer's overall marketing strategy, but it should become another element in the promotional mix that allows stores to communicate with and influence consumer purchasing decisions. Social media should be used to broaden the reach of existing marketing initiatives. For example, if a retailer has an ad campaign running on TV, they should also post it on Facebook, Twitter, and other social media platforms and include a link to a YouTube clip of the commercial. The difficult task will be in finding the right balance between using social media and the other elements of the promotional mix.

Social Media Strategies

Many retailers are already using social media channels like Facebook, Pinterest, and Twitter to advertise, respond to customer service questions, and drive sales with "buy now" buttons. Some retail buyers are also using data gathered on social media platforms combined with other data to better gauge consumer perceptions and potential buying behavior. In fact, mobile and social media are keys to the promotional efforts of many retailers.

For example, the beauty retailer Sephora has implemented mobile marketing efforts as a means to enhance retail sales in their stores. In fact, management views mobile technology as the ultimate bridge between the in-store and digital shopping experiences of their customers. The company targets its customers with a mobile app that allows customers to shop, as well as providing them with video and scanning capabilities. Shoppers using the app can scan bar codes for product information as well as how-to videos, and they are able to access the breadth of products available on Sephora's website while they are in the store. The mobile app also allows customers to immediately see what is new and what the retailer is "buzzing" about. In addition, shoppers can also scan a product in the store and find out what other customers think about that product. Moreover, when using the mobile app, customers are also provided deals and special sale prices that may be available only to them, and the app even uses GPS to help them find the nearest Sephora store. Customers can also read product ratings and reviews, retrieve information on their previous purchases, access their account, and even create shopping lists.

Nordstrom is another retailer that has implemented an effective social media strategy. Nordstrom, which achieves 21 percent of its sales online (a very high percentage for a traditional retailer), has spent hundreds of millions of dollars on things like distribution centers and inventory management software to integrate stores with its digital operations. The company sends news to shoppers on Twitter and showcases its fashions on Instagram. Discussions between the retailer and consumers are hosted on Facebook. Pinterest opens the door for some shopping, while Snapchat allows Nordstrom's shoppers to interact with each other and have a role in producing the content. Moreover, in all these social media strategies, Nordstrom has moved carefully so the efforts do not come across as a blatant commercial for the company.

Target, Nordstrom, H&M, and Sephora have all conducted successful marketing efforts with Snapchat, the social media platform that lets people share images or video clips with friends for a brief period of time. By some estimates, Snapchat has over 100 million daily users, with over half of them ages thirteen to thirty-four. The goal of companies implementing such a strategy must be about interacting with consumers in a fun way while creating a unique experience that is associated with the retailer.

Kate Spade, Jack Threads, and Warby Parker are just some of the brands experimenting with Instagram's shoppable-photo strategy. These brands have added a "tap to view" icon to company images that conveys additional information for the consumer, such as price and available colors, making it easier for customers to make a purchase decision on the spot. To learn more about how Levi Strauss has used social media to promote its stores, read the Snapshot titled "Levi Strauss: Cashing in on Social Media and Mobile Technology."

Have you interacted with any retailers using a social media platform? More and more companies will be doing so because the future of retailing looks a lot more social. Social media is a powerful connector capable of creating lasting and meaningful partnerships between retailers and consumers, and the most astute retailers are implementing unique social media strategies to influence the shoppers they covet the most (Figure 1.6).

Research showing that many consumers heavily rely on social media when making a purchasing decision has rendered social media indispensable, but as retailers build these social connections, they must realize that there is no one-size-fits-all strategy.

Figure 1.6
Social media has the potential of creating partnerships between retailers and consumers.

Whether they connect using Snapchat, Instagram, Pinterest, or Facebook depends on the shoppers that retailers are targeting. Review Table 1.1 to learn about the percentage of consumers using various social media platforms.

TABLE 1.1

WHICH SOCIAL MEDIA PLATFORMS ARE YOUR CUSTOMERS USING?

	Percentage of U. S. Internet users who access this site weekly	Percentage of users on the service ages 18-34
Facebook	70%	36%
Instagram	32%	46%
Twitter	30%	40%
Snapchat	25%	53%
Pinterest	25%	38%
Tumblr	18%	50%
Linkedin	17%	36%

Source: *Time*, March 13, 2017

Importance of Mobile and Social Media Strategies

Even though shoppers may ultimately make a purchase on their computer or in a traditional store, retailers must have a mobile-first mind-set because a vast majority of consumers' first impressions occur using mobile technology. In fact, research has shown that nearly half of store purchases are influenced by digital interactions.

An effective mobile and social media strategy can provide retailers, and especially retail buyers, a wealth of information about their customers and potential buying preferences. But, in order to tap into the true power of such strategies, retailers must listen to their customers, analyze their findings, and take appropriate actions to meet their needs. Through **social listening**, or tracking conversations about the brand on social media, retailers can gain a better understanding of which issues are gaining importance among consumers. Social media data can then provide retail buyers with details that aid in making purchasing decisions. Mobile and social media are shaping retail industry trends and will probably continue to do so in the coming years, especially as more and more companies move to omnichannel retailing approaches.

OMNICHANNEL RETAILING

Today's shopper is a consumer whose purchasing experiences are characterized by connectivity using multiple touchpoints with retailers, that is, bricks-and-mortar stores, cell phones, laptop computers, and social media platforms. As customers interact across various retail channels, retailers must implement a strategy that creates a unified message for their customers across every channel. Let's more closely examine strategies retailers are implementing to seamlessly connect these various touchpoints.

Omnichannel Strategies

Just twenty-five years ago, retailing was synonymous with bricks-and-mortar stores, but with the development of online retailing in the '90s, a second channel was created where consumers could interact with retailers. On the internet, they could purchase products and experience the brand to some degree; however, most retailers made the decision to implement different approaches with these two channels. In fact, most retailers only offered limited inventories to support their e-commerce sites.

As more retailers moved to a multichannel approach, many of them began some integration between the bricks-and-mortar part of their business and their e-commerce side. Then, mobile technologies added a new touchpoint allowing retailers and consumers to interact in much different ways. A new approach was needed to fully integrate these different channels—an **omnichannel** approach. The omnichannel concept (Figure 1.7) is focused on consumers being able to interact with the retailer from whatever touchpoints (i.e., laptop, smartphone, social media platform, or a bricks-and-mortar store) are appropriate to them wherever they are in the purchasing process—from learning about a product to making the final purchase to providing feedback on how the product performed. Read the Trendwatch titled "Omnichannel Retailing Done Right" to learn more about how some retailers have implemented omnichannel strategies.

Figure 1.7
The omnichannel concept is focused on consumers being able to interact with the retailer from whatever touchpoints are appropriate to them.

Need for an Omnichannel Strategy

Most products that consumers purchase are not made on impulse; they typically develop their shopping preferences through a series of activities. Engaging with sales associates, browsing e-commerce sites, reading advertisements, seeking advice from friends who have used a product, having conversations on social media platforms, and purchasing the same or similar products in the past are just some of the touchpoints that lead to a consumer's interest in a product and their making the final purchase.

In the omnichannel world, ease of access across all channels is paramount for consumers, and that requires integration of all a customer's records regardless of where they are accessed. An omnichannel approach provides retailers an opportunity to insert themselves along all these touchpoints, creating information and content that educates and excites consumers wherever they may be, and retailers must build systems, solutions, and operations to deliver content and experiences seamlessly across any of these touchpoints. This will mean that consumers choose how they want to relate to the retailer, rather than the other way around. Whether customers shop online, in the store, or on a mobile device, they have the same expectations of the purchasing process. If these expectations are ignored at any of these touchpoints, the retailer will probably lose both customer loyalty and revenue growth.

How important is an omnichannel approach to retailers? Walmart reports that an average store-only customer spends approximately $1,400 a year at its stores, compared to $200 among customers who shop only online. However, customers who shop using multiple channels spend $2,500 a year—clear evidence of how important an omnichannel approach can be in driving retailers' revenues.

Above all, retailers want to establish a conversation with consumers. Technology gives retailers the opportunity to extend their reach far beyond the typical bricks-and-mortar stores and even their computers. Mobile technologies have created an entirely new arena for retailers to reach consumers, most of whom do not leave their home without their smartphones—tools that can be used by retailers and consumers to interact with each other. Smartphones also give retailers the ability to target messages and promotions to consumers wherever they are.

Challenges of Omnichannel Strategies

Omnichannel retailing has also created new challenges for retailers. With the evolution of new integration strategies, such as "buy online and pick up in store" and "same-day delivery," retailers now need to have greatly improved visibility of inventory in all channels and better tools for predicting future demand for products. Moreover, retailers must be concerned with the costs associated with offering these services to customers. They must also ensure that safety stock levels in the store are not jeopardized by online orders to "pick up in the store."

In the expanding omnichannel world of retailing, the challenge of keeping customers loyal is accelerating. Retailers can no longer manage each of their channels as a collection of unconnected processes. Customers want retailers to remember what they have purchased in the past, and they want some sense of personalization. Customers feel better about the experience when they are remembered, regardless of the touchpoint they are using to interact with the retailer. If retailers tell customers an item is in stock, it needs to be in stock; excuses about separate computer systems that do not communicate with each other will not be accepted.

Remember that the cost of keeping a current customer happy is exponentially lower than that of attracting a new one; therefore, it pays to invest in a retail technology platform that can handle customer needs at any touchpoint they have with the retailer. In fact, Walmart is now focusing on enhanced omnichannel customer experiences through seamless shopping that includes initiatives such as online ordering and curbside pickup, a faster fulfillment network, and building new data capabilities to enhance shoppers' experiences at all customer touchpoints with the company.

As e-commerce becomes a greater percentage of total sales for most retailers, they will be forced to view inventory management quite differently at their warehouses. In fact, many retailers now make an effort to process e-commerce orders not from the warehouse, but from the store that is closest to the customer. Done properly, this process may be the most cost-effective way to support "next-day or same-day pickup" that many retailers have begun offering their customers.

Most retailers also opt for an easy and generous returns policy to stay competitive. Omnichannel makes it easier for customers to make a return, but it also makes the returns process more complicated for retailers. For example, a product bought online in North Carolina and shipped from an Atlanta distribution center could be returned to a store in South Carolina and then sent to a returns center in Ohio. As retailers move toward a seamless shopping experience for their customers, failures or shortcomings in the returns process can have a dramatic impact on the company. For example, some research suggests that only about half of returned products are resold at full price; however, 70 percent of customers who make an in-store return make another purchase—which does not occur with online returns. As they implement omnichannel strategies, many retailers are also rethinking merchandise assortments, which consumers to target, how best to reach their target customer, and the ideal number of stores they need.

Future of Omnichannel Retailing

Some industry experts are now determined to eliminate the word "omnichannel" from retailers' vocabularies and to break them of the habit of referring to e-commerce as a separate business channel. For them, the real challenge is to concentrate on shoppers' definition of retailing, which has nothing to do with channels and everything to do with delivering great products, on time, and at a fair price. Customers do not think about a shopping experience from an omnichannel point of view; instead, customers interact with retailers using a variety of methods. Regardless of whether a customer enters a store, shops through a website, uses a mobile app, or browses social media platforms, they want the shopping experience to be smooth and consistent, regardless of the channel. In fact, one retail analyst suggests that soon such customer experiences will overtake price and product as the key differentiator between retailers. As part of this process, customers expect a certain experience from the brand, and they expect that experience to be the same, regardless of which mode of interaction they choose. Shoppers expect a seamless shopping experience that easily shifts from digital to physical stores.

If they have not already done so, retailers must make an omnichannel approach a core element of their future strategies. An effective omnichannel strategy will help them create improved company awareness, generate greater customer retention and loyalty, and lead to higher sales revenues. But, failing to make the shopping experience seamless will hurt both customer satisfaction and revenues.

THE FUTURE OF RETAILING—TRENDS

As you have read, retailing has changed dramatically in the past twenty-five years. In today's fast-changing market, retailers need to identify and quickly respond to trends and challenges. A **trend** involves change or movement in a general direction. The ability to predict trends and deal with them before they fully influence the market is critical in retailing. The only way retailers can plan for the future is to anticipate the forces that will have an impact in the decades ahead. Then they must develop effective strategies in response to those changes if they are to survive.

Retailing is being revolutionized, and success in retailing will require strong decision makers who have a clear vision of what they want to do. All retailers must position themselves as shopping destinations rather than places into which consumers wander. Buyers, through their merchandise selections and other merchandising decisions, will play a key role in making their stores a shopping destination for consumers.

The history of retailing has always been one of change, and dramatic, if not revolutionary, changes must occur if many of today's retailers are to survive. Read the Trendwatch titled "Pop-Ups: Stores That Will Not Be Here Tomorrow" to learn more about the strategy being used by some retailers to open temporary storefronts. Customers' expectations are rising—they want what they want, when they want it, how they want it, and they want it fast. Moreover, resistance to change will probably be the major reason some retailers will not survive. Let's examine some of the future trends that retailers will be facing and strategies that they may be using to drive customer traffic, revenue, and profits while enhancing customer satisfaction.

Customers Becoming More Empowered

Today, the customer is in control. The twenty-first-century customer is "informationally empowered," is actively engaged in the marketing process, demands instant gratification, and seeks quality. One problem for retailers will be to determine which services their customers want. At Nordstrom, customer service may mean trained sales associates who coddle shoppers. At Walmart, it may mean having enough low-priced merchandise in stock and keeping checkout lines short so customers do not leave frustrated. No matter what service means at each retailer, keeping shoppers happy will be ever more important.

High-performing retailers will compete on the basis of value rather than price. Low price may be an important element of their retail strategy, but never the only element. The top performers give customers what they want—in other words, they give them their money's worth. For example, Home Depot's success is not just a function of good prices and selection; it is also a function of staffing the stores with personnel who can teach consumers how to be "do-it-yourselfers." IKEA's success is not just a function of low-priced furniture; it is a function of low-priced furniture that is well constructed and sleekly styled (Figure 1.8).

Figure 1.8
IKEA's success is not just a function of low-priced furniture; it is a function of low-priced furniture that is well constructed and sleekly styled.

New Experiences for Shoppers

New shopping experiences will be used to draw customers to stores. As sales at bricks-and-mortar stores decline in proportion to online sales, retailers will initiate new experiences that will build a better in-store engagement with customers. For example, one such idea, Reserve & Try, is already being implemented at some Nordstrom stores. Using their mobile phones, customers can select merchandise they would like to try on and schedule a time for their next store visit. The merchandise they have selected for fittings is placed in a dressing room right before the customer has scheduled to arrive at the store. In addition, these customers will find even more personalization when they find their name posted on the dressing room door to which they have been assigned. Developing in-store experiences like these that expedite and personalize the shopping experience will be critical for success in the future. Above all, these new shopping experiences will be less about entertainment and more about creating engagement and relevancy for customers.

To broaden their merchandise assortments and enhance customer experiences, many retailers will have more **concessions** in their stores—vendor partners who take over selling space. Macy's, Bloomingdale's, and Nordstrom are just some of the department stores that are already using these partnerships to reduce their investment in inventory. In European stores, concessions can be 60 to 70 percent of a store's selling space, while in the United States it averages only about 10 percent. Macy's is one retailer that has already implemented this trend by converting athletic shoes (Finish Line), caps (Lids), and sunglasses (Sunglass Hut) to concessions, and Bloomingdale's also has a group of leading designers, including Armani, running concessions in its stores. While concessions give a different character to stores, they can ensure a smooth, fast flow of merchandise direct from the manufacturer. In addition, concessions assure fresh merchandise, reduce markdowns, and guarantee the retailer a steady income stream.

Retailers Becoming Destinations for Consumers

Forward-looking retailers are becoming differentiated retailers—deciding what they want to stand for in the marketplace and staking out that role. Consider the following retailers—Target, Neiman Marcus, Forever 21, Walmart, and IKEA. Each of them can be characterized as filling a very specific role or marketplace niche—each has an identity, a personality. In other words, their stores are differentiated from similar retailers.

The key for retailers, then, is to view, define, and position themselves as **destination stores**—shopping destinations for customers. That is, retailers must strive to become focused, presenting a clear picture of merchandise and service to a distinct audience, so that they become stores for customers to consciously seek, rather than places for customers to wander into. Retailers can also use store layout and displays to position themselves as shopping destinations (Figure 1.9).

Everyone in the retail firm, particularly buyers, must also have a clear vision of the store—what it is and what it is not; what makes it special to customers. Outstanding retailers have a clarity of purpose that is demonstrated throughout the organization. Retailers cannot be all things to all people, but they need to be the right things to their customers.

Stores Becoming Mini-Fulfillment Centers

Lots of retailers will be transforming their bricks-and-mortar stores into mini-fulfillment centers. In 2016, for the first time ever, online shopping outpaced in-store shopping during the Black Friday weekend—a strong signal that a real shift in customers' shopping habits has occurred. As online sales growth continues, bricks-and-mortar stores will need to capitalize on one of the biggest advantages they have—the physical stores themselves. Stores can become mini-fulfillment centers that blend the digital and physical shopping experiences for customers. Shoppers can order online and pick up and return merchandise to a store near them. Even Amazon has recognized

Figure 1.9

Apple is one retailer that has positioned itself as a destination store.

the advantage of having some physical presence and has begun to build some bricks-and-mortar stores.

To make way for these mini-fulfillment centers, selling space will shrink as stores concentrate on profitable core product categories. For some retailers, the number of stores will also shrink. For example, as online sales of apparel and accessories saw robust growth online, several retailers, including Ann Taylor stores (women's apparel and accessories retailer), realized that the future of apparel retailing was e-commerce and there was little reason to open new stores. Thus, Ann Taylor has been closing some stores to reposition itself for omnichannel retailing. The remaining bricks-and-mortar stores would serve normal customer traffic as well as being an online fulfillment center. Ann Taylor is just one of many retailers that have come to terms with the fact that the shift in customers' shopping preferences is permanent, resulting in the closing of many retail stores.

There will continue to be a shaking-out period as retailers, many times painfully, adjust the size and number of their stores to accommodate the new normal. The winners will be those retailers who can quickly and efficiently right-size that footprint and make customer interactions seamless, store visits special, and order fulfillment optimized.

Faster and More Efficient Shopping Experiences

Shoppers are expecting faster and more efficient experiences. Walmart, for example, offers curbside pickup for customers who order online. Customers never have to enter the store; they simply park in a preassigned numbered space and their purchases are brought out. Amazon is experimenting with a no-check-out grocery store where customers are automatically charged for their purchases through a combination of artificial intelligence, computer vision, and data pulled from multiple sensors. If making the purchasing process faster and more efficient improves customer satisfaction and builds loyalty, other retailers must act and innovate quickly.

Greater Use of Data Analytics

The use of **data analytics** will increase dramatically in retailing. Unlimited computing capacity in the cloud and advanced analytics have enabled retailers to overcome the challenge they have faced in the past—collecting and analyzing huge volumes of different types of data, such as customer databases and social media trend reports. Until recently, when making decisions, retailers have had to rely on insights gained from their own experiences, forecasts based on past sales, and customer feedback, which were basically high-quality educated guesses.

The frustration that retailers face about not being able to distill value from data quickly enough to drive business performance will be reduced by the speed and accuracy that retail analytics can provide. Modern retail analytical software can package customer data, trend analyses, and supply chain data into a single view of what is occurring at a retail store. Putting all relevant data into a form that is easy to understand and use will help retailers, and particularly retail buyers, design strategies that will improve a store's performance, allowing them to have the right products available for customers at the right place and time. Data analytics can also be used to identify potential customers, decide which customers should receive a particular offer, and reactivate a customer's spending at a store.

Although data analytics were once the preserve of big retail chains with deep financial pockets, today the falling cost of computing power allows almost any retailer to move into this area. However, just having lots of information about customers stored away somewhere is not enough; strategies based on that information must be developed. Accepting the influence of analytics is critical for many retailers to remain vibrant.

More Effective Measurement of Marketing and Social Media Efforts

Marketing efforts to reach shoppers will also continue to change and evolve. Social media platforms, such as Facebook, YouTube, LinkedIn, Google+, Pinterest, and Twitter, will not be going away in the near future, but the massive amounts of media attention and hype will probably cool. Retailers will need to monitor the impact of social media on their sales. However, measuring the effectiveness of social media efforts presents new challenges. What should the retailer be measuring? For example, website "hits," mentions on other sites, number of "likes," traffic on a site, and the number of new customers making a purchase are just some of the variables that can be measured. Other factors, such as internet "buzz," may be impossible to measure quantitatively. On the other hand, podcasts and online video sites, such as YouTube, offer retailers the potential to deliver polished, high-quality content to better educate their customers and build sales.

Forecasts and Predictions Will Still Involve Risk

Predicting all future trends and challenges is impossible, but retailers must work to anticipate trends and then prepare and execute strategies that will allow them to adapt to the fast-changing marketplace. In 2009, one national retailing publication made the following predictions—"the recession would end by the second quarter of 2009," "sales of private-label merchandise would decline," and "the electronic wallet would become a reality." In 2009, they were wrong on all counts! Retailers will continue to make incorrect forecasts and predictions about the future, but they must lessen the degree of their errors. That will take a mix of improved retail knowledge, listening to retailing experts, analyzing retail analytics, endless hours of research, and even some reliance on "gut feelings."

As they reassess the future, retailers must find innovative ways that will allow their stores to grow while still operating profitably as they offer merchandise that attracts customers who want to buy what is being offered. The challenge will be to adapt as quickly as possible and capitalize on new opportunities. Finally, keep in mind that better merchandising begins with buyers who understand the products they stock and the customers to whom they sell. Better merchandising will require buyers who understand the value of new technologies, and who recognize them only as tools to facilitate customer satisfaction. It will require buyers who understand that taking risks is part of successful retailing. Are you ready to become that retail buyer?

Summary Points

- Retailing operates in an ever-changing environment; therefore, buying, a key function of retailing, must deal with the continuous changes in the marketplace.

- Online retailing continues to grow and thrive, with more than half of Americans preferring online to in-store shopping.

- Increasingly, the lines between online and in-store shopping are blurring.

- Online and mobile shopping have changed the retail environment quickly, and social media platforms have empowered consumers.

- Social media is not going to replace a retailers' overall marketing strategy; yet, retailers are quickly implementing strategies to attract customers and sell products using social media platforms.

- Retailers are replacing multichannel approaches with omnichannel approaches.

- Buyers must recognize and anticipate trends that are currently developing in retailing. They must develop the vision that will allow their stores to become destination stores for customers.

- Better merchandising will require buyers who not only understand the value of new technologies, but who also recognize them only as tools to facilitate customer satisfaction and increase revenue growth.

Review Activities

Developing Your Retail Buying Vocabulary

Consult the glossary if you did not add the following terms to your vocabulary.

bounce rate	data analytics	retailing	touchpoint
bricks-and-mortar	destination store	reverse showrooming	trend
buying	omnichannel retailing	showrooming	
clicks-and-mortar	online retailing	social listening	
concessions	pure play retailers	social media	

Understanding What You Read

1. Cite examples of retailing that do not require stores.

2. Explain reasons for growth in online retailing.

3. Identify benefits of online shopping for customers.

4. Identify benefits of online shopping for retailers.

5. Cite reasons given by consumers for not shopping online.

6. Explain why shoppers are reluctant to purchase high-end items online.

7. List four expectations online shoppers have of websites they visit.

8. Present examples of how online and in-store retailing have blurred.

9. Identify the largest online retailer in the United States, and describe strategies the company has used to achieve that ranking.

10. Explain why smartphones provide such an important opportunity for retailers.

11. Explain how social media platforms have empowered shoppers.

12. Describe how retail buyers can make decisions using data collected from social media platforms.

13. Describe the retail buyer's role in the development of destination stores.

14. Differentiate between multichannel and omnichannel retailing.

15. Describe the challenge for retailers when accepting returns in an omnichannel environment.

16. Explain why some analysts want to eliminate the word "omnichannel" from retailers' vocabularies

17. Explain what is meant by "informationally empowered" customers.

18. Describe why retail buyers have been reluctant to use analytic tools in the past.

19. Explain how retail success on social media platforms can be measured

Analyzing and Applying What You Read

1. The number of department stores is declining. Develop retail strategies that you would implement to turn around this decline.

2. One of the biggest trends facing retailers in this decade will be greater customer use of social media. Develop specific strategies on how a retail buyer could implement this trend in their retail strategy.

STUDIO

Spreadsheet Skills

Throughout this text, you will have the opportunity to develop your spreadsheet skills using numerous assignments presented at the end of selected chapters. The STUDIO accompanying this text contains assignments that can be printed using Microsoft Word. You will also find Excel files that will allow you to design and construct your own spreadsheets.

Being able to use and interpret spreadsheets is a critical skill that all buyers must possess. The goal of these assignments is to enhance your abilities in this area. Visit this book's STUDIO product at www.BloomsburyFashionCentral.com and print Assignment A. This assignment is designed as a tutorial to provide you with a quick review of spreadsheet operations. Answers to these practice activities are provided at the end of the assignment.

Internet Connection

1. Locate an online site for a retailer with whom you are familiar—one that also has a bricks-and-mortar presence. Develop a chart that compares the similarities and differences between the two, comparing such dimensions as product assortments offered, prices, image, and so on.

2. Visit the book's STUDIO to watch videos about omnichannel retailing, future retail trends, and advanced retail technology.

SNAPSHOT: Levi Strauss: Cashing In on Social Media and Mobile Technology

In a recent two-year period, Facebook users who visited Levi Strauss's fan page each month increased from 180,000 to over a million fans visiting the site. What changed so dramatically? The company changed its online strategy to be more than just an e-commerce site; Levi Strauss redefined how the company related to its customers through social media and mobile technology.

Retailers have always known that customers' word-of-mouth drives their businesses, but it has always been the part of the marketing mix that has been hardest to manage. And, today a company's marketing mix is increasingly more complex than ever. While traditional media, such as broadcast and print, are still an integral part of most companies' marketing mix, they have an increasing number of digital and mobile channels from which to choose.

Today, consumers use Facebook and other social media outlets to connect with their friends and family on a daily basis, and these social media outlets are finding ways to manage word-of-mouth of their users. They are providing a platform for their users to become advocates for a business or product. For example, Facebook has found that promoting a product with a friend's endorsement—a like or positive post—creates a more powerful marketing tool.

Levi Strauss is one company that has taken full advantage of the new technologies as it has sought to revamp its image in recent years. Working with developers at Facebook, features of the social media site were integrated into the Levi.com e-commerce site. Now, when shoppers log onto the Levi's site with their Facebook credentials, they are able to view what their friends have liked and purchased. Through this Levi Friends Store, Facebook users have the opportunity to influence their friends' purchases. A "see it" or "buy it" button also appears next to each product listed. A random list of likes from strangers appears if none of the customer's Facebook friends have liked any jeans recently. The user is also invited to be the first among their friends who like the product. As a way to spark additional sales, an ad on the page shows which friends are having a birthday soon.

Facebook was also used to alert fans about each stop for Levi's "Wear the Pants Tour." A vintage Airstream trailer was used to visit cities with lots of free items, coupons, and entertainment sponsored by Levi's. Twitter followers who tweeted with the hashtag #wearthepants also received coupons for Levi's gear. For those fans who could not meet the tour in person, there was an app for a game, which encouraged a hands-on experience with the company's products.

Mobile social interactions have certainly become a powerful marketing tool for retailers such as Levi Strauss, and will probably continue to gain importance as that commercialization grows. Levi Strauss's use of social media has been to link its Facebook fan page to its e-commerce site; however, some other retailers sell on Facebook directly. For example, 1-800-FLOWERS opened one of the first storefronts on Facebook.

Social media and mobile technology have allowed Levi Strauss to maintain a sustained conversation with its customers. The company is doing well with engaging their customers when measured by their comments, likes, and shares on social media sites. What is less clear is the impact on sales. At present, Levi Strauss declines to reveal sales generated by its Facebook connection.

Now that they have their customers engaged, their next step will be to increase that engagement and carefully track its impact on company goals such as sales and customer traffic. While implementing social media as part of its promotional mix, Levi Strauss must also be concerned with the privacy of its customers' information. As technology firms like Facebook increasingly deploy users' data to create more personal advertisements, they must realize that such practices can alienate users and open companies to invasion-of-privacy suits.

BASED ON:

Koppelman, Charles. (2017, February 14). 5 reasons why American giant is the new Levi Strauss. *Forbes.com*.

Marikar, Sheila. (2014, March 17). Papa's got a brand-new tag. *Fortune, 64*.

Parnell, David J. (2015, June 15). Levi Strauss & Co. CEO Chip Bergh, on managing the intersection of tradition and innovation. *Forbes.com*.

Raymond, Noah. (2013, October 28). Advertisements starring. . . you. *Time*, 16.

Vanian, Jonathan. (2016, May 20). Levi Strauss and Google's new jacket will rule your smart phone. *Fortune.com*.

POP-UPS: STORES THAT WILL NOT BE HERE TOMORROW

Staying open for business for only a few weeks would be considered a major flop for most retail stores. But some retailers are opening their stores in just such a manner. In fact, these temporary retail operations—pop-up stores—are springing up all over the country.

Pop-up stores are retail spaces—usually in the form of a kiosk or temporary store in an empty building or empty mall storefront—designed to operate for only a few days or a few months. Moreover, these stores are part of a deliberate and innovative retail strategy that has spelled profits for many merchants.

The growing popularity of pop-up stores is partly due to store closings by retailers causing many retail storefronts in the United States, particularly at malls, to remain vacant. These increased vacancy rates have caused many property owners to be more receptive, compared to past years, to leasing commercial space on a short-term basis.

The concept of using temporary space to clear excess or seasonal merchandise is not new. In the past, the pop-up store concept of "now you see it, now you don't" has more often been associated with holidays such as Halloween and Christmas, but in recent years, these stores have flourished regardless of the time of year. Retailers, such as Toys "R" Us, have also used pop-up stores to sell both discounted merchandise from their traditional retail stores and value-priced items specifically made for these outlets. Other retailers return to pop-up locations in malls year after year. For example, Calendar Club and Hickory Farms have become fixtures every year for a few months during the Christmas season—the time of year when almost all of their sales occur.

More often, retailers are using pop-up stores to generate buzz and excitement around a new product launch. Gap opened a pop-up store in one trendy shopping area in Los Angeles to promote its new premium denim line, and celebrities including Halle Berry and Ashlee Simpson turned out for the store's launch party. When Kanye West brought his tour to New York, he needed somewhere to sell merchandise, and instead of a concert booth, he opened a pop-up store for four days. When the tour left town, the store was quickly emptied, but not before generating lots of media coverage.

Pop-up stores have also become a popular way for emerging designers to generate buzz around their brand and test if the brand can stand on its own. Comme des Garçons designer Rei Kawakubo started the trend in 2004 with shops popping up everywhere from Berlin to Barcelona. Other fashion retailers and designers have also demonstrated the success that pop-up stores provide in generating buzz about new brands and designs.

Toys "R" Us also offers another sign that the pop-up store is part of mainstream retailing. The retailer opened hundreds of Toys "R" Us Express stores across the country for several weeks during the Christmas season. The temporary stores gave Toys "R" Us a much broader reach, doubling the number of locations nationally. Moreover, about half of Spencer Gifts' annual sales now come from its pop-up stores, Spirit Halloween, which are only open two months a year.

Pop-up locations can be a successful part of a retail strategy. They can alert traditional retailers on how to continuously change their merchandising mix and product selections to best fit the needs of their customers. Sales and store traffic at pop-ups can also provide the retailer with enough information to not only decide to deploy a permanent storefront nearby, but also have enough information on what to stock there and what customer experience they should provide.

A potential downside to pop-up stores is that a retailer may find an ideal location, but it cannot return there in the future. New tenants may move in who are willing to sign a long-term lease for higher rent. It may also be more difficult to merchandise a temporary location; the retail buyer has to carefully decide just what limited products will be sold and in what quantities they will be purchased based on no past sales records. The goal would be to completely sell all products by the time the pop-up closes.

Pop-up stores are here to stay. They have become a vital part of the retail strategy for many merchants. And for many consumers, there is something exciting about shopping at a store that will only be around for a few weeks.

BASED ON:

Cheatam, David. (2017, January 24). Stores closing are just doors opening to a new age in retailing. *ChainStoreAge.com*.

Gustkey, Constance. (2016, March 30). Pop-up stores thrive in a world of failing retailers. *NYTimes.com*.

Kim, Eugene. (2016, September 9). Amazon is doubling down on retail stores with plans to have up to 100 pop-up stores in US shopping malls. *BusinessInsider.com*.

O'Connor, Clare. (2013, October 11). No trick, just treat: Halloween pop-ups now account for half Spencer Gifts' annual sales. *Forbes.com*.

Stein, Joshua David. (2013, December 20). No space too small, no lease too short. *NewYorkTimes.com*.

OMNICHANNEL RETAILING DONE RIGHT

One of the big "buzz" words in retailing right now is "omnichannel." Retailers know what the term means, but it is not always clear how to implement the concept. Here are several companies that are doing omnichannel retailing right.

Crate & Barrel realizes that many of its shoppers switch from the company's website to a smartphone to a tablet when learning about products and making purchases. So when customers are signed in, the Crate & Barrel app saves their e-commerce shopping cart so they can access their information across multiple devices and browsers. It does not matter which device they may switch to; customers can pick up where they left off if they were interrupted or had to delay purchasing. Crate & Barrel provides the same seamless experience for shoppers using the company's wedding and gift registry. Customers can even create and monitor their registries online or in-store by scanning bar codes to add items. In addition, customers can use the app on their mobile device to edit their registry and even see purchases made in real time.

Oasis, a fashion retailer in the United Kingdom, has fused their e-commerce site, a mobile app, and several bricks-and-mortar stores to provide customers with a great omnichannel shopping experience. Sales associates at Oasis are provided with iPads, allowing them to give shoppers on-the-spot information on product availability as well as handling a customer's purchase from anywhere in the store. And, if the item requested is not available in the store, the sales associate can use the iPad to place the order on the company's e-commerce site. The reverse can occur for online shopping. If online shoppers find that an item is sold out online, they can use the "Seek & Send" app that searches the brick-and-mortar stores for the item's availability there. The customer receives an email notifying them of the status of the search, and if it is available, the item ships it to the customer. Then, customers can track their delivery using a code provided on an email sent to them.

Starbucks is another retailer providing a seamless experience for their customers across all channels. For example, customers can add to their Starbucks card balance by using their smartphone, visiting the company's website, or going to any store. Any changes in the customer's balance or their profile when using one channel are also updated in real time across all the other channels. Additionally, any rewards that the customer earns are automatically reflected in the account without any action on the customer's part.

Sephora, the beauty retailer, has successfully used an omnichannel approach to implement the "My Beauty Bag" rewards program. Members can use their smartphones or computers to view and track both their purchases and rewards. They can add items to their shopping list, save items for a future purchase, and easily reorder items. Customers can also access Sephora's app when they are in the store if they do not have their smartphone with them.

Chipotle Mexican Grill is another retailer utilizing the omnichannel approach to enable customers to place orders from wherever they are. In addition, if customers create an account, they will be able to track past orders and save their favorites for faster reordering in the future.

At Bed Bath & Beyond, management has seen consumer preferences shifting from in-store purchasing to browsing in the store and purchasing online. To leverage this trend, the company has strengthened its e-commerce channel with investments in technology. It invested heavily by upgrading its online site, creating new mobile apps, and installing a new data center. To integrate the in-store and online experience, Bed Bath & Beyond is also offering options to customers that include the ability to buy online and pick up and return in-store. New stores are experimenting with an area called the "Beyond Room," for customers to work with in-house experts that provide decorating services. They also encourage customers to schedule appointments online, which should attract more customers to the physical stores.

These are just a few of the retailers who have successfully implemented an omnichannel approach to conducting business. They have allowed customers to do whatever it is they need to do throughout their shopping experience, no matter what device or platform they are on.

BASED ON:

Brady, Sean. (2017, January 4). Creating customer centricity in 2017: Omnichannel marketing and mobile. *Multichannelmerchant.com*.

Hamdani, Zeke. (2016, March 4). Winning customer loyalty through omnichannel loyalty perks. *Multichannelmerchant.com*.

O'Brien, Mike. (2017, January 13). Retailers continue omnichannel pivot as stores struggle. *Multichannelmerchant.com*.

Wilson, Marianne. (2017, January 10). First-of-its-kind store for Bed, Bath & Beyond. *ChainStoreAge.com*.

CHAPTER 2

THE BUYING FUNCTION IN RETAILING

Performance Objectives

- **Recognize factors that will affect the scope of the buyer's job.**
- **Describe the duties and responsibilities of the buyer, assistant buyer, and merchandise manager.**
- **Identify the qualifications needed to become a buyer.**
- **Outline career paths related to buying careers.**
- **Identify trends that will affect buying careers in the future.**
- **Explain how a buyer's performance is evaluated.**
- **Calculate individual and cumulative markup percentages—quantitative performance objectives used to evaluate a buyer's performance.**

As you read in the last chapter, retailing is an ever-changing environment. Because of those constant changes, working in the field is both exciting and challenging. One of the most challenging functions of retailing is buying. As the name implies, purchasing merchandise is a key task performed by buyers, but they also must spend time analyzing market data and reading the latest publications and trade journals to keep abreast of what is happening in the market. Purchasing merchandise occurs only after buyers thoroughly understand their customers, the market, their products, and their competition—and that takes careful study and analysis.

As you read this chapter, you will have the opportunity to closely examine what buyers do and the qualifications you will need to be successful in the field. Possible career paths and current employment forecasts are presented to assist you with career planning. If you choose a buying career, you will find it demanding, but you probably will not mind so long as you are doing something you really enjoy.

THE BUYER'S JOB

Often, buying appeals to college students because they see the glamour associated with frequent travel to exciting places, such as New York City, Los Angeles, Paris, Hong Kong, or Milan, for buying trips where they get to spend hundreds of thousands of dollars, and in some cases even millions of dollars, on the newest styles and fashions. Travel may be exciting, but often all that a buyer may see of a city is the view from a taxi on the way to a hotel or a merchandise mart. Nor does the hectic pace of a market week allow much time for sightseeing. Deciding what merchandise to buy with those thousands of dollars can be stressful. Because of this financial responsibility, the buyer's job is pressure packed. Many people, however, thrive on the pressure that comes from having the responsibility to make decisions. If you like such challenges, consider buying as a career option. However, if you like quiet contemplation, little stress, and routine activities, buying is probably not for you.

It is difficult to generalize about what a buying career will involve because of the diversity of the types of retailers that exist. The trends and changes that you read about in the previous chapter also have an impact on the activities buyers perform.

Factors Affecting the Scope of the Buyer's Job

Individuals in the retail organization whose primary job is to purchase merchandise are **buyers**. As you will learn in this chapter, their job is much more complex than purchasing merchandise. Three factors affect the scope of the buyer's job: (1) merchandise carried, (2) organizational structure, and (3) size of the retail organization.

Merchandise Carried

The merchandise carried by the retailer determines the responsibilities of a buyer. Buying **basic merchandise** will be much different from buying **fashion merchandise**. Basics are those products that a business always wants to have in stock. Basics tend to have stable consumer demand, so sales vary little from year to year. An analysis of last year's sales records and the current year's sales trends and marketing plans will determine the amount of basic merchandise that a buyer needs to purchase. That is not true for fashion merchandise. A fashion that sold extremely well last year may not sell at all this year. Buying fashion requires much greater reliance on forecasting consumer demand and market trends.

Today, there are fewer and fewer basic items in most retail stores; fashion is affecting almost all merchandise assortments. For example, kitchen appliances come in a multitude of colors and styles, there are various designer sheets and sunglasses, and automobile styles change yearly.

As shown in Figure 2.1, fashion buyers spend plenty of time in the market scouting for just the right merchandise that will provide their stores with unique items or fashion looks that the competition does not carry. They also seek items that their stores can receive before the competition. Fashion buyers may even have to seek out resources that will produce private brands just for their stores.

Buyers for discount stores may only be concerned with finding merchandise at the best possible price. Uniqueness is not a key factor; they are more interested in buying merchandise with proven sales records.

Organizational Structure

The type of organizational structure that a retailer uses also determines the duties and responsibilities of buyers. Many retailers today have centralized the firm's buyers at corporate headquarters. In these situations, buyers have little or no direct daily contact with the stores. Activities such as management of sales associates and inventory control are performed by managers at the store level. Large chain stores, such as J.C. Penney, Macy's, Forever 21, and Gap, conduct buying in this manner.

In small independent stores, the owner usually performs all the buying duties, in addition to all the other responsibilities required in operating a retail business. They may be responsible for varied activities such as scheduling and evaluating sales associates, developing promotional activities, and maintaining inventory records. In addition, they must buy for all product categories carried by the store.

Size of the Retail Organization

The size of the retail organization is another factor affecting the scope of a buyer's job. In small retail stores, the buyer may be responsible for buying all the merchandise for several departments. For example, a buyer may purchase all men's and boys' apparel. In large retail stores, however, buyers become more specialized; they are responsible for buying product categories—such as boys' jeans—rather than every product for a department.

The Buyer's Job: Duties and Responsibilities

Even though a buyer's duties and responsibilities vary at different retail firms, there are basic duties and responsibilities that most buyers will perform. Most retail organizations will develop a job description for buyers that would probably include most of the following tasks:

- Develop merchandising strategies for a product line, department, store, or the entire retail organization.
- Keep abreast of current market trends and economic conditions.
- Develop an awareness of fashion trends.
- Understand and identify needs and wants of consumers.
- Analyze and interpret reports.
- Follow social media streams to detect applicable trends.
- Make regular market trips.
- Plan and select merchandise assortments.
- Represent the store or retail organization to vendors.
- Negotiate with vendors for favorable terms and services.
- Plan and develop private brands (sold only by that retailer) and/or import programs for the store or chain.
- Price merchandise to generate desired profits.
- Experiment with new merchandising trends and vendors.
- Identify fast-selling and slow-selling products.
- Maintain well-balanced stocks and assortments.
- Control planned purchases, stock levels, and deliveries to stay within merchandise plans.
- Review and periodically revise basic stock programs.
- Contact or visit stores; consult with sales associates and store managers.
- Select merchandise for promotion activities; develop a point of view for presentation of merchandise.
- Shop and analyze competing stores in the trading area to evaluate their merchandise assortments, prices, and merchandise presentation.
- Achieve quantitative performance goals such as sales, markups, markdowns, gross margin, and turnover.

Role of Assistant Buyers

In large retail organizations, buyers may have one or more assistants to help perform these duties. **Assistant buyers** may be considered buyers in training. College graduates pursuing a buying career will usually hold this job after completing a management training program.

Assistants can be assigned much of the clerical and routine parts of the job. By turning over such time-consuming activities to assistants, buyers are better able to complete tasks that take them out into the market.

Duties that are typically assigned to assistant buyers include the following:

- Prepare daily reports to identify best sellers and slow sellers.
- Replenish basic stock.
- Complete markdown records and reports.
- Review inventory records.
- Follow up with vendors on merchandise orders to ensure prompt delivery.
- Supervise returns to vendors.
- Analyze daily sales reports.
- Write purchase orders with information provided by the buyer.

In some retail organizations, a **planner** monitors stock levels by store and tracks key items by sales. The primary role of the planner is to maximize the entire chain's stock efficiency through appropriate location planning (Figure 2.2) and distribution of merchandise; however, the planner does not select product or develop promotional strategies.

Part of your job as a buyer will be to develop capable assistants. Make assistant buyers and planners a part of your team; do not treat them as competitors for your job. You can develop an atmosphere of teamwork by allowing them to review merchandise lines with you in the store or on trips to market showrooms. When you return from market trips, review with them current trends you found. Let them provide input for the merchandise selection process, and keep your assistant buyers informed on how the department or product category is performing.

You and your assistant buyers have a common goal—the success of your department or product category. As a team, you will be able to accomplish more, and at the same time, you will be contributing to the development of a future retail buyer or manager.

Role of the Merchandise Manager

The manager of the buying function in most retail organizations is the **merchandise manager**—the buyer's direct superior. This position may also be referred to as a divisional merchandise manager. Merchandise managers set the direction of styles, product lines, and image for their area and oversee its budget, but their major duty is to supervise buyers and allocate resources among them. Usually, the duties of merchandise managers can be divided into four areas: (1) planning, (2) directing, (3) coordinating, and (4) controlling.

Figure 2.2

Planners will be responsible for deciding upon shelf space allocation for products.

Planning

Even though merchandise managers are not directly involved in the actual purchase of merchandise, they formulate policies and set standards related to the merchandise areas for which they are responsible. The merchandise that buyers purchase must meet requirements established by merchandise managers, as well as fit the store's image that management has developed.

Another key planning task for merchandise managers is budget development. Buyers must make purchases within financial guidelines developed by merchandise managers, and they must also have merchandising plans approved by them. Merchandise managers are also involved with developing standards (such as sales goals, stock levels, or markups) against which a buyer's performance is measured. When developing these standards, merchandise managers should make every effort to seek involvement from buyers in the planning process. Resentment is likely to develop when performance standards are simply imposed from above; most employees want to have input into such decisions. In addition, input from buyers is vital in the budget preparation process.

Directing

Supervision of buyers also involves training new buyers. Many times new buyers require counsel from someone with a broad perspective. New buyers are often timid about taking markdowns; others, if left unrestrained, may want to overbuy. Merchandise managers may need to prod buyers into taking markdowns to move merchandise out of the store and help them maintain a sense of balance as they make purchases. Merchandise managers, however, must remember that their function is to advise. In most situations, the buyer is probably more of an expert on buying specific categories of merchandise than is the manager.

Merchandise managers will also want to keep buyers up to date on business and economic trends. Many buyers are knowledgeable about product and fashion trends but are less aware of overall economic and market conditions.

Coordinating

Because merchandise managers usually supervise a number of buyers, much of their time is spent coordinating all the buyers. They must unify their efforts to achieve the image and sales that management desires. Purchases for which different buyers are responsible must also be coordinated. For example, the color and design of a new purchase of scarves must complement apparel purchases made by another buyer. Many times, merchandise managers are involved with coordinating promotional campaigns that involve merchandise from several departments, and there are times when they must coordinate merchandising plans with other divisions such as finance and operations.

Controlling

Merchandise managers are directly involved in reviewing the performance of merchandise areas under their control. They must also evaluate each buyer's performance. If a buyer is not meeting performance standards, merchandise managers must take corrective action that could mean working with a buyer on a problem area, such as too many markdowns, or removing a buyer from a job he or she is incapable of performing.

CHANGING ROLE OF THE RETAIL BUYER

The world of today's buyer is more of a numbers game than ever before. Technology is providing buyers with access to increasing quantities of data, making buyers' jobs more scientific than they were years ago. Today, buyers must do much more than scour the market for the most appropriate merchandise and negotiate the best deals. Buyers must analyze numbers (Figure 2.3), in real time and historical formats, and then make purchasing decisions based on trends and past product performance.

New Challenges and Expectations

Buyers can no longer rely solely on the right "hunch" about which products might sell the best. Successful buyers must become competent researchers and forecasters. Because the job has changed, some retail analysts believe that the term "buyer" may be obsolete. In some retail organizations, buyers are now referred to as "category managers," while other firms view the buyer as the "purchasing agent" for a store's customers. Read the Trendwatch titled "Employment Forecasts: What Are the Projections for Jobs in Retail Buying?" to learn about future job forecasts in buying and purchasing.

There are positives and negatives as to how the buyer's job has changed. Although an abundance of data can assist buyers in making more appropriate decisions about quantities to order and inventory levels, buyers can also become inundated with too much data. In fact, many buyers feel overwhelmed with the enormous amount of information that can be easily generated; they receive more data than they can ever actually use or implement.

Much of the data generation is being fueled by consolidation in the retail environment. Fewer, but larger, retail firms mean each corporation is under constant pressure to increase profits. Today, a large part of a buyer's evaluation is not based solely on number of sales, but on the profitability of those sales.

Figure 2.3
Before making purchase decisions, buyers must spend time analyzing numerical data.

Buyers must also know how to bring new products into their stores with minimal risk. This has made product testing and evaluation a growing part of the buyer's role. They must possess a keen eye for fashion—even if they are not buying fashion per se. Products like cell phones and computers also have a fashion element because they come in many colors and models.

Buyers today must be knowledgeable about logistics. They need to understand the cost of moving merchandise, including delivery costs and delivery times, across town or across the globe. There is an increasing emphasis on developing partnerships between vendors and retail buyers and making these relationships far more collaborative than in the past—which takes effort and time.

Buyers must have the skills to utilize an ever-growing list of available technologies. That list includes everything from complex, mathematical computer programs to weather forecasts, email, social media (such as Twitter, Pinterest, YouTube, LinkedIn, Google+, and Facebook), and the internet. These technologies allow buyers 24/7 communications with resources and customers around the world. However, they have some drawbacks. Because many of them are so easy and inexpensive to use, retail buyers can quickly become overwhelmed with the mass of communications and data received each day. Yet, they must spend a great deal of time filtering through these communications to gain a clear picture of who their customers are and what products they want. Does all of this data analysis make buyers today more mechanical and less creative? Some in the industry feel that is indeed the case. Buyers, however, may also be required to look beyond the information provided to them by information technology and data analytics. Their best "educated guess" still may be needed after they have assimilated and analyzed all the data at hand. The buyer who succeeds gets the product first, turns it around fastest, and replenishes it quickest, all the while keeping costs down and providing customers with retail prices they are willing to pay.

Impact of Technology on the Buyer's Job

Technological advances are rapidly changing the buyer's role in many retail stores. Computerized Quick Response systems have been adopted by many retailers. The use of computers has allowed many stores to implement **automatic reordering systems**. Currently being used for basic merchandise, automatic reordering generates weekly orders based on sales in relation to model stock plans. These plans, in turn, have been developed based on past sales and current trends.

Implementation of computer technology and the use of automatic reordering have caused several trends in buying patterns to develop:

- Stronger partnerships are developing between retailers and vendors.
- More frequent orders in smaller quantities are being placed.
- Orders are being made closer to the selling season.
- Replenishment of basic merchandise is based on actual sales, forecasts, and trends.

Automatic reordering systems give the buyer more time to concentrate on other buying activities such as the selection of merchandise and the development of merchandising programs. Some retail organizations are even removing control for the replenishment of basic merchandise from buyers' responsibilities. Automatic reordering allows retailers to turn basics into a replenishment operation as opposed to a buying operation. Buyers can focus more attention on understanding customers and planning purchases more carefully. For example, at Dillard's department stores, buyers do not have to deal with writing orders for basic merchandise because automatic reordering systems have been implemented. At these stores, inventory management is being shifted to the store level.

Information technology is also having a major effect on many other aspects of buyers' jobs. Computers are handling most of the routine tasks—enabling buyers to concentrate mainly on the analytical aspects of the job. For example, computer programs are used to obtain instant and accurate product and price listings, track inventory levels, process routine orders, help determine when to make purchases, record the history of vendor performance, and issue purchase orders. Computerized systems have dramatically simplified many of the routine acquisition functions and improved the efficiency of determining which products are selling. For example, cash registers are point-of-sale computer terminals, allowing retail organizations to maintain centralized, up-to-date sales and inventory records. This information can then be used to produce weekly sales reports that reflect the types of products in demand.

Buyers also use computers to gain instant access to the specifications for thousands of commodities, inventory records, and their customers' purchase records. Some firms are linked with manufacturers or wholesalers by electronic purchasing systems. These systems improve the speed of selection and ordering and provide information on availability and shipment, allowing buyers to better concentrate on the selection of goods and suppliers.

PLANNING FOR A BUYING CAREER

Now that you know what buyers do, you may have more firmly decided on buying as your career choice. As with any job that you are considering, you need to compare your qualifications with those of people who already have the job. Successful buyers share very definite traits and skills. Decide which qualifications you possess, and then make an effort to sharpen the ones you already possess and develop those you lack.

Qualifications Needed

Qualifications needed to become a buyer include (1) appropriate personality traits, (2) human relations skills, and (3) merchandising knowledge and skills. Each area is vital to your future success as a buyer.

Personality Traits

Most retail managers will select new buyers based on whether or not they possess the following personality traits.

Enthusiasm.
You must be enthusiastic about the merchandise you are purchasing, your job, and the company. When you make market visits, you must be able to feel the thrill of discovery when you find just the right merchandise for your customers. Enthusiasm is infectious; it will rub off on everyone with whom you come in contact. That enthusiasm will eventually find its way to your store's customers.

Drive.

Ambition and hard work are usually prerequisites for success in any retailing career. Buying requires perseverance—the ability to stay with a job until it is completed. Often, long hours may be required.

Vision.

As a buyer, you will always be looking ahead—to next season or to next year. Doing just what you did last year may guarantee failure. Consumer demand, fashions, and market trends are constantly changing. As a buyer, you must be alert to these changes and anticipate them before they occur. In business, the most profit is usually made by the firm that has the merchandise first.

Goal-Setting Ability.

Management will be looking for individuals who have set a path to a goal and reach it. Completing college is such a goal. A large part of a buyer's job involves planning, so management will want individuals who can prioritize their time to attain high but realistic expectations.

Ability to Work Under Pressure.

Management will be looking for individuals who work well under pressure. In buying, as soon as you have completed one task, others will be waiting. In fact you will probably be juggling multiple tasks at the same time.

Creativity.

Even though much of the job is numerical and analytical, buyers must also be creative; they must be innovative. In other words, they must give direction to merchandising decisions that are made to distinguish their merchandise areas from those of competitors who may be selling similar products. Merchandise selection also allows buyers a certain degree of self-expression as they choose products to meet consumers' wants and needs. Buyers must also use creativity in solving many of the day-to-day problems they face.

Curiosity and imagination are the source of all innovation. Buyers must exploit those traits in themselves and employees with whom they work. They should be willing to consider new ideas from wherever they come. Even customers often have great ideas for changing and showcasing products. The secret to real innovation lies not in doing things just to be different but in doing things to be better.

Human Relations Skills

Another fundamental qualification for a buyer is having the capacity for teamwork. Working with a variety of people is an essential part of the buyer's job. Buyers must be able to work well with superiors (merchandise managers), subordinates (assistant buyers), vendors, department managers and sales associates, and other managers in the organization with whom they coordinate buying activities. Buyers have to value people and demonstrate that they care. Often just by listening, buyers can show that they recognize colleagues' importance to the company. Working with each of these audiences requires a unique set of skills (Figure 2.4).

Figure 2.4
Working with a variety of
people is an essential part of the
buyer's job.

Communications.

Communication is essential for buyers because they have constant contact with people. Communication is vital as they channel product information, trends, and enthusiasm from the market to the selling floor and the customer. Communications may also involve oral presentations on product information or written product reports and bulletins sent to store personnel. Advertising may be created based on your reports and bulletins, so it is important that you be clear and concise. You will also need to develop a technical vocabulary that can be used clearly in your communications.

Because stores and vendors are scattered worldwide today, clear and concise written communications are crucial. You must learn to effectively present information in faxes, memos, and emails.

Leadership.

As a buyer, you head a team. You must be able to provide leadership for your merchandising area. Management wants individuals who can innovate and motivate. Another crucial task is to ensure that other staff members follow through on directives. Many times you will have to use your leadership skills to enlist the help and support of others to plan and implement merchandising decisions.

Leadership demands flexibility—the ability to handle the many changes that are certain to occur every day. For effective buyers, it means keeping their fingers on the pulse of the competitive landscape, monitoring changing consumer trends, being aware of what is happening in the economy, and most importantly, anticipating how all these changes will affect them and their stores. Buyers must have the leadership skills to be able to move quickly to modify their strategy and correct their course when conditions warrant. Buyers cannot rest on past accomplishments, because what worked yesterday may not work today, and it almost certainly will not work tomorrow.

Merchandising Knowledge and Skills

In addition to personality traits and human relation skills, buyers will usually be selected based on the merchandising knowledge and skills they already possess. Buyers have to develop an understanding of customers' wants and needs and be prepared to satisfy them. Even though training and internship programs are conducted by most retailers to train buyers, management usually looks for the following qualifications.

Education.

A college education is more the rule than the exception for hiring buyers today. Many retailers prefer a four-year degree, but outstanding two-year graduates may be given consideration. Generally, retailers seek buyers who have majors in retail management, fashion merchandising, marketing, or closely related business programs. Courses in marketing, economics, sales, computer applications, personnel management, retailing, and merchandising are essential.

Some liberal arts majors are considered because of their strong background in psychology or sociology. Both of these areas give graduates extensive insight into what motivates customers. Even though they may not have the merchandising skills, their education has developed their self-discipline and sharpened their intellectual abilities.

In addition, rapid technological developments require that buyers be able to adapt to change. Training and retraining are likely to be an ongoing part of the job.

Analytical Ability.

Buyers must be decision makers. Pricing, merchandise selection, and vendor selection are just three of the decisions they make daily. A strong math background is a prerequisite, with a solid understanding of retail math calculations. Your performance as a buyer will be measured in numerical terms, so you need skill with numbers. Strong analytical skills give buyers the confidence to act decisively. In these days of instantaneous communication overload, buyers have to be able to cut through the clutter using all the tools at their disposal, combined with their own judgment and intelligence, to make informed decisions. Above all, they have to balance decisiveness and analytical skills to avoid "paralysis by analysis." Long response times are a luxury retail buyers seldom have. To meet customers' needs and exceed their expectations, buyers must make decisions frequently and quickly.

You will frequently need to work with budgets and make merchandise plans. Both tasks require that you be able to analyze and present information in numerical terms. You will also have to translate numerical reports into merchandising strategies.

Computer Literacy.

Information technology has made the buyer's job even more numerical and statistical than it used to be. Familiarity with computer programs is essential for most buyers today. More importantly, buyers must be able to read and interpret computer output.

Experience.

When selecting new buyers, management will desire some actual retail experience. Sales experience is preferred because it provides you with firsthand knowledge of consumers' wants and needs; however, if you do not have extensive retail experience, emphasize any experience you have had. For example, instead of simply describing your duties on a résumé, emphasize performance that is measurable in numbers and percentages. Buyers are always being evaluated against such performance standards.

Qualifications may vary from one retail organization to another, so it will be important to investigate specific firms with which you are interested in working. A want ad stressing buyer qualifications is shown in Figure 2.5. Examine the ad to determine what skills you may already possess.

If you take a job as a buyer, you will need to be observant, beginning with the first day on the job. Nothing is wrong with showing eagerness as you assume new responsibilities;

Figure 2.5
Do you possess the skills needed to apply for this buying job?

Buyer

Area of Interest:	**Corporate**
Location:	**NY - New York**

Description

POSITION SUMMARY:

a leader in the luxury good industry is seeking a Buyer. The Buyer is responsible for selecting and assorting the product for US market as well as managing boutique sales/stock plans, OTB preparation, analysis and inventory management.

POSITION RESPONSIBILITIES:

- Develop and execute strategic business initiatives to drive full price sales.
- Project sales and stock plans by boutique.
- Monthly Open-To-Buy preparation: sales and stock projections.
- Select and assort collections.
- Manage continuative businesses.
- Inventory management: stock to sales, obsolescence mark-downs.
- Buy preparation.
- In-boutique training and business meetings.
- Manage an Assistant Buyer.

POSITION REQUIREMENTS:

- The ability to be proactive in finding ways to maximize business opportunities and grow the business in each market.
- The ability to look at information and interpret it in a clear and concise fashion and suggest an action plan.
- Communication with management on store performance, issues, needs, etc.

Minimum Education:

- 4 year college degree.

Minimum Years of Experience:

- 5 years in a buying related job.

SKILLS AND KNOWLEDGE:

- Analytical skills.
- Retail math.

be a good observer, and ask the right questions. Pay attention to the dress codes and the style in which others interact to get work done. All these factors will also play a part in how successful you will be as a buyer.

Career Paths

Rarely do college graduates enter retailing as buyers. Most buyers begin their careers in a **management training program** or as assistant buyers. In either situation, the emphasis of your training will probably be on selling. Buyers must know the products they are purchasing as well as understand customers' wants and needs. Time spent in such training programs will vary from one company to another. Read the Snapshot titled "Nordstrom's Internship Program" to learn more about internships offered by Nordstrom. Similar programs are offered by many retailers. Internships are a great way to enter management training programs.

Most retailers believe strongly that working in the aisles and waiting on customers extends the knowledge base of management or buyer trainees. You really need the store experience to fully know and appreciate the scope of the retail store. Customers can be great educators, and employees are probably the best source of ideas to improve the way things are done.

The main reason that college graduates need to start their careers in retail stores is that working directly for the customer is essential to a retailing orientation. The experience develops empathy toward the customer and sensitivity to store personnel. When buyers move to the corporate office, they are better prepared to deal with the needs and requirements of store employees and customers—they are more emotionally attuned to both of these groups.

Job promotions can mean that you, as a buyer, will be given additional product classifications or departments for which to buy, or you may take on major departments with corresponding increases in pay and pressure. Other promotions could lead to your becoming a merchandise manager or head of the merchandising division for an entire retail organization.

In some retail organizations, jobs in buying may lead you to a management career. Many retail buyers make career changes by moving into the store as department managers. From there, future promotions may take them to management positions in personnel, merchandising, or operations. Some successful buyers could eventually become store managers. Typical career paths found in many retail stores are illustrated in Figures 2.6 and 2.7. These job progressions are called **career ladders** or **paths**. Realize that there is nothing carved in stone about suggested career paths; they merely represent how individuals might advance in a career area.

Buying provides excellent training and background for other fields, too. You could enter a job as a fashion coordinator, comparison shopper, product tester, or product designer. You may even have a strong entrepreneurial inclination and decide to open a retail business of your own. Jobs at businesses associated with buying, such as buying offices and apparel manufacturing plants, may also present opportunities for career advancement. Many of the skills that retail buyers possess could also be used to seek employment as purchasing agents for industrial products. Many of these types of jobs are listed and briefly described in Table 2.1.

Many career paths and options are open to you. Select one that interests you, and sharpen and develop the skills you will need to succeed in that area.

Figure 2.6
Sample career path in merchandising.

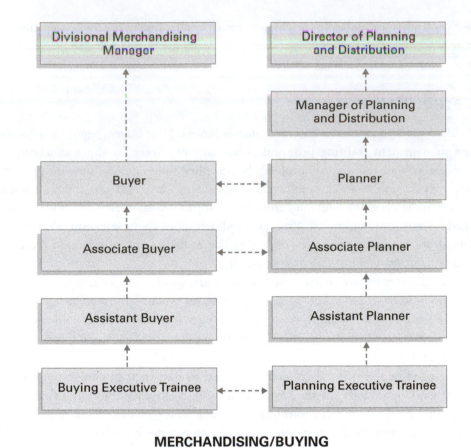

MERCHANDISING/BUYING

Figure 2.7
Merchandising career paths can also lead to store management positions.

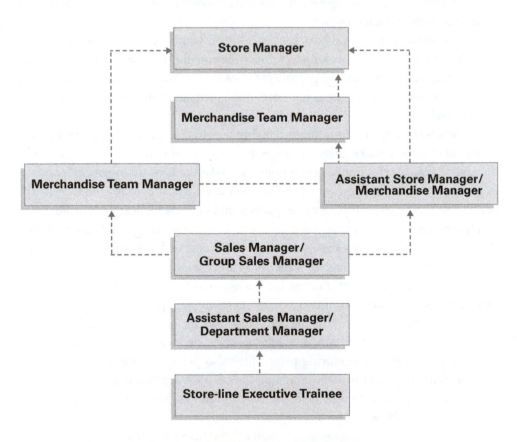

STORE MANAGEMENT

TABLE 2.1

OTHER JOBS IN RETAILING

Job Title	Description
Assistant Buyer	Works under the direction of a buyer, usually in a specific product category. Assists in sales analysis, handling reorders, and purchasing some merchandise.
Assistant Department Manager	Works under the supervision of a department manager. Assists in managing personnel, controlling inventory, and other store operations.
Assistant Store Manager	Helps in implementing merchandising strategy and policies. Works with personnel and overall store operations.
Catalogue Manager	Selects merchandise for inclusion in catalogues. Works with vendors, places orders, and monitors order fulfillment.
Department Manager	Responsible for a department's merchandise displays, analyzing merchandise flow, and the training and direction of sales associates.
District Manager	Responsible for management personnel, sales generation, merchandise presentation, expense control, and customer service at all stores in the district.
Fashion Coordinator	Directs buyers in evaluating fashion trends.
Fashion Director	Responsible for developing and maintaining a retailer's overall fashion perspective.
Management Trainee	First position for most college graduates entering retailing. Involves company orientation, classroom and on-the-job training, and contact with all facets of the store.
Marketing Research Director	Acquires and analyzes relevant and timely information that assists executives in making important decisions. Heavily involved in research methodology and data collection.
Merchandise Analyst	Plans and evaluates merchandise allocation to stores to ensure merchandise is delivered at the right time and in proper assortments. Develops assortment plans based on trends and past performance histories.
Merchandise Manager	Plans, manages, and integrates buying for an entire merchandise division composed of several departments or product categories.
Sales Promotion Manager	Plans and enacts special sales, themes, and sales promotion tools, such as contests.
Store Manager	Oversees all store personnel and operations in a particular store. Coordinates activities with other units of a chain. Responsible for customer service, merchandising, and human resource policies.
Vice President for Merchandising	Responsible for developing and evaluating the performance of all product categories. Has responsibility for growth and profit.

Getting a Job as a Buyer

Because buying jobs vary, you may need to investigate specific retail firms to determine how buying is conducted there. In addition, there may be differences from one geographic region to another. A key step in career planning involves research. Discover as much as you can about jobs in which you are interested. The best way to do that is not by reading, but by talking with individuals who work as buyers. When you talk with them, ask questions that will reveal what it takes to be a buyer in that retail organization. The following are possible questions:

- "How do you spend your time during a typical work week?"
- "What skills or talents are most essential to being effective in your job?"
- "What are the toughest problems you face?"
- "What is most rewarding about the work itself, apart from salary or fringe benefits?"
- "If you decided to leave your job, what would drive you away?"

Questions such as these give you insight into both the positive and negative aspects of the job. Realize, however, that changes in retailing will change the buyer's job in the future. Information is presented in Table 2.2 about some of the key reasons why applicants lose out on a job in retail buying. Identify your weaknesses and develop plans to begin eliminating them today.

Staying in touch—with colleagues, friends, neighbors, customers, suppliers, and just about anybody else—will be one of the keys to your getting a job as a buyer. In other words, networking will be critical to identifying job leads. **Networking** involves identifying and communicating with individuals who can be helpful in your job search.

Once you have identified a job opening that looks promising, realize that your résumé and job interviews cannot be approached haphazardly. For example, instead of just describing your past or current job duties, describe what you have accomplished on the job, especially performance that is measurable in numbers and percentages.

TABLE 2.2

WHY APPLICANTS LOSE OUT ON JOBS IN RETAIL BUYING

- Poor scholastic record—low grades and/or low level of accomplishments.
- Personality problems—poor attitude, lack of poise and self-confidence, timid, too introverted.
- Lack of goals or objectives—poorly motivated, indecisive, no specific career plans.
- Lack of enthusiasm—lacking drive, little evidence of initiative.
- Inability to express ideas verbally.
- Failure to get information about the company—lack of preparation for the interview.
- Unrealistic salary demands—more interest in salary than opportunity, unrealistic expectations.
- Poor personal appearance.
- Lack of maturity—no evidence of leadership potential.
- Inadequate preparation for a buying career—inappropriate background.

If you instituted a safety program, stress the reduction in on-the-job injuries. As you apply for jobs at many retail organizations today, you may also be required to take a pre-employment test, which typically measures your retail math competencies. Read the Trendwatch titled "Pre-Employment Tests: Will You Be Ready?" to learn more about these tests.

There are many online services today where college graduates can post their résumés. Job seekers at these online services, such as AllRetailJobs.com, can conduct a free search for career opportunities by job category, location, salary range, and keywords. Moreover, when potential job candidates apply for these jobs online, their résumés are automatically emailed to the appropriate companies. Candidates can also receive weekly emails that alert them to all new jobs that meet their specifications. In addition, recruiters can maintain an electronic log of all candidates who apply for jobs.

Management or buying careers will place enormous responsibilities in your hands that are tied directly to the financial success of the retailer. In fact, you may be responsible for purchasing millions of dollars' worth of merchandise that has to generate the desired profit. There is stress, but there are also rewards. Can you handle the pressure?

EVALUATING BUYERS' PERFORMANCE

Buying is a retailing job for which **quantitative performance measurements** can easily be developed. Standards can be established in numerical terms, such as having a certain sales level while maintaining a specific markup percentage. How effectively buyers meet these standards will determine how fast they advance in the firm, or, possibly, whether they will keep their jobs. A buyer's goal, for example, may be "To secure a maintained markup of 45.2 percent with sales of $56,000 and markdowns of $2,000" for a department or product category. Precise goals also make it easier to evaluate buyers' performances and reward buyers who achieve their goals.

There are a number of quantitative performance measurements against which retail buyers can be evaluated. Each of these measurements will be discussed in various chapters of this text as related topics are introduced. These measurements may vary with different retailers but are likely to measure such standards as the following:

- net sales,
- individual markup percentages,
- cumulative markup percentages,
- markdown percentages,
- gross margin percentages,
- open-to-buy,
- stock-sales ratios,
- stock turnover, and
- profit percentage.

In addition to quantitative performance measurements like the ones found on this list, buyers' performances will also be measured by how well they handle relationships with assistants, other management personnel, vendors, and store managers. A key part of the buyer's job is to create a team atmosphere.

In this chapter, two of the performance measurements listed above will be examined closely; others will be examined in later chapters of this textbook. You will have the opportunity to develop your skills in calculating individual markup percentages and cumulative markup percentages, and examine more closely how they will be used to evaluate your success as a retail buyer.

Performance Measurement: Individual Markup Percentages

One of the key performance measurements on which retail buyers are evaluated is **markup**, which is the difference between merchandise cost and its selling price. The markup that is established must cover all operating expenses for a business or department in addition to providing a reasonable profit. Of course, the actual sale price may be below the targeted retail price, so the actual markup is determined when an item is sold. Although it is important to know the dollar amount of markup, it is usually more important to know the markup percentage. Usually retailers state performance goals for a store or department in percentage terms rather than in dollars. Also, in making comparisons, dollar figures are usually not very meaningful.

The **individual markup percentage** is calculated by first determining the dollar markup on an item, which is found by subtracting the cost of the item from its retail price. The dollar markup is then divided by the retail price. All these components are expressed in the following formula:

$$\text{Markup \%} = (\text{Retail} - \text{Cost}) / \text{Retail}$$

Illustrative Problem

An item cost a retailer $56.32. If it sold for $112.00, what was the markup percentage?

SOLUTION
Markup % = (Retail − Cost)/Retail
Markup % = ($112 − $56.32)/$112
Markup % = $55.68/$112
Markup % = 0.4971428
Markup % = 49.7%

Performance Measurement: Cumulative Markup Percentages

Even though markup percentage can be calculated for individual items, retailers more commonly report markup percentages for a product category, a department, or an entire store for an extended period of time. In these situations, markup is referred to as cumulative markup. **Cumulative markup** is the markup achieved on all merchandise available for sale in a given period. Using cumulative markup is also more useful when comparing merchandising performance with established goals, with past sales records, or with the performance of other stores.

A cumulative markup goal is often planned for a group of merchandise, but some individual items are usually given higher markups than this goal, while a lower markup is applied to other items. The cumulative markup is found by dividing the total markup in dollars (on all merchandise) by the total retail in dollars for all merchandise.

Buyers must plan cumulative markup goals for their store or departments. Typically, the cumulative markup percentage on all merchandise in a department is one of the most critical goals for the buyer to plan and establish. To effectively reach this goal, merchandise must be purchased and priced in such a way that at the end of the season, the cumulative markup goal will be achieved.

By defining their goals, buyers give themselves a way to measure their performance. In addition, buyers must change their strategies when goals are not being met. By periodically measuring their progress toward reaching their cumulative markup goal, buyers can make changes in their merchandising strategy before the end of the selling season, when it would be too late to achieve their goal.

Illustrative Problem

At the start of a season, a buyer's inventory of scarves had the following values:

Total Cost $3,000
Total Retail $5,800

During the month, the following purchases were added to inventory:
   50 scarves, costing $20 each, to retail at $40 each.
   100 scarves, costing $10 each, to retail at $19 each.
   What is the cumulative markup percentage to date?

SOLUTION		
	Cost	Retail
Beginning Inventory	$3,000	$5,800
Purchases	$1,000 (50 × $20)	$2,000 (50 × $40)
Purchases	$1,000 (100 × $10)	$1,900 (100 × $19)
Totals	$5,000	$9,700

Next, calculate total markup in dollars by subtracting total cost from total retail:

$$\$9,700 - \$5,000 = \$4,700$$

Finally, calculate cumulative markup percentage by dividing total markup in dollars by total retail:

$$\$4,700 / \$9,700 = 48.5\%$$

The cumulative markup percentage is 48.5 percent.

Pricing merchandise would be simple if the same markup were applied to all items that are purchased during a season; however, this seldom occurs. Some items will carry higher or lower markups for a variety of reasons. Some items carry a higher markup because there is a greater risk of theft. Fashion merchandise is usually given a higher markup than basic items. Demand for some fashion items changes quickly, and a product that sells quickly today may be tomorrow's big markdown. Also, when an item is first introduced, a lower markup may be used to build store traffic. Later, retail prices on the item would probably reflect a higher markup. Other factors may also affect the markup that is used during the season. Wholesale prices may have been increased by a manufacturer in the middle of the season, or some retail prices may have been reduced during the season to meet competitors' prices.

As a season progresses, buyers must track cumulative markup on their purchases. Any of the occurrences described earlier could result in different markups for merchandise in a department; therefore, in order to achieve the planned cumulative markup percentage, different markups will have to be used on the balance of purchases made during the season. For example, if the cumulative markup to date is slipping below the departmental goal, higher markups will be required on future purchases. Buyers must be able to estimate what this new markup should be to realize the planned cumulative markup for the season. Buyers can easily make that estimate using some of the basic concepts you have already learned.

Buyers will use calculations such as individual markup and cumulative markup to continually monitor the store or department's performance for a specified period of time. They will compare these figures against (1) established goals, (2) past records for the department or store, or (3) industry averages.

At most retail stores, performance appraisals are formal processes based on documentation. Because buyers plan and establish quantitative goals for their merchandise areas, their performance can easily be measured. Therefore, it is imperative for buyers to constantly monitor performance measurements such as individual and cumulative markups, and other performance factors that will be examined in other parts of this text.

Summary Points

- The key function of the buyer is purchasing merchandise, but that requires analysis and interpretation of data and trends. Buyers must thoroughly understand their customers, the market, their products, and the competition before decisions can be made.

- Buying offers an attractive and challenging career for individuals who like being responsible for making decisions. Buyers must also like working with products, as well as people.

- The buyer's job will vary in different types of retail stores. The merchandise carried, the organizational structure of the store, and its size will all have an impact on the buyer's job.

- Buyers perform many activities in and out of their offices. Many buyers have assistant buyers on their staff to perform many of their routine activities.

- The buyer's job is changing at many retail stores. Computerization has allowed buyers to implement automatic reordering systems for many basic merchandise items.

- Merchandise managers are the immediate superiors of buyers in most retail stores. Their duties can be grouped into planning, coordinating, and controlling.

- There are specific personality traits, human relations skills, and merchandising knowledge that potential buyers should possess. A college education is usually a prerequisite.

- Buyers can advance along career paths in both merchandising and management tracks in many stores. Buyers can also advance into occupations related to their field such as fashion coordination and product testing.

- Forecasts for buying occupations indicate slowed employment growth.

- Buyers are evaluated against quantitative performance standards. Two of the most critical performance measurements for a retail buyer are markup and cumulative markup.

Review Activities

Developing Your Retail Buying Vocabulary

Consult the glossary if you did not add the following terms to your vocabulary.

assistant buyer

automatic reordering system

basic merchandise

buyer

career ladder/path

cumulative markup

fashion merchandise

individual markup percentage

management training program

markup

merchandise manager

networking

planner

quantitative performance

    measurements

Understanding What You Read

1. List and categorize positive and negative characteristics of the buyer's job.

2. Identify reasons why college students may initially be attracted to a job as a buyer.

3. List the factors that affect the scope of a buyer's job in retail organizations.

4. Distinguish how buying basic merchandise differs from buying fashion merchandise.

5. Summarize how buying may be different in large and small retail stores.

6. Identify activities that a buyer can do to ensure that an assistant buyer feels part of the merchandising team.

7. How have automatic reordering systems changed the buyer's job?

8. List the benefits that automatic reordering systems provide the retailer and the buyer.

9. Summarize the planning duties of a merchandise manager.

10. What is the key reason that many buyers lose their jobs?

11. List quantitative performance standards that can be used to evaluate a buyer's performance.

12. Describe how "vision" is an important trait needed by all buyers.

13. List the different groups with whom the buyer must communicate.

14. Explain how buyers use written communications on the job.

15. Describe why a college degree is required of prospective buyers by many retailers.

16. Identify how college graduates would probably spend their first weeks of employment in a management training program to become a buyer.

17. Outline one career path that a buyer could pursue.

Analyzing and Applying What You Read

1. Should extensive travel opportunities be viewed as a positive or negative feature of the buyer's job? Explain.

2. Predict how the buyer's job will change with increased monitoring of social media by retail firms.

3. Will there be a need for buyers in retailing thirty years from now? Explain.

4. Develop a job description for a merchandise manager detailing specific tasks they perform.

5. Assume that you are applying for a job as a buyer. Describe how you would ensure that the interviewer knew you possessed the following personality traits: enthusiasm, vision, and goal-setting ability.

6. Interview an individual at a local retail store who is responsible for buying merchandise. Ask questions similar to the ones presented in the text to determine traits and qualifications needed for the job as well as the person's duties. In class, compare and contrast your findings with those of other students.

Retail Buying Math Practice

1. An item cost a retailer $62.12. If it sold for $125.00, what was the markup percentage?

2. An item retails for $150.00. If it cost the store $71.25, what was the markup percentage?

3. At the beginning of the season, a buyer's inventory of socks had a total retail value of $5,600. The socks had cost $2,750. What is the cumulative markup percentage for these socks at the beginning of the season?

4. At the beginning of the season, a buyer purchased 700 scarves for $8,000. A retail price of $20 was placed on each scarf. What is the cumulative markup percentage for the scarves at the beginning of the season?

5. At the beginning of the season, a buyer's inventory of white T-shirts had the following values:

    Total Cost: $5,400

    Total Retail: $10,000

    The following purchase was added to inventory: 600 T-shirts costing $3,000. A $12 retail price was placed on the T-shirts. What is the cumulative markup percentage to date?

6. Beginning inventory for a department is $59,345 at cost and $120,500 at retail. New purchases have been received with a cost of $8,456 and a retail value of $26,112. What is the cumulative markup percentage to date?

7. At the beginning of the season, a buyer's inventory of sweatshirts had the following values:

    Total Cost: $2,433

    Total Retail: $4,500

    Two new purchases have just arrived: 100 sweatshirts costing $25 each will be added to inventory and retail at $55 each. And, 100 sweatshirts costing $21 each will be added to inventory and retail at $55 each. What is the cumulative markup percentage to date?

8. At the beginning of the season, a buyer's inventory of tank tops had the following values:

    Total Cost: $765

    Total Retail: $1,750

    Three new purchases have just arrived. Fifty tank tops costing $564 will be retailed at $20. One hundred tank tops costing $1,020 will also be added to inventory at a retail price of $20. Finally, 200 tank tops costing $1,950 will be added to inventory at a retail price of $20. What is the cumulative markup percentage to date?

STUDiO

Spreadsheet Skills

In this assignment, you will use a spreadsheet to calculate individual and cumulative markups—two of the quantitative performance measurements that can be used to evaluate a retail buyer. Visit this book's STUDIO product at www .BloomsburyFashionCentral.com and open and print Assignment B. Record your answers on the tables provided on the assignment sheet that you print.

Internet Connection

1. Go to http://www.nordstrom.com and locate specific procedures for applying for one of the available internship programs offered by the company. Locate one other online retailer offering an internship program. Describe the features of that internship (eligibility, length of internship, pay, etc.).

2. Go to http://www.AllRetailJobs.com and use the search function on the site to identify retail opportunities that are listed for your area.

3. Visit the book's STUDIO to watch videos about what buyers do, and to learn about retailing internships.

Nordstrom, headquartered in Seattle, Washington, is one of today's leading fashion specialty retailers selling clothing, shoes, and accessories for men, women, and children. They have 349 stores in forty states and Canada. Customers are served at 122 full-line stores, 216 Nordstrom Rack locations, seven Trunk Club clubhouses—a personalized styling service—two Jeffrey boutiques, and two clearance stores. They also serve customers worldwide through Nordstrom.com and the nordstromrack.com site, which operates in partnership with their private sale site, HauteLook.

The company has also been in the top fifty on *Fortune* World's Most Admired Companies list for six years in a row, and one of the reasons that the company has achieved those rankings is the strength of its strong reputation for customer service. One way the company strives to continue that reputation for customer service is by investing in a sound internship program.

With such a respected reputation in the marketplace and the continued growth in the number of stores, Nordstrom is certainly a retailer that you should investigate as you plan internships and future employment in the field. Determining if this company matches your needs and aspirations will take effort and research. Internships with Nordstrom, or any retailer, should not be just a part-time summer job. So, let's learn a little more about the Nordstrom internship program before you begin your own in-depth investigations.

The Nordstrom internship program is open to active college juniors and seniors who are enrolled in accredited institutions with applicable degree programs. Usually, applications for merchandise and planning internships at company headquarters are accepted online during mid-December before the summer of the internship. After that time, applications for retail management internships at specific stores are open until positions are filled. So, you need to start planning early for this internship program. In fact, the internships are highly competitive; Nordstrom receives hundreds of intern applications each year.

The Nordstrom internship program is a summer-long, paid experience that allows students to explore the retail industry and learn more about how the company operates. Internships focus on store management, product design and development, and buying, which provides interns with a wide range of experiences. During the program, interns will:

- be mentored and learn from highly experienced and dedicated professionals;
- participate in hands-on, meaningful work experiences;
- gain valuable experience through sales and customer service activities;
- get exposure to Nordstrom's culture and operating procedures while meeting key leaders in the company;
- gain exposure to a wide range of management responsibilities; and
- have the opportunity to be considered for a career at Nordstrom upon college graduation.

Qualifications for this internship program are broadly stated as follows:

- Applicants should possess a real passion for retailing by keeping up with current trends and seeking to learn more about the company and the retailing industry.
- Applicants must be able to commit to a full-time schedule.
- Applicants should be high-achieving students. The merchandising and planning internship requires a minimum cumulative GPA of 3.2.
- Applicants should be strong team players.

Do you have the qualifications for this internship? If so, you can complete an online profile on the company's website. Remember, with this internship or any other one in which you might participate, approach it as the beginning of a career: make personal and professional connections, network, ask questions, and explore all your opportunities with the firm. Do not just go through the motions and view the experience as another activity that needs to be completed before you graduate. When you find and apply for the internship that is best for you, be prepared to show that you are both goal-driven and self-motivated.

The Nordstrom internship program is a great experience for interested students. Through the program, Nordstrom can continue to enhance its reputation built on customer service by training and hiring the best prepared employees.

BASED ON:

Fairchild, Caroline. (2014, April 7). Service with style. *Fortune*, 22.

Loretto, Penny. (2013). A great program for students interested in retail. *About.com*.

Loretto, Penny. (2013). An interview with Nordstrom's northeast regional recruiter. *About.com*.

Internship program requirements. (2017). *Nordstrom.com*.

PRE-EMPLOYMENT TESTS: WILL YOU BE READY?

One retail industry trend that will impact a future job seeker like yourself is the greater use of pre-employment tests by human resource departments to screen applicants. Particularly, as you pursue a career in merchandising and buying, you will probably find that you will be required to take a retail math pre-employment test. In fact, when looking at help wanted ads or job descriptions for almost any job in retailing, you will probably find retail math skills listed as a job requirement. Math is used at every level of retailing—from the part-time salesperson to the executive suite.

Will you be ready to take a retail math test during a job application process? When you finish this course and the activities provided in this textbook, you should be prepared. However, for a lot of students in your shoes, the term "math" conjures up horrible memories from their experiences in high school, especially if calculus was part of the curriculum. They are already intimidated by math before they sit down to take a pre-employment test in retail math. Relax; you do not have to be an accountant or a mathematician to handle retail math calculations, and you will not be using calculus. Yet, numbers are extremely important in retailing. In a merchandising and buying career, you will be calculating and analyzing numbers daily to help make the best business decisions possible.

At its simplest, retail math is basic arithmetic—that's the math you were doing in school before you started algebra. Addition, subtraction, multiplication, and division are the only math functions required. You will also be working with fractions, decimals, and percentages. So a little practice and review may be needed to re-familiarize yourself with math skills you may not have used recently. Basically, you will need to know which numbers to use in retail math calculations and how to interpret the results. In other words, you have got to understand how to make retail math calculations and know how to use the calculations to make decisions. If you are concerned about whether or not you will be ready to take a pre-employment test in retail math, the practice activities and experiences provided by this course will provide you with the preparation needed.

What kind of questions could you find on a retail math pre-employment test? The two questions below are examples from a retail math pre-employment math test given by a major national retailer. See if you can answer them.

Question 1. Calculate turnover using the formula that follows if Sales = 75,000 and Average Inventory = 20,000.

TURNOVER = SALES / AVERAGE INVENTORY

A.   2.75

B.   3.25

C.   3.50

D.   3.75

Question 2. Daily sales for one week at Frank's Lemonade Stand are listed on the chart below.

Day of Week	Glasses of Lemonade
Monday	100
Tuesday	150
Wednesday	150
Thursday	200
Friday	400
Saturday	500
Sunday	300
Total	?

If the weekend sales consist of Friday through Sunday sales, what percentage of the total week's sales were weekend sales? Round to the nearest percentage.

How did you do? You should have answered D for question 1 and 67 percent for question 2. Remember, however, that careers in merchandising and buying jobs will require that you do more than make calculations; you must be able to make decisions based on your calculations. For example, in question 2, should more advertising be considered for the first part of the week to increase sales? Or, would other inducements, such as a price decrease on Monday, increase sales and not decrease profit? For question 1, retail buyers would need to compare the achieved turnover with their goal to determine if they were successful. If the goal was not met, what could the buyer do to improve turnover? This course will prepare you not only to make retail math calculations, but to make decisions based on those calculations.

Good luck on that first retail math pre-employment test that you have to take. You'll be ready.

EMPLOYMENT FORECASTS: WHAT ARE THE PROJECTIONS FOR JOBS IN RETAIL BUYING?

One of the key skills needed by retail buyers is the ability to accurately make forecasts or predictions. In addition, they must be able to interpret forecasts and apply them in their daily decision-making activities. As you pursue a career in retailing, you can already start honing your skills in obtaining and interpreting forecasts in an area that will be very important to your future—future employment predictions. You will probably find various forecasts for local, state, and national levels, and sometimes your sources may even contradict each other. Just like a retailer, you will have to interpret your data and apply that interpretation the best that you can to your specific situation.

Each year the Bureau of Labor Statistics in the US Department of Labor makes national forecasts about employment change and the job outlook in various occupations. Remember that they are making predictions based on an examination of volumes of research and data, but forecasting is not an exact science. Also, when examining the bureau's forecasts, you must also understand that they are national projections. Forecasts would vary for different parts of the country and for specific types of businesses. However, the data presented give a snapshot of future job prospects that potential employees like you need to examine as part of their career planning process. The data will need to be supplemented by collecting forecasts from other local or state agencies.

Information from the bureau is presented yearly in the *Occupational Outlook Handbook* and is available online. The publication groups the following job categories together: purchasing managers, buyers, and purchasing agents. Data presented below for buyers includes both wholesale and retail buyers. Jobs in this occupational category are similar in nature; therefore, skills are usually easily transferable as employees switch between these jobs. All these occupations involve buying products for organizations to use or resell. Primary duties include evaluating suppliers, negotiating contracts, and reviewing product quality. Employees in these occupations accomplish these by primarily studying sales and inventory records and keeping abreast of changes in the marketplace that affect the supply and demand for products they sell.

In 2014, purchasing managers, buyers, and purchasing agents held about 443,200 jobs in the United States. Overall, the Bureau of Labor Statistics predicts that employment in this entire job category will increase 2 percent during the 2014–2024 decade, which is slower than average for all occupations that are surveyed. Remember, these projections are in relation to job growth; jobs will also be available as employees retire or switch to other jobs.

Data are also presented about earnings potential for this occupational category. In 2015, the median annual wages of wholesale and retail buyers were $59,620. Keep in mind, this is the national average. Wages will vary by geographic area.

Are there reasons that buying jobs are growing more slowly than other occupations? Demand for buyers will be limited by the increased use of technology, which has eliminated much of the paperwork that was previously required. Also, a growing number of purchases can now be made electronically much quicker and more efficiently. Mergers and acquisitions have also caused buying departments to consolidate. In addition, large retail chains are eliminating local/regional buying departments and creating a centralized buying department at their headquarters. Further, there have also been many retail store closures in the last few years; some retailers have vanished from the scene entirely.

As you prepare for a career in retail buying or any other occupation, you must monitor employment forecasts like the *Occupational Outlook Handbook* in order to accurately prepare yourself for jobs that will be available in the future.

BASED ON:

Bureau of Labor Statistics, US Department of Labor. (2015). *Occupational Outlook Handbook*, 2016–2017 edition.

Retail buyer: Job outlook & career information. (2017). *Study.com*.

BUYING FOR DIFFERENT TYPES OF STORES

CHAPTER 3

Performance Objectives

- Describe the differences between buying hard lines and soft lines.
- Describe the differences between buying fashion merchandise and basic merchandise.
- List and describe retail formats for which buyers make purchases.
- Describe centralized buying.
- Identify advantages and drawbacks of centralized buying.
- Identify types of centralized buying.
- Describe how buying is conducted for a single independent retailer.
- Explain the rationale for departmentalization at retail organizations.
- List and explain the types of departmentalization.
- Recognize the need for buyers to coordinate activities with other departments in a retail organization.
- Calculate and use profit percentages as a quantitative performance measurement to develop and implement retailing strategies.

As you learned in the previous chapter, the key duty of the buyer is to purchase merchandise for the store that will meet customer needs. This is true of all retail stores, regardless of their size or organizational structure or what products they sell. As you also learned, a key measurement of the buyer's performance is sales volume; however, in most retail stores today, the individuals who buy merchandise are separate from the individuals who sell the merchandise. As you will learn, separation of buying and selling has both advantages and drawbacks for the buyer. This chapter focuses on how the buying function is performed in different types of retail stores. Departmentalization is also described, along with a discussion of the coordination that must occur between the buyer and other departments.

BUYING DIFFERENT TYPES OF PRODUCTS

Almost all the duties that are described in the last chapter are performed by a buyer at any type of retail store—no matter what products are sold. As you start to plan your career in retail buying, one of your first decisions should be to determine the types of merchandise that would interest you the most. Are you more interested in soft lines or hard lines? **Soft lines** are typically the apparel and accessory product categories and fashions for the home such as linens, curtains, and bathroom items. In most stores, the remainder of the merchandise would be classified as **hard lines** and would include such product categories as hardware, sporting goods, appliances, furniture, toys, and lawn and garden products. Each of those areas could be further subdivided, depending on the size of the store. Soft lines could include women's, men's, and children's clothing. Even these categories could be further broken down—for example, men's jeans or men's dress pants. At large retail chains, some buyers may be responsible for only one product type—boys' jeans, for example.

Another way of further subdividing these two broad categories would be to classify merchandise as fashions or basics. Basic merchandise includes items that customers buy year in and year out; they expect the store to have these items in stock at all times. For example, black socks, men's white shirts, and blue blazers would be considered basics in soft lines. In hard lines, basics would include products such as Barbie dolls, dictionaries, or votive candles. Fashion merchandise, however, includes products that have high demand over a relatively short period of time—usually one selling season. Fashion merchandise includes most apparel items but also many hard lines. The newest aroma candles, the "hottest" color for cell phone covers, or a "special edition" Barbie doll would all be considered fashion merchandise. These items will be in the store for only a few months before being replaced by the next trend or newest model.

New buyers will find that forecasting for basic merchandise is much easier than for fashion merchandise. Sales for basics tend to vary little from year to year; that is not true with fashion merchandise. Fashions come on the market quickly and are gone just as quickly. Fashion buyers must be able to *predict* what their customers will buy this year without having last year's sales figures available because the merchandise is entirely new to the store. Even looking at similar products from last year may not provide valuable information. A trend that sold well last year may not sell at all this year.

Fashion buyers must always be seeking out new and innovative products to buy. Their buying decisions will involve many more risks than decisions of buyers who handle only basics. For many fashion buyers, these are the reasons that make buying fashion merchandise exciting and challenging. In addition, because of the pressure of taking these risks, fashion buyers are paid more than buyers who purchase only basics. Having the "right" fashion products in a store can be very profitable.

As you enter a career in retail buying, your first job will probably be buying basic merchandise. As you make purchasing decisions for that product category, you will be able to develop and hone your buying skills before having to deal with the risks and uncertainties of buying fashion merchandise. Which types of products interest you the most as you start your buying career?

BUYING AT DIFFERENT RETAIL FORMATS

After you decide which types of products interest you the most, you need to make a choice about the type of retail store for which you would like to be a buyer. By looking around your community, you can identify many types of retailers for whom you could work. Some of those stores may be located in malls or in downtown areas. Others may be stand-alone stores or located in strip shopping centers. These stores probably range from small independents to large stores that may be a part of a chain found in communities across the country. Examine the types of stores that interest you. Who performs the buying duties? Do they have buyers at the local store or are all buying duties performed by individuals at corporate headquarters? The answers to these questions may narrow your list of potential employers.

Do your career interests lie more with large retailers or small independents? Or are you interested in one day owning your own retail store? Before making your choice, you need to carefully examine the various kinds of retailers—their similarities as well as differences. First, you may want to examine the largest retailers in the country. These firms probably offer many employment opportunities due to their size and expansion plans. Review Table 3.1 to identify the top ten retailers in the United States. You are also provided with information on how fast these retailers are growing.

On the other hand, you may be more interested in starting your buying career at a local independent store that is not part of a chain. Such a decision certainly offers benefits. You will probably face less pressure and be better able to know your customers' wants and needs. But you will probably have to make purchases for the entire store or an entire department. You will be dealing with many different products, and that requires broad product knowledge. Also, at small independent retail stores, opportunities for advancement probably will come more slowly. No matter where you work, however, retail buying will provide you with an exciting and rewarding career.

As you make your decision about where to start your buying career, you need to examine the different types of retail formats that exist. Stores today are quite different from the way they were only a few years ago, and retailing tomorrow will look much different from the way it does today. One of the biggest changes has been in classifications of retail stores themselves. Already the lines between many retailers have blurred. For example, discounters and some department stores have added food lines

TABLE 3.1

TOP US RETAILERS, 2015

Retail Sales Rank	Company	2015 US Retail Sales ($000)	USA Sales Growth (2015 vs. 2014)	# US Stores 2015
1	Walmart	$353,108,000	2.8%	5,182
2	Kroger	$103,878,000	.8%	3,747
3	Costco	$83,545,000	4.8%	476
4	Home Depot	$79,297,000	6.9%	1,965
5	Walgreens	$76,604,000	6.0%	8,052
6	Target	$73,226,000	.8%	1,774
7	CVS	$72,151,000	6.2%	9,659
8	Amazon.com	$61,619,000	23.1%	N/A
9	Albertsons	$58,443,000	4.8%	2,311
10	Lowe's	$57,486,000	4.9%	1,805

Source: Stores, June, 2016.

to their product assortments. Target now sells groceries, and grocery stores sell flowers and greeting cards, and both have added on-site pharmacies. In the new millennium, new retail formats are likely to emerge to compete with traditional retailers for the customer's shopping dollar. What new formats do you see appearing?

As you will learn, old formats are changing, but general retail formats still exist, many times in an altered state. Review Figure 3.1, which illustrates recent sales growth and decline in some of these retail formats, and then, let's examine some of these broad retail classifications and identify the power players in each one.

Discounters and Mass Merchants

Mass merchants and **discount department stores** emphasize one-stop shopping to meet the needs of all family members and tend to appeal to consumers who value savings over service. Discounters typically offer an extensive selection of national brands in a modest setting with only a few sales associates on hand to offer customer service; emphasis is on selling products at low prices. Merchandise is organized to encourage self-selection by the customer. Typically, these retailers do not carry broad categories but tend to concentrate on the fastest-moving merchandise. Giants in the field include Walmart, Kmart, and Target. Amazon may not sell everything consumers want to buy, but the company sells enough different kinds of merchandise to warrant inclusion as a mass merchant retailer. For example, they dominate book sales and may soon be the largest retailer of apparel products. There seems to be a limitless array of products in Amazon's marketplace.

Since most of these retailers concentrate on basics, buying may be an easier task than at stores that also sell the latest trends and fashion-forward merchandise. It is much riskier to attempt to forecast sales for the newest fashion than it is for a basic product whose sales will probably be similar to sales from the previous season.

Department Stores

Originally, **department stores** were businesses that also sold all kinds of merchandise for the individual and the home, but today many of these stores have altered their product assortment as well as changing their customer base—they no longer try to offer something for everyone. Nordstrom, for example, focuses on apparel for men,

Figure 3.1

Percent of Sales Growth/ Decline by Retail Segment, from 2011–2016. Sales for some retail segments, like off-price and beauty, have grown, while other segments, such as department stores and office supply stores, have declined.

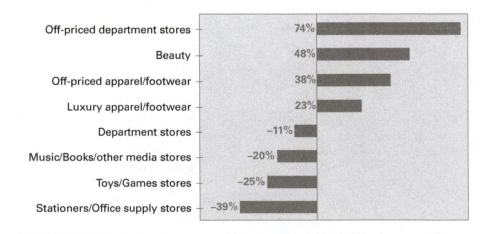

Off-priced department stores	74%
Beauty	48%
Off-priced apparel/footwear	38%
Luxury apparel/footwear	23%
Department stores	−11%
Music/Books/other media stores	−20%
Toys/Games stores	−25%
Stationers/Office supply stores	−39%

women, and children as well as shoes, handbags, accessories, and beauty. J.C. Penney has expanded its apparel lines, offered more national designer brands, and eliminated other product categories such as hardware and appliances. But, recently the company is reintroducing appliances at some stores. Changes like these will probably continue for most stores in this category.

For years, Sears was not only the dominant department store in the United States, it was also the dominant retailer—advertising itself as "where America shops," offering something for everyone. Today, however, many retail analysts question whether or not Sears will survive, and other department stores, such as Macy's and J.C. Penney, are also closing hundreds of stores. Read the Snapshot titled "Belk: Modern, Southern, Style" to learn more about how this department store has succeeded by defining itself regionally.

Recently, off-price and online retailers have siphoned sales from traditional department stores, and department store sales as a percentage of total retail sales have declined in the United States—from 2005 to 2015, department store sales fell 31 percent. Department stores realize that they must change with the times if they are to survive. Read the Trendwatch "Macy's: Are Department Stores Really Dead?" to learn about the techniques this store is using as it fights declining sales trends.

Mergers have affected the decline in the number of department stores, which will impact the number of retail buying jobs in this sector. In addition, department stores now have to adjust to new realities in the marketplace and to the changing preferences of shoppers. For example, many department stores lost their one-stop-shopping appeal as product categories were eliminated from their mix. Some department stores have shown an overdependence on products that can now be easily found online or in other stores. The next ten years will be critical for department stores as many of them seek strategies to simply survive.

Years ago, each department store chain had a different point of view, with many of them setting fashion trends of the day. Today, however, many of them are virtually interchangeable—looking nearly identical with the same product assortments and layouts. Moreover, their locations have also impacted sales negatively. Today many department stores are found at locations that many customers believe to be inconvenient—in traffic-bound malls.

Retail buyers at department stores will play a big role in finding ways to differentiate their stores from other retailers. They must create stores offering product assortments that will attract and retain customers whose shopping behavior continues to change.

Specialty Stores

Specialty stores primarily sell a few specific product categories and are based on the concept of meeting the needs of a narrower market segment. In fact, there is a specialty store for almost every product category. Let's examine some of the largest specialty segments and some key retailers in each segment.

- *Apparel.* Many of the most successful apparel retailers today implement a fast-fashion approach—moving merchandise much more quickly from the design concept to a product for sale on the store floor. Zara, H&M, and Forever 21 continue to be successful with this approach. On the other hand, some other apparel retailers have experienced a slump in revenues as online apparel sales increase. For example, to cut costs, Victoria's Secret has downsized its corporate offices and will stop publishing its catalog. Eliminating the catalog—300 million of which were printed annually—should save the company up to $150 million a year. Most apparel specialty stores are facing similar financial decisions. Although they also sell items for the home, TJX, parent of T.J. Maxx and Marshalls, now is the biggest general apparel seller in the United States.

- *Health and Beauty.* In the last ten years, beauty has been the second fastest growing segment of retailing. Within that segment, Ulta has been one of the big success stories by using an unusual business model (Figure 3.2). The stores offer mass (Nyx, Maybelline, and Revlon), prestige (BareMinerals, Urban Decay, Smashbox), and private-label products as well as salon products and services under one roof. The store is expected to add approximately 100 stores annually for the next few years. Read the Snapshot titled "Ulta: A Retail Success Story in the Beauty Market" to learn more about what has made this company so successful.

- *Hobby and Craft.* This retail segment is dominated by two retailers—Hobby Lobby and Michaels. Hobby Lobby recently opened its 700th location and plans to add fifty stores. Moreover, the stores seem to have a unique customer base. In a recent survey, two-thirds of their customers indicated they would rather shop in stores than online, and 18 percent did not even know they could make purchases online. Even so, Hobby Lobby is redesigning its website to make it more mobile-user friendly. Michaels Stores is also expanding by purchasing thirty stores from a crafts retailer in the Midwest and adding thirty-three more new stores.

- *Sporting Goods.* Currently, turmoil probably best describes the sporting goods retail segment. Sports Authority ceased operations and liquidated its stores. Eastern Mountain Sports and Sports Chalet have also filed for bankruptcy. In addition, Cabela's was recently purchased by Bass Pro Shops. All of these closures and consolidations leave companies like Dick's Sporting Goods eying some of the vacated storefronts as they seek to fill the void in the market.

Figure 3.2
Beauty retailers, like Ulta, have been big success stories in retailing.

- *Footwear.* Foot Locker is the power player in this segment with sales more than double those of runner-up DWS. The company operates a number of different formats and is constantly adjusting its locations by opening, closing, relocating, and sometimes rebranding its stores. In recent years, the company has generated record sales as well as improving earnings.
- *Drug Stores.* The two key power players in this segment are CVS and Walgreens, who are battling for dominance in the market. Both companies are implementing technology that allows customers to order items online (but not prescriptions) and pick them up in the store. Both also continue to expand product offerings beyond the pharmacy. They continue to add to food offerings and have made aggressive moves for the beauty market.
- *Hardware and Home Improvement.* Home Depot, the fourth largest retailer in the United States, continues to grow and expand while growth at its major competitor, Lowe's, has slowed. In fact, Lowe's has faced major layoffs both at corporate and in the stores recently. Home Depot has continued to attract customers to its bricks-and-mortar stores, even though many of the products it sells can be purchased for less online. Moreover, they have continued to enhance their own online sales with their buy online, ship to store program.
- *Entertainment and Electronics.* Even though e-commerce, downloads, and streaming have had a negative impact on the sales of books and media at bricks-and-mortar stores, Barnes & Noble remains somewhat strong as Borders ceased to exist and Books-A-Million closed many of its stores. However, even sales at Barnes and Noble have decreased 12 percent since their 2008 peak. Management's vision for the future is to make the company a "lifestyle brand" with stores stocked with not just books but also giftware, gadgets, games, and toys. The stores will be about learning, personal growth, and development. Best Buy remains the power player in electronics, as its competitors have closed many of their stores.
- *Supermarkets.* Two of the top ten retailers in the United States are supermarkets— Kroger is the second largest retailer in the United States and Albertson's is number nine. And, they face competition from other formats on the top ten list who have enhanced their grocery offerings, such as Walgreens, CVS, and Target. Supermarkets have broadened their product lines to include nonfood items such as hardware, health and beauty aids, housewares, stationery, and even some apparel. Consolidation and retrenchment have also marked supermarket retailing. For example, Kroger has purchased Harris-Teeter, a large grocery chain in the southeast, and Piggly Wiggly keeps retrenching in the few states where their stores remain. Dutch-controlled Ahold and Belgian-owned Delhaize are combining to create a network of supermarkets along the East Coast. These chains include Stop and Shop, Martins, Hannaford, and Food Lion.

Outlet Stores

Many traditional retail stores have established **outlet stores** across the country where they sell slow movers and out-of-date merchandise. Nordstrom with its Nordstrom Rack stores is an example of one retailer that has entered this retailing format. Many manufacturers also have established outlet stores to sell factory overruns, usually at deep discounts. In fact, buyers at outlet stores often have the responsibility of developing specifications for products that will be sold only at the outlets—new merchandise not offered in traditional stores. The buyers must work in tandem with other buyers so that the two lines are complementary.

Some outlets may even sell the same merchandise being offered at traditional retail stores near the end of the selling season. Other outlet stores are also used as test markets for new styles or models coming into the market. Polo, Bose, Eddie Bauer, UnderArmour, and Tommy Hilfiger are just a few of the manufacturers that have been selling merchandise through this retail format that has seen modest growth.

Superstore Retailing

The term **superstore** refers to just about any store that is bigger than what would normally be found selling a particular category of merchandise. These stores tend to be the largest stores of their type in a geographic area and include warehouse clubs, supercenters, and specialized superstores.

- *Supercenters.* Supercenters are mega-supermarkets and general merchandise stores that stock everything from food to appliances under one roof. Examples include Walmart, Big Kmarts, and SuperTargets. The strategy behind supercenters is to have on hand the products that represent 80 percent of customers' regular needs and to avoid specialty or slow-moving merchandise. The brand-name merchandise assortment is tailored to middle-income consumers; however, supercenters avoid being too fashionable because inventory requirements and risks are so large.
- *Warehouse Clubs.* Warehouse clubs are huge warehouses that sell just about everything, typically in large-sized quantities. They offer no frills, little sales assistance, and no special décor. Customers may even have to dodge forklifts as they shop. Most warehouse clubs operate as members-only stores where customers pay an annual fee. In fact, nearly one-third of these members are retail store owners who are buying in bulk for their own stores. Three firms now account for about 90 percent of the market: Sam's Club, BJ's Wholesale Club, and Costco (Figure 3.3).

Figure 3.3

Costco is one of the top three warehouse clubs in the United States.

- *Specialized Superstores.* Specialized superstores typically offer one to three categories of merchandise in tremendously large assortments at discount prices that are unmatched by any other retailer in the area. They are also known as "category killers" because of the way in which they totally dominate the market for a specific product category. Toys "R" Us was the first retailer to prove this type of store could work. Since then, superstores have come onto the retail scene in many different product categories, such as books (Barnes and Noble), electronics (Best Buy), pets (Petco), office supplies (Office Depot), and even crafts (Hobby Lobby).

As you pursue a career in retail buying, realize that most of the buying skills and competencies you learn will be transferable among the various retail formats. Keep your eye on the marketplace; understand which formats are growing and which ones are declining or restructuring. Table 3.2 illustrates a number of retailers who have experienced rapid sales growth in recent years.

Retailing formats will continue to change, and it is imperative that you recognize the changes that are occurring and which retailers are the power players of the future within each retail segment.

BUYING FOR CHAIN STORES

With mergers and expansion of many independent retail stores, there has been a tremendous growth in the number of chain stores. A **chain store** is two or more stores under single ownership. Typically, a chain store has a central headquarters that manages and buys merchandise for all stores in the chain. It is hard to generalize about chain store organizations because they are so complex. Some have two or three stores, whereas others have hundreds. Chains can be located in one city, one state, one region, or nationwide. Some chains own all their units, whereas others franchise part of their operations.

TABLE 3.2

SELECTED RETAILERS EXPERIENCING SALES GROWTH, 2014–2015

Retailer	US Retail Sales (000)	Sales Growth 2014–2015	Number of Stores 2015
Dollar Tree	$19,930,000	138%	13,626
Wayfair	$1,943,000	88%	N/A (online)
H&M	$3,938,000	48%	415
Kate Spade	$764,000	26%	159
At Home Stores	$622,000	25%	100
Amazon	$61,619,000	23%	N/A (online)
Ulta	$3,715,000	21%	874
Ollie's	$762,000	19%	203
Skechers	$627,000	17%	390
Lululemon	$1,453,000	16%	260

Source: Stores, August 2016.

As retail stores grow and expand, management looks for ways to increase control as well as profitability of their stores. Standardizing merchandise assortments and store operations in all stores of the chain has become an approach that is frequently used. Buyers are removed from individual stores and placed at the chain's headquarters. By purchasing the same merchandise for many different stores, the chain also has the advantage of mass buying power, providing the opportunity for increased profits. In fact, some of the largest national chains purchase the complete output of certain manufacturers.

There are chains that carry varied assortments of merchandise such as grocery, department, discount, and drugs; but some chains specialize in a single line of merchandise such as shoes, men's clothing, candy, jewelry, toys, tires, or sporting goods. Buyers for such specialty stores may have responsibility for only one line or brand of merchandise.

Buyers for a chain store plan sales goals, seek out sources of merchandise, and purchase merchandise to be sold in all the chain's stores. In most chain stores, selling is separate from the buying function. Buyers have very little responsibility for sales personnel and practically no personal contact with them. Removal of selling responsibility enables them to devote their entire time to product and market knowledge; therefore, they become product specialists. Because of the separation of buying and selling, buyers must keep in contact with stores and sales associates through bulletins and other communications because the buyer's performance is still measured by the amount of merchandise sold in the stores.

Centralized Buying

Centralized buying occurs when all buying activities are performed from the store's central headquarters. Buyers there have the authority and responsibility for the selection and purchase of merchandise for all stores. The primary advantages of central buying include the following:

- A steady flow of merchandise is provided to the store because buyers are able to spend more time in the market. They are able to make frequent small shipments to keep store assortments complete and balanced.
- Sales forecasts for all stores in a chain are more reliable than forecasts for each separate store. Centralized data allow buyers to be more accurate in predicting consumer trends because examining a small number of sales in each individual store may not be enough to detect trends.
- A specialist is making the buying decisions. Centralized buyers make merchandise decisions for only a few products rather than a multitude of items, allowing them to be more knowledgeable about that merchandise.
- Expenses are reduced because each store does not need individual buyers. Travel expenses to markets are also reduced.
- Purchasing power is consolidated at headquarters, and this leads to lower merchandise costs because the chain will be in a better position to take advantage of quantity discounts.

Types of Centralized Buying

Central buying usually occurs in one of two forms: (1) central merchandising plan and (2) warehouse requisition plan.

Central Merchandising Plan

Under the **central merchandising plan**, a central office representing a group of stores has complete responsibility for the selection and purchase of merchandise for all the stores. Stores using this plan include major department stores such as J.C. Penney and Macy's, as well as national specialty store chains such as Victoria's Secret, Lane Bryant, Old Navy, and Gap. Each store receives whatever the corporate office considers appropriate; however, these decisions are not made haphazardly. Buying decisions for each store are based on factors such as sales history and average ticket sale. Centralized buyers spend a great deal of time collecting and analyzing sales and inventory data collected from each store. Because of a dependence on reports, there is a tremendous reliance on computer output.

The chief disadvantage of this approach is that individual store needs may not be met. Managers may be less enthusiastic about selling merchandise that they had no choice in selecting and may even be critical of the merchandise received. Some store managers may even blame the buyers for slow-selling merchandise.

Warehouse Requisition Plan

The **warehouse requisition plan** attempts to overcome some of the limitations of the central merchandising plan; however, it is typically used only by stores carrying basic merchandise. Regional distribution centers are established to serve a number of stores in the area. The buyer at headquarters still determines the assortment of merchandise carried in the warehouse; however, each store manager is allowed to requisition the assortment that he or she wishes for the individual store. This plan allows managers to eliminate items they feel are unnecessary for their store, or items that will not sell well in their locality. Requests for merchandise are sent directly to the warehouse, which many times is located less than twenty-four hours from the store. Chain stores that decide to use this plan must have a sufficient number of stores in one area to make the establishment of a distribution center cost-effective.

The plan provides several advantages. Usually, shipping distances from the distribution center to each store are short so that orders can be filled quickly. Using the warehouse requisition plan also reduces the amount of inventory that must be carried by each store. Because stores can obtain quicker reorders, less merchandise has to be kept in stockrooms, freeing additional space for sales.

This plan is used extensively by food, drug, and discount chains. Department stores such as Sears and J.C. Penney have also established warehouses for many of their lines; however, this plan is not usually effective for fashion items. Fashion items change so quickly that they need to come directly from the manufacturer. Fashion goods have too short a selling life to permit storing them for a time in a warehouse.

Drawbacks of Centralized Buying

As you have read, buying and selling have become separated in most retail stores. Advantages are gained with increased profitability, standardized operations, and improved control, but there are drawbacks to central buying.

The most evident challenge is that adjusting merchandise selection for local conditions may be difficult. Larger sizes and different colors may sell at various rates in particular areas depending on characteristics of the population. Timing of seasonal goods also varies from one part of the country to another. Winter comes earlier to some sections of the country than others. However, this may not be as serious as it sounds. Except for weather variations, demand in all parts of the United States today is remarkably uniform, no doubt due to mass media advertising and the large amount of consumer travel. Centralized buyers also have a wealth of store data to analyze, even though they are not in the area where an individual store is located.

Centralized buying can lead to a lack of cooperation between buyers and store managers. There is a difficulty in fixing responsibility when merchandise does not sell well. In fact, some managers may be apathetic or prejudiced against the merchandise sent by buyers at headquarters because they did not have a choice in its selection.

Sometimes, centralized buying makes it difficult to maintain enthusiastic and knowledgeable sales associates. The merchandising division and the buyers are still judged by the amount of goods sold, but the use of centralized buying has removed control of sales associates from the buyer. In fact, except for an occasional visit to a nearby store, many buyers may never have been in the vast majority of a chain's stores.

Buyers have the responsibility for informing the stores of the manner in which the merchandise is to be sold. Because this cannot be done orally, a constant flow of written communication is required. Written bulletins, however, are a poor substitute for the enthusiasm built up by actual involvement in the selection of goods.

To overcome these drawbacks, some chains have moved toward decentralization. Some duties that once were performed at headquarters are delegated to the stores. For example, both the warehouse requisition plan and the price agreement plan give each store manager more choice in merchandise selection.

Almost all national chains use centralized buying today. Because it has become so dominant in the retail industry, fewer complaints are heard at the store level. Most store-level associates have never known buying to occur any other way.

ORGANIZATIONAL STRUCTURE AND THE BUYING FUNCTION

At large retail operations, job functions are assigned to different sets of employees—they are departmentalized. **Departmentalization**, organizing different store activities into departments or divisions, results in managers who are directly responsible to the store or chain's manager.

Types of Departmentalization

Usually, departmentalization is based on job function, but it may occur based on product line or geographic location. The size of the firm usually determines which approach is used.

Functional departmentalization is one of the most commonly used methods by which work is organized in retail stores. With **functional departmentalization**, activities of a similar nature are grouped together into a major area of responsibility and headed by an individual who reports to the owner or chief executive of the firm.

A basic four-function plan of store organization known as the "Mazur Plan" has been used by most retailers since 1927, when Paul M. Mazur recommended it to what is now the National Retail Federation. The four functions he presented occur in every retail store organization, regardless of size or number of people employed:

- *Control.* This department would be responsible for safeguarding the firm's assets and is usually divided into accounting, credit, and financial control.
- *Promotion.* Responsibilities of this department would usually include advertising, visual merchandising, public relations, special events, and fashion coordination.
- *Operations.* This department would typically be responsible for the stockroom, maintenance, delivery, receiving, and customer services.
- *Merchandising.* Duties of this department would be to forecast the type, quality, and price of merchandise that will be wanted by the store's customers, and then to purchase these goods as economically as possible.

Today, the organizational structure of many retail stores also includes the function of personnel or human resource management. This department is responsible for interviewing, placing, and terminating employees as well as maintaining employee records and conducting training programs.

Product line departmentalization occurs at some retail stores that have a varied product offering. Stores using **product line departmentalization** group merchandise by categories such as furniture, appliances, children's wear, or jewelry. Large food stores are all departmentalized this way, with departments such as grocery, meats, produce, deli/bakeries, and health and beauty aids. An individual is responsible for all business operations affecting a particular product line, including buying and selling.

Using product line departmentalization, a buyer could be in charge of a single product category or several. Other store functions can also be departmentalized this way. For example, control can be divided into accounts receivable and accounts payable; however, the focus of this chapter is on the merchandising function.

Stores could also decide to departmentalize based on both function and product line. An independent department store, for example, may establish a merchandising division for the store, with buyers directly responsible to this division manager. Each buyer would be making purchases for specific product lines.

Geographic departmentalization can be found at many retail chains that have expanded nationally. **Geographic departmentalization** breaks the organization down by region of the country. For example, some national firms may have a north, south, east, and west division, each headed by an executive. Under this executive would be various other managers, each with a different area of responsibility. Usually, these areas are the functional areas presented previously.

Some retail firms are so large they may use all three types of departmentalization—functional, product line, and geographic departmentalization. This type of combined organizational structure is presented in Figure 3.4.

Figure 3.4

The organizational structure
for some retail stores
combines several types of
departmentalization.

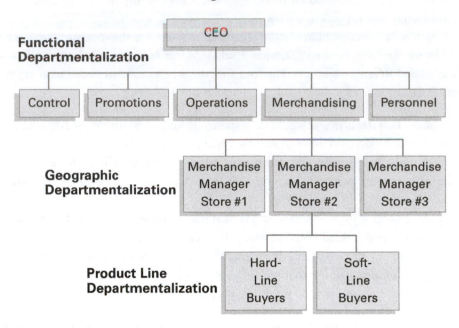

Combined Organizational Structure

Relationship of Merchandising to Other Departments
===

Relationship of Merchandising to Other Departments

To be successful as a buyer, you must understand the relationship of your job duties to other jobs in the organizational structure of your firm. In particular, you must understand the relationship of the buying and selling functions within your store. Many firms design an **organizational chart** of their internal structure that indicates all the employees and their relationship to one another. Seldom are any two retail stores organized in exactly the same manner; however, there are many common elements in every retail organization, as well as differences.

There must be communication and cooperation between departments of any business if it is to operate efficiently. Each department's functions must be clearly defined and understood by every employee. This section, however, focuses on the relationship of the merchandising division to the other store functions. As a buyer, you must be ready to coordinate your efforts with those of others in the firm.

Buyers should know the relationship of the merchandising division to all the other departments that make up the store's organizational structure. As a buyer, you should have specific knowledge of other departments in the store and a working knowledge of the duties that each employee performs. For example, in many large independent stores, sales associates may be hired by the personnel department, but the merchandising division may be given the responsibility of providing them with product knowledge training.

Buyers must also work closely with the promotion department by providing information on products that need to be advertised or promoted. Buyers must also ensure that the store has merchandise in stock before an ad breaks.

The control department will develop the record-keeping and control systems used by the store. Buyers should have input so that records and reports will be useful to them as they keep track of inventory levels and make purchasing decisions. The buyer's budget is also approved by the control department. Before going to market, some stores require that this department approve the buyer's merchandise plan. Invoices are also paid by this department, and their prompt payment will allow the buyer to take advantage of cash discounts offered by vendors. Many retailers have established **IT (information technology)** departments to handle the technology needs of the entire store. Today, IT departments at many retailers also develop and monitor the store's social media programs, which generate lots of reports about customer attitudes and behaviors in relation to the store and the products offered.

Operations are another key partner for the buyer. The department is responsible for receiving and marking merchandise and getting merchandise to the selling floor promptly and correctly marked. It also has responsibility for merchandise in the stockroom. The merchandise purchased by buyers cannot be sold if it is not on the sales floor.

As the organizational structure for retail stores becomes larger and more complex, buyers must understand the internal store environment in which they are working. Buyers cannot perform their jobs in isolation. There must be cooperation and coordination with all departments if the buyer is to succeed and the store is to satisfy the needs of its customers.

BUYING FOR YOUR OWN STORE

Your community probably has many independent firms such as a neighborhood grocery store, hardware store, furniture store, clothing store, or shoe store. Single, small, independent stores are a vital part of our economy. In fact, almost half the businesses in the United States are operated entirely by one or two people, usually the owner and a spouse, partner, or employee.

In small independent stores, the owner is responsible for all aspects of the business operations, *including all buying duties*; therefore, he or she must have a thorough understanding of the buying process. Store owners not only decide what to purchase for the store, but also they will probably receive, check, and mark the merchandise when it is delivered and will probably be responsible for selling it.

Because buying and selling activities are both usually performed by the store owner, selecting merchandise that customers want and need is probably easier than at most national chains because of the owner's direct day-to-day contact with customers. Moreover, because store owners purchased the products being sold, they are probably very knowledgeable about the merchandise and enthusiastic about selling it.

The combination of a changing consumer and aggressive big retailers has been very tough on small independent retailers. Do they have a future? The answer is yes, but not without some dramatic changes in behavior. Blocking the big-box stores, such as Walmart, from communities is only delaying the inevitable. Keeping out big retailers is not the answer; small retailers must differentiate themselves in such a way as to reduce or quite possibly eliminate comparisons with their big competitors.

Strategies for Competing with Big-Box Retailers

Independent retailers must examine their market segments carefully. They need to find out where else their customers shop—small as well as **big-box retailers**. Then they need to learn as much as they can about those stores. A toy retailer should understand Toys "R" Us. Apparel retailers must frequently visit stores like Forever 21 and H&M and understand why customers are shopping there. Read the Snapshot titled "Forever 21: Providing Fashion Faster" to learn more about how this apparel retailer has become so successful. The more that independent retailers learn about their big-box competition, the better they will be able to compete. Most small independents will not be able to compete on price and depth of assortment. If customers want the lowest price or a large assortment, the big-box stores win. Small independents cannot look and act like big stores; these retailers must act differently. Small independent retailers must know where they can win and where they cannot. They cannot buy merchandise at the same price paid by big-box retailers. They cannot consistently sell at low prices. They cannot obtain the concessions from vendors and suppliers that big-box stores can. They cannot instantly replenish inventory. Nor can they operate their business as inexpensively as the big-box stores can. There are, however, some strategies they can implement.

Many big-box stores carry merchandise that is not fashion forward; it is safe but boring. Independents must seek out and buy from fresh, new, innovative vendors. They must avoid carrying too much basic merchandise. Even though it is dependable, it does little for the merchandise mix and their profitability. The products they select should add personality to the store and set it apart—not be the same brands carried by the big stores.

Many big-box stores offer little or no customer service. This is the real opportunity for independent retailers to distance themselves from their big competitors. They need to provide real customer service to their shoppers. Sales associates must be available who know the products they are selling.

Most big-box stores are technology-dependent. Small retailers need to take advantage of existing technology, but not become its slave. Contact with sales associates at small stores should be an inspiring experience for customers. These associates should be able to make the sale, even if the computer crashes.

Many big-box retailers present a "low price" image to their customers. Small independents should use price as a weapon as little as possible. Clearance sales should be really special events with aggressive price cutting and promotions. The goal is to sell out the old merchandise fast and get new products in as quickly as possible.

One of the critical success factors for small retailers is expertise in, and enthusiasm for, the merchandise being offered the customer. Sales expertise is not dead at large chain stores, but it is rarely outstanding. This void creates a perfect opportunity for small independent retailers who really know their product.

Unique merchandise is another critical success factor for small retailers (Figure 3.5). Most chains are not able to implement merchandise plans that are wildly unique. Their size tends to make them conservative, even though they first rose to success because of a unique approach to business. One of the most unique merchandising ideas does not belong to a chain but can be found at Stew Leonard's supermarket in Connecticut. Stew offers a "Disneyland" of activities for the store's customers—from a petting zoo to mechanical singing animals. It is an approach that is working—parking lots are filled to near capacity most days.

Probably the most important critical success factor for a small business is dedication to customers. Many retailers give lip service to the customer being king; few are able to implement the idea really well. Once small retailers know what they want to be, marketing and advertising will become much easier; they will more easily identify new

Figure 3.5
Offering unique merchandise is critical to small independent retailers competing against large chains.

product opportunities for the store. More importantly, customers will be satisfied and keep returning. They will have been given reasons to shop there rather than at the big retailer a few miles away.

Measuring the Success of Strategic Decisions

How will independent retailers or big-box retailers know if the strategies they have implemented are successful? As you learned in the last chapter, there are numerous quantitative performance measurements that can be used (i.e., cumulative markup percentage, stock turnover, sales, and profit). Because small business owners need to monitor more than just the purchasing/buying functions of their firm, they will probably examine profit calculations first. **Profit** is the amount of money that remains after operating expenses have been subtracted from **gross margin** (sales minus cost of goods sold). Most retailers will probably have an accountant to track profit for the firm on a periodic basis. Management, however, must still be able to determine what strategic changes are needed to improve the overall profit picture.

Typically, profits are shown on **income statements** or **profit** or **loss statements**, which contain five key components:

- **Net sales** represent the real volume of sales that have occurred. In other words, net sales equal total sales minus returns made by customers.
- **Cost of goods sold** represents the actual cost of the merchandise that was sold during the period.
- **Gross margin** is the difference between the cost of goods sold and net sales; it represents money remaining to cover the store's operating expenses and anticipated profit.
- **Operating expenses** are expenses incurred in operating the business. Salaries, rent, advertising, and utilities would be operating expenses. The cost of the merchandise is *not* an operating expense.

- **Profit** is the amount of money that remains after operating expenses have been subtracted from gross margin. If the operating expenses of a business are greater than gross margin, a loss results.

Detailed operating statements contain many more components that retailers would examine in detail; however, most buyers and merchandisers make decisions that probably will only affect net sales and cost of goods sold. In this chapter, we will examine only the five key components listed above. The following formula illustrates how these components are used to determine the profit calculation as a dollar figure:

Net sales — Cost of goods sold = Gross margin — Operating Expenses = Profit / loss (before taxes)

However, raw numbers like these make comparisons difficult for the buyer or store owner. For example, sales may have dramatically increased from one period to another, with a corresponding increase in operating expenses. Profit dollars in such a situation may be larger but represent a smaller portion of total sales. Therefore, it is more important to calculate these components as percentages that are calculated by dividing the dollar amount for each component by the dollar amount of net sales. The sample problem that follows shows how this formula is used.

Illustrative Problem

During the year, net sales for a florist were $200,000. Cost of goods sold was $105,000, and operating expenses totaled $75,000. Complete an income/profit or loss statement, showing both dollar amounts and percentages for each of the components.

Solution

First, substitute into the operating statement the information you already know, as follows:

Net sales	$200,000
— Cost of goods sold	$105,000
= Gross margin	
— Operating expenses	$75,000
= Profit	

Next, determine gross margin by subtracting cost of goods sold from net sales; therefore, gross margin equals $95,000 ($200,000 – $105,000). Then, calculate profit by subtracting operating expenses from gross margin. In this example, profit would equal $20,000 ($95,000 – $75,000).

Now you need to convert these dollar amounts to percentages as follows:

Net sales	100.0% (calculated by $200,000/$200,000)
Cost of goods sold	52.5% (calculated by $105,000/$200,000)
Gross margin	47.5% (calculated by $95,000/$200,000)
Operating expenses	37.5% (calculated by $75,000/$200,000)
Profit	10.0% (calculated by $20,000/$200,000)

If the profit percentage does not meet the retailer's expectations, a careful examination of each of the components of the formula will assist them in making future strategic decisions. This basic formula suggests that there are three ways to improve the profit performance for the firm: (1) increase sales, (2) decrease cost of goods, and (3) decrease operating expenses. Retailers may decide to alter their strategy on one or all of these components. However, decisions must be made carefully so that profit is not negatively impacted.

For example, retailers can typically increase sales by lowering retail prices or advertising more; however, both of these strategies involve spending money. Increases in sales must compensate for the increase in advertising or reduced income from a lower retail price. Retailers may look for less expensive strategies to increase sales—for example, moving the merchandise to a better location in the store or providing better training to sales associates so that they increase their average sales.

The formula also suggests that profits can be increased by decreasing the cost of goods sold. Again, retailers must carefully examine any strategy they decide to implement. For example, cost of goods could be reduced by finding different vendors who sell similar products for a less expensive price; however, the new product may not appeal to customers and sales may go down rather than increase. Obtaining quantity discounts from the vendor is another way to achieve a lower cost of goods.

Finally, based on the formula, reduced operating expenses will increase profits. Again, retailers must examine each of their expenditures and analyze the impact a change would have on sales. For example, operating expenses can be reduced by reducing the number of employees. That move could result in less customer service and possibly less sales, resulting in less profit.

Quantitative performance measurements, such as cost of goods percentage, gross margin percentage, and profit percentage, alert retailers that a change may be required in their strategy if they are not meeting established goals in these areas. Various strategic decisions can be executed; however, making too many changes in strategy at one time may not be beneficial because it will be difficult to determine which change had an impact on profits. Retailers, from both large and small stores, must continually monitor performance measurements like these and examine the impact of their decisions on the overall success of the business.

Summary Points

- **The way in which individual stores are organized contributes to their uniqueness. A store's organizational structure will also influence how buying is conducted in that store.**

- **In many small independent stores, the owner typically is responsible for both the buying and selling functions; however, as a store grows and expands, there is a need to departmentalize.**

- **Three types of departmentalization can be found in retail stores—functional, product line, and geographic. A retail store can use a combination of any of these types of departmentalization in its organizational structure.**

- **As stores expand, owners start to identify ways to make their operations more profitable. Many chains use centralized buying, where all buying activities are handled from the store's headquarters.**

- **Centralized buying usually occurs in one of two forms—central merchandising plan or warehouse requisition plan.**

- **Few retail stores are organized in exactly the same manner. As a buyer, you must understand how the store you work for is organized as well as obtain a general understanding of how each department operates.**

- Buyers must coordinate their activities with other departments if they are to be successful.
- Store owners/buyers at small independent retail stores must calculate and use profit percentage figures as quantitative performance measurements to evaluate the success or failure of strategic decisions.

Review Activities

Developing Your Retail Buying Vocabulary

Consult the glossary if you did not add the following terms to your vocabulary.

big-box retailer	functional	mass merchant	profit or loss statement
central merchandising plan	departmentalization	net sales	soft lines
centralized buying	geographic	operating expenses	specialized superstore
chain store	departmentalization	organizational chart	specialty store
cost of goods sold	gross margin	outlet store	supercenter
department store	hard lines	product line	superstore
departmentalization	income statement	departmentalization	warehouse club
discount department store	IT (information technology)	profit	warehouse requisition plan

Understanding What You Read

1. Identify reasons that might cause buying to be easier for the owner of a small independent retail store than for a centralized buyer.

2. Compare and contrast the three types of departmentalization. Identify components of a retail strategy.

3. Identify specific areas of coordination between the merchandising division and other departments.

4. Identify the key disadvantages of centralized buying.

5. List and discuss the major advantages of centralized buying.

6. Compare and contrast the two types of centralized buying.

7. Which centralized buying plan gives the most freedom to store managers? Explain.

8. Describe how centralized buying can improve a store's merchandise offerings.

9. Describe the importance of written communications to buyers at headquarters.

10. Identify the differences between department stores and discount department stores.

Analyzing and Applying What You Read

1. Are the disadvantages of centralized buying serious enough to prevent retail chains from growing and expanding in the future? Explain.

2. Describe how buyers, removed from direct customer contact, can make better merchandise selections than store or department managers.

3. Outline the steps you would take as a buyer located at your firm's headquarters to build enthusiasm among managers and sales associates for merchandise you have purchased.

4. Develop a plan that you could implement as a buyer located at headquarters that could involve managers in the merchandise selection process.

Retail Buying Math Practice

1. During the month, net sales for a menswear store were $215,768. Cost of goods sold was $105,800, and operating expenses totaled $80,980. What profit (before taxes) was achieved by the store for the month?

2. Based on the income profit/loss statement that follows, calculate the percentage that each element represents.

Sales	$567,100
Cost of Goods Sold	$251,000
Gross Margin	$316,100
Operating Expenses	$285,500
Profit/Loss	$30,600

3. A store has the following figures available: sales were $220,000; cost of goods sold was $160,000; and operating expenses were $70,000. Calculate gross margin and profit for this store.

4. Based on the information that follows, calculate the components of an income/profit or loss statement as a dollar amount and as a percentage.

Sales	$250,000
Cost of Goods Sold	$118,500
Operating Expenses	$105,200

5. Based on the information that follows, calculate the components of an income/profit or loss statement as a dollar amount and as a percentage.

Sales	$600,253
Cost of Goods Sold	$301,112
Operating Expenses	$256,825

STUDIO

Spreadsheet Skills

In this assignment, you will use a spreadsheet to calculate components of the operating statement—key quantitative performance measurements that can be used to evaluate retail buyers, managers, and store owners on how well they implemented a retail strategy. Visit this book's STUDIO product at www.BloomsburyFashionCentral.com and open and print Assignment C. Record your answers on the tables provided at the end of the assignment.

Internet Connection

1. Choose one of the top ten retailers listed in Table 3.1 and use the internet to locate current sales and number of stores for that retailer. Describe any rationale given for increases or decreases in either of these areas.

2. Use the internet to locate an organizational chart for a major retailer. Describe the type of departmentalization the firm is using.

3. Visit the book's STUDIO to watch videos about retail buying and merchandising at TJX stores and the business of fast fashion.

SNAPSHOT: Forever 21: Providing Fashion Faster

Forever 21 is an American chain of specialty clothing stores (selling fashion and accessories for young women and men) with branches in the United States and around the world. In a short time, the chain has gained a reputation for providing faster fashion and cheaper chic to its customers. The firm was founded in Los Angeles, California, in 1984 by South Korean Dong-Won Chang and his wife, Jin Sook. By 1997, there were forty stores in the chain, and expansion began in Canadian and Asian markets. Most recently, new stores have opened in Great Britain, Ireland, Spain, and Austria.

Sales at department stores may be sluggish, but specialty stores selling low-priced and fast-fashion brands seem to be booming, and Forever 21 is one of the leaders in this area. How have they accomplished such rapid growth? While it takes most designers several months to get clothes into stores after their debut on the runways, Forever 21 delivers their interpretations of the same looks within six weeks. By relentlessly chasing trends and catering to an ever-widening market, Forever 21 has positioned itself as a retail powerhouse, now competing with fast-fashion emporiums like European-based Zara and H&M. Wider assortments are also offered. In the United States, stores are typically 25,000 square feet, roughly five times that of many Anthropologie or Gap stores. Their success may also be attributed to the firm's ability to tailor assortments to local communities; they do not carry the same merchandise at each store. The trendiest items, for example, are offered only at select locations.

Management has also taken steps to widen the chain's appeal beyond its core teen and young adult market. Two of the largest stores in the chain (85,000- to 90,000-square-feet mega-stores) are in California and New York. The stores are modern and sleek, with white lacquered and mirrored walls, crystal chandeliers, and Lucite display cases. The merchandise assortment ranges from the trendy to the more sophisticated, and includes a children's line, a plus-size line, shoes, makeup, and all kinds of accessories. The chain has also launched a line of cosmetics with no item costing more than ten dollars. And, the store has tested the designer waters with a T-shirt collection by Brian Lichtenberg and other collections by Petro Zillia and Rory Beca.

Management is making changes to help guarantee continued growth. Yet, many questions remain. Will the chain be able to keep fresh new designs in the stores, offering customers fast fashion and a cheaper chic? Will Forever 21 be able to dominate the market? Rivals like American Eagle and Abercrombie are both making a concerted effort to also become fast-fashion stores, reducing their times from design to store within forty-five to sixty days. Will the chain over-saturate the market with such an ambitious expansion plan?

BASED ON:

Berthiaume, Dan. (2016, May 19). Forever 21 seamlessly credits loyal customers. *ChainStoreAge.com.*

Heller, Laura. (2014, April 28). The real cost of fast fashion. *Forbes.com.*

Heller, Marc. (2014, July 9). As pace of teen retail picks up, Abercrombie looks set to prosper, Forever 21 could flounder. *Forbes.com.*

Soltes, Fiona (2016, December 5). Staying ahead of fast fashion. *Stores.org.*

SNAPSHOT: Belk: Modern, Southern, Style

Belk, one of the country's largest regional department store chains, will have been conducting business for over 130 years as the decade ends. In addition to investing heavily in refurbishing existing stores and enhancing its e-commerce site, the company has also refreshed its visual identity with a new corporate logo, color palette, and tagline—Modern, Southern, Style. According to Belk representatives, the new brand clearly communicates what the company is today and aspires to be in the future.

To meet these goals, Belk has improved its use of in-store technology and that also includes the use of mobile technology by customers using smartphones while shopping. Primarily, the stores have been redesigned to better appeal to female shoppers. In addition, the company's e-commerce site has been upgraded to improve the store's digital footprint as well as online sales. The overall goal is to establish Belk as the brand leader in the southern market.

While the company continues to meet the needs of its traditional customers, there will be a focus on meeting the fashion needs of modern consumers. That focus includes expanding product assortments to attract new customers who are looking for modern, updated brands and styles. The goal is for the modern southern woman to think about Belk first when making purchases for herself and her family.

Redefining the company involved time and money. The rebranding process took over a year and involved extensive research in Belk's primary markets, which included hundreds of associates and a survey of more than 30,000 customers. Moreover, approximately $80 million was spent on rebranding and marketing efforts, including $25 million for the installation of new logo signs in all the company's stores.

Currently Belk, headquartered in Charlotte, North Carolina, is located in sixteen southern states—Alabama, Arkansas, Florida, Georgia, Kentucky, Louisiana, Maryland, Mississippi, Missouri, North Carolina, Oklahoma, South Carolina, Tennessee, Texas, Virginia, and West Virginia. In those markets, store sizes vary widely, ranging from 40,000 to 300,000 square feet, depending upon the location. The average store is 92,000 square feet. Name recognition and sales growth are also occurring outside the south. About 20 percent of e-commerce sales are outside Belk's sixteen-state footprint.

Store growth has primarily occurred through acquisitions. In 2005, Belk acquired forty-seven Proffitt's and McRae's stores, and in 2006, thirty-nine Parisian Department Stores were acquired. To maintain a southern focus, some of the acquired stores were sold to the Bon-Ton stores because they were not in Belk's trading area.

Traditional sales are growing. Recently, company revenues increased 7 percent over the previous year. And, internet sales are growing even faster. In a single year, the chain experienced an 87 percent increase over the previous year. The company's goal is to reach 6 billion dollars in sales within the next few years.

With solid leadership over the years, the company has expanded and continues to embrace change. Today, Belk is a retail success story in an environment where many department stores have ceased to exist.

BASED ON:

Cornatzer, Mary. (2013, March 8). At 125, Belk is expanding and embracing change. *NewsObserver.com*.

Loeb, Walter. (2013, May 3). Belk stores—A jewel in the South grows with the Internet. *Forbes.com*.

Moultrie, Dalondo. (2013, August 10). Belk sets its eyes on lone star state with New Braunfels store. *Herald-zeitung.com*.

Reda, Susan. (2013, April). Redefining modern southern retailing. *Stores.org*.

At a time when major retailers are closing hundreds of stores, Ulta has become one of the hottest success stories in retailing. In fact, Ulta now ranks as the country's biggest specialized beauty retailer, overtaking Sephora. And, there are plans to nearly double their store count to 1,700 locations in the next few years.

The company's rapid growth can be attributed to several factors. This success has come in part due to the company's decision to sell products across the price spectrum—from mass market to high-end premium. Ulta offers services too, allowing customers to have their hair done, get a facial, and then buy a curling iron and moisturizer to maintain their new look at home. In addition, the company also offers an industry-leading customer loyalty program.

In 1990, the founders of Ulta opened their first five stores "to save women time." This concept may sound obvious today, but it was not the norm when the first stores opened. The company founders believed that busy customers did not want to go to a drugstore (for low-priced beauty basics), then a mall (for high-end beauty products), and finally to a beauty salon to purchase all their beauty needs. One-stop shopping was their response.

Most of the first locations were opened in suburban strip shopping centers due to less expensive rents available there, and it also sped up Ulta's ability to expand. Today, typical stores are approximately 10,000 square feet, with about 10 percent of that space occupied by the salon. On the sales floor, about 20,000 different products are available covering the pricing spectrum, including products such as an $8 Revlon eyeliner to an Estee Lauder lipstick selling for $32.

Gradually, Ulta is moving store locations from strip shopping centers into shopping areas that include stores like T.J. Maxx and Target, which also attract the middle-class customers that Ulta wants to target. Ulta has also begun expanding into urban areas with stores about half the size of their traditional stores. In fact, the first Manhattan store recently opened.

Another key to Ulta's success has been its Ultamate customer loyalty program, and those members fuel about 80 percent of the company's sales. In fact, its nearly 21 million members exceeds Starbucks' loyalty program. Moreover, Ultamate provides data to buyers and managers about what products to stock, and more data from Ultamate provides better analytics for deciding on new product offerings. The company has also enhanced its online presence. Ulta's mobile app, for example, includes a feature called Glam Lab that allows shoppers to take selfies and apply virtual makeup before they make a purchase.

Aggressive expansion for Ulta really began in 2007 when the company went public. Speeding up expansion is the fact that Beauty is a fast-growing market, with annual sales growth forecasted at around 5.3 percent through 2019. In fact, beauty specialist retailers are the second fastest growing retail segment in the United States. Expansion has also been fueled by Ulta selling products at all price points, giving the company the ability to capture market share from a wide range of retailers, from drugstores to high-end department stores. But, what does the future hold?

As traffic and sales at department stores and malls continue to flounder, Ulta is boosting its premium product offerings. Companies like Estee Lauder, which once relied mainly on department stores for sales, are much more receptive to expanding their lines in specialty retailers like Ulta. Brands like this used to shun Ulta because of its down-market locations in strip centers where stores could be possibly found next to dollar stores.

Ulta's competitors are also making aggressive moves for the beauty market. Walgreens, Target, and CVS have all made improved beauty sections at their stores a priority, and J.C. Penney is modernizing its 850 hair salons while rolling out more Sephora cosmetics boutiques in its stores. Even Macy's is speeding up the expansion of its Bluemercury luxury-beauty chain.

To maintain is rapid growth, Ulta must focus on keeping customers happy by making the stores a "fun beauty destination." Buyers must keep the company's product line fresh and offer products and experiences that customers cannot get anywhere else. The brands and services offered must continue to drive customer excitement and allow Ulta the ability to stand out in a very crowded retail segment. By changing the way women shop for beauty products, the future looks bright for this rising star in retailing.

BASED ON:

Wong, Hoi-Nga Stephanie. (2017, January 27). Selfie generation turns make-up chain Ulta into rare retail star. *Bloomberg.com*.

Wahba, Phil. (2015, August 19). How Ulta outruns bigger retailers in the beauty-products race. *Fortune.com*.

Wahba, Phil. (2016, September 15). How Ulta and Mary Dillon are winning the beauty battle. *Fortune.com*.

Wahba, Phil. (2016, October 14). Ulta plans to double its store count as sales soar. *Fortune.com*.

MACY'S: ARE DEPARTMENT STORES REALLY DEAD?

Have department stores, like Macy's, outlived their purpose? Retail sales are generally up, but Macy's has experienced both declining sales and store closures in recent years. And, it is not just Macy's that is facing these challenges. Retailers like Sears, Kmart, Staples, and Kohl's are facing similar declines. Adding to the pressure facing Macy's is the fact that customer traffic at many malls has continued to decline. Moreover, the company's sales are also being impacted by fast-fashion chains like H&M and Forever 21 as well as online sales from companies like Amazon.

All retailers are looking for novel and integrated shopping experiences that will stem declines in sales. For example, the success of Apple stores has shown that face-to-face retailing still has a place in a retail environment, and Sephora, the cosmetics retailer, is winning new converts by giving customers the opportunity to try out products without typical interactions with a commissioned salesperson. These two examples indicate that there will not be a single answer for retailers facing declines in sales; each of them must identify unique shopping experiences that will appeal to their customer base.

Macy's, the largest department store chain, has seen a radical shift in how customers shop; they are buying more and more frequently online and at discount fashion retailers like T.J. Maxx and Steinmart. In fact, online sales at Amazon have grown so rapidly that it may soon become the nation's top seller of apparel. Management at Macy's acknowledge that their stores in the future will have to be more exciting and inviting in order to have customers come into the store rather than making purchases online. To face these challenges, the company has decided to focus on 150 of its best stores for enhancements and remodeling in what executives call "Top Door" strategy.

The cosmetics department, for example, will get a makeover with completely new counters and fixtures. In addition, a Bluemercury shop, which Macy's recently purchased, will be added, and will feature salon services like microdermabrasion, brow tinting, facials, and waxing. Event space will be added in the front of the store to prominently feature store brands, with classes for customers so that floor space will not just be about selling. The philosophy behind the changes is to let customers experience the products—giving them a reason to come into a Macy's store.

Elsewhere in the reconfigured "Top Door" stores, thirty mannequins will be lined up to showcase the newest fashions. There will also be a Connect@Macy's kiosk for one-to-one service as customers walk into a store. Moreover, more convenient locations will be established for customers to pick up orders they have placed online rather than having to go to customer service and face long lines there. There will also be heavy promotion for MyStylist@Macy's—the company's personal shopping service.

Another strategy that the company is implementing involves bringing together products like men's and women's activewear, yoga gear, healthy snacks, and cookbooks in an area called the "Restore, Nourish and Strengthen" department. It will include such brands as Fitbit and Finish Line, which will be operated as a store-within-a-store. Management indicates that more space in the stores will also be leased to outside specialty retailers. For example, Best Buy boutiques in some stores have really enhanced Macy's electronics offerings. Other such partnerships include Lids and Sunglass Hut. To compete with stores like T.J. Maxx and Marshalls, Macy's has also launched Backstage, the company's own chain of off-price fashion stores.

Some of these initiatives are also being made by Macy's rivals, which are facing similar challenges. The next few years will tell if efforts like these will have turned the tide on declining sales. Or will there be more store closures in the future for Macy's?

BASED ON:

Colvin, Geoff, & Derousseau, Ryan. (2017, January 5). Macy's falls for innovation's trap. *Fortune.com*.

Wahba, Phil. (2016, June 15). Inside the Macy's store of the future. *Fortune.com*.

Wahba, Phil. (2016, June 23). Macy's next CEO hints how he plans to shake the retailer out of its sales slump. *Fortune.com*.

Wahba, Phil. (2016, November 10). Macy's to redevelop 50 more stores. *Fortune.com*.

Yu, Howard. (2017, January 11). Why the Macy's death spiral isn't the end of retail. *Fortune.com*.

PART II

GETTING READY TO MAKE BUYING DECISIONS

CHAPTER 4

OBTAINING ASSISTANCE FOR MAKING BUYING DECISIONS

Performance Objectives

- Describe how retail buyers use marketing research.
- Identify the differences between primary and secondary data.
- Identify the sources of the assistance available to buyers.
- Identify internal and external sources of information for making buying decisions.
- Explain the importance of buying offices to buyers.
- Differentiate between the different types of buying offices.
- List and describe services performed by buying offices.
- Outline the process for selecting a buying office.

As a buyer, you will not want to make decisions alone in your office. Buyers typically use some form of marketing research before they make decisions. Various internal and external sources of information will be available to help you in predicting consumer demand and making purchases, and you will want to seek out and use information from as many sources as possible. It is doubtful, however, that any one source alone will be sufficient to provide all the information you need.

MARKETING RESEARCH

Marketing research is a systematic process of gathering, recording, and analyzing information about problems related to marketing. Good marketing research must be conducted in a comprehensive, step-by-step process; it cannot be haphazard. Marketing research involves using information, or **data**, from many different sources. As a buyer you must be able to do more than locate information; you must be able to analyze and use the information that you collect.

Using Marketing Research

One of the most frequent uses of marketing research is to locate information that describes current economic and market conditions that would help you better understand the environment in which your store operates. In addition, many stores want to develop a profile of their customers with respect to characteristics such as age, income, education level, and spending patterns. Developing a customer profile will help you make day-to-day business decisions, such as selecting products to purchase and choosing which types of promotion to use. You will also be interested in information about the size of a potential market and where those customers are located. Marketing research can also be used to determine an area's unemployment rate, new housing starts, or similar economic data that can be used to make forecasts about future sales. Examples of economic data that buyers could use are shown in Table 4.1. As you can see, many times buyers are faced with conflicting data when making a decision.

TABLE 4.1

TYPES OF ECONOMIC DATA THAT BUYERS CAN USE TO MAKE FORECASTS

Building Permits	↓ −0.02%
Monthly total building permits issued.	
Unfilled Orders for Durables	↑ +0.23%
Changes in manufacturer's unfilled orders for durable goods.	
Commodity Prices	↓ −0.04%
Change in sensitive materials' prices.	
Stock Prices	↑ +0.13%
Average for 500 common stocks.	
Consumer Confidence	↑ +0.03%
Consumer expectations of economy's health.	
New Plants, Equipment	↓ −0.22%
Contracts and orders, plants and equipment.	
Unemployment Claims	↑ +0.15%
Weekly claims on unemployment insurance.	

Marketing research is essential for all businesses if they are to remain competitive in the marketplace and satisfy customer wants and needs. Your key to success will be to know your customers better than your competitors do. Good marketing research allows you to anticipate and capitalize on changes occurring with customers; failure to adequately monitor what is going on with them may lead to some bad decisions. Above all, marketing research should help take the guesswork out of your decision making.

The size of your store will affect how marketing research is conducted and used. Most small retailers cannot afford the money or the time to conduct and analyze hundreds of customer surveys. They typically rely on general findings reported in newspapers or magazines. Some retailers use informal surveying extensively—they observe their customers or have sales associates ask them simple questions as they are completing their purchases. Many large retailers have their own marketing research departments and are continuously monitoring their customers and the marketplace. As you will learn in this chapter, there are also many private firms that specialize in marketing research activities, and many retailers purchase these services.

Marketing research does not have to be time-consuming and expensive. Simply comparing sales figures from this year with sales at the same time last year is marketing research. Observing the colors teens in the mall are most often wearing is marketing research. Keeping a file of newspaper and magazine articles about product trends is marketing research. Marketing research activities will be vital to your success as a retail buyer.

Collecting Data

To help you make decisions, your marketing research may involve primary data, secondary data, or both. Your first step should be to locate all relevant secondary sources. **Secondary data** consist of data that already exist—someone else has done the work for you. Government agencies are an excellent source of secondary data, as are trade journals, newspapers, and trade associations. In addition to being able to obtain most secondary data quickly, you will be able to obtain a wealth of information at little or no cost. Some secondary data, however, may not be suitable for your purposes—they are too general or incomplete. Other secondary data may be dated or obsolete. Census data, for example, are only collected every ten years. In many situations, secondary data cannot provide all the information you need to make a decision; you may then need to collect primary data.

Primary data consist of information collected for the specific purpose at hand. The key advantage of using primary data is that this information specifically relates to the problem being researched and is usually collected by interviewing consumers, either individually or in small groups. Obtaining primary data, however, may be time-consuming and expensive to collect, so it is used infrequently by retail buyers.

Analyzing and Interpreting Data

When you conduct marketing research, you are looking for answers, not just information. Your job is to study the data that you have collected and determine their meaning. For example, if several sources of secondary data were obtained, you must compile and summarize the relevant information. If you conducted a customer survey, you will need to analyze the data once all responses are tabulated.

By themselves, data that you have collected usually will not lead to an immediate solution to your questions. You must draw conclusions and make recommendations based on your interpretation of the data collected (Figure 4.1). In other words, you must make decisions: How many will you buy? What styles and colors will you buy? From which vendors will you make your purchases? What models will be stocked at which stores? What merchandise should be eliminated from stock? What new products should be added? The list of questions you will face as a buyer will be endless, but with good marketing research and assistance from other sources, you will be able to answer them.

In your search for information, there will be various internal and external sources available to you. Use as many sources as you can, and do not be afraid to ask for help. Read the Trendwatch titled "Using Different Retail Formats to Extend Target Markets" to learn how retailers are experimenting with different formats based on marketing research findings.

INTERNAL SOURCES

Key sources of internal information include (1) store records, (2) management, and (3) sales associates. Each of these sources can provide you with valuable information as you make buying decisions.

Store Records

In most buying situations, past sales and inventory records may be your most important source of information. Analysis of store records is essential for all buyers, but especially for buyers who are located at the headquarters of a retail chain. These buyers may not have easy access to managers and sales associates at the store level. Increasingly, retailers are tracking much more information about customers than just total sales. For example, information recorded in store records may indicate types of products that

Figure 4.1
Buyers must draw conclusions and make recommendations based on their interpretation of the data collected.

customers generally purchase together. Data may reveal characteristics of customers who purchase a particular product. These situations involve data warehousing and data mining and are examined in Chapter 5.

The key limitation to relying on sales and inventory records to predict consumer demand is that they reveal only what your customers have purchased or not purchased in the past. What happens when customers visit your store or department and do not make a purchase? Sales and inventory records do not reflect what the customer would have purchased if the merchandise had been in stock. Such sales data cannot reveal what sales might have been made to customers who were seeking items that were temporarily out of stock or were not carried by your store.

Some stores operate a formal **want slip system** in which a form is completed each time a customer requests a product not in stock. If you use such a system, you will need to impress upon sales associates the importance of keeping accurate records and taking the time to complete the form when customers ask for an out-of-stock item or one not carried by your store. You cannot, however, meet every customer request. Analysis of want slips could help plan future merchandise assortments if a large number of your customers are making similar requests.

Sales and inventory records should be made to work for you. Retailers using loyalty cards can provide a wealth of information for store management and retail buyers. Loyalty cards allow stores not only to track what products are selling but also to obtain specific information about who is buying those products. With such a massive amount of data on shoppers being collected through loyalty cards—from the types of cola bought to whether they shop late at night—retailers are getting smarter at tracking consumer trends. By knowing who joins loyalty card programs, buyers can adjust their merchandise offerings, store layouts, product adjacencies, and advertising efforts. Theoretically, through these programs, retailers can gather information about consumer purchases and target individuals with communications offering them something that is directly relevant to them.

Even though store records are likely to be your most important source of information, they are not sufficient by themselves. You need to use other internal sources, as well as external sources, before making your final buying decisions.

Management

In large stores, you probably need to consult with your merchandise manager as you plan your purchasing decisions. Before approving your merchandise plan, your merchandise manager may suggest changes. He or she should also be able to offer you valuable assistance in predicting future economic and market trends. The controller or finance officer will also need to be consulted for approval of the budget for your buying plan.

Buyers located at corporate headquarters will want to seek input from store managers. Short phone calls to these managers can make them feel more involved in the buying process and probably more enthusiastic about selling the merchandise you will order. Important information about consumer demand that may not be readily detected from store records can possibly be found. Small store owners probably have no other management personnel from whom they can get advice; therefore, it will be critical that they use external sources.

Figure 4.2
Sales associates may be able to tell buyers *why* a product is selling or not selling.

Sales Associates

Whenever possible you should obtain input from the store's sales associates. Records may reveal what merchandise is selling or not selling, but only sales associates may be able to tell you *why* it is selling or not selling (Figure 4.2).

Sales associates are in constant contact with customers and can be aware of their wants and needs, which may not be reflected in sales records. In fact, because they are typical customers, sales associates are probably good judges of the sales potential for new products being considered. Some sales associates, however, may not be able to distinguish their personal likes and dislikes from those of their customers.

Sales associates are the store's personal representatives to its customers, and in such a role, they are in a position to conduct primary research for you. If your store does not use want slips, consulting with sales associates may reveal if they have been asked for merchandise that the store does not sell. Also, sales associates can quickly and easily ask questions that will be important to you. For example, they can ask about a customer's satisfaction with past purchases, or they can get requests for items not carried by the store.

During telephone conversations or at store meetings, you should be able to determine which sales associates are the most insightful and can offer you genuine feedback. Discuss with these sales associates what should be in stock, and allow them to inspect new product samples and give their opinion as to whether they should be purchased. Their opinions may support what you have already learned from other sources or give you an entirely different perspective that could cause you to alter your plans.

If possible, visit the sales floor. Buyers located at a store's headquarters should regularly visit stores nearby to observe customers in action. While visiting the sales floor, observe cues about the kinds of styles, colors, and fabrics that are popular with your customers. The problem with making personal contacts is that you may be so completely absorbed with merchandising activities that visits are difficult. Store visits, however, are likely to provide benefits to you in the form of more enthusiastic sales associates and more specific knowledge for you to consider when making your buying plans. If you solicit opinions and suggestions from sales associates, take the time to extend a personal word of thanks to them describing how their suggestions were acted on.

Once you have exhausted sources inside your store, seek assistance from external sources. Remember, however, that information from these sources could reflect national or industry trends rather than local trends.

EXTERNAL SOURCES

Many sources outside your store will be available to help you when making purchasing decisions. They include (1) customers, (2) magazines and trade publications, (3) vendors, (4) trade associations, (5) comparison shoppers, (6) fashion forecasters, (7) reporting services, (8) the internet and social media, and (9) buying offices. The type of merchandise that you are selling and the time you have available will determine how many and which sources you will use.

Customers

Some large retailers are able to conduct formal marketing research involving questionnaires to determine consumer wants and needs; however, consumer research can be quite informal. You or other employees of the store may simply talk with customers on the selling floor, or just observe them while they are in the store. Both activities involve informal marketing research.

Are your customers quick to experiment with new fashion trends? Or do their tastes tend toward the classic or traditional? Are they price conscious when they shop? Or are they more interested in quality and fashion? Extensive customer questionnaires will probably be needed to adequately answer these questions. Some simple questions, however, may reveal a lot about your customers. An example of a survey that customers may be asked to complete is shown in Table 4.2, "Style Assessment." Take a minute to complete and score the survey to determine your own attitude toward fashion. Do you think the results described you correctly? For the survey results to have meaning to a retail buyer, hundreds of customer responses will probably need to be completed and tabulated.

Some stores organize consumer advisory groups. Teen boards are an advisory group that many department stores use. They are established by selecting student representatives from local high schools or colleges to serve as advisers for the store. Teen board members may also serve as fashion show models and provide assistance with special promotions. Some members even wear new merchandise from the store on their school campus.

Other stores may establish **consumer advisory panels** consisting of typical customers who make suggestions about store policies, services, and merchandise assortments. The panels usually meet weekly for a few hours to provide their input by offering opinions and suggestions about store activities and merchandise assortments.

TABLE 4.2

STYLE ASSESSMENT

Sections 1 and 2: Rate yourself on a scale of 0 to 10 for each of the following questions. Assign higher numbers to the statements that strongly represent your feeling.

SECTION 1   Score (Assign 0 to 10)

  1. I keep up to date on the latest styles and fashions.   _____

  2. I like to buy top designer brands of clothes.   _____

  3. I am an individualist and like my clothes to project attitude.   _____

SECTION 2   Score (Assign 0 to 10)

  4. When I shop, I look at the price tag first.   _____

  5. I like a store where I can shop for the whole family.   _____

  6. I try only to buy things that are on sale.   _____

SECTION 3   Circle Your Response

  7. I like to indulge myself.   Agree/Disagree

  8. I usually talk things over with other people.   Agree/Disagree

  9. Women should offer to split the cost when they go out with men.   Agree/Disagree

10. I would choose to do my own housework, even if I could afford help.   Agree/Disagree

11. Success at school or work is important to me.   Agree/Disagree

12. I am a fun-loving person.   Agree/Disagree

How to Score

  1. _____   Add up your points from Section 1.

  2. _____   Add up your points from Section 2.

  3. _____   In Section 3:

If you agreed with statements 7, 11, and 12, add one point for each "agree" to your total score in Section 1.

If you agreed with statements 8, 9, and 10, add one point for each "agree" to your total score in Section 2.

  4. _____   Subtract the total score in Section 2 from the total in Section 1. (Score may be a minus.)

  5. _____   If your score is:

+10 to +30 you are an Updated (Fashion Forward) Shopper;

+9 to −15 you are a Classic or Traditional Shopper;

−16 to −30 you are a Conservative Shopper.

Magazines and Trade Publications

As a buyer, you have to stay ahead of what is selling on the floor. You must be aware of changes in styling, new materials, new models, and other innovations long before they are available to customers. You will need to read several publications to update your knowledge of current trends in new product developments, resource information, economic conditions, and other market news that will enhance your understanding of customers. You will also want to subscribe to the local newspaper as well as an out-of-town paper from a large metropolitan area. If you are in a small town, examining retail ads appearing in these out-of-town papers will alert you to trends and styles that may eventually be accepted by your customers.

Fashion news is reported in many consumer magazines. *Vogue*, *Harper's Bazaar*, *Elle*, *Glamour*, *Mademoiselle*, and *GQ* are several magazines you can pick up at your local newsstand to keep abreast of changes in fashion (Figure 4.3). Other publications such as the *Wall Street Journal*, *USA Today*, *Business Week*, *Fortune*, and *Forbes* are excellent sources of information about economic and market trends. Several of these publications also feature columns on new product innovations. Reports on trends, technological developments, marketing plans of various companies, and the impact of economic developments on business areas are frequently reported.

You should also subscribe to trade magazines directly related to product categories for which you are buying. In fact, almost every retail activity has some trade publication associated with it. Some of these include *Stores*, *Women's Wear Daily*, *Chain Store Age*, *Furniture Age*, *Footwear News*, *Progressive Grocer*, *Hardware Age*, and *Home Furnishings Daily*. These publications can provide you with valuable information about the products that you are buying. For example, most of these publications conduct national surveys and report information about typical customers for specific products.

Vendors

Your merchandise suppliers, **vendors**, will be able to inform you about what merchandise is being heavily ordered by other retailers. Also, the information they have about merchandise reorders will give you an excellent indication of customer acceptance of specific products. Vendors are usually eager to pass on useful information because they have a stake in the success of your store too; however, there is a distinct difference between accepting advice and letting the vendor make your decisions. As a partnership develops between you and the vendor, you will be able to put more confidence in these suggestions.

Trade Associations

You or someone from store management will want to join and actively participate in a **trade association** related to your area of retailing. These organizations of businesses with similar characteristics usually publish newsletters updating members on current trends and market conditions. They also provide the opportunity for you to make important personal contacts and discuss matters relevant to a particular retailing area. The National Retail Federation is the largest and most important trade association to which most retailers belong. The organization covers areas of interest for both large and small retailers, providing them with publications, videos, and periodicals. You can find a trade association for every area of retailing. For example, the Accessories Council

Figure 4.3
Consumer magazines like the ones pictured keep buyers informed about changes in the fashion world.

stimulates consumer awareness and demand for fashion accessory products and the American Apparel & Footwear Association represents apparel, footwear and other sewn products companies in the global marketplace. The Footwear Distributors & Retailers of America is another footwear trade association. You should also consider joining the merchants' associations at your state and local levels. Another positive feature of trade associations is that they typically sponsor trade shows as part of conferences where vendors exhibit new products.

Comparison Shoppers

You should also study the promotion campaigns of competing stores. Study their print and broadcast ads as well as their online advertising to obtain information on price and quality. If possible, you will want to visit competing stores to see what is being stocked and what is featured in displays, as well as what appears to be selling. Observe prices, assortments, services, and customer response to the merchandise stocked. Comparison shopping reports also give you information about products not carried by your store.

If you do not have the time to conduct comparison shopping activities yourself, you may need to assign this task to assistant buyers or department managers or hire **comparison shoppers**. These firms shop competing stores to provide information on the merchandise assortments, prices, and promotion policies of other retailers in the area. They are located in many large cities and charge their clients based on the services provided.

Do not spend so much time watching competitors that you forget the work to be done at your own store. Few retailers are successful if they merely copy someone else with their prices and merchandise assortments. Some stores have found that it is not necessary to make adjustments each time a competitor makes a price change. They build their reputation on the services they provide to their customers. However, many retailers stress in their advertising that they will "meet or beat" the competition's prices. For these stores, comparison shopping is extremely important.

If possible, obtain information on stores similar to yours in other geographic areas. At trade association meetings, you can network with buyers from noncompeting stores in other locations. They are frequently happy to exchange information because it will help them make better buying decisions, too.

Fashion Forecasters

Fashion forecasters are business consultants that you or your firm can hire to help predict fashion trends months in advance. Fashion items change frequently, and buyers must be aware of trends so the store has the right products to meet the wants and needs of its customers. On a weekly or monthly basis, fashion forecasters provide their clients with a report on predicted consumer trends. These services are most helpful with long-range planning.

There are hundreds of fashion forecasters available to retail buyers. Two of these firms include Youth Intelligence and Pantone. Youth Intelligence, a company that forecasts fashion and other trends involving young consumers, advises Levi's, Calvin Klein's CK line, and Benetton. Reporters for the firm find trends by following fashion-forward designers; scoping out the streets of London, Los Angeles, and New York; and monitoring eclectic boutique wares. Pantone is a forecasting firm that predicts color trends for the future. Many retailers often consult more than one forecasting firm. Forecasting services may be expensive, but most major retailers agree that they cannot afford not to use them.

Reporting Services

Reporting services are organizations that report on constantly changing market trends that will have an impact on the products you purchase. Changes occur most frequently and most rapidly for fashion merchandise, so it is extremely important that fashion buyers keep current. Several reporting services conduct market research valuable to buyers and email their analyses to clients on a weekly or monthly basis. Today, the internet has made the immediate delivery of information possible; breaking news no longer has to wait for the next issue of a newsletter. Articles describe topics such as the latest fashions from Europe, economic indicators, or the latest colors and fabrics for the new season. There are several online sites that provide 24/7 sources for news coverage related to the retail industry. They include RetailingToday.com, ChainStoreAge.com, RetailSolutions.com, and Retail-Merchandiser.com. Many search engines also provide news feeds related to retailing.

The Internet and Social Media

The internet may be the most important research tool that buyers can use. Millions of pages of information are archived and available at the click of a computer mouse. More importantly, buyers are able to obtain up-to-the-minute news and information about their industry or products they are buying. At no time in the past have buyers had such a wealth of information at their fingertips. Following interactions on social media platforms will also provide buyers with information on current consumer attitudes and behaviors.

For example, at Apparelsearch.com, buyers can find information on customers, conversion charts, trade shows, apparel news, and designers—all at the click of a mouse. At Fashion.net, they can find daily fashion news, view runway videos, or read fashion profiles. And, at apparelresources.com, buyers can find a directory of apparel exporters from India. Information that once took weeks and months to collect can now be located in minutes. The internet has proved a very powerful tool for buyers.

Buying Offices

Buying offices are organizations that provide consulting services to retailers. Because they are used by both small and large retailers, they are described in depth in the next section.

BUYING OFFICES

A buying office is an organization located in a major market center for the purpose of providing buying advice and other market-related services to client stores. Essentially, they serve as researchers and advisers to save the store buyer time and money. Few stores can afford to have a permanent staff in central markets. For that reason, many retailers use the services of buying offices. Today, many buying offices consider themselves as merchandising consultants.

Purpose and Importance

By using a buying office, you are able to "feel the pulse" of the market without being there, and you will no longer have to rely on just an occasional visit to the market to make your purchasing plans.

Buying offices vary in size from a one-person operation to giant offices employing hundreds of people. In the United States, buying offices are located in major market cities, such as New York and Los Angeles. Buyers can also find buying offices in major market centers worldwide.

Mergers and acquisitions have made the Doneger Group one of the strongest buying offices in the country. The firm has been able to broaden its client base as well as develop many specialized services. Table 4.3 shows the various divisions of the Doneger Group and provides a brief description of the services performed.

A buying office is employed by a retail store to act as a buying specialist and adviser. They become your "eyes and ears" when you are not in the market by constantly scouting the market for new merchandise, new resources, and the best prices.

TABLE 4.3

DIVISIONS OF THE DONEGER GROUP, A NEW YORK BUYING OFFICE

MERCHANDISING	
Doneger Merchandising	This is the core business of Doneger and provides retailers with extensive consulting services, seasonal merchandising direction, and current business and market analysis in all classifications, sizes, and price levels for women's, men's, and children's apparel, accessories, and footwear.
Directives West	Doneger's West Coast merchandising team provides market analysis, extensive retail and street coverage, and insight into the West Coast lifestyle as it relates to fashion and the consumer.
Price Point Buying	With a focus on women's, men's, and children's apparel, accessories, footwear, and home, Price Point Buying presents clients with outstanding opportunistic buys and facilitates business relationships in the value-driven marketplace.
TREND SERVICES	
Doneger Creative Services	Doneger's lifestyle, trend, and color forecast offering is composed of a broad range of products and services devoted to the apparel, accessories, footwear, beauty, home, and lifestyle markets.
TOBE	TOBE is Doneger's consumer-centric fashion think tank. TOBE defines the influence fashion and aesthetics have on the consumer, delivering creative strategies in the areas of business development, marketing, customer engagement, design, and presentation.
Doneger Consulting	Offers customized projects tailored to clients' individual needs. Projects are planned and executed to provide clients with strategies to meet their specific needs in areas such as lifestyle profiling, industry analysis, customer color and trend research, and product line creation.
Online Services	Provides members with an online platform that delivers information as soon as it is available. Information is provided on trend concepts, market reporting, runway analysis, and global retail and street photography.

Adapted from *www.doneger.com*, April 2017.

Buying offices are important to retailers for the following reasons:

- Many retailers are placing an increasing importance on fashion products, and the rapidity with which fashion changes requires that a buyer have constant contact with the market.
- Many buying offices are able to make group purchases for their client stores so that merchandise costs are reduced.
- Retail stores represented by buying offices can have their buyers make fewer and shorter trips to market, thereby reducing expenses.
- Many times, buying offices will be able to obtain exclusive merchandise for client stores. Most stores want to carry some products that are unique to their trading area.
- Finally, being a client of a buying office brings retail stores together to pool their information and knowledge. Information can be shared freely, because a buying office will not represent competing stores in a trading area.

Reasons to use a buying office will probably vary from one retailer to the next.

Services Provided by Buying Offices

Buying offices communicate vital market information to client stores through bulletins and reports and give much-needed assistance to buyers when they visit the market. While buyers are at their stores, representatives of the buying office can do the following:

- Answer requests for information on such topics as market conditions, prices and styles available, and location of new resources.
- Place orders on request of the store's buyer. The buyer specifies the type, price, and quantity of merchandise desired and leaves the selection of the vendor and specific styles to the representative of the buying office. Store buyers still have the primary responsibility for purchasing.
- Keep on the lookout for merchandise a buyer may find of interest, such as new products and new styles. Calls are frequently made to store buyers about new merchandise offerings.
- Follow up and check on deliveries. Manufacturers may be more motivated to ship quickly if pressured by a buying office because of its size and location in the market.
- Handle adjustments and complaints. Again, a buying office may be able to apply more pressure than retailers can by themselves.
- Save the retailer money by pooling orders from several member stores to make purchases at one time for a lower cost.
- Locate new resources. Most buyers are constantly seeking fresh merchandise to satisfy the needs of their customers. It may not be possible for the store buyer to thoroughly scout the market to seek out new resources. Representatives of a buying office are more capable of performing this function. In fact, many manufacturers seek out buying offices because of the number of stores they represent.
- Recommend hot items. A **hot item** is a product that the buyer cannot keep in stock because of great demand by customers. All buyers are interested in products that will provide a quick return on the store's investment.
- Secure private brands for the retail store. Many buying offices have developed private branding programs to assist their member stores to meet the competition and provide store individuality.

- Provide fashion forecasts on style, color, and fabric trends and new market offerings.
- Prepare promotional activities. Most small retailers have neither the specialized talent nor the capital to develop promotional campaigns. Many buying offices supply their member stores with promotional materials such as ideas for window displays, interior display hints, or sample ad layouts. Even canned fashion show commentary may be provided.
- Provide research findings to client stores. Information may be from informal studies, which might involve conversations with representatives of key stores to find out what is selling, or from more formal market research activities involving questionnaires and interviews. Market and economic trend analyses are also provided by most buying offices.
- Maintain foreign connections so that they can offer expertise to the retailer who is interested in importing merchandise.

Once the store buyer is in the market, the buying office helps by carefully planning the market trip so that the visit is productive. Representatives of the buying office can locate merchandise and resources in advance of the buyer's market trip and schedule his or her time so it is used most productively. Most buying offices provide office space and sample rooms for buyers of their member stores. These offices will usually collect samples from vendors so they are easily accessible to buyers while they are in the market. Having samples readily available saves buyers' time during the rush of market week because they do not have to visit manufacturers whose samples are inappropriate for their needs.

Representatives of buying offices may even accompany store buyers to market showrooms on request. Such a service, however, may not always be available if a large percentage of the buyers from member stores are in the market at the same time. Many buying offices also make hotel and transportation reservations for store buyers. These services may be provided at reduced prices because the buying office is representing a large number of stores and probably qualifies for a group discount. Finally, buying offices can vouch for the credit standing of member stores when buyers are in the market. Read the Snapshot titled "Equatoriale: The Italian Buying Office" to learn more about how buying offices operate in other countries.

Types of Buying Offices

Buying offices can be grouped into two broad categories: (1) independent buying offices and (2) store-owned buying offices. Buying offices in both categories essentially provide the same type of services.

Independent Offices

Most buying offices are **independent buying offices**—they are privately owned and operated. Store buyers use independent offices just as they would any other business consultant. Two variations of this type of buying office are (1) the salaried (fixed-fee) office and (2) the merchandise-broker office.

The **salaried** or **fixed-fee buying office** is paid directly by the retail stores the firm represents. The retailer signs a contract with the buying office and agrees to pay a fee based on a percentage of the store's annual sales volume. This fee typically ranges from 1/2 to 1 percent of sales and is paid monthly. Smaller stores, with low sales volume, may pay a flat fee each month.

The salaried office is mainly used by store owners and buyers who do not have the time to spend away from their stores to make frequent market visits. Some stores may be so far removed geographically from the market that it would be too costly for the owner to make regular market trips.

The **merchandise-broker** office provides similar advice and services to retailers, but it is paid by the manufacturers represented by the firm. From 2 to 4 percent of the client store's purchases are paid to the buying office by the manufacturer. Many brokers represent several noncompeting manufacturers.

Merchandise brokers offer another avenue for manufacturers to broaden their contact with small stores because representatives are able to visit store owners in the field who seldom come to market. Merchandise brokers are extremely important to retailers who cannot afford the services of salaried buying offices. You must realize, however, that conflict of interest may be present. Brokers are interested in selling the lines they represent, even though they may not be the best ones for your store. Most merchandise brokers, however, will give good service because they are interested in keeping your continued patronage.

Store-Owned Offices

Some buying offices are owned by the store or stores they represent. Large department and specialty stores generally use this type of service.

Private buying offices are maintained in market centers by some large retailers. These offices require a large financial investment, which is warranted if the retailer's sales volume would require an extremely high fee to be paid to a salaried buying office. Therefore, establishing their own buying office is more economical for these stores. These buying offices perform the same functions as independent buying offices except there are no other stores with whom to exchange information.

Selecting a Buying Office

How will you go about selecting a buying office? First, you need to determine if your store needs the services provided. Then you will need to screen the possible choices from which you have to select. Make a thorough search, and do not be afraid to ask questions. Ask for references and speak to some of the buying office's clients. Following are some of the typical questions you will want to ask:

- What kind of merchandise lines are represented by the buying office? Does its merchandising approach fit your store's image?
- Is the buying office too small or too large for your needs?
- Do you feel an atmosphere of compatibility when communicating with representatives of the buying office? Are they the kind of people with whom you feel you can do business?
- Is the staff of sufficient size to give adequate service?
- Does the buying office provide references?
- Who are the buying office's current members? You want to be associated with stores that are similar to yours because information exchange is beneficial. For that reason, you may not be able to be represented by a buying office already representing your competitor. Exchange of information might divulge company secrets.
- Which manufacturers does the buying office deal with regularly?

- What is the scope of services provided?
- What standard, regular services can you expect that will help save time, avoid needless market trips, and provide professional buying assistance?
- What will joining the buying office cost?
- How is the fee determined? What kind of contract arrangement is required?
- Can you afford the costs?
- Will the buying office treat you as an individual?
- How will your store benefit?

Once you have selected a buying office, make use of the services it provides. Read the bulletins, online updates, and reports that are sent to you. This will be the buying office's primary means of communicating with you. You can learn about products with which other stores have had success and also obtain information on new resources.

Get to know the various representatives at the buying office who will be assigned to your store. Develop a close working relationship with them. Communicate your ideas and problems on a regular basis through phone calls or letters. By knowing you and your situation better, the buying office will be more effective in working for you.

Let your representatives at the buying office know well in advance of any market trips that you are planning. Communicate to them your particular needs and the merchandise categories that you will be purchasing. Advance notification will allow someone at the buying office to block out time to devote to you.

Participate in group activities that have been organized for you by the buying office. Much of the strength of a buying office is based on member stores sharing their experiences with one another. These activities provide an opportunity for you to gain insight into general market conditions and trends as well as specific information on vendors and merchandise availability. Share information about successful and unsuccessful merchandise in your store.

Communicate with representatives of the buying office when you are not in the market. Work toward developing a long-term partnership that will be mutually beneficial for both you and the buying office.

Trends Influencing Buying Offices

In the past, retailers were small and scattered throughout the country, so manufacturers and vendors found it difficult to contact stores directly; therefore, buying offices developed to serve as a link between retailers and the market. Today, however, the major retail stores have grown so large through mergers that it is possible for manufacturers to contact all their major customers and prospective customers directly. Also, retail store closures have eliminated many buying office accounts. One day the buying office is doing business with a retailer, and the next day that retailer is part of a chain that has its own buying office or an account with a competing buying office. For these retailers, there has been less reliance on buying offices.

Buying offices, however, offer much-needed assistance for any retailer that cannot easily perform the services offered. As many retailers become larger, there will be a very strong need felt by smaller retailers to band together to compete. They may need the services of buying offices just to remain competitive.

What does the future hold for buying offices? Will their role change? Some retail analysts feel that buying offices should begin performing some new functions with which most have never dealt—services related to the use of technology, store planning, site selection, and human resource management. Such services, however, may be beyond the realm of expertise for most buying offices. Some retail analysts are already starting to question whether or not buying offices really possess the talent to make a difference, and this may be one of the main reasons why retailers are using them less often.

The most recent trend has been the use of the internet to maintain constant contact between a buying office and member stores. New developments can be relayed instantly, as can information on a manufacturer's price break that retailers must take advantage of quickly. Most buying offices now maintain online sites that members can access with passwords.

Buying offices have consolidated, and many have gone out of business, but those that remain seem to have a strong position in the marketplace. Most fashion retailers need a buying office so they have someone to cover the market for them on a day-to-day basis, to tell them what is hot and what is not. Using buying offices is especially important today because it is so costly to send buyers to markets in large metropolitan cities and foreign countries. Above all, buying offices help small retailers compete with industry giants.

Summary Points

- Buyers do not make decisions alone. They seek out and use as much information as possible before making purchasing decisions.

- Retail buyers use some form of marketing research to help them make decisions, even if it is very informal. They seek out secondary data first before trying to obtain primary data on their own.

- Store records, such as sales and inventory, are key sources of information for buyers; however, such information shows a buyer only what sold or did not sell. Buyers should contact sales associates and store managers for assistance in determining why customers purchased or did not purchase merchandise in the store.

- Buyers can seek information from customers through formal surveys or advisory groups.

- Buyers need to read to keep up to date. Consumer magazines and newspapers are required reading, as are trade magazines directed toward their specific retailing area.

- Vendors are sources of information and assistance but should not make decisions for the buyer. Buyers must coordinate their activities with other departments if they are to be successful.

- Buyers must continually monitor the competition through comparison shopping trips or through similar information provided by comparison shopping bureaus.

- Buyers can use the services of fashion forecasters and reporting services to monitor trends and changes in the retail market. Such services are especially useful for recognizing long-range trends.

- Buying offices serve as consultants and advisers to buyers and provide many market-related services to their member stores. Buying offices provide assistance to buyers while they are in their store and when visiting the market.

- Buying offices are either independent or store-owned. They all offer similar services to stores but vary in how they are paid and who becomes a member.

- Buying offices are changing as retailing changes. Consolidation has occurred; many buying offices are no longer in business. Today, the internet provides an immediate connection between buying offices and their clients.

Review Activities

Developing Your Retail Buying Vocabulary

Consult the glossary if you did not add the following terms to your vocabulary.

buying office
comparison shopper
consumer advisory panel
data
fashion forecaster

hot item
independent buying office
marketing research
merchandise-broker office
primary data

private buying office
reporting service
salaried (fixed-fee) buying
   office
secondary data

trade association
vendor
want slip system

Understanding What You Read

1. Describe some simple approaches to marketing research that buyers can use to answer questions and make decisions.

2. What are the advantages that secondary data provide the buyer?

3. For the buyer, what are the problems with using primary data?

4. What is probably a buyer's most important source of information when making purchasing decisions?

5. Describe why contact with store managers and salespeople is critical for a buyer.

6. What is the limitation of using only sales records to make purchasing decisions?

7. Identify the two individuals who will likely need to approve a buyer's purchasing plans in large retail stores.

8. Describe how centralized buyers receive feedback from store managers and salespeople.

9. Describe why visits to the sales floor are vital to buyers.

10. Identify the purpose(s) of teen boards.

11. What is a buyer's purpose in subscribing to an out-of-town newspaper from a metropolitan area?

12. What information should a buyer obtain from comparison shopping that will assist in making purchasing decisions?

13. List two reporting services, and describe the information they provide to clients.

14. Describe why buying offices are important to retailers.

15. Describe specific services that buying offices can provide to buyers when they are in the market.

16. Describe the difference between fixed-fee buying offices and merchandise brokers.

17. When might retailers choose a merchandise broker over a fixed-fee buying office to represent them?

18. Describe how being a member of a buying office can save the store money.

19. Identify general trends that are affecting the operation of buying offices today.

Analyzing and Applying What You Read

1. What reasons could explain why most retailers do not collect want slips?

2. You are a centralized buyer for a large specialty store chain. Outline a plan that you would implement to encourage involvement in the buying process from store managers and sales associates.

3. You are a new buyer at a local hardware store. Briefly describe the specific steps you would take to seek external information to aid in making purchasing decisions.

4. The owner of the small menswear store that you manage is considering using a buying office. Categorize the pros and cons of hiring a buying office.

5. Do you feel that buying offices should offer services related to the use of technology, store planning, site selection, and human resource management? Explain.

6. A buying office that specializes in menswear has experienced declines in billings each of the past three years. What changes would you recommend that this buying office consider?

Internet Connection

1. Visit the Doneger Group buying office online at http://www.doneger.com.

   a. Record information about any market trends it is providing visitors to the site.

   b. Describe the process that a retail store would use to join the buying office.

   c. Use an internet search engine to locate the home page of another online buying office. Read and analyze the information provided at the site.

   d. Describe the similarities and differences of the two sites.

2. Visit the book's STUDIO to watch videos about trend forecasting.

SNAPSHOT: Equatoriale: The Italian Buying Office

Retail buyers can also use the assistance of buying offices in other countries. For example, if your firm was interested in purchasing products from Italy, Equatoriale is one buying office that you might consider. Equatoriale was established in 1946 in Milan, Italy, to serve as a buying office for retailers around the world—including chain stores, department stores, catalog firms, wholesalers, and importers. They are not a merchandise broker for suppliers and manufacturers; they work exclusively for their clients—retail and wholesale buyers. The firm's areas of expertise include apparel, ready-to-wear, knitwear, woven goods, accessories, lingerie, hosiery, shoes and leather goods, textiles, furniture, and giftware.

Equatoriale stresses there are several key reasons that retail buyers would want to make purchases of products made in Italy. First, the country has a deep-rooted tradition in fashion, and Italian designers and craftspeople are among the most skilled and versatile in the world. Italians have a history of being innovative and creative, generating a strong and steady flow of new ideas, concepts, and designs that set the trends and fashions. Italian manufacturers are also available to help buyers improve and modify their products instead of merely reproducing them. Finally, the delivery lead time of Italian manufacturers is considerably shorter than those of many other markets in the world. This allows retail buyers to make up-to-the-minute changes in production, lowering their risk as they stay on top of market changes and new trends.

Equatoriale provides assistance that buyers need to accomplish their goals from the start to the finish of the purchasing process. The firm's contacts include established vendors, so they are able to assist buyers in locating the right suppliers at the right price. The firm prides itself on continuously sourcing and tracking new and upcoming manufacturers and brands to keep up with the latest market trends so that they can determine the most suitable suppliers in order to satisfy the specific needs of each buyer.

Equatoriale also provides professional staff to retail buyers when they make a buying trip to Italy. These representatives prepare for the buyer's trip before their arrival, accompany them during their buying trips, help negotiate effectively with suppliers for the best prices and terms, and follow up on orders all the way through to final shipping. The firm's goal is to plan every detail of the buying trip so that buyers can concentrate and maximize their purchasing goals.

The firm also schedules appointments with manufacturers to effectively make use of the buyer's time in the market. They can also make all of a buyer's travel arrangements: providing them with a car and driver for local trips or providing train and plane bookings. They can also book hotels or make suggestions for ones providing corporate rates.

Once the order is placed, Equatoriale maintains contact with the suppliers selected to ensure they are complying correctly with instructions and delivery deadlines. They also provide progress reports to buyers on the status of the production, delivery, and shipment of their purchases.

When you need guidance and assistance in making purchases in other countries, take the time to locate and investigate buying offices such as Equatoriale.

BASED ON:

Information provided at *equatoriale.it*.

USING DIFFERENT RETAIL FORMATS TO EXTEND TARGET MARKETS

Today many retail firms are making attempts to extend their market reach by offering different store formats that appeal to very different target markets. Some retailers are even opening retail stores that nurture potential customers before they are attracted to the firm's core business. Moreover, other retailers are offering formats that attract customers after they age out of the firm's core business. On the other hand, some retail chains are offering different formats in the same market to appeal to different demographic characteristics. How successful have such stores been in extending their target market?

Abercrombie & Fitch nurtures its future teen shoppers with Abercrombie Kids, another division of the chain aimed at preteens. Then, Abercrombie & Fitch and Hollister stores target these same customers during their teen and college years. Several years ago, the chain also opened about two dozen RUEHL units aimed at shoppers (ages twenty-two to thirty-five) who had just graduated from college and were heading out on their own. The format was designed to retain customers after their teen years. However, this concept did not succeed, and all RUEHL locations were closed. Management cited the poor economy as the reason for the closings. With sales slowing in recent years, Abercrombie & Fitch plans to shift its marketing, product assortments, and pricing as the company moves its focus from teens to college students. Concurrently, the firm also plans to rebrand its Hollister stores as a fast-fashion retailer, which involves providing the latest apparel styles favored by teens. It also means a quick supply chain turnaround and teen-friendly pricing.

Like Abercrombie & Fitch, American Eagle also honed a strategy to extend the company's brand to older demographics. In 2006, the firm debuted Martin + Osa stores, skewing to twenty-five- to thirty-five-year-olds. In a similar way to what happened with Abercrombie & Fitch's RUEHL stores, American Eagle closed its Martin + Osa store formats. It was determined that these stores were not achieving performance levels that warranted further investment. After recent disappointing sales results, American Eagle retrenched even farther by announcing that more stores were closing in North America.

Gap has used a different strategy to extend the chain's target market. Many times all three of the chain's formats—Old Navy, Gap, and Banana Republic—can be found located near each other. Each format is designed to appeal to a different market segment. Old Navy appeals more to families and value shoppers, while Gap stores have long appealed to younger customers with a stylish bent. Banana Republic offers stylish apparel at a higher price point. Yet even this retail chain ran into problems trying to extend its target market of Gap stores. For several years, Gap attempted to reach a broad range of consumers—teens to baby boomers. The store's lack of focus did not resonate well with customers, and the chain had to refocus on identifying just who was their target market.

Efforts to extend target markets have also occurred with major discount stores. Target has opened its smallest format store in downtown Minneapolis near the University of Minnesota. The new format, called TargetExpress, features an edited assortment of merchandise, including fresh produce, grab-and-go food and snacks, pharmacy, home, seasonal, electronics, and beauty. Target has also opened another type of small-format store in downtown locations in Los Angeles and San Francisco. These urban stores, called CityTargets, are larger than TargetExpress stores and carry fresh groceries, household basics, and other product categories found in standard Targets that have been tweaked for city residents and commuters. Walmart has also experimented with smaller store sizes, opening Neighborhood Markets and Walmart Express stores with mixed success. Another format being tested is a 2,500-square-foot store located on or near college campuses called Walmart on Campus.

Today, retailers are faced with heavy competition from many sources. One attempt by established retailers to meet that competition and increase sales has been to create new store formats to extend their brand. As you have seen, some attempts at extending a firm's target market by opening new formats have not been successful.

Have retailers gone too far in trying to extend their target markets beyond their original core business? Do retail buyers

USING DIFFERENT RETAIL FORMATS TO EXTEND TARGET MARKETS (CONTINUED)

really understand these new target market extensions and provide products that have distinct appeal to the needs of that new audience?

BASED ON:

Ausick, Paul. (2014, March 22). Walmart now has six types of stores. *247wallst.com.*

Berthiaume, Dan. (2014, March 7). Report: Abercrombie to rebrand Hollister as fast-fashion chain. *ChainStoreAge.com.*

Berthiaume, Dan. (2014, March 10). Report: Abercrombie to target collegiate shoppers. *ChainStoreAge.com.*

Berthiaume, Dan. (2014, March 18). Gap to open five Old Navy franchise stores in Philippines. *ChainStoreAge.com.*

Berthiaume, Dan. (2014, May 21). American Eagle to close 150 stores. *ChainStoreAge.com.*

Gustafson, Krystina. (2016, October 5). Target is chasing Walmart with its smaller stores but using a different playbook. *CNBC.com.*

Wilson, Marianne. (2014, July 25). Video tour of new TargetExpress; four more locations on tap. *ChainStoreAge.com.*

CHAPTER 5

UNDERSTANDING YOUR CUSTOMERS

Performance Objectives

- Use positioning and targeting to develop retail strategies.
- Identify methods used to target retail customers.
- Cite recent demographic and behavior changes in the consumer market.
- Cite recent psychographic changes in the consumer market.
- Identify the different types of buying motives.
- Describe data warehousing and data mining.
- Cite examples of how data mining is used by retail buyers.
- Identify how buyers can use the information maintained in data warehouses.
- Describe database marketing and identify its goals.
- Recognize methods buyers can use to learn more about their customers.

As you learned in the last chapter, marketing research can be used to help buyers make decisions. In this chapter, you will concentrate on learning more about consumers. Knowing and understanding consumers will be vital to your success as a buyer. A wealth of information from secondary sources will be available as you identify and track changes in the consumer market. More importantly, retailers today are using technology that allows them to know more information than ever about their current customers. And, it will be critical that you understand why your customers are buying—what motivates them to purchase a specific product or shop at your store. This information is invaluable to buyers as they make purchase decisions.

In this chapter, you will learn about some of the changes occurring with consumers; demographic, geographic, behavioristic, and psychographic trends are explored. You will examine the basic reasons why customers make purchases as you learn about data warehousing and data mining techniques. Finally, database marketing is examined to illustrate how retailers can make use of all the customer data they collect.

A MARKETING ORIENTATION

A retailer's success is directly dependent on consumer satisfaction; therefore, as a buyer you must be responsive to the wants and needs of consumers. Let's review some key marketing concepts that affect all retailers today.

Developing a Consumer Orientation

In recent years, retailing has become more consumer-oriented. In fact, a philosophy about the way in which retailers want to conduct business has developed—the belief that all business activities should be geared toward satisfying the wants and needs of consumers. As a buyer, you must identify what consumers want and then offer merchandise that will satisfy their wants and needs at a price they are willing to pay.

Customer satisfaction cannot be obtained without planning. A **retail strategy** is an overall framework or plan of action that guides a retailer. Usually, the store's owner or management team outlines the philosophy, objectives, target customer, tactics, and control activities that will guide the store's employees for a period of time, typically one year or more. Customer-driven stores have consistently better stocks of merchandise, more customer satisfaction, and broader and deeper assortments of styles and sizes than do stores that are concerned primarily with the profitability of each item sold.

A successful strategy helps retailers distinguish themselves from competitors and develop a merchandise assortment that appeals to a specific group of consumers. Making the effort to design a strategy also allows the retailer's total efforts to be coordinated. Management must develop an integrated strategy that coordinates factors such as store location, merchandise assortments, pricing, and promotion. Buyers, for example, may select the best products available that customers want, but a poor store location could mean few sales.

Positioning a Retail Store

Retailers must go beyond developing strategies; they must also determine how consumers perceive the store's **image**. For example, consumers may view your store as innovative, conservative, exclusive, budget, high-priced, or a fashion leader. Their perception may or may not agree with your planned strategies.

Virtually all retailers are concerned with how they are perceived by consumers. A key part of developing a retail strategy will be how to create and maintain an image that you want consumers to have of you. Every retailer positions itself in the market with activities such as selecting merchandise assortments, pricing policies, and promotion activities. **Positioning** involves identifying a group of consumers and developing retail activities to meet their needs. For example, a menswear store could be positioned as upscale, mid-priced, or discount. Neiman Marcus positions itself toward upper-class, status-conscious consumers. It offers exclusive brands of high-quality merchandise, charges relatively high prices, and uses very distinctive print ads. In contrast, Walmart targets middle-class, value-conscious consumers by utilizing discount prices and advertising that features a wide assortment of merchandise.

Targeting Consumers

The first step in positioning is to identify possible markets for your products. A **market** is a group of people with the ability, desire, and willingness to buy—in other words, your potential customers. Markets come in all shapes and sizes—some are large, while others are small. Regardless, markets are the target of your retail strategy. Read the Snapshot titled "The Chinese Consumer—Nearly One and A Half Billion Strong" to learn more about why retailers are so interested in this market.

Few retailers can serve every consumer because consumer needs and wants are so varied. Today, rather than trying to please everyone, successful retailers attempt to serve a **market segment**, a group of potential customers who have similar needs or other important characteristics (Figure 5.1).

Dividing the total market into segments is known as **market segmentation**. When retailers segment the market, they are attempting to identify and serve a particular group of customers with common characteristics. By identifying and understanding these groups of possible customers, buyers can tailor their merchandise assortments to meet the exact needs of those groups. Four types of data are typically used to segment markets: (1) demographic data, (2) geographic data, (3) behavioristic data, and (4) psychographic data.

Demographic Data

Consumer characteristics, such as age, sex, family size, income, education, occupation, and race, are known as **demographic data**. Retailers identify their potential customers in terms of those characteristics that would have an impact on purchasing products they have for sale. For example, consumers of all ages may purchase a specific product, but most of those consumers have incomes of more than $30,000 per year. In this instance, a retailer would want to make sure there were a sufficient number of individuals in the area earning more than $30,000 before purchasing the product.

Figure 5.1

Can you identify market segments that would purchase these products?

Geographic Data

Information on where consumers live, such as ZIP codes, neighborhoods, cities, counties, states, or regions, is known as **geographic data**. As a buyer, you must determine if there are enough potential consumers in your geographic area who will purchase products you are buying. For example, a product may have high sales in an urban setting but not be purchased by customers living in a small town.

Behavioristic Data

Information about customers' buying activities composes **behavioristic data**. For example, most retailers attempt to determine information such as the time that most customers make purchases or the average dollar amount of their purchases. Knowing this information can help buyers ensure they have adequate amounts of merchandise when and where customers want to purchase it.

Psychographic Data

Information on the lifestyle, interests, and opinions of consumers is termed **psychographic data**. In some cases, customers' personality characteristics influence what and where they make purchases. For example, shoppers who make purchases regularly at Walmart may be motivated by savings.

Most retailers use one or more of these data sources to segment their customers into groups or market segments. Retailers try to develop a profile of the consumers they will attempt to serve in order to buy the right merchandise and to present and promote it in the most effective manner.

Because market segments have different consumption patterns, products that are satisfactory for one group may not be appropriate for another group. For example, an urban professional has dissimilar needs from a retiree in Florida. These differences require you to segment your total market into more manageable pieces.

Types of Target Marketing

Mass marketing is no longer the norm; the US market is composed of many smaller segments, or **niches**. Retailers must create a competitive advantage by matching their strategies to specific market segments. After you have identified the characteristics of your market and divided the market into segments, you will want to identify your **target market**, the specific group or groups of consumers on which your store will focus. Typically, retailers use one of the following approaches to target their customers: (1) undifferentiated, (2) concentrated, or (3) multisegment.

Undifferentiated Target Marketing

An attempt by retailers to please all consumers is known as **undifferentiated target marketing**. Conventional supermarkets and drugstores are examples of retailers that use undifferentiated target marketing; they broadly define their potential customers. In the past, most department stores also used undifferentiated target marketing; however, many of them have changed this focus today. For example, J.C. Penney has narrowed its target market in recent years by eliminating many product categories.

Concentrated Target Marketing

Focusing on one segment of the market involves **concentrated target marketing**. A women's shoe store or an upscale deli are examples of retailers that have selected a well-defined consumer group that they wish to target. A retailer focusing on one market segment does not attempt to appeal to every consumer.

Multisegment Target Marketing

Retailers that focus on more than one consumer segment are using **multisegment target marketing**. They offer distinct merchandise aimed at several different groups of consumers. These groups, however, could have some similar characteristics. For example, big-and-tall menswear stores appeal to two distinct but similar groups. In some situations, appeals may be directed toward quite different market segments. For example, supermarkets may stock microwave dinners for both working mothers and singles. In such instances, different advertising strategies and product assortments will be needed to reach both groups.

Today, most retailers have taken steps to distinguish themselves by identifying and appealing to specific target markets. Targeting is a technique that catalog retailers use extensively. L.L. Bean is only one of many catalogers that have made effective use of target market concepts. In addition to one general catalog, it now has other catalogs aimed at very different retail niches. Separate catalogs are focused on men, women, plus-sized collections, children, travelers, fishermen, and hunters.

As a buyer, developing and implementing your plans will be directly linked to your store's retail strategy. Management must clearly define the store, identify target customers, identify an image, and position the store in the marketplace. If management has successfully completed these tasks and the store is perceived as offering customer satisfaction, your job as a buyer will be much easier.

IDENTIFYING CHANGES IN CONSUMER MARKETS

Consumers in the United States are changing, and they will continue to change. Current population numbers are known; future population trends can be forecasted. The number of people who will be over sixty-five and the number of teenagers ten years from now can be accurately predicted. Those customers are already born, and because forecasters have a good idea of mortality rates, these predictions are more than guesses. Retailers can safely use population and other demographic forecasts as they make future plans. Buyers can accurately use the numbers when forecasting the size of potential markets. What cannot be forecast with as much certainty are the tastes and attitudes of consumers. How will consumers in the future want to live? What products will they want to purchase? Examine Figure 5.2 to find a list of the green products that consumers have most often purchased.

Forecasts can be made in these areas, although with much less accuracy. By looking at the numbers that can be accurately forecast, buyers can ask questions about what these groups will want from retail stores in the future. There is no mystery to collecting the data; this information is available from a wide range of sources. Such statistics are reported every day by government reporting agencies, private market research firms,

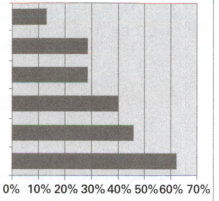

Figure 5.2
Recent green activities of consumers.

Bought a fuel-efficient automobile
Installed low-flow plumbing fixtures
Purchased energy-efficient appliances
Switched to paperless bank statements
Started paying bills online
Installed more energy-efficient lightbulbs

0% 10% 20% 30% 40% 50% 60% 70%

Source: *Green Decisions,* Success, February 2010.

business magazines, and daily newspapers. The difficulty is putting the data together to develop plans. For example, knowing that the over-fifty-five market is growing at a rapid rate does not mean that retailers should drop their juniors and young men's departments and concentrate on merchandise assortments for the older consumer.

The population of the United States is far different today in terms of geographical distribution, racial and ethnic composition, age mix, family types, and economic circumstances from what it was just a decade ago. Four trends have had a great impact on these shifts. The US population has shifted south. More than half the nation's population growth during the past decade occurred in the south. A "browning" of America has also occurred. Nonwhites accounted for an estimated 85 percent of the US net population growth during the past decade. Additionally, there has been a "graying" of America. About 8,000 Americans will turn sixty-five every day over the next five years, and they will live longer than previous generations. Also, a gender shift has occurred in the US market. Women now hold nearly half of all paid jobs in this country and own 40 percent of all businesses. Identifying shifts like these is important to retailers and buyers, but more importantly, they must be able to identify the implications to their businesses.

Demographic trends related to consumer characteristics change very slowly, and retailers cannot look at such trends and make immediate changes in their strategies. Recent consumer demographic trends are illustrated in Table 5.1. Buyers will want to closely examine growth rates for specific age groups. The most successful stores are the ones that are consumer-driven and adjust their focus season to season by listening to their customers.

Most retailers have been adept at targeting a consumer segment and providing merchandise assortments to meet the wants and needs of those individuals. Too many retailers, however, have not been adept at forecasting changes in their customers. They must respond to events such as:

- changes in the tastes and attitudes of customers;
- declines in the size of their target market; and
- changes in spending patterns of customers.

Market size, consumer attitudes, and future spending patterns of consumers depend on many factors that can be forecast based on an analysis of major demographic trends.

TABLE 5.1

US POPULATION BY AGE GROUP: 1950–2050

Age/Year	1950	1975	2000	2025	2050
Number (rounded)					
Total	152,272,000	215,972,000	281,171,000	357,452,000	439,010,000
0–19	51,673,000	75,646,000	80,576,000	94,254,000	112,940,000
20–64	88,202,000	117,630,000	166,522,000	199,290,000	237,523,000
65 +	12,397,000	22,696,000	35,074,000	63,907,000	88,547,000
Percentage in Age Group (rounded)					
0–19	33.9	35.0	28.6	26.4	25.7
20–64	57.9	54.5	59.0	55.8	54.1
65 +	8.1	10.5	12.4	17.9	20.2

Source: US Census, 2010.

Also, when analyzing trends, buyers must realize that a general trend for the country may not be valid for a particular city or region. These trends are useful only as guidelines in preparing forecasts of what customers at a specific store will want in the future.

As a retail buyer, you must have a thorough knowledge and understanding of who your customer is, as well as general trends occurring in the marketplace. A discussion of some of the most prevalent trends that will affect the decisions you make as a buyer follows. These trends are designed as a starting point; as a retail buyer, you will need to identify and examine specific trends related to your store's target customers. Buyers will need to analyze each trend and ask themselves, "What are the implications for my store, department, or product category?" Let's examine some of the more important consumer trends that will be affecting future purchases.

Demographic and Consumer Behavior Trends

As buyers begin to learn more about consumers, they usually begin by identifying trends related to their characteristics and lifestyles. Once they identify relevant information, buyers must then be able to use that information in making purchasing decisions.

Marital Status and Birthrates

Single-person households are showing the greatest increase in numbers, and that trend is projected to continue. Projections to the year 2020 show a dramatic increase in the number of middle-aged singles. The birthrate has remained relatively stable since 1994. Overall, population growth in the United States will continue to slow.

Households

The growing percentage of working women means that department and specialty stores will need to offer more career clothing, while grocery stores will need to offer more convenience foods—prepared foods from in-store delis and microwavable foods. Work also puts time constraints on customers, limiting when and where it is convenient for them to shop.

Increasingly, today's homemaker has a "five o'clock shadow." Research shows that the percentage of male "homemakers" (defined as the person in the household who does most of the shopping) continues to increase. Women, however, will continue to make the majority of purchasing decisions—from big-ticket items to small items, from clothing to food.

Age Groups and Spending Patterns

As more responsibility is placed on younger children because of latch-key lifestyles, they are learning savvy shopping skills, along with gaining confidence in their role as shoppers. Children and teens today greatly influence family purchases (Figure 5.3). Read the Trendwatch titled "Generation Z: The Most Technologically Advanced Generation Yet!" to learn more about this young generation.

The baby boom generation is reaching retirement age. By 2020, that cohort will number 115 to 120 million people. Research indicates that this group of "seniors" will be much healthier than previous generations, and marketers are finding that as the boomers age, these older consumers are still big spenders. Older households, with their higher incomes, are spending more. Retailers have found, however, that baby boomers vary markedly in their attitudes and values, and thus cannot be looked at as a single market segment. Because they are typically well educated, this group tends to spend lavishly on their children, buying millions of dollars worth of educational toys, video games, and children's books.

As the population ages, retail buyers will have to carefully select products for this older market segment. Products appealing to older customers will probably need to

Figure 5.3
Teens and children greatly influence family purchases.

focus on comfort, security, convenience, sociability, and old-fashioned values. Some products have already positioned themselves for this market. Levi's Action Slacks are cut for fuller bodies, Bulova is offering watches with larger numerals, and a host of home security companies have taken aim at this market segment. In addition, many retailers today are offering discounts to seniors on special days of the week.

Ethnic Origin

Europeans are no longer the most numerous ingredient in the ethnic mix of the United States. The non-Hispanic white population will increase more slowly than other racial and ethnic groups. In fact, whites are projected to become a minority (47 percent) by 2050. The Hispanic population, already the nation's largest minority group, will triple in size and will account for most of the nation's population growth through 2050. By that year, Hispanics will compose 29 percent of the US population, compared with 14 percent in 2005. J.C. Penney and Macy's were among the first retailers to target ads specifically to this market, focusing on attitudes such as a strong commitment to family. Table 5.2 illustrates the growth in the nonwhite population of various generations, such as Generation X, millennials, and Generation Z.

Lifestyle Trends

In addition to demographic trends, buyers must also be able to identify **psychographic trends** related to consumers' lifestyles, attitudes, and opinions. For example, information presented in Figure 5.4 indicates baby boomer opinions about future purchases. What trends could account for this? General trends in these areas are difficult to identify, but there are some general directions.

"Busy, Busy, Busy" Lifestyles

Juggling multiple tasks is common among harried Americans, but it has taken its toll on their physical and mental well-being. Many individuals are reevaluating their lives and restructuring them to find more personal time. Most people feel a time crunch, even when there is none. They seem to always be under pressure and feel they do not have enough time to do all the tasks they need to accomplish. For many consumers,

TABLE 5.2

U. S. POPULATION THAT IS NON-WHITE BY GENERATION (LATINO, BLACK, ASIAN, OR OTHER RACE)

Generation	Born Between	Percentage Nonwhite
Swing Generation	1933-1945	21.4%
Baby Boomers	1946-1964	27.0%
Generation X	1965-1976	36.3%
Millennials	1977-1994	38.1%
Generation Z	Born since 1995	41.5%

Source: U. S. Bureau of Census, 2010.

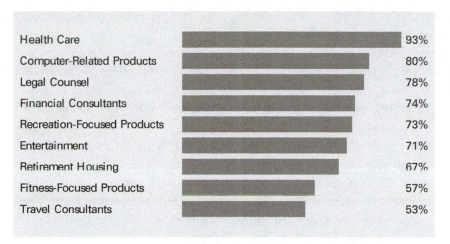

Figure 5.4
What baby boomers say they will be purchasing when they reach sixty-five.

Health Care	93%
Computer-Related Products	80%
Legal Counsel	78%
Financial Consultants	74%
Recreation-Focused Products	73%
Entertainment	71%
Retirement Housing	67%
Fitness-Focused Products	57%
Travel Consultants	53%

Source: Benefits of Marketing and Advertising to Baby Boomers, SCnewspapernetwork.com, 2010.

shopping has become a chore—an activity that many hate. In fact, most consumers are spending less time shopping at retail stores.

Retail buyers are reacting to this trend with the products they purchase. Many are stocking and promoting items directed at calming and relaxing customers. Aromatic candles, relaxing teas, crystal jewelry, bath soaps, and small-home-size water fountains are just some of the products being promoted to relieve the stress that consumers are feeling.

Computer and Social Media Junkies

The younger generation has grown up with computers, just as the baby boomers grew up with television. And, both groups have quickly embraced social media as a communications tool. Today, members of this younger generation are plugging into their computers, smartphones, and social media sites more often than they watch TV.

For retailers, increased usage of social media and mobile technologies can have a positive impact, giving retailers the potential to enlarge their market and communicate on a more personal level with their customers. No longer are retailers limited to a market within a certain trading area. Now, shoppers worldwide are potential customers. Retailers have responded to these new technologies by integrating their e-commerce sites and their presence on social media. As the mass market evaporates into smaller and smaller niches, traditional forms of advertising through TV, radio, newspapers, and magazines have become less effective. The internet and social media have allowed retailers to narrowly target specific consumer groups and be able to advertise and communicate with them almost on a one-to-one basis. Retailers will have to be where shoppers are, and as consumers move to mobile technologies and social media for work and play, retailers must take their products and promotional messages there too.

"We're Living Large" Lifestyle

Today, retirement is creeping up on baby boomers, who feel they need to reward themselves for the daily stresses they face. They have purchased huge, overstuffed furniture for houses that are three rooms bigger than they were two decades ago, with an "urban assault" vehicle in the garage. Americans are bigger too, with one-third of the US population tipping the scales as obese. Big, comfortable clothes are available, as are big meals—seventy-two-ounce drinks, two-foot pizzas, tubs of popcorn, and huge servings at most restaurants.

The "good life," according to Roper Starch Worldwide, has seen changes in the past twenty years. Happy marriages, a steady job, a home, and college for their kids were on the wish list of Americans in the twentieth century. Today, the list of material desires is considerable, including a second car, travel, a swimming pool, and a pile of money. Americans seem to want it all.

These trends affect individual retailers and specific products differently. Even different geographic locations of the same store within a chain could be influenced differently. Retailers must interpret the national trends based on a complete knowledge of their local customers. State and local forecasts need to be obtained, and if necessary, direct customer surveys may be required to determine what your customers want and the reasons why they buy.

UNDERSTANDING WHY CONSUMERS BUY

Once buyers have an understanding of how consumer markets are changing, they must determine "what products and brands are they most likely to purchase?" and "what causes targeted consumers to make purchases?" Each year, *Stores* magazine publishes research conducted by Prosper Insights & Analytics related to these questions, asking consumers what they can and cannot live without—in other words, what products and services do they view as expendable and which ones do they view as untouchable? Such information is critical to retail buyers as they make purchase decisions. Many personal indulgences, such as luxury handbags, high-end jewelry, and gourmet foods were perceived to be expendable, yet 80.1 percent of US consumers considered internet service to be the top item that was untouchable—the one item they could not live without. In fact, the top five items that consumers listed as untouchable provide strong evidence of the way they spend their time. All five were communications related—internet service, mobile phones, and cable TV. The list of "untouchable" items is shown in Table 5.3.

TABLE 5.3

PERCENTAGE OF US CUSTOMERS WHO CANNOT LIVE WITHOUT THE PRODUCT

Product	%
Internet service	80.1
Basic mobile service	59.0
Advanced mobile service	50.1
Basic cable/satellite TV	48.0
Upgraded mobile device	41.0
Haircut/color	39.0
Discount apparel	38.0
Vacation	35.0
Charitable contribution	35.0
Fast food	35.0

Source: Prosper Insights & Analytics, *Stores*, April 2017.

TABLE 5.4

PERCENTAGE OF US CUSTOMERS WHO CAN LIVE WITHOUT THE PRODUCT

Product	%
Luxury handbag	88.3
High-end jewelry	88.1
Club/social membership	87.7
Costume jewelry	87.6
Maid service	87.0
High-end cosmetics	86.6
Gourmet foods	86.0
Specialty apparel	86.0
Facials	85.6

Source: Prosper Insights & Analytics, *Stores*, April 2017.

Consumers provide an extensive list of items they can live without. The list of "expendable" items is shown in Table 5.4. Topping that list were luxury handbags, maid service, high-end jewelry, and club/social memberships. Changes in any of these trends in the future will have an impact on what consumers will be purchasing.

Retail buyers must also understand consumer buying motives, their reasons for making purchases. Read the Snapshot titled "Lego: A Fast-Fashion Company Thinking Inside the Box" to learn more about how this company has thrived on gaining a better understanding of its core customers. As a buyer making purchasing decisions, you will need to determine the reasons why customers would buy each product you have purchased for your store. Such knowledge will be critical when planning promotional campaigns and providing product knowledge to sales associates. Typically, buying motives can be grouped into three categories: (1) rational, (2) emotional, and (3) patronage.

Rational Buying Motives

Rational buying motives are concerned with basic human needs such as food, clothing, and shelter. Such needs would correspond to the physiological needs on Maslow's hierarchy, which include hunger, sex, and thirst. Consumers tend to satisfy these needs first, but once they are met, they will seek to satisfy needs on the other levels. An illustration of Maslow's hierarchy is presented in Figure 5.5.

Rational buying motives are based on a customer's ability to reason in logical terms. Typical motives of customers that fit into this category could include economy, savings, durability, dependability, reliability, and gain.

Emotional Buying Motives

Customers may purchase food, clothing, and shelter to satisfy rational needs, but those needs can be satisfied with minimum purchases. What causes consumers to purchase several sweaters or two coats? These purchases can be explained by **emotional buying**

Figure 5.5

Can you identify products that would satisfy consumers at each level of Maslow's hierarchy?

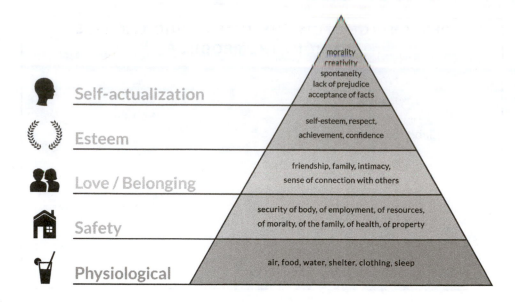

Self-actualization — morality, creativity, spontaneity, lack of prejudice, acceptance of facts

Esteem — self-esteem, respect, achievement, confidence

Love / Belonging — friendship, family, intimacy, sense of connection with others

Safety — security of body, of employment, of resources, of morality, of the family, of health, of property

Physiological — air, food, water, shelter, clothing, sleep

motives, which involve customers' feelings rather than logical thought. Examples of emotional buying motives could include social acceptance, curiosity, change, sex appeal, self-esteem, and group approval.

Patronage Buying Motives

Patronage buying motives explain why consumers choose one store over another. This information is vital to the retail buyer because customers have to enter the store before they can buy products the buyer has purchased. Some key factors customers use include the following:

- *Convenience.* The location of your store may be the deciding factor for the consumer. Customers may select stores at shopping malls because of easy parking. Parking may be expensive as well as difficult to find at many downtown locations.
- *Value Received.* Value received is important to all consumers but from different perspectives. For some consumers, value is associated with low price. For others, price is no object if they feel they are receiving a quality product. Consumers return to stores where they feel they receive the most value for their money.
- *Assortment of Merchandise.* Most consumers shop at stores that provide them choices; however, they can become confused when too many choices are provided. Also, many consumers buy in places where they can make all their purchases at one stop. Mall locations are appealing for this reason, and one-stop shopping is the concept on which warehouse clubs and hypermarkets are based.
- *Services Offered.* Many consumers may decide to make purchases at a particular store because of the services offered, such as credit, delivery, gift wrapping, or alterations. For example, a consumer could buy a recliner anywhere but may choose the store that offers free delivery. Providing services is a key method retailers can use in distinguishing themselves from competitors.

- *Experienced and Courteous Sales Associates.* Consumers will usually return to stores where they find friendly, courteous, and experienced salespeople who are crucial to the image that a retailer is attempting to develop. Many customers return time after time to their favorite salesperson. Nordstrom has built an industry reputation on the high level of service provided to customers by its sales associates.

LEARNING MORE ABOUT YOUR CUSTOMERS

In addition to identifying and examining trends related to the general population, most retail decision makers, and specifically buyers, are now using techniques that allow them to identify, analyze, and take advantage of trends prevalent among their own customers. These techniques include data warehousing and data mining.

Data Warehousing

Retailers have searched for ways to efficiently collect the wealth of information they gain from customers every day and to use that information to develop better retail strategies. **Data warehousing** involves electronically storing all this information. Retailers have generally used the data for financial and accounting purposes only and ignored the value of the data for making merchandising decisions. Typically, this data had been kept by many different parts of the retail organization. With data warehousing, there is only a single source of data. Data warehousing acts as a comprehensive single source for sales, margin, inventory, and other key merchandising performance measures.

The process of building a data warehouse requires retailers to transfer significant amounts of data from operational computer systems to analysis systems. This data transfer makes vital sales data more readily accessible to decision makers and buyers in the store as well as its vendors. Data warehousing provides them all with access to the vast amount of information that is stored on the computer system. The result is usually strengthened partnerships with vendors, an improved selection of merchandise in the store, and more effective promotional campaigns. Using data warehousing can also effectively boost the retailer's potential to offer the right merchandise at the right time. Additionally, retail buyers and other decision makers in the company have a unified understanding of the company as a whole.

Benefits and Uses of Data Warehousing

Storing and using data are more important than ever for most retailers as they seek ways to improve their businesses through technology. Rather than using a broad brushstroke to market all products to all customers, retailers want to maximize purchase decisions and promotion efforts by directing them to the consumers who are most likely to buy. Data warehousing allows retailers access to detailed customer, inventory, and financial data on a perpetual, real-time basis. With a data warehouse system in place, very specific analyses can be performed, such as determining how well a particular product is selling in a specific store, as well as making merchandise replenishment decisions based on facts rather than intuition. Data warehousing provides all retail decision makers with the tools to understand their business in detail, not just in summary.

For example, each day, information from Lands' End order processing and customer mailing systems is added to the company's data warehouse. Detailed information is kept on approximately 20 million customers, enabling management to find and analyze data by customer, product, and transaction. The system can also track what customers ordered that was not in stock. Williams-Sonoma, another cataloger, uses its data warehousing system to improve its bottom line by better targeting customers who generate sales and eliminating from its mailing list individuals who seem unlikely ever to order anything.

Data warehousing has a strong foothold in large retail firms but is also gaining popularity among midsized and even small chains. Some firms have seen a payoff of ten to seventy times their initial data warehouse investments through more effective decision making. Walmart, for example, currently operates the world's largest commercial data warehousing system. Their decision support system now has more than five terabytes of online storage and is used to store sixty-five weeks of sales data by item, store, and day. The surge of data warehousing is due to a growing recognition that it is a tool that provides retailers with the best means of understanding and satisfying the needs of their ever-more-demanding customers. Data warehouses, running on ultrafast computers with specialized software using files now stored on the cloud, are the basis on which companies hope to operate in real time—instantly adjusting such factors as product mix, inventory levels, and marketing programs.

Data Mining

Technology is not the difficult aspect of implementing data warehousing. The hard part is deriving meaning from the data. Significance must be extracted from the blizzard of numbers, facts, and statistics. **Data mining**—searching through warehoused data to find trends and patterns that might otherwise have gone unnoticed—is a cutting-edge technology that uses the information already maintained in the firm's data warehouse. Data mining software has enough built-in "intelligence" to detect meaningful patterns and relationships on its own. These trends might otherwise take many years to detect by retail buyers or other decision makers sifting through all that information.

Typically, buyers have used a firm's database to supply answers to such simple questions as "What was the sales volume for stores in the southeast region last month?" Data mining reaches much deeper into databases. Software tools are used to dig through and analyze information as well as extract its meaning; computer tools find patterns in the data and make inferences from them. Those findings can then be used to guide decision making and better forecast the effect of actions being considered.

Using Data Mining Techniques

Most analysts agree that past behavior is more predictive than age, sex, and income; but with hundreds of behavioristic variables to choose from, the difficult question becomes "Which techniques will help retailers understand the customer better?" Effective data mining almost requires an explorer's mentality—retailers never know what they are going to find and what changes may result. Data mining, however, produces some general types of data:

- *Associations.* The system links occurrences to a single event. For example, data mining analysis may reveal that customers buy a new tie 65 percent of the time when dress shirts are regularly priced, but 85 percent of the time when dress shirts are on sale. Having mined this information, retailers can evaluate the profitability of various promotional strategies.

- *Sequences.* The system links events over time. For example, 50 percent of customers who purchase a suit may then purchase shoes within thirty days. This information lets the retailer formulate more informed buying, merchandising, and promotional decisions.
- *Clustering.* Data mining tools can discover groups within the data. For example, decision makers may be better able to pinpoint customer groups most likely to use the retailer's e-commerce site.
- *Forecasting.* Tools can be used to analyze data to predict whether a customer will continue to shop at the store, and even forecast future purchases based on patterns within warehoused data.

Clustering customers into segments is one of the top objectives of data mining for management at Fingerhut catalog. At that firm, data mining has led to the creation of new catalogs. In one analysis using data mining, decision makers found that customers who changed their residence tripled their purchasing in the three months after their move. The company developed a new "mover's catalog" filled with targeted products for that consumer segment. At the same time, it saved money by not mailing other catalogs to these customers right after they moved.

Data mining allows retailers to understand what customers buy and when they buy it; therefore, retailers are able to do a better job of marketing to those customers. For example, a new mother goes to her local pharmacy to fill a prescription for postnatal vitamins. After her profile has been collected at the store, management can then send a steady stream of coupons for products that she will need at each stage of the baby's development. Such product selections can easily be based on results of data mining that have shown what products similar customers have purchased over time.

Generally, data mining can be used by management, buyers, and other retail decision makers for a number of purposes. They include the following:

- *Competitive Price Analysis.* Data warehousing and mining allows for a better interpretation of competitive price data collected by comparison price shoppers. The system can use mathematical formulas to identify overpriced and underpriced items and product categories on a store-by-store basis.
- *Markup/Markdown Opportunity Identification.* Mathematical formulas in data mining techniques allow retailers to single out stock-keeping units (SKUs) that have rapidly accelerating or decelerating sales volumes, compare the prices of these items with prices charged by competitors, and recommend new price points.
- *Promotional Price Analysis.* Data warehouses and data mining techniques can be used to compare average prices in local markets with the buyer's suggested promotional price. The system then reviews promotional sales history to understand item movement at various price points and generates a promotional price.
- *Private Brand Analysis.* Data warehouses and data mining can be enlisted to calculate the price points at which consumers will switch from a national brand to a competing private-label product.
- *Promotional Performance Analysis.* Data warehousing allows retailers to scrutinize their promotions at an item level to isolate products that yield the greatest promotional sales increase or that customers buy without making any other purchase in the store or department. Insight into individual items and product categories that are more likely to be cannibalized by promoted items can also be gleaned.

- *Affinity Analysis.* Data warehousing can identify products and merchandise classifications most commonly purchased together, such as those shown in Figure 5.6. The result can be better in-store product adjacencies, improved promotional display effectiveness, and more effective advertising campaigns.

Effective use of data warehousing and data mining techniques results in a sharper competitive edge, a selling and merchandising approach based on real data, a marketing plan that correlates with customers' needs, and reduced operational costs. But above all, retailers must remember that computer-generated reports do not provide all the answers. Decision makers who implement data mining must be people with a solid knowledge of the marketplace.

EXAMPLES OF DATA MINING IMPLEMENTATION

Today, more and more retailers are using data mining techniques to market to their customers. Even very small business owners are developing their own customer databases to learn more about their customers so they can build a lasting relationship. Examples of how retailers and buyers have effectively implemented data mining are described below. These techniques are based on analyzing and understanding customers and their behaviors through data analysis.

Targeting Current Customers

Against the backdrop of today's highly competitive retail environment and low single-digit sales growth, the importance of understanding all customers—from the most loyal to the most indifferent—is critical. Retailers know that selling to an existing customer is generally easier and less expensive than converting a new customer, but too often retailers fail to use targeting techniques with their existing customers resulting in customer attrition, or **churn**. Reducing that churn often involves offering promotions

Figure 5.6
Buyers must coordinate the purchase of items like the ones pictured.

and incentives such as discounts to customers identified as likely to defect. The tricky part is determining who should be targeted. One technique is to classify current customers based on the following framework:

- *Disciples.* Shoppers do most of their shopping at your store. They frequent multiple departments regularly.
- *Secure.* Shoppers do most of their shopping at your store and consider it acceptable. These shoppers also frequent multiple departments.
- *Susceptible.* Customers shop regularly with you but do not really like it compared to the competition. These shoppers do it because it is convenient or close to home or work, or no other store has made the right appeal.
- *Vulnerable.* Customers shop your store regularly at more than one department. But they really do not like it; in fact, a large percentage of this group is actively looking for a better alternative.
- *Disgruntled.* Shoppers patronize one department in your store but do most of their shopping elsewhere. They do not really like the other store where they usually shop but prefer it to your store. Many times these shoppers are actively looking for a more acceptable alternative.

Placing customers into groups, such as these, can be based on information from the store's database of credit card purchases. For example, parameters can be set in the database to trigger if a decline in a customer's shopping and spending is detected over a predetermined period. For example, you may find that a customer who had been spending $150 a month with your store is now making purchases only totaling $25.

Once these customers are identified, the next step would be to implement strategies that could help retain shoppers who may be straying and use that information to enhance the customer's relationship with the store. More extensive surveying may also be needed. You need to determine why these shoppers are vulnerable, where they are spending their money now, and where they would shop if they defected. Once all the data is available for analysis, you can explore what can be done to ensure that a store's most vulnerable shoppers do not defect.

The greatest opportunity targets are customers who are on the verge of leaving your store—susceptible, vulnerable, and disgruntled. If you focus on these groups with appeals that hit their hot buttons, your store can do a better job of retaining them as loyal shoppers. Today, retailers wanting to connect and maintain relationships with their customers are also developing effective social media campaigns using sources such as Facebook, Instagram, and Twitter. And, email continues to offer a cost-effective method of providing different messages and incentives for each group identified above.

The fundamental challenge of implementing such a plan will be having data available about your customers' shopping patterns. Remember that it takes about five times as much effort to get a new customer as it does to retain an existing one. Such targeting efforts may be worth the time and expense.

Market Basket Analysis

Sales data provide a view of what customers are purchasing but do not provide a view of how they are buying—in what combinations and in what quantities. One data mining method that is being used to better determine how customers are buying is market-basket analysis.

Market-basket analysis is a term that describes data mining solutions that identify the correlations among items in a customer's shopping basket. Buyers and merchandisers can apply these findings and respond to customer demand more effectively by making better space allocation and product placement decisions. Their first step is to associate the products in the customers' market basket with a product category. Through analysis, the percentage that each category represents is calculated. For example, if there are ten items in a market basket and five are cosmetic products, 50 percent of the basket is represented by the cosmetics category.

Management predetermines a percentage to represent a customer in a particular purchase profile. For example, a retailer may determine that having more than 25 percent of items in a product category places a customer into the profile. In the preceding example, the customer would be categorized as belonging to a "Beauty Conscious" shopper profile. A market basket with more than 25 percent of the items related to photographic equipment and supplies would be categorized as a "Photographer," and so on for each type of basket found. In essence, the analysis captures the key reason that the customer was in the store.

The category becomes more than a product grouping; it becomes a shopper profile. For example, makeup, cotton balls, hair dye, and cologne may be in different product categories and in different physical locations within a store, yet they are all part of the "Beauty Conscious" purchase profile. By using this analysis, retailers are not trying to pin labels on customers; they are attempting to categorize shopping experiences and analyze how customers collectively behave while shopping.

Once customer purchase profiles are identified, the next step is to provide information to decision makers, such as buyers, on which they can act.

A gross margin figure is calculated for each profile. This figure can then be used to base decisions about key areas of the business. For example, the data can provide information to the retailer about how to spend advertising dollars. "Beauty Conscious" may generate $15.24 in profits per market basket, whereas the "Photographer" generates only $2.55. Obviously, advertising dollars should be spent on the products that generate the most profit. Further study may show that the store is spending money on product categories that bring in the least profit.

Another way in which market-basket analysis can be used is to make fact-based decisions about space allocation and product placement. Space allocation needs to be correlated with customers whose purchase profiles generate the most profit. Also, product placement decisions can be made by determining affinity purchases. This concept involves using market-basket analysis to determine what items are most frequently purchased with other items in the same market basket. For example, analysis may reveal that in the "Beauty Conscious" shopping basket, greeting cards were found 25 percent of the time and seasonal candy was found 16 percent of the time. Such data would indicate that sales of these two products would increase by moving them adjacent to a primary beauty care area. By using affinity analysis, a store can be moved from being a product-driven business to being a customer-driven business.

Decisions may not always be made using the results of market-basket analysis. For example, new fathers with no time to go out and socialize tend to pick up a six-pack of beer when buying disposable diapers. This is an exploitable relationship that is not obvious at first glance; however, it is doubtful that any retailer would stock diapers alongside beer. But if acted on properly, effective market-basket analysis can bring increased sales, a stronger in-stock position, and increased customer satisfaction.

Figure 5.7
Market-basket analysis uses information on what products customers purchase together in their shopping cart.

Knowing the customer better leads to a more personal relationship between a retailer and the customer. As a retail buyer, you should realize that every customer transaction tells a story (Figure 5.7). Implementing a market-basket analysis is one way to reveal the details of that story.

Database Marketing

This concept has several names—**database marketing**, relationship marketing, one-to-one marketing—but in all cases it involves collecting mountains of information about customers, analyzing it to predict how likely customers are to buy a product, and using that knowledge to develop a marketing message designed to best match customers' wants and needs.

Database marketing has evolved over time, and computer technology has dramatically expanded its implementation by retailers. First, there was the mass market—the vast, undifferentiated group of consumers who received identical, mass-produced promotional messages. Then, retailers started using market segmentation, which divided consumers into smaller groups with common characteristics. Today, more powerful software programs are enabling retailers to zero in on ever smaller niches of the population. They are taking aim at the smallest consumer segment of all—the individual.

Retailers increasingly are recognizing that past customer behavior, as recorded in actual business transactions, is a good indicator of future buying patterns. For example, knowing customers' ZIP codes or income levels yields less insight and opportunity than knowing that they just purchased a new house. Such a move signals the need for lots of new purchases, such as window treatments, carpets, and furniture, and retailers can better stock their stores and design promotional messages based on that information.

The fundamental principle that should guide retailers who use database marketing is that a retailer's most important asset is a satisfied customer. Satisfied customers stay with the store, and it is much less expensive to keep existing customers than to find new ones. Examples of database marketing are varied. For example, one men's specialty retailer may find itself with too many suits in size 42-regular. After electronically sorting through its database, previous customers who have purchased that size are sent promotion offers to buy a suit at a reduced price. The retailer is able to clear excess inventory while also building customer loyalty among its customer base. Many national chains track credit card holders who spend more than a predetermined dollar amount at the store each year. Those customers who meet or exceed the required purchasing amount are sent special offers, advance notice of sales, and discount coupons. Some retailers have found that loyal customers are not always motivated by the most expensive rewards. One of the most popular benefits at Neiman Marcus is a chance to have lunch with the store manager and attend a private fashion show.

Database marketing starts with information about the customers from databases maintained at the store or corporate level; today those data are typically stored on the cloud. The initial building block of information is data on each sale. Items from credit or debit card purchases can provide even more information. The retailer can then mix in data from other sources. Research consultants can glean vast amounts of data from public records—auto registrations, drivers' licenses, and tax records. Even income can be estimated based on mortgages and automobile registrations. Retailers must be aware, however, that obtaining such information is not inexpensive.

Consumers, consciously or unwittingly, also offer retailers lots of information about themselves. Most product warranty cards ask a gamut of questions such as age, income, occupation, education, and marital status, but many go on to ask many psychographic questions, such as what sports the purchaser plays or whether he or she participates in other specific activities.

Challenges Facing Database Marketing

Analysts point to problems and challenges facing the spread of database marketing. Too many retailers have jumped into the field without a complete understanding of the basic concepts. Some retailers are uncertain of its benefits, while others lack a strategy for coordinating database marketing with other traditional approaches. Stores are also faced with the resistance of consumers and consumer groups that feel having stores collect and use information on their shopping habits constitutes an invasion of privacy.

Goals of Database Marketing

Clearly, any retailer implementing database marketing programs must have specific purposes for using the technique. Survey research has revealed the following nine basic goals that most retailers have for database marketing programs:

1. Targeting promotional offerings to specific customers.
2. Gaining a better understanding of customers.
3. Strengthening the store–customer relationship.
4. Gaining a more detailed understanding of the best customers.
5. Tailoring merchandise offers to specific customer segments.
6. Reducing the cost of new customer acquisition.
7. Improving customer service.
8. Assisting in the merchandise selection process.
9. Preventing customer defections.

As more retailers are learning that customer databases can be developed, organized, and mined successfully to encourage customer loyalty, such programs are likely to continue to grow. Fueling the move toward database marketing is a paradigm shift away from the idea that consumers can be marketed to as one huge market and toward the idea that consumers want customization. In other words, they "want it their way." Above all, these programs help build store traffic, improve customer service and merchandise strategies, and, for omnichannel retailers, develop synergies among store, catalog, mobile, and online sales.

Summary Points

- The most successful retailers are consumer-driven. They know who their customers are and listen to them.

- Retail stores cannot please everyone, so they target specific market segments based on demographic, geographic, behavioristic, and psychographic data.

- Positioning and targeting are key marketing tools that retailers use to develop their image and retail strategies.

- Retailers typically identify market segments they wish to serve using undifferentiated, concentrated, or multisegment target marketing.

- Retailers must monitor changes in the consumer market, particularly demographic and lifestyle changes.

- Buyers must do more than identify consumer trends; they must understand the implications for their store or department. Identifying consumer trends will help buyers make better decisions.

- Buyers must identify local and regional trends that have a direct impact on their customers. These trends may be very different from national trends.

- Reasons that customers make purchases can be grouped into three categories: (1) rational, (2) emotional, and (3) patronage buying motives.

- Many retailers are using data warehousing techniques to store a wealth of information about their customers.

- Retailers and buyers are implementing data mining technology to extract meaning from the information stored in data warehouses.

- Many retailers use database marketing techniques to target specific customer groups. Such efforts have the potential to strengthen store–customer relationships.

- Technology is playing a critical role in enabling buyers to learn more about their customers.

- Data mining tools can be used to categorize current customers, identifying those customers who are shopping less and less frequently. These tools can be also be used to analyze customers' total purchases identifying products most often purchased together.

- Most importantly, data mining can be used to develop database marketing programs that can lead to one-to-one promotion programs for individual customers.

Review Activities

Developing Your Retail Buying Vocabulary
Consult the glossary if you did not add the following terms to your vocabulary.

behavioristic data	demographic trend	market segmentation	rational buying motive
churn	emotional buying motive	multisegment target marketing	retail strategy
concentrated target marketing	geographic data	niche	target market
data mining	image	patronage buying motive	undifferentiated target
data warehousing	market	positioning	marketing
database marketing	market-basket analysis	psychographic data	
demographic data	market segment	psychographic trend	

Understanding What You Read

1. List four types of data retailers use to segment consumer markets.

2. List and describe three types of target marketing.

3. Identify demographic trends that are occurring in the United States related to (a) the number of single-person households, (b) the median age for marriage, (c) the birthrate, (d) US population growth, and (e) the number of male homemakers.

4. Identify behavioristic trends that are occurring in the United States related to spending patterns of (a) children, (b) baby boomers, and (c) Hispanics.

5. Describe lifestyle changes that are occurring in the consumer market.

6. Describe the differences between rational and emotional buying motives.

7. How do customers select one store over another when making a purchase?

8. List types of data maintained by retailers in data warehouses.

9. Describe how retailers use data mining.

10. Describe how associations are using data mining to learn more about customers.

11. How is data mining used for affinity analysis?

12. List some of the challenges retailers face when using database marketing. What is a buyer's purpose in subscribing to an out-of-town newspaper from a metropolitan area?

13. List the basic goals of using database marketing.

Analyzing and Applying What You Read

1. You are the buyer for a grocery store. Describe the implications related to your purchase decisions of knowing that there are (a) more single-person households and (b) more women working than you projected.

2. You are the owner of a used-car dealership and have just purchased 100 small cars. Your advertising agency is preparing your next promotional campaign. Because you purchased the cars, the agency has requested that you supply reasons that customers would purchase them. Provide rational, emotional, and patronage buying motives that prospective customers could have.

Internet Connection

1. Go to www.census.gov. Locate the following information about consumers in your state and community: (a) the population of your state and (b) the population of your city or community. Then locate data related to the number of individuals in different age categories.

2. Use the internet to locate new information about one of these specific consumer groups—Generation X, baby boomers, Asian Americans, male homemakers, or Latinos. Identify major trends that are occurring with the group you research.

3. Visit the book's STUDIO to watch videos about the changing face of the American consumer and Generation Z.

SNAPSHOT: Lego: A Fast-Fashion Company Thinking inside the Box

Lego bricks are played with by millions of kids and adults around the world, offering them endless opportunities for creative fun. Today, Lego, a Danish company that is over eighty years old, is the world's number two toy company, behind Mattel. In reaching that milestone, the company manufactures over 45 billion plastic elements annually and escaped two brushes with bankruptcy in the early part of this century. To achieve this success, Lego has adopted business approaches from fast-fashion retailers such as H&M and Forever 21 while still thinking inside the box for their core customers.

Lego had its humble beginnings in 1916 in a craftsman's workshop in the small town of Billund, Denmark. The company's name was based on Danish words for "play well." Up until the 1990s, demand for the product was so high that it was difficult for the company to keep up with sales. But then, the toy market shifted drastically. Big-box retailers, like Walmart and Toys "R" Us, dramatically lowered prices, which resulted in a lot of small toy stores closing. In addition, birth rates were declining, and it seemed that those children had less time to play—wanting instant gratification for their efforts.

To combat the changes in the marketplace, the company undertook efforts to change its product offerings and increase sales by using approaches similar to those used by fast-fashion apparel retailers. New Lego products hit store shelves rapidly and the basic Lego building sets became less of a focus for the company. A line of Lego-branded children's wear was created, along with book, movie, and TV deals. At the same time, Lego building sets became increasingly more complex as many unique components were added.

However, as the number of Lego-branded items grew, profits did not, and in 1998 the company had its first financial loss. Adding more elements to the building sets also began to choke the company. It became more difficult to assemble all the new construction elements, and sales forecasts for different products were harder to determine, making inventory levels harder to manage. There was too much inventory of some items or no inventory at all, creating a lot of disgruntled customers. And, Lego was losing its core customers, who had seen the toys as outlets for personal creativity.

Additionally, the company also signed licensing deals with Marvel Entertainment and representatives of the *Harry Potter* and *Star Wars* franchises. While many of the new tie-in products were a hit, the big successes only occurred in years when there was a movie. In 2003, for example, when there was no movie from either franchise, sales tanked, and the company started losing money rapidly.

Many of its core customers felt that Lego had lost its way. The new *Star Wars* and *Harry Potter* kits came complete with step-by-step instructions and stated objectives. For them, Lego products were no longer about imagination and creativity; they were merely about replication. As profits continued to decline, management was faced with changing the company yet again.

However, rather than trying to innovate with "new" product elements, Lego managers started thinking "inside the box." They went back to their origins and focused on police stations and fire trucks, which the company's core fans were buying and which were very profitable since they were not tied to the whims of movie-going consumers. In doing so, Lego rediscovered its niche of loyal customers: devoted Lego fans who stayed that way even after they became adults by purchasing Lego sets for their children. Management found that one of the most powerful assets that the company had was these loyal fans, who became a big part of the firm's comeback from near bankruptcy.

The company has achieved a balance between continuing to add new products as fast-fashion retailers have done and retaining an emphasis on its core products and the fans that purchase them. Lego still extends its name to hit movies and the occasional flop—*The Lone Ranger*, for example—but the company emphasis has returned to its core business.

Lego has found that growth and success are about balance and controlling complexity. Moreover, they clarified the core of the business: a product for kids that provides them with creative thinking-in-action and, when playing with Lego, those kids should only be limited by the boundaries of their own minds and, possibly, by the number of Lego bricks they have available.

BASED ON:

Knowledge@Wharton. (2013, August 26). How Lego stopped thinking outside the box and innovated inside the brick. *Forbes.com*.

Starvish, Maggie. (2013, March 18). How Lego grew to global dominance. *Forbes.com*.

Venables, Michael. (2013, March 12). Behind the legendary Lego, Part one: The public relations, family values and product quality. *Forbes.com*.

Venables, Michael. (2013, April 20). How Lego makes safe, quality, diverse and irresistible toys everyone wants: Part two. *Forbes.com*.

Wieners, Brad. (2013, December 16). How Lego became a fast-fashion company. *BusinessWeek.com*.

Nearly one and a half billion people are a lot of potential customers for retailers, and that is what they are looking at in China, the world's most populous country. As retailers look to the bulging China market for growth and expansion, retail buyers in these global companies must gain a full understanding of who these customers are—their likes, dislikes, and purchasing habits. Above all, buyers must determine what product assortments will appeal to these customers and how they can best be presented to the Chinese customer.

First, the sheer size of the China's population is staggering. It is estimated to be 1.42 billion by 2020, and 1.45 billion by 2030. However, these consumers differ widely. Most Chinese consumers still live in rural areas making low incomes, but the government continues to support more urbanization. In fact, in the next four years, more than 13 million Chinese are expected to move to cities from rural areas. Such shifts in the population are producing a rapidly expanding, brand-conscious middle class. Currently, there are approximately 109 million Chinese people with a net income between $50,000 and $500,000, and in the next five years that number could surpass 500 million.

The aspirations of this fast-growing middle-class market in China are a big draw for retailers around the world. Some retailers are already cashing in on the popularity of many Western brands to the Chinese consumer. New Look, a British clothing store, is preparing for rapid expansion in China with plans to manufacture clothes there to ensure they cater to local tastes and get to stores quickly. In 2016, H&M opened more stores in China than anywhere else in the world, and the country is already Zara's biggest market outside of Spain.

Sales have indicated that many of the new middle-class Chinese consumers purchase brands from abroad because many foreign brands carry a better reputation than their Chinese competitors. Such attitudes have been fueled by toxic chemicals being found in Chinese-made food and cosmetics. For products that "touch the skin," like cosmetics, diapers, and personal care products, Chinese shoppers place a premium on foreign brands. While Chinese consumers may admire foreign brands, they may not initially buy these products. For example, some global retailers in the China market have had to develop how-to videos for teaching consumers how to best use foreign products with which they may be unfamiliar, and Robert Mondavi wines found they had to offer single-serving bottles of wine to encourage shoppers to try wines they had never purchased before. Growth in luxury markets has also occurred in China. Sales of both expensive Swiss watches and Porsches have increased recently, and Tiffany has also reported strong growth for its products.

The world's most populous country, however, is aging at an accelerating pace. Projections indicate that about 25 percent of China's population will be sixty or older by 2030. That's up from 13.3 percent of the population in the country's latest census in 2010. This has huge implications for economic growth—the nation's expenditures for public services, insurance, and health care must sharply increase. Moreover, older consumers tend to purchase less, which puts a big dent in domestic consumption, and a shrinking labor force has also slowed consumption.

To combat this graying of the population, China's government recently scrapped the more than three-decade-old one-child policy for couples. Couples are now being told they would be permitted to start having two children. As of yet, however, births in the country have fallen short of official projections. For retailers, this change in policy could offer a great opportunity for expansion. Hamley's, a toy retailer in the United Kingdom, is already implementing aggressive expansion efforts in China that could result in more than 100 new stores there. Toys "R" Us is also planning to double the number of its stores in China, to 200 shops. And with more children on the horizon, it is not just toy retailers seeking to expand; vendors of diapers, kids' clothes, and baby food have indicated interest in expanding in the China market.

All is not rosy for foreign retailers, however. Some Western brands have struggled in attracting the Chinese consumer, including Gap, Abercrombie & Fitch, and Marks and Spencer. Sometimes, the fit is just too different for the Chinese consumer. Yet, for most global retailers, expansion into the world's largest consumer market is well worth the risk. It will be crucial, however, that retail buyers for these companies fully understand the Chinese consumer and make needed adjustments in products and assortment offerings that will offer the greatest appeal in the marketplace.

BASED ON:

Einhorn, Bruce & Wei, Daniela. (2017, January 25). The Chinese rediscover luxury. BusinessWeek.com.

Rao, Leena. (2015, December 29). Why Alibaba wants Chinese shoppers to buy American. Fortune.com.

The world's most populous country is turning gray. (2017, January 26). BloombergNews.com.

This retail tycoon wants to open 500 stores in China in three years. (2016, October 21). Fortune.com.

Toh, Michelle. (2016, October 7). The end of China's one-child policy is helping this UK toy store. Fortune.com.

GENERATION Z: THE MOST TECHNOLOGICALLY ADVANCED GENERATION YET!

They would rather text than talk. They prefer to communicate online, many times with "friends" they have never met. They cannot imagine life without smartphones. They prefer computers to books and want instant gratification. They grew up in an economic recession and are under constant pressure to succeed. These are just some of the characteristics of Generation Z.

This generation has begun receiving widespread attention in the press. For years, the media mostly focused on the preceding generations—baby boomers, Generation X, and Generation Y (also referred to as millennials). In fact, there is not even a clear-cut agreement on the name to assign this particular generation. Generation Z has also been referred to as Generation Net or iGen, because they have never known a world without the internet.

Generation Z is roughly defined as anyone born between the late 1990s and the present day, and although many of them are still too young to have their own income, they have significant control over household purchases such as toys, groceries, and clothing. In addition, the average allowance for members of this market segment is $70 a month, which generates an annual purchasing power of $44 billion.

One thing is certain: new generational groups are emerging more frequently than in the past. Baby boomers, for example, most often thought of as those born from 1946 through 1964, lasted almost twenty years. But Generation X, born from around 1965 through 1980, was five years shorter. And Generation Y appears to span about ten years.

Many members of Generation Z have not even graduated from high school and marketers and retailers are already trying to determine how this generation will be different from their predecessors. We know they are the most tech-savvy generation of all time—preschoolers can maneuver their way through YouTube and some first graders can put together a PowerPoint presentation. But beyond that, who are they really?

Most experts in the field agree it is just too early to know for sure. But that has not stopped marketers from trying to figure out this young group of consumers—the future of their businesses may depend upon developing that understanding.

From a product perspective, we know this group has huge expectations when it comes to technological gadgets, whether they are smartphones, laptops, or the latest version of the iPod or iPad. In many instances, their parents are getting them those gadgets. Using technology is one of the easiest ways to delineate this generation, but analyzing their mind-set is another. For members of Generation Z, everything is customized and individualized to "me." Their music choices are customizable, as is what TV programs they watch and when they watch them. Products they purchase in the future, such as jeans and perfumes, must also be customizable to just them. They want their world individualized.

From a communications perspective, they want to be constantly connected and available in a way that even their older siblings do not quite understand. For Generation Z, portability is the key for communications devices. They are inseparable from their wireless devices; they are constantly connected. Many of this generation admit they check their smartphones constantly for messages, and they access Twitter, Instagram, Snapchat, and Facebook accounts as part of their daily routine. News and product recommendations come from these connections, creating a lot less brand loyalty than with past generations. At the same time, however, this constant communication creates more individualized promotion opportunities for retailers and marketers in the future. What does Generation Z care about? They love finding and sharing "stuff." In fact, they have become more than consumers; they have become curators. From tweets to Facebook and Instagram posts, they like to tell the world about what they find. And, retailers must make it easy for them to share their information and opinions about their experiences with stores and products because Generation Z relies heavily on the opinions and recommendations of their peers when making a purchase decision.

Retailers must start today to develop plans as to what products Generation Z will purchase in the future, and seek to gain a better understanding of which types of technology will work best to communicate with this group in order to promote the company and its products. And, above all, those communications must be honest and transparent.

BASED ON:

Begley, Sarah. (2017, March 27). How to work with Generation Z. *Time*, p. 24.

Forbes Agency Council. (2017, March 24). Think beyond millennials: 12 ways your brand can engage Gen Z. *Forbes.com*.

Knoepp, Lilly. (2017, March 22). These brands are proving gender-fluid is the future of fashion. *Forbes.com*.

Peterson, Hayley. (2014, June 27). Generation Z is a complete nightmare for retailers. *Businessinsider.com*.

Start preparing your business for the generation after millennials. (2014, July 14). *Entrepreneur.com*.

Wilson, Marianne. (2017, January 23). Study: Retailers need to pay attention to Gen Z. *ChainStoreAge.com*.

Wong, Venessa. (2014, May 12). What comes after millennials? *Businessweek.com*.

CHAPTER 6
UNDERSTANDING PRODUCT TRENDS: WHAT CUSTOMERS BUY

Performance Objectives

- Recognize that the merchandise mix offered must be geared to satisfying customer wants and needs.
- Identify product categories based on availability and durability.
- Recognize that fashion is a powerful force in almost all retail stores.
- Describe how retailers establish a fashion image.
- Distinguish between fads and trends.
- Identify stages of the product life cycle.
- Describe merchandising decisions occurring at each stage of the product life cycle.
- Identify theories of fashion adoption.
- List buyers' methods for differentiating products they purchase from those sold by competitors.

Once buyers have an understanding of customer behavior, they must decide which products to purchase that will best satisfy the wants and needs of their customers. The store image that management has established will greatly influence these purchases.

In this chapter you will learn more about how customers decide which products they will purchase. You will also gain an understanding of product life cycles and fashion adoption theories and how they help buyers make merchandising decisions. And you will identify techniques that buyers use to differentiate the products they purchase from those competitors are offering.

PRODUCT SELECTION DECISIONS

As a buyer, you must plan and control the kinds of products that will be offered in your store or department. In other words, you must be concerned with the **merchandise mix**—the types or mix of products that are available for customers to purchase. The merchandise mix that you select should meet the specific needs of your customers. It must be frequently monitored because an appropriate mix today might not contain the right products tomorrow.

After you determine the types of products that will be offered, you must determine the product lines that you will be carrying. A **product line** is a group of products that are closely related because they function in a similar manner. For example, New Balance has several lines of athletic shoes, and Samsung offers several lines of televisions. Buyers typically want to provide a variety of products for their customers. You may also have to think in terms of which products customers associate with other products. If they purchase New Balance shoes, will they also purchase New Balance caps and jackets?

The image that your store is attempting to project will also have a direct impact on the types of products that you will purchase. Decisions made by top management in the following areas will determine the image that the store projects to its customers:

- *Target Market.* The types of products that you purchase must be matched to the wants and needs of your store's identified target market. Read the Trendwatch titled "Men's Grooming Is Booming" to learn more about how the grooming products being purchased by men have changed in recent years.
- *Competition.* Management may decide to sell merchandise similar to that of the competition or carry entirely different products that appeal to a different market from that of your competitors.
- *Store Location and Layout.* Store location, layout, store design, fixtures, lighting, and display all will have an impact on the product assortment desired by management, as illustrated in Figure 6.1.
- *Merchandise Selection.* Brand names carried in the store will also influence the store image. For many customers, national brands denote higher quality than private

Figure 6.1
Store fixtures, lighting, and displays will all have an impact on the product assortment a store offers.

brands; however, private brands create exclusivity—a goal of all stores. Merchandise selected can also create a fashion image. High-quality products tend to bring a higher profit per unit than low-quality goods, but they usually represent slower turnover.

- *Personnel.* Skilled, knowledgeable personnel are necessary when stores offer some products such as designer gowns, cameras, or computers.

In addition, stores that wish to develop a fashion image must be known for offering new and unique products in the marketplace. Today, more and more stores are attempting to establish a fashion image. For example, mass merchants and discounters are promoting brands to develop a fashion image. J.C. Penney has added many national brand names, while Rooms to Go has developed private brands such as Sofia Vergara to create a more fashionable image for the store.

As a buyer, you must make decisions about merchandise selection that require understanding your customers' desire to purchase new, innovative, or fashionable products. Generally, stores attempt to attract upscale customers by offering high-quality and fashionable merchandise that will also tend to be more expensive. Other stores use moderately priced items that have mass appeal to cater to middle-class customers, while inexpensive items are used to attract bargain-conscious customers.

As you select merchandise for your store, you must be aware of trends in the marketplace. Identifying trends will allow you to make the most appropriate product selections for your store or department. Customers continually change. If you can capitalize on opportunities created by that change by quickly identifying emerging trends, you will provide your store with a competitive advantage.

TYPES OF PRODUCTS CUSTOMERS PURCHASE

As a buyer, you must thoroughly understand the trends that will have an impact on the products you are purchasing. You will also need to understand how your customers make their product purchases and be able to answer questions such as the following:

- What types of products do your customers most often purchase?
- How much time are customers willing to spend buying a particular product?
- What are customers' expectations about durability and product quality?
- Are your customers fashion forward?
- Do customers expect your store to have "new" and cutting-edge products?
- Will your customers purchase the latest fads and crazes?

Purchases Based on Availability

Availability refers to the amount of effort customers are willing to exert to obtain a particular product. Today, products offered at one retailer in the community can probably be found at several other retail outlets, too. If customers cannot find exactly what they are looking for at one store, will they accept a substitute? For some products, they will; for other products, they will never accept a different model or brand.

Products purchased by consumers can be grouped into four broad categories: (1) convenience products, (2) impulse products, (3) shopping products, and (4) specialty products. As a buyer, you need to categorize the products you purchase into one of these areas to have a better understanding of how customers view them.

Convenience products are those products that the customer is not willing to spend time, money, and effort in locating, evaluating, and purchasing. Easy and quick availability of these products is paramount to the customer. For convenience products, if a particular brand is not available, customers will easily switch brands as well as stores. Customers usually purchase convenience products frequently—with little planning and comparisons. Examples include batteries, candy, toothpaste, white socks, and gasoline—to name a few. Convenience products are usually low priced, and suppliers place them in many retail outlets to make them readily available when customers need to purchase them.

Impulse products are purchased by customers because of an often irresistible urge. Impulse purchases are sudden and spontaneous, without much deliberation by customers. Many retailers have seen sales skyrocket of some items simply by the placement of the products in the store so that they create the impulse purchase. Batteries and candy at the cash registers of most grocery stores are prime examples. Stimuli, such as smell and touch, often trigger the purchase of these types of products. Seeing a product demonstrated in a store stimulates impulse purchases of many products, such as the latest kitchen gadget, and window or in-store displays can also stimulate consumers to make purchases they had not planned for during a shopping trip.

For **shopping products**, customers make price, quality, suitability, and style comparisons. They are willing to spend considerable amounts of time, money, and effort in obtaining shopping products. What constitutes a shopping product, however, varies from one customer to another. Customers purchase shopping products less frequently than, and make careful comparisons to, similar products based on suitability, price, and style. Examples of shopping goods include furniture, designer clothing, automobiles, and major appliances. Customers may be willing to accept a substitute product if their comparisons indicate it would better suit their purposes. Manufacturers usually distribute these types of products in few retail outlets.

Specialty products are those products for which customers' buying behavior is geared to obtaining a particular product without regard to time, effort, or expense; and, they will not accept a substitute. Again, which products fall into this category would vary among customers. Examples could be a particular brand of perfume customers always use or the newest Barbie doll for their collections.

Purchases Based on Durability and Quality

The quality level and durability of products that you, as a buyer, purchase must support your store's positioning strategy in the marketplace as well as meet the needs of your target customers. Most retailers rarely try to offer the highest-quality products—few customers want or can afford the high levels of quality offered in products such as a Rolls-Royce or Rolex watch.

Durability refers to how long a product will last. **Durables** are products (such as cars, furniture, and appliances) that are capable of surviving many uses and usually last for years. These products are relatively expensive, and customers purchase them infrequently. In fact, during difficult economic times, consumers tend to stretch the life of durables and hold onto them as long as possible. **Nondurables** are products that are used up in a few uses or simply become out-of-date as styles change. Consumers tend to make frequent and regular purchases of these products if they are fresh, new, unique, current, or fashionable. Food products represent the largest category of nondurables.

Quality and durability can also be related to the features that a product provides. Products can be offered with varying features—from a model with only a minimum number to one with all the extras. Product features offer retailers a competitive tool for differentiating products in their store from those of competitors. Buyers must identify which product features available are most desired by their customers. To learn about customer wants and needs, customers can simply be asked questions like these:

- "Which new features would improve the product?"
- "Which features do you like the most?"
- "Which other features would make this product more appealing to you?"

Purchases Based on Fashion Appeal

Another way to add value to a product is through distinctive product style and design—making it more "fashionable" or making it a better product. **Style** is a basic and distinctive mode of expression—the appearance of a product. Styles can be eye-catching, or they may never excite shoppers (Figure 6.2). A sensational style may generate attention, but such products may not perform better. A **fashion** is the currently accepted or popular style. Many people confuse fashion and style. Style is the characteristic or distinctive way a product looks: the combination of features that makes it different from other items. For example, a bow tie is a style of tie, a four-door sedan is a style of car, and a turtleneck is a style of sweater.

Conversely, good design contributes to a product's usefulness as well as to its appearance. For example, men's shirts are available in "wrinkle-free" fabric. Appearance, as well as the usefulness of the shirt, is improved for customers when this fabric is used by designers and manufacturers.

Almost every product sold today is influenced by fashion. In fact, almost all retailers are increasingly in the fashion business. Fashion occurs in all areas of retailing, not

Figure 6.2
What factors would affect sales of products like these in a sporting goods store?

just apparel—automobile dealers offer new styles every year, appliances now come in a multitude of fashion colors, and many fashion designers have their own line of sheets and bedspreads. Therefore, all buyers should have a general understanding of what fashion is and how it works. As a buyer, you must realize that customers determine fashion. That is why building your forecasting skills is so important to your success, and being able to predict the future depends to a large extent on understanding what has happened in the past. Manufacturers and retailers cannot dictate what products will become fashion; customers make that decision when they make purchases. Many times, customers are wearing an entirely different look from what is being promoted by the retailers and manufacturers; or, they may not rush out to buy the newest style automobile that is being heavily promoted.

Fashion is a powerful force in our society because a desire to change is a part of us all. Fashion satisfies the desire for change and gives customers the opportunity to identify with certain groups and be accepted by their peers. That is why customers reject many useful products when they are no longer fashionable. In fact, today's biggest sellers may be tomorrow's biggest flops because they are no longer "in fashion."

Fashions change because people's ideas and behaviors change. As a larger portion of women entered the workplace, their clothing changed. As more firms accepted "casual Fridays," clothing changed. Read the Trendwatch titled "Men's Socks: No Longer Just Black and Navy" to learn more about this fashion trend.

Political and leisure activities also influence fashion changes. New clothing or accessories worn by the First Lady show up in retail stores the next week. Designs worn by stars at award ceremonies make their way to the mass market within weeks. Products that customers see in movies or TV programs are on their "must have" list the next day. Fashions also change because of technology. New fibers have altered most apparel. And technology itself spreads the word on new fashions and trends—TV, the internet, and social media platforms have greatly increased the speed of new fashion awareness and acceptance by customers. Examine Table 6.1 to read about how many of the fashion trends in the past started with a movie.

Change is inevitable in retailing and a vital component of the industry. Buyers must understand fashion by remaining up to date on current trends and make merchandising decisions based on an understanding of their customers. In previous chapters you learned about the importance of reading magazines, trade publications, newspapers, and other sources in order to forecast trends. Buyers need a firm grasp of the dynamics of fashion trends. They need to know what fashion involves, how it moves, and how to forecast the impact of fashion on a store or department.

Fashion encourages customers to buy new products and discard the old, but at varying speeds. Some fashions change every few months, whereas others change only after several years. While making purchasing decisions, you must be alert to **obsolescence**— the outmoding of a product due to a change in fashion before its usefulness has been exhausted. Fashion apparel, cameras, computers, and home electronics are examples of products that typically remain useful when customers decide to purchase replacements.

Carrying fashion items also gives your store or department a competitive advantage. A consumer may not replace some basic items until they are worn out. Because American consumers quickly tire of what they are wearing or using, purchasing new products makes them feel a sense of change and renewal. Purchasing new fashion items provides for this sense of change.

TABLE 6.1

FILM FASHION THAT MADE AN IMPRESSION

Film	Fashion Impact
Letty Lynton (1932)	Broad-shouldered power suits designed for Joan Crawford's character.
It Happened One Night (1934)	Clark Gable's Norfolk jacket, V-neck sweater, and trench coat.
Pat and Mike (1952)	Katherine Hepburn's gender-bending menswear style.
Rear Window (1954)	Edith Head's haute couture designs in everyday wear, and square overnight bag designed for Grace Kelly—the predecessor to the "Kelly Bag" that Hermès would name for her.
Rebel Without A Cause (1955)	James Dean's T-shirt and red jacket.
And God Created Woman (1956)	Brigitte Bardot's bikini, ballet flats, and cotton gingham beach dresses with an open neckline (later called the "Bardot neckline").
Breakfast at Tiffany's (1961)	The little black dress is the film's greatest fashion achievement, but triple-strand pearls, sleeveless dresses, and oversized sunglasses also became trends.
Bonnie and Clyde (1967)	Theodora van Runkle's "'30s retro chic" look worn by Faye Dunaway; berets also hit the mainstream.
The Thomas Crown Affair (1968)	Three-piece suits designed by top English tailor Douglas Hayward, showcased with high-end accessories, like a Patek Philippe pocket watch and tortoiseshell Persol sunglasses with blue lenses.
Shaft (1971)	Three-quarter-length black leather jackets as worn by Richard Roundtree.
Annie Hall (1977)	Renewed women's obsession with the menswear look.
Saturday Night Fever (1977)	John Travolta's white disco suit inspired a wave of form-fitting clothes in bright colors.
Flashdance (1983)	Activewear as fashion, including sweatshirts, leg warmers, Spandex pants, headbands, and high tops.

Source: The State, 2010

You must also realize that new fashions create "ripple effects" with new customer needs. When the length of skirts changes, women will probably purchase new slips, shoes, and hosiery. So, as you make new product purchases, you must determine the impact on other products that your store is selling.

Increased fashion importance also causes problems in reordering and timing of purchases, but most buyers welcome the addition of fashion items into their inventory because new products tend to stimulate sales and enhance the store's image. One area where fashion is having a tremendous impact on the type of merchandise available is products for the home. Many home items are being recast as décor merchandise—items that are high in fashion but low in function. Most notable are crafts and silk flowers; both are linked with the color themes of the home.

The broad fashion decisions for a store will probably have been made by top management as merchandising policies were established. In fact, management may have already identified "looks" that are expected to be acceptable to your customers. Your job will then be to execute how these looks will be expressed in your merchandise selections.

Purchasing "New" Products

Buyers are constantly besieged with a barrage of "new" products and must evaluate each of them before making a decision about whether to purchase them for the store. Following are some factors that should be considered before adding new products:

- The compatibility of the new product with existing products carried by the store.
- The potential profitability of the new product.
- The placement of existing products within the product life cycle.
- The appropriateness of the new product for your customers.
- Do customers expect your store to have "new" and cutting-edge products?
- The ability of the competition to offer the same or similar products.

Today, new products arrive in the marketplace frequently. Most "new" products simply offer improvements over existing products. For example, the "newest" camera or computer has many more features that will probably make these products more useful to customers. Some "new" products, however, are really new—they have not been available before in any form. Wine coolers, when they were first introduced, were an example of one such product.

Buyers must be aware of the world around them and sensitive to the changes that are constantly occurring. They must be aware of trends. Even though product changes are constantly occurring, those changes tend to be evolutionary rather than revolutionary— most changes tend to be made slowly. For example, men's ties become narrower or wider slowly from year to year, sometimes almost imperceptibly. Occasionally, new products become revolutionary—a very quick change. In the 1970s during the oil crises, small cars moved into general acceptance almost overnight. Today, as concern for the environment escalates, hybrid automobiles have gained quick acceptance. However, such revolutionary changes are rare. If current products differ too dramatically from those in the past, they will not fit in with what customers already own.

Buyers have to create excitement on the sales floor, and they do that with newness. New products make customers want to buy; new and innovative products create store traffic. There are always customers who want something different, and there is always something new available in the market for buyers to purchase. Some buyers are reluctant to purchase new and untried products because they may not understand newness and hesitate to make such purchases—causing a lot of staleness on the sales floor. Every year there are many new products available in the market, but it is up to the buyer to want to take the chance on them. When the economy slows, buyers tend to become even more cautious in their purchasing.

As a buyer, you will face a tremendous selection of new products every time you enter the market. Knowing what consumers want—before they know themselves—can make the difference between your purchase decisions being a hit or flop. Consumers may not even be aware of the availability of new products before you purchase them and place them on the sales floor. In fact, the pace of new products appearing in the market is speeding up because many companies are reducing the time involved in product development. Moreover, products survive in the market for a shorter time because competitors are introducing rival products at a more rapid pace as well. Stores that offer any new product today have only a three- to six-month head start on the competition.

One reason for all these new products is that stores can command a higher price for them than for standard items. Japanese consumer electronics companies continually strive to make their existing products less expensive while at the same time adding new features so they can sell them at the same price. The result of incremental innovation is that many products are not totally new, but they are packaged differently and have a new idea added.

Buyers must also decide how innovative or fashionable their merchandise selections should be. Several factors should be examined before making this decision:

- *Target Market.* You will need to evaluate whether your target market is conservative or progressive. Will the newest, most fashionable products on the market be accepted by your customers?
- *Store Image.* The kinds of products a retailer carries are influenced by its image, and the level of innovativeness should be consistent with this image. Consumers may look to your store as an innovator—the first in town with new products and styles. Or your store may wait to see which products are accepted by the public before making the purchases. The more clear-cut your store is in establishing its image, the more confidently you can make purchases.
- *Competition.* You must also decide if you want to lead or follow the competition. You must decide to undertake fashion leadership or wait until a product is widely accepted.
- *Fashion Trends and Theories.* You will also need to understand the theories that apply to fashion adoption. A useful tool for assessing the potential for a new product is the product life cycle, a helpful planning tool used to develop buying strategy. Sales and inventory data must be analyzed to chart trends as they develop. Adequate store records reveal how fast or how slowly product classifications have sold, how frequently they had to be reordered, or whether they had to be marked down. Examining all the best sellers may reveal characteristics that each of the products has in common. For example, popular colors with your customers may be determined using past sales data. You will also want to become a shrewd observer of people. Your own observations will substantiate trends you have already detected or may reveal entirely new trends.

Buyers must also be aware that some products are **classics**—styles that are in demand continuously even though minor changes may be made in the product. Cardigans, button-down collars, and jeans are examples of classics. Classics appeal to a great number of people for a long period of time.

Purchasing Fads versus Trends

One of the most challenging tasks facing a buyer is being able to distinguish between fads and trends. **Fads** are products that enter the marketplace quickly, are purchased with zeal, and then have sales that decline quickly. Fads have invaded every area of retailing and present several merchandising problems to buyers. There is the problem of obtaining enough supply while the fad is strong, and then there is the problem of disposing of the leftover stock when the fad quickly dies. Fads require that buyers carefully watch for trends. For example, when goods are offered in all types of stores at constantly lower prices, the end is near for the fad. Wise buyers forgo profits late in the selling season and cut the fad from stock early. If your store serves a fad-prone group, such as teenagers, you will need to keep in the closest possible touch with them.

Fads, however, are a key ingredient of the product mix for many retail buyers. They can hit fast and furiously, providing buyers with one shot at making quick profits. The danger is that buyers can overestimate a fad's long-term appeal and be left with lots of worthless inventory. But overlooking or dismissing a product that develops strong consumer appeal can lead to a stodgy reputation for the retailer. Although fads are only a small blip in relation to the sales longevity of other products, they have a disproportional importance in terms of store image and customer appeal.

Fads help buyers keep their stores vital and attract new customers; however, the sales cycle for a fad is vastly different from that of regular products. Sales of fads generally show a meteoric rise, followed by an equally dramatic drop. Trends show gradual sales growth that eventually evolves into stable business. It is imperative that buyers identify fads and then closely monitor inventory levels and sales for those products. What is critical is the amount of inventory the store has left when the fad dies.

Each generation embraces its own fads, from slap bracelets and cabbage patch dolls to pet rocks and Pogs. Some fads fizzle and fade quickly, while others demonstrate a more lasting appeal. One of the most recent fads to hit the market was Silly Bandz, colorful rubber bands in shapes such as animals and sports figures, made of silicone and die molded, allowing them to return to their original shape when stretched. In the toy market, fads come and go yearly. Read the Snapshot titled "Hoverboards: From Boom to Bust in a Short Time" to learn more about how hoverboards (Figure 6.3) went from boom to bust so quickly. Is your favorite toy from childhood still on the market? Or did it drop out of stores at the end of its first Christmas season?

The consumer marketplace is characterized by rapid changes that provide opportunities for buyers if they anticipate those changes and use them to create a competitive advantage for their stores or departments. However, early identification of trends requires sound judgment and the ability to analyze data. If you miss the

Figure 6.3
One recent fad: hoverboards.

emergence of a trend by thinking it as a fad, you will play catch-up with the competition. For many years, the US auto industry paid the price for missing or ignoring changes in US consumers. In contrast, many firms have been able to capitalize on trends by identifying them early. For example, having identified the growing health and fitness trend in the marketplace, Nike exhibited fantastic growth with athletic shoes, and Lean Cuisine redefined the market for single-serving, healthy frozen food.

There are also benefits to identifying a fad as a fad. Your store can make a lot of money quickly, but you must get out when the fad has reached its crest. If you think the fad will be a trend, you may keep purchasing merchandise and get caught with a lot of unsold inventory.

All buyers face the challenge of correctly identifying fads and trends. Today, for example, almost all areas of retailing are being impacted by "green" products. Clothing purchasers are faced with recycled apparel and the use of more natural fibers like organic cotton, wool, hemp, bamboo, and coconut-based blends. Will green products be the next big trend or will they die the quick life of most fads? Only time will tell. Read the Trendwatch titled "Wearable Technology: The Next Big Thing or Only a Fad?" to learn more about several new products hitting the market.

How do you identify a trend? Fads tend to be inflexible. There are few, if any, ways to alter the product. The "pet rock," for instance, was such a fad. Trends, however, tend to be more flexible with many ways of expression, but some products may appear to be a fad when they enter the marketplace. The first microwave, known as the "Radarange," came to market in 1947; weighing in at 750 pounds and standing five-and-a-half feet tall, it cost $3,000. In 1967, Amana introduced a countertop version for $495. But between high prices and anxiety about radiation, it took years for microwave sales to explode and the product to become more than a fad. Gradually, technology improved and prices came down; at the same time, consumers' hurried lifestyles demanded speed. These days, a microwave can be found in almost every American home. Many households have two, and they come in a variety of fashion colors. In addition, the microwave has transformed the food industry. Microwave popcorn and microwavable meals, for example, are now multimillion-dollar industries.

In the final analysis, when trying to identify trends, retail buyers must remember that consumers are extremely complex and notoriously difficult to categorize, and this can be frustrating even to professional trend watchers. It seems that for every trend that is identified, there is also a corresponding countertrend. For example, today's consumers continue to shop for low-fat foods, at the same time as there has been a return to self-indulgence, and that often means foods with more fat and taste. The average consumer may eat fat-free pretzels for a mid-afternoon snack, have salad and mineral water for dinner, and top it off with a bowl of chocolate ice cream. Additionally, light beers continue to sell successfully, but it is the hot microbrews that are stealing the spotlight with their richer, darker, and more calorie-filled taste.

Moreover, some surveys suggest that cooking from scratch is dead, that kitchens have become museum pieces, and that people only venture there to use a microwave. But on the countertrend side, TV cooking shows are growing in popularity, and online recipe sites have burgeoning visitors. Kitchen remodeling trends include induction-heat cooktops, professional stoves, and restaurant-style refrigerators. What is more, as the size of the formal dining room shrinks, big kitchens remain more popular than ever.

Retail buyers must constantly try to detect and monitor trends in the marketplace. They should, however, also attempt to detect any countertrends that may be occurring.

PRODUCT LIFE CYCLES AND FASHION ADOPTION THEORIES

Through strategic planning and understanding the market and consumers, buyers can learn to develop effective retail strategies. Planning is especially crucial in dealing with inevitable product changes. An understanding of product life cycles and fashion adoption theories aids buyers in making many merchandising decisions.

Demand for and sales of all products move in cycles, and the lengths of these cycles vary. One product may have a very short sales cycle, while others remain on the market for years or even decades. When customers have rejected a product, however, stores must clear out the merchandise as quickly as possible.

Product Life Cycle

To improve their forecasting skills, buyers must understand the life cycle of each product they are purchasing—particularly its impact on sales. The **product life cycle** illustrates the expected behavior of a product over its lifetime. The traditional product life cycle has four stages: (1) introduction, (2) growth, (3) maturity, and (4) decline (Figure 6.4). Products move through this cycle at various rates. **Velocity**, or the speed at which products move through the product life cycle, must be a concern of buyers. Some products, such as women's clothing, have a high velocity, completing the cycle in a few months; other items, such as luggage and furniture, move through the cycle much more slowly.

A buyer's chief concern is that risks are greater the faster a product moves through the cycle. Yet rewards are there for successful products with fast sales and higher-than-average profit margins—which is why there seems to be constant pressure to introduce fashion into traditionally basic items such as sheets, men's underwear, and appliances.

Products pass through several stages in their lifetime, and sales performance varies at each stage. Knowing which stage a product is in helps the buyer judge both its existing and future sales potential. Each stage of the product life cycle also suggests different retailing strategies.

The Product Life Cycle

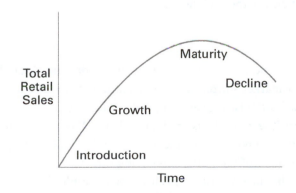

Figure 6.4
The product life cycle.

Introduction Stage

In the **introduction stage**, products are characterized by low sales and losses, as well as high risk. Many products never make it out of the introduction stage. For example, new perfumes are introduced every year, but only about 10 percent are hits with customers. During the introduction stage, the risk is great because buyers are gambling on an unproven product. During this stage, buyers generally utilize a high-price strategy and develop promotion activities that are designed to tell the customer about the new product. For most retailers, new products are essential for their image.

During the introduction stage, products are usually accepted by a limited number of customers. Buyers should anticipate a limited target market composed of high-income or innovative customers. **Innovators** are those customers who are more likely to purchase a new style. In the past, new styles appeared first among the wealthy and slowly reached other groups; however, that is not as true today. Teenagers may be the first group to purchase a hot new product. As an increasing number of consumers accept a product, it moves into the growth stage.

Growth Stage

When innovative consumers purchase products and recommend them to friends, the product enters the **growth stage**. The most desirable products for retailers are those in this stage because they are characterized by accelerating sales and the highest profit levels of any stage. Ultra HD televisions and virtual reality devices are two products currently in the growth stage.

In the growth stage, product variations begin to appear, and the number of retailers carrying the product expands. Usually, there is also an increased number of suppliers. In this stage, **early adopters** are those customers who purchase the products in its early rise stage. The majority of customers finally make the purchase as it reaches the last rise and peak of the cycle.

Maturity Stage

In the **maturity stage**, sales increase at a slower rate and finally begin to level off. Characteristics of this stage are a highly competitive market, falling prices and profits, and more intensive advertising. CDs and DVDs are currently in this stage. They can now be purchased at stores like Target and Walmart at very low prices. Low, discounted prices may signal that such products may be headed to the next stage of the product life cycle. Maturity is the most competitive stage, and price is prominently mentioned in promotions. In this stage, **late adopters** accept the product when it is past its peak, while **laggards** adopt it during the decline stage.

Decline Stage

Buyers, as a rule, will not be purchasing products in the **decline stage**. During the decline stage, the target market shrinks, and price cutting minimizes profit margins. Normally, products reaching this stage are dropped, and heavy markdowns are taken on remaining inventory. These products are high-risk and low-reward items. At this stage, the target market is composed of price-conscious individuals and laggards. Most stores cut back on the variety of their offerings during this stage, while many retailers drop the product altogether before customers abandon it completely.

The product life cycle can easily be applied to fashion apparel. Several different product life cycles are illustrated in Figure 6.5.

Fashion Adoption Theories

Buyers who purchase fashion merchandise must be familiar with theories of fashion adoption and how they affect products they are purchasing. There are three theories that attempt to explain how fashion is adopted.

Downward Flow Theory

The downward flow theory maintains that fashion innovators are those people at the top of the social pyramid, such as royalty, world leaders, and the wealthy. Over time, fashion that this group accepts moves to progressively lower social levels. For example, hats and jewelry worn by many First Ladies become a fashion statement for the masses. Fashion is passed from the upper to the lower social classes through three vertical stages: (1) distinctive—original, custom-made designs are worn by high society; (2) emulation—original designs are modified and carried by finer department stores, and they appeal to the middle class; and (3) economic emulation—the original design is mass-produced and mass-marketed.

Many fashions start their life cycle as **haute couture** from designers such as Chanel, Givenchy, and Christian Dior (Figures 6.6a–c). Every year a few thousand women pay $30,000 and up for handmade, one-of-a-kind creations. Although these gowns are glamorous, they are only marginal moneymakers. These designers rely on related items, such as fragrances and accessories, to generate profits. In addition, many European couture houses and prestigious US designers are developing "secondary lines," which are designed by couturiers but cost from $100 to $900—within reach of the middle class, although still expensive.

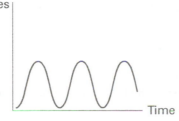

Figure 6.5
Variations of the product life cycle.

Figures 6.6a–c
Haute couture looks from Chanel, Givenchy, and Christian Dior.

One problem designers will have to deal with is the possible damage that the less expensive lines could have on the haute couture image. Designers such as Halston lost much of their luster when they attached their names to too many products. Although some designers are shying away from secondary lines, many may have no choice if they expect to remain profitable.

Horizontal Flow Theory

The horizontal flow theory maintains that fashion adoption moves horizontally within groups. In each group, there are innovators who are willing to try the new product. When other members of the group see the fashion being worn, they are more likely to make a similar purchase. If fashion is adopted in this manner, it does not matter what the upper classes are wearing or purchasing. Within each social class there are innovative customers who act as opinion leaders. Once they accept a fashion, they convince other members in the same social class to accept it as well.

Upward Flow Theory

This theory is the opposite of downward flow and maintains that the fashion innovators are the young. For example, T-shirts, for a long time part of the teenager's basic wardrobe, are now a part of many designers' lines. Today, considerable fashion influence is exerted by young consumers.

Each of these theories is based on the concept that fashion innovators and fashion followers exist. Understanding each theory and determining which one is most appropriate for your customers and the products you are purchasing will enable you to predict future adoptions. Most buyers use all three theories to predict what styles are likely to become fashion successes.

Using Product Life Cycles and Adoption Theories

Understanding product life cycles and fashion adoption theories can assist buyers in making many merchandising decisions, including those of timing, forecasting, and product elimination.

Timing

Knowing your target market allows you to determine when new products, particularly fashion merchandise, should be introduced in the store at a time when your customers will be ready for them. Product selection must reinforce the store's reputation as either a leader or a follower. Stores attempting to establish a fashion image cannot continue to carry fashion merchandise after customers are tired of it without giving the feeling of staleness.

Forecasting

Understanding these theories also helps you predict the merchandise that will be desired by specific groups of consumers. You can obtain general forecasts from trade publications, reporting services, buying offices, or consumer publications. By knowing what the innovators are purchasing, you may be able to pick the next "hot" product for your customers.

Product Elimination

Knowing the stage of the product life cycle in which the product happens to be also allows you to determine when products should be eliminated from stock. You should begin considering substitutes as new products begin appearing on the market. Before eliminating products entirely, however, you may want to consider other strategies such as revisions in marketing strategies or price cutting.

Sharpening your product sense is a matter of increasing your sensitivity to your customers' readiness to accept new products. Combining that sensitivity with a knowledge of the marketplace will allow you to make the most intelligent buying decisions.

CREATING PRODUCT DIFFERENCES

As a buyer, you will want to purchase products that can be differentiated by your customers from what the competition is offering. Typical ways to do this are by adding private-label merchandise, licensed products, and mass-customized products to your merchandise mix.

Brand Names

Customers rely on brand names to distinguish products among the massive number from which they have to choose. In essence, consumers use brand names to help them make a product choice. **National brands** are products that are sold almost everywhere—Ragu spaghetti sauce, Arrow shirts, Levi's jeans, Ford Mustangs, and the list goes on. National brands dominate the product selections at most retail stores, creating a sameness at stores that all sell identical brands.

An increasing number of retailers are creating their own **private brands** (or **store brands**). For example, Sears sells Craftsman tools, Kenmore appliances, and DieHard batteries—all are private brands that are available only at Sears. Private brands belong to the store and can be found on products sold exclusively at that store. At some retailers, such as Eddie Bauer and Lands' End, almost everything sold is a private brand. J.C. Penney has developed its Arizona jeans label, Kmart has Jaclyn Smith apparel, and Walmart has Sam's Choice. Most grocery stores usually have at least one private brand. Private brands are also gaining prominence in home fashions. Some private labels on fashions for the home have the added benefit of appearing on apparel and other merchandise, so customers are already familiar with them. For example, Dillard's uses its long-running Daniel Cremieux apparel brand on home goods.

Some stores offer generic brand products. **Generic brands** attach no significant identity to the product through the name. Generic products are usually found at grocery stores and drugstores and are typically promoted to price-conscious customers. For example, the cost of a generic bottle of aspirin may be half that of the same size bottle of Bayer aspirin.

Consumers view brand as an important part of a product, and brand names add value. For example, most customers would perceive a Ralph Lauren Polo knit shirt as a high-quality product. But the same shirt without the logo and brand label would probably be viewed as lower in quality, even though it is identical. Brand names can even be found at produce counters in grocery stores. Sunkist oranges, Dole pineapples, and Chiquita bananas are several products in an area that continues to be unbranded.

Branding helps buyers in several ways. Brands help customers identify products that might benefit them. Brands also indicate something about product quality to most customers. Shoppers who always buy the same brand know that they will get the same features, benefits, and quality each time they purchase the product.

Licensed Products

Another way buyers create differences in their merchandise mix is through purchasing **licensed products** that are designed and sold through identification with a celebrity or corporate name, logo, slogan, or fictional character (Figure 6.7). For an extra cost, buyers have an instant and proven brand name. Cartoon and story characters are the most popular among children, with Mickey Mouse being the leading character. Names of sports stars and teams have also been very popular on licensed products. As expected, sales vary by the region in which the team is located, but some teams, such as the Dallas Cowboys and the New York Yankees, have national appeal.

While licensed products run the gamut from trinkets to expensive collectibles, apparel products dominate the list. Licensed products also tend to be higher quality today, with a wider assortment of items being offered. In the past, quality was not always

Figure 6.7
Cartoon and storybook characters are popular licensed products for children.

the chief concern with licensed products because a new, hot cartoon character or sports celebrity would hit the market within a few weeks. Today, licensed products adorn expensive jackets and denim shirts. Most licensed apparel is "fashion right." The shift to higher quality merchandise has resulted in many licensees producing two lines—one that is sold to discounters and the other to department and specialty stores. However, some licensees, such as Hello Kitty and Blue's Clues, want to keep an upscale image and are producing most of their products for upscale stores.

Licensed products for the bed and bath market continue to be a viable and growing area for sales. Throughout all areas there is an emphasis on classics such as Mickey Mouse, Bugs Bunny, and Superman. For both discounters and department stores, classics are "safer" purchases. On children's products there is an almost endless list of character names and images on toys, clothing, school supplies, cereals, lunch boxes, and many other items. In fact, almost half of all toy sales come from products based on TV shows and movies.

Buyers must evaluate licensed products as they would any other merchandise, looking for quality, design, price, and compatibility with the store image and customer wants and needs. The uncertainty of whether licensed names will catch on with customers makes choices difficult for buyers. Furthermore, in recent years, the novelty of these items has diminished.

Buyers must also be particularly alert to the timing and markdowns of licensed products. Disney items may be strong sellers for years, but other products typically have sales that peak and then fall precipitously. For example, sales of merchandise with the Olympics logo fall dramatically as soon as the games are over.

The biggest challenge for every retail buyer is selecting the right license. The anticipated release of a big summer movie will have all buyers guessing. Will the success of the new movie measure up to the hit of last summer? Will that appeal translate into customers wanting to purchase licensed products based on the new movie? Movies that do not meet their expectations mean heavy markdowns on licensed products promoting characters or symbols of the movie. For example, many retailers got stuck with lots of yellow raincoats when *Dick Tracy* was not the hit movie it was expected to be. Licensed products based on movies do not have the same staying power as those linked with TV shows that people see regularly for many years.

Buyers also have to be careful when making purchases of sports-licensed products. A bad season for the team will probably mean a bad season for sales. Yet being the first retailer in town with sports apparel featuring the local team that just made the play-offs can generate high-volume, as well as high-profit, sales.

Licensed products have broad appeal, particularly among younger consumers, women, and households with limited incomes. The appeal of licensed products wanes rapidly as customers grow older. People over fifty have little interest in purchasing such items for themselves.

Mass Customization

Many retailers are discarding the one-size-fits-all philosophy that has guided them for decades. They are beginning to experiment with **mass customization**, which involves efficiently providing customers with unique products that give them "exactly what they want." Mass customization is based on harnessing technology to narrowly target products to the needs of the individual shopper. Customers choose their options, and the product is assembled according to their specifications. The challenge is to offer enough options for the customer to feel that the product is custom-made, without substantially increasing costs.

Making custom-made products can be efficient. Inventory is reduced, saving warehouse space and the expense of monitoring stock in order to maintain a wide assortment. And there is little leftover merchandise on which markdowns must be taken. Although mass-customized products are more expensive to make, their profit margins tend to be much higher.

Mass customization is also occurring in other areas of retailing. General Nutrition Centers (GNC) have installed machines in some of its stores that custom-mix daily vitamins, shampoos, and lotions. The revolution has spread to the internet, where greeting card retailers allow customers to customize their cards with personalized remarks. Many bricks-and-mortar retail stores have also begun offering different types of customization with in-store kiosks. For example, Yankee Candle now provides customers the opportunity to create a personalized label for candles using pictures from their smartphones.

Many retail analysts predict that mass customization may become as important to the twenty-first century as mass production was to the twentieth century. It provides one way for retailers to give customers exactly the products they want. Buyers must constantly be alert to techniques that will allow them to differentiate their product offerings.

Summary Points

- A store's merchandise mix must meet the specific needs of its customers.

- Four broad categories of products based on availability are convenience, impulse, shopping, and specialty.

- Fashion occurs in all areas of retailing, not just apparel.

- Even though fashion presents problems in reordering and the timing of purchases, most buyers seek fashion additions to their lines because these products tend to stimulate sales and enhance the store's image.

- Stores attempt to establish a fashion image through such factors as merchandise selection, store location, visual merchandising, fixtures, and store personnel.

- To understand the impact of fashion on customers, buyers must be able to distinguish between fads and trends.

- The product life cycle includes the introduction, growth, maturity, and decline stages.

- All products are continuously moving through product life cycles at varying and individual rates. Fashion adopters during the cycle can be described as innovators, early adopters, late adopters, and laggards.

- Fashion adoption theories include downward flow, horizontal flow, and upward flow.

- Buyers differentiate the products they purchase from the competition by using private brands, licensing, and mass customization.

Review Activities

Developing Your Retail Buying Vocabulary

Consult the glossary if you did not add the following terms to your vocabulary.

availability	fashion	late adopter	private brand
classic	generic brand	licensed product	product life cycle
convenience product	growth stage	maturity stage	product line
decline stage	haute couture	mass customization	shopping product
durability	impulse product	merchandise mix	specialty product
durables	innovator	national brand	store brand
early adopter	introduction stage	nondurables	style
fad	laggard	obsolescence	velocity

Understanding What You Read

1. Why should buyers constantly monitor their merchandise mix?

2. Explain how products that buyers purchase influence personnel decisions for a store.

3. What have J.C. Penney and Rooms to Go done to establish a fashion image?

4. List five examples of convenience products.

5. Describe how department stores can sell kitchen gadgets as impulse items.

6. Give two examples of specialty products.

7. When do customers tend to stretch the life of durable products?

8. What is the difference between a style and a fashion?

9. Explain why buyers cannot determine fashion.

10. Why do many buyers welcome the addition of fashion items into their inventory?

11. Provide examples of how fashions have changed because of technology.

12. Describe how new fashions may create a "ripple effect" with the sale of other products.

13. Provide examples of how movies have influenced "new" products on the market.

14. What problems do fads present for buyers?

15. How can buyers distinguish between a fad and a trend?

16. List the four stages of the product life cycle.

17. Describe differences in pricing strategy between the introduction and decline stages of the product life cycle.

18. Describe the downward flow theory of fashion adoption.

19. How can knowledge of the product life cycle help buyers decide which products to eliminate from their merchandise mix?

20. Why do buyers add private brands to their merchandise mix?

21. Why is the timing of markdowns on licensed products crucial for buyers?

22. What is the primary reason for the move to mass customization?

Analyzing and Applying What You Read

1. Why is it important for buyers to identify and capitalize on trends early?

2. Identify the stage of the product life cycle at which each of the following products is found: records, cassette tapes, CDs, VHS tapes, and DVDs.

3. Give reasons as to why new apparel fashions are not just first appearing among the wealthy as they did in the past.

4. How will you determine if an item is moving into the decline stage of the product life cycle? What could a buyer do to prolong the life of that product?

5. Which do you feel has more relevance in today's apparel market—downward or upward flow theory? Explain.

Internet Connection

1. Go to http://www.etoys.com, http://www.toysrus.com, or a similar site that sells toys. Identify the hottest trends in the toy market.

2. Visit the book's STUDIO to watch videos about wearable technology and "hoverboards."

SNAPSHOT: Hoverboards: From Boom to Bust in a Short Time

Just a few short years ago, some of you (like thousands of others) may have been zipping along sidewalks on two wheels known as hoverboards. They looked somewhat like a Segway minus the pole and handlebars—riders stood on a platform and used subtle shifts in their weight to steer the motorized devices. Of course, they did not actually hover. If hoverboard riders were agile and well-coordinated, they could be zipping past pedestrians in a just a few minutes, but for others, more time was required to remain upright.

At first, hoverboards were expensive and not readily available at retailers, but then a few celebrities starting Instagramming their hoverboard exploits. Jamie Foxx even wheeled onto the *Tonight Show* set on his hoverboard. All this unleashed a wave of buying by both gadget-savvy consumers and average teens. In fact, at one point, 40,000 boards a month were arriving in the United States from China. However, within a year, hoverboards turned into one of the fastest boom-to-bust cycles in modern business. What happened?

To take advantage of the new craze, hundreds of manufacturers of hoverboards sprang up in China, and not all of them produced the boards to stringent safety standards. China has become known as a country where small factories can quickly convert their manufacturing operations to new products like selfie sticks or hoverboards, allowing them to churn out copycat products in record time. But, with hundreds of manufacturers of hoverboards in China, the real differentiator became price. To make their hoverboards less expensive, many of those factories cut corners on safety standards, often substituting cheaper parts and potentially flammable batteries. Keep in mind, however, that this is not a reflection of the quality of all Chinese manufacturing—practically every high-quality Apple product is produced on a Chinese assembly line. Also contributing to the huge number of copycat manufacturers was a lot of confusion as to who held the patent for hoverboards.

As sales boomed, lots of problems surfaced. Over one ten-week period the U.S. Consumer Product Safety Commission (CPSC) received nearly sixty complaints of hoverboard fires, causing over $2 million in property damage, including destroyed bedrooms and even entire homes. The scary part was that there was no single reason causing the hoverboards to explode, even though most fires were caused by defective batteries and chargers. Moreover, there was no particular brand causing the problems. Additionally, US emergency rooms were reporting an increase in injuries due to falling from hoverboards. A big problem facing importers and retailers when hoverboards starting arriving in the United States was that no safety standards for the product existed. Standards existed for motorized scooters and toys, but hoverboards did not really fit.

As safety concerns increased, the US airline industry banned hoverboards on flights, and the US Postal Service stopped shipping hoverboards as well. Then, retailers like Amazon, Target, and Overstock.com stopped selling hoverboards. In the United Kingdom, it became illegal to ride hoverboards on public roads or walkways, and thousands were seized by the government and destroyed for safety concerns.

Sales plummeted, and they never recovered. The final blow to hoverboards came when the CPSC notified hoverboard manufacturers, importers, and retailers that they must meet new safety standards or face recall or seizure at ports. The warning, however, did not ban hoverboards. In fact, consumers can still find hoverboards for sale at a few online sites that are produced by a few remaining manufacturers in China. Today, many of the small Chinese manufacturers who are no longer building hoverboards have now nimbly converted their operations to the next big trend—drones.

Manufacturers and retailers had expected a much longer life span for hoverboards. It was a product that seemed right for the times and to fit perfectly with products desired by a tech-savvy generation. Even if new hoverboards are produced with more reliable parts, it is doubtful that their sales will ever rebound. With so many safety concerns and negative media coverage that ensued when they hit the market, it will be nearly impossible to change most customers' image of hoverboards. When adding new products, such as hoverboards, to their inventory assortments, what must retail buyers do to prevent such a rapid boom-to-bust cycle?

BASED ON:

Breen, Marcia. (2016, February 19). U.S. government agency declares hoverboards unsafe. *NBCNews.com*.

Cendrowski, Scott. (2016, March 1). Boom goes the hoverboard fad. *Fortune.com*.

Hollister, Sean. (2016, July 9). Here are the reasons why so many hoverboards are catching fire. *C-Net.com*.

WEARABLE TECHNOLOGY: THE NEXT BIG THING OR ONLY A FAD?

Fashion and technology are merging. Consumers can now take their calls on smartwatches and have their email sent to their Google glasses. Purses are available with built-in smartphone chargers, and a new line of jackets is designed to cool wearers down and warm them up again. Some shirts and sports bras are even being manufactured with body sensors that monitor the wearer's vital signs. And, solar power engineers in the Netherlands are rolling out a new line of clothing called "Wearable Solar" that has flexible solar cells on the surface of the clothes that can even charge a wearer's smartphone.

In addition to major companies such as Google, Samsung, Sony, and Apple, many smaller boutique manufacturers are also entering the market promoting their electronic fashion accessories. The battle for space on consumers' bodies with wearable technology has begun.

The first waves of wearable technology focused on a person's wrist. As smartphones have increasingly made watches obsolete, manufacturers and designers have jumped at the opportunity to grab those empty wrists. And, fitness has been a huge area for this wearable tech, with heart rate monitors, step counters, exercise trackers, and calorie counters—all designed to help measure and potentially improve consumer lifestyles.

One of the major players in the field, Fitbit, is a fitness tracker that measures steps and turns them into calories. When launched in 2011, the device sold out within a day. Positive reviews and word-of-mouth publicity have helped increase sales over the last few years. The technology provides something that the consumer can use in daily life.

However, some attempts to merge technology with fashion may be nothing more than a fleeting curiosity. A British designer has created shoes inspired by *The Wizard of Oz*. The shoes are fitted with global positioning microchips (GPS) and are activated when the heels of the shoes are clicked together. Once the wearer's chosen destination is uploaded to the shoes by means of a USB port, LED lights on the toe point the wearer in the right direction. Another company with offices in the Netherlands and China has produced a dress called Intimacy that becomes translucent when it senses changes in a woman's heartbeat indicating that she is sexually aroused.

Some retail analysts predict that wearable tech fashions are going to be one of the key growth areas in mobile technology. However, despite sustained attention in the media, sales of wearable tech products have not yet gained tremendous traction. Some analysts suggest that the problem may not be about marketing but more about product design. For example, right now, most of the fitness tech wearables on the market have the same black rubber bracelet look—which is typically fine for men but may not fit women's fashion needs. Style changes, however, are beginning to occur. Designer Tory Burch is collaborating with Fitbit to design an exclusive collection for them, in which her trademark prints will be incorporated into the devices. Such "fashion" options are probably needed for all wearable technology. In addition, it may take years before manufacturers can reach the economies of scale needed to bring prices for high-tech clothing within reach of the masses of the population.

It is unlikely that wearable technology will dominate the aisles of retailers tomorrow. But, will it become more than a fad? Several questions remain to be answered. How will wearable tech evolve from a style and fashion perspective? Will more fashion designers collaborate with technology companies?

Retail buyers must constantly monitor the marketplace for answers to these questions. They cannot ignore fads because without them, they are positioning their stores in the vast sea of retail sameness. But neither can buyers jump on every new product on the market. In the final analysis, knowing the customer and market conditions are the most important factors as buyers select products that may become "the next big thing" for their stores.

BASED ON:

Best wearable tech of 2017. (2017, March 28). *cnet.com.*

Fischler, Marcelle Sussman. (2013, April 6). The latest in smart fashion is wearable technology. *Forbes.com.*

Gaddis, Rebecca. (2014, February 10). Wearable technology and fashion: Can they merge? *Forbes.com.*

Grossman, Lev, & Vella-Cpertino, Matt. (2014, September 22). iNeed. *Time,* 41–47.

Kharif, Olga & Edwards, Cliff. (2013, October 31). Wearable tech inspires a shoe, clothing design push. *Businessweek.com.*

McNew, Bradley Seth. (2016, December 13). The most expensive wearable fitness device of 2016. *FoxNews.com.*

Pentland, William. (2013, December 12). Solar-powered apparel may be coming to a store near you. *Forbes.com.*

Sharma, Rakesh. (2014, June 12). Of stupid smartwatches and gimmicks: Wearable tech's design problems. *Forbes.com.*

Slade, Holly. (2013, November 19). Tap, tickle, flex and bond—Startups want to grab your naked wrists. *Forbes.com.*

Smith, Sandy. (2016, November 7). Wearable technology migrates to the rest of the ensemble. *Store.org.*

Spence, Ewan. (2013, November 2). 2014 will be the year of wearable technology. *Forbes.com.*

MEN'S SOCKS: NO LONGER JUST BLACK AND NAVY

Men's socks are one of the fastest growing segments of the men's apparel market, and they have moved from being simply a basic in men's closets to being a fashion statement. In fact, sales for men's socks have been growing three times faster than sales for all men's apparel. What has caused this dramatic increase?

It seems that men from all age categories are updating their sock drawer. Boredom with black, navy, and other conservative solids is probably the main culprit. Many men have said their wardrobes lack color, and colorful socks can provide a nice accent. Wearing these socks is one way of personalizing standard business attire. Today, many men are leaving safe colors in the drawer in favor of bright colors like purple and orange, as well as bold stripes and dashing prints.

Images in the media also support this surge toward colorful socks. On the TV program *Mad Men,* one of the advertising partners walked around the office shoeless, showing off his pastel argyle print socks. Even former president George H. W. Bush wears colorful socks. Recent pictures in the news showed him sporting pink power socks at the dedication of his son's presidential library.

Celebrities and retailers have also jumped on the bandwagon. Rob Kardashian rolled out his line of attention-getting socks at Neiman Marcus, and sales have tripled since they were first introduced. At Jack Threads, a members-only men's apparel website, the selection of men's socks increased by 600 percent in during one year to meet increased demand. Retailers from Macy's to Target are also stocking their shelves with these new colorful and fashionable socks.

These new socks can also mean more profit for retailers. First, men will be updating their socks more frequently, which means more sales, and typically these fashionable socks are more expensive. Even though some can be purchased as inexpensively as three pairs for $10 at Gap, men can pay much more. At high-end retailers like Paul Smith, they can cost $55. A cashmere pair at J. Crew goes for $80, while the Elder Statesman brand sells for $350 at Barney's in New York. And, at Harry's of London, a pair of 100 percent cervelt socks made from New Zealand red deer can be purchased for $1,500.

For most men, colorful socks are probably more than the "new necktie." Even the most timid dressers can put their feet into this new trend. Colorful socks are not as shocking to others as brightly colored ties. Other people will only get a teasing glimpse of the orange camouflage print that someone else is wearing. It is a way for all men to engage in a little whimsy in what they are wearing.

It would appear that men's socks have become a fashion accessory and are no longer just a basic. But, retail buyers must keep a watchful eye on trends such as these. What new colors and prints will be "hot" next year? And, at some point, will men start cycling back to basic black and navy?

BASED ON:

Cheng, Andria. (2014, May 4). More men step out in stylish socks. *WallStreetJournal.com.*

Dayler, John. (2014, June 15). Men's socks: From commodity to luxury. *CBSNews.com.*

Foot fashion forward: Socks are the new neckties. (2014, June 14). *CBSNews.com.*

Monget, Karyn. (2013, June 13). Ath-leisure socks drive sales. *WomensWearDaily.com.*

Pesce, Nicole Lyn. (2013, May 19). Fashion-conscious men are making bold statements—with their socks. *NewYorkDailyNews.com.*

MEN'S GROOMING IS BOOMING

Beauty is the second fastest growing segment of the retail market in the United States, and contributing to that growth are men's beauty/grooming products. In the past, men's grooming products may have only been considered a niche segment, but today they have become a huge mainstream market. Traditionally, the men's grooming products carried by many retailers were limited to deodorants and shaving products. These companies are now offering a widening range of products in categories like hair care and skin care, and there is also a strong focus on men's bath and shower products.

Men seem to be more body-conscious than ever, causing a shift in men's grooming culture. Many bathroom cabinets today brim with moisturizers, facial cleansers, bronzers, concealers, anti-aging creams, and even mud masks—all designed specifically for men. In fact, 25 percent of males in the United States use some kind of facial skin-care product. And, a big bonus for retailers is that these male shoppers tend to be more brand-loyal than women when purchasing similar products.

Why has there been such a dramatic shift in sales of men's grooming products? Retail analysts point to these four reasons: (1) there has been an increase in the number of males employed in the service industries, (2) there is increased competition in the workplace for promotions, (3) younger men are influenced by changing standards of exactly what is male beauty, and (4) aging baby boomers are eager to stay youthful.

Overall, there seems to be a shift in men's perception of grooming. While many of them still view tasks like shaving and getting a haircut as mundane chores, there seems to be a growing number of men who not only take greater pride in maintaining their appearance but also view such grooming activities as pleasurable.

Sales of men's grooming products are booming. In fact, sales of men's toiletries in the United States were expected to hit $3.2 billion in 2016, up from $2.6 billion in 2012, and globally that figure is expected to exceed $21 billion. Two of the trends that are playing out in the market are the growth of online sales of men's grooming products and the continued popularity of beards. Both trends will have a big impact on future sales of men's grooming products.

There has been stellar growth in online sales of men's shaving products, with razors and blades accounting for the vast majority of those sales. In fact, the largest online seller, Dollar Shave Club, now boasts more than 3 million subscribers; however, the online market is becoming overcrowded quickly. Gillette has a new online shave club in addition to other players such as Harry's, 800Razors, and several others. To differentiate themselves, Dollar Shave Club and Harry's are branching out beyond razors into other men's grooming products, such as shaving cream and hair care products. Currently, less than 10 percent of American men are currently members of an online shave club, and that leaves plenty of potential for continued growth.

One of the other big trends in men's grooming over the past decade has been the popularity of men growing beards. Some analysts disagree over how much longer this trend will last, but it has had and continues to have an impact on the sales of men's grooming products—both positive and negative. Although beards may look unruly to those who do not have one, they usually require a lot of grooming, and that has increased sales of products to care for beards, such as trimmers and oils. But, stagnating razor blade sales can also be attributed to the rise in the number of men with beards. These are the situations that present the most challenges to retail buyers. As they purchase men's grooming products for next year, they will have to decide how this trend will play out; they do not want to make the wrong decisions and have their stores stuck with grooming products that their customers no longer need.

How are retailers capitalizing on these trends? Ulta recently rolled out in-store boutiques called the Men's Shop; some CVS drugstores now feature "Guy" aisles; and both Macy's and Nordstrom are devoting more space to men's grooming products, even creating separate sections

MEN'S GROOMING IS BOOMING (CONTINUED)

dedicated exclusively to men. One department store has even opened a Men's Grooming Zone with a barber, flat-screen TV, and free Wi-Fi along with a wide selection of men's grooming products. As more retailers cater to this market segment, experts advise them to steer clear of descriptors like "makeup or men's cosmetics" or using packaging that veers too close to the feminine side.

Men's grooming is certainly a segment of the beauty market that seems primed for continued growth.

BASED ON:

Bye, bye beard-y? (2016, December 16). *GlobalCosmeticIndustryMagazine.com*.

Castro, Alexis. (2016, January 16). The men's grooming industry is booming, estimated to bring in over $21 billion in 2016. *Complex.com*.

Garcia, Denise. (2016, January 16). Beards boom, and so do businesses catering to them. *NBC.com*.

Garrison, Scott, & Sharma, Sourabh. (2015, March 4). Sex appeal: Four tips for marketing men's products to guys and the women who buy for them. *GlobalCosmeticIndustryMagazine.com*.

Graham, Luke. (2016, January 28). New standards of male beauty are emerging in the men's cosmetics sector. *CNBC.com*.

What's growing the male grooming category. (2016, July 6). *GlobalCosmeticIndustryMagazine.com*.

Why men's grooming/shaving startups are beating established brands. (2016, October 18). *GlobalCosmeticIndustryMagazine.com*.

PART III

PLANNING AND CONTROLLING MERCHANDISE PURCHASES

CHAPTER
7

FORECASTING

Performance Objectives

- Recognize the value of accurate forecasting to the buyer.
- Identify the benefits of developing sales forecasts.
- Describe internal and external forces affecting sales forecasts.
- Identify uses of primary and secondary data in developing sales forecasts.
- List the steps involved in developing a sales forecast.
- Describe methods used in forecasting inventory needs.
- Predict sales based on stock-to-sales ratios and stock turnover.
- Recognize that buyers need quantitative skills.

After collecting information from the sources described in the previous chapters, buyers must use the data to make forecasts about what will happen in the future. **Forecasting** involves predicting what consumers may do under a given set of conditions. Buyers most often make forecasts concerning consumer demand, sales, and required inventory levels. To make these forecasts, they must collect and analyze information from a number of sources, including forecasts that other people have made. Many forecasts and predictions concerning the entire retailing industry were described in Chapter 1.

In this chapter, you will learn more about forecasting. How buyers identify consumer trends and anticipate changes in market conditions will be described and the steps used to make a forecast examined. Then you will learn how buyers use these skills for sales forecasting and stock planning.

SCOPE OF FORECASTING

Buyers typically develop forecasts to answer questions such as these:

- How much of each product will need to be purchased?
- Should new products be added to the merchandise assortment being offered?
- How much inventory is needed to support the planned sales?
- What price should be charged for each product?

Answers to these questions are based on predictions of what you believe the customer will do in the future. Just like a prediction about tomorrow's weather, your forecast will not always be correct, but steps can be taken to improve your forecasting ability. Read the Trendwatch titled "Using Weather Forecasts to Improve Retail Forecasts" to learn more about how long-term weather forecasting is being used as a tool to improve retail forecasts.

First, you need to obtain past sales records. In making a forecast, most buyers start with information on past sales to predict future sales, but you cannot stop there. You must also consider other internal forces that are operating in your store such as expansion of sales space or reduction in the number of sales associates. Then you need to examine external forces such as competition and economic conditions. As you probably realize, no sales forecast will match actual sales exactly. You may purchase too much of some items and not enough of others, but if you keep accurate records, you have the opportunity to improve your future forecasts.

Once you have identified all the sources of assistance that are available to you, you are ready to collect and analyze information about market conditions and your target consumers to develop forecasts. The most important forecast you will make is the **sales forecast**, a prediction of future sales for a specified period under a proposed marketing plan. The sales forecast can be a prediction of total sales volume, or sales can be forecast for:

- specific products or services (brands or models);
- specific consumer groups (males, over sixty-five);
- time periods (weekly, monthly); or
- specific store locations.

A sales forecast is made for a specified period of time that can cover a few weeks or even years. **Short-term forecasts** usually include a period of up to one year. Buying fashion merchandise usually requires developing a sales forecast for a six-month period. Grocery stores and drug stores that deal with more basic merchandise may have to forecast sales for only a few days or a week. **Long-term forecasts** extend for more than a year.

The time period for which the sales forecast is made will have a great impact on its accuracy. Forecasts that attempt to predict sales many years into the future may be much less accurate than a forecast for sales during the next two months. Existing market conditions may remain the same for a few weeks; however, these conditions could drastically change by the end of the season. Customers' tastes could also change rapidly. If the market is volatile and changes quickly, long-term forecasts may be meaningless.

Forecasting is a crucial planning tool for buyers. Preparing sales forecasts requires them to think in detailed terms about (1) target market groups the store is trying to serve, (2) existing and potential competitors, and (3) future trends occurring in the market and the economy. In other words, they must make a thorough examination of the store and its markets before preparing a sales forecast and developing merchandise buying plans. In addition, sales forecasts do the following:

- *Stimulate Planning.* Without a sales forecast, buyers could not make other critical decisions such as inventory levels required and retail prices to charge customers.
- *Promote Coordination.* A sales forecast becomes a target for all members of the merchandising team. Buyers, store managers, and sales associates must all tailor their activities to reach the desired sales goal.

- *Support Control Activities.* The sales forecast becomes the basis for measuring the success or failure of the buyer's efforts. It provides a quantitative measurement against which the buyer's performance can be measured for pay raises, promotion, or dismissal.

Because they play such an important role, sales forecasts need to be as accurate as possible, but because forecasting is an attempt to predict the future, they can be inaccurate. In the final analysis, accuracy of sales forecasting tends to improve as more data analysis and interpretation are applied.

Buyers must have confidence in forecasts they make, and that confidence increases with a thorough understanding of all the forces that can have an impact on sales. Forecasts should be based on facts, not guesswork! Before developing a sales forecast, buyers must first identify their target customers, understand why they buy, and gain an understanding of trends affecting these markets.

DEVELOPING SALES FORECASTS

Forecasting sales requires that buyers identify and understand the internal and external forces that will have an impact on those sales.

Examining Internal Forces

Before developing a sales forecast, you should carefully examine all **internal forces** within the store that probably will affect sales. For example, future sales can be affected by increasing or decreasing advertising expenditures, liberalizing or tightening credit policies, and increasing or decreasing retail prices. Even changes in store hours or physical facilities will affect future sales. You must estimate the impact of such changes on projected sales before any sales forecast is developed.

Examining External Forces

Before making a sales forecast, you must also analyze **external forces** that may affect sales. You will need to examine changes in economic conditions, demographic trends, and competitive conditions.

Economic Conditions

Both the national and local economic climate should be analyzed, but you must realize that economic conditions will not affect all businesses in the same way. For example, during economic slowdowns, sales at some stores, such as do-it-yourself home stores, actually increase. Plant closings and employee layoffs are local economic conditions that will generally cause sales to decline. Headlines from the newspaper, such as those presented in Figure 7.1, provide information that should be considered when you are making a sales forecast. You must also realize that during inflationary periods, increases in dollar sales may occur without a corresponding increase in unit sales.

Demographic Trends

Demographic factors should also be analyzed before you develop a sales forecast. The movement of people into or out of your store's trading area can have an impact on

Figure 7.1

How would each of these headlines affect buyers' decisions?

Stocks Slide as Rate Fears Grow
REUTERS

Stocks End Day Slightly Higher

Dow Loses Ground in Mixed Market

Tokyo, Hong Kong Shares Tumble

Crawling Out of Recession
EDITORIAL DESK

Net Up at Two Retail Firms

European Stock Market Close Lower AP Associated Press

Women's Wholesale Apparel Prices See 0.2 Percent Drop in February

future sales. Sales forecasts should be adjusted downward if the store's trading area appears to be losing a large number of residents.

Changes in the composition of the population may also affect sales. A firm that relies on purchases by eighteen- to thirty-five-year-olds may find that the most rapidly growing segment in its trading area is over sixty-five, requiring forecasts to be adjusted downward.

Even lifestyle changes in your target market need to be examined. For example, your customers may become more conscious of environmental issues and start purchasing only products that are environmentally sound. You must be alert to all demographic trends and changes in your customer base before making your sales forecast. Read the Trendwatch titled "Data Mining Using Social Media" to learn more about how retailers use data accumulated from social media to improve sales forecasts.

Competitive Conditions

Competitors may enter or leave your market area at any time, and sales forecasts need to be adjusted accordingly. Your competitors' promotional strategies may also change. For example, a competitor may decide to increase advertising or introduce a new contest, and if they are effective, both could cause decreased sales for your store.

Acquiring Needed Data

To make sales forecasts, you need to locate and use information; therefore, you must be knowledgeable about the types of data available and how to obtain them. Many of these sources were described in Chapter 4. Your first decision is whether primary data collection will be needed. To make that decision, you must thoroughly examine secondary data sources because they can be the most cost-effective to use.

Primary data originate with the specific research being undertaken. In other words, you collect the information to solve the current problem at hand. Direct customer surveys are the chief means used to obtain information on your customers' attitudes and opinions. Secondary data are data that have been gathered for some other purpose but are applicable to solving your problem. Business records produced by other departments in your store and information that is obtained from books and magazines are examples of secondary data. Let's more closely examine these data sources and the uses that can be made of each one.

Primary Data Sources

Many retailers spend both time and money to collect information from their customers on a perpetual basis. Stew Leonard's, the famous Connecticut food store, relies heavily on primary data collection to improve its service and product offerings to customers. Holding weekend focus group sessions, reading comments from the suggestions box (which customers actually use), and simply walking the aisles speaking with customers and employees are techniques the company has used since it opened its first store. Management is constantly on the lookout for ways to improve customers' shopping experience. They do not wait until sales decline before making changes; they know that without careful attention to the desires of the market, sales could change quickly.

The National Retail Federation and similar retail associations sponsor primary research related to customer attitudes about shopping and release these findings to their member stores. For example, a recent report examined buying triggers and influencers, as well as the impact of economic fluctuations on purchase decisions among multiple generations. And the report gave insight into how trending attitudes among the groups can be taken into account when building merchandising and marketing strategies. Several of their findings follow.

- Fewer than one in four consumers in Generation X consider the newest trends and styles personally important when it comes to shopping for clothing. A somewhat stronger focus on traditional, conservative looks will be appealing to the largest share in this generation.
- More than four in five baby boomers, who are largely still working and preparing for future retirement, had a renewed focus on eating at home. For retailers, this can mean more trips to the grocery store but fewer visits to neighborhood restaurants, and also an emphasis on making smart purchase decisions in other spending areas.

Retailers and buyers must use findings like these from primary sources to forecast future buying patterns. They must also determine what keeps current customers shopping at their stores.

Secondary Sources

Searching for external data may be quick or extensive. For example, the only information that you may need is the average annual sales of men's suits by stores with less than 2,500 square feet. A single trade journal will be able to provide this information to you. Other questions that deal with consumer opinions may require obtaining as many sources as are available.

Business Publication Rates and Data is an index published by the Standard Rate and Data Service, Inc., which will be a great help to you in identifying trade sources. Every major industry has one or more magazines specifically aimed at its member firms.

Professional and trade associations are also good sources of forecasting data. *The Encyclopedia of Associations* lists associations' names, addresses, number of members, and, most importantly, their publications.

General business publications and newspapers should not be overlooked when you need to locate information on market trends or economic conditions. There are even specific sources that report and forecast customer purchasing patterns. *Consumer Expenditure Survey*, published by the Bureau of Labor Statistics, contains valuable information on state and local markets. Data are provided on population, household incomes, and retail sales. *Consumer Buying Indicators* is issued quarterly by the Bureau of the Census and contains six-month and twelve-month expected purchase estimates (in units) of automobiles, homes, furniture, carpets, major appliances, and home improvements.

If you use secondary data in making sales forecasts, you must realize there are several shortcomings of this information. Some of the data may be out-of-date. There is no rule as to when data are out-of-date, but in volatile times, data more than five years old are of questionable value. Also, you need to determine the bias of the source that collected the data; be aware of who collected the data and for what purpose. Numbers can usually be twisted to defend almost any side of an argument.

There is a huge amount of secondary data available to you. Seek out what you need and make use of it. However, you may be forced to collect primary data in situations where available information does not fit your specific needs.

Making Sales Forecasts

When developing a sales forecast, a step-by-step process should be followed that analyzes both internal and external forces that will affect sales. This process involves the following steps:

1. Review past sales.
2. Analyze changes in economic conditions.
3. Analyze changes in sales potential for specific products or markets.
4. Analyze changes in marketing strategies of your firm and the competition.
5. Forecast sales.

Let us more closely examine each of these steps.

Review Past Sales

A review of past sales records will determine if there are any patterns or trends in the sales figures. Sales will need to be compared with those of last month as well as last year during the same period. This information will give you an initial estimate of any change that might be expected during the coming year if everything else remains the same—which rarely happens. From this information you can answer the following questions:

- Have sales shown a pattern of increase or decrease over the past several years?
- If a pattern is present, what is the average percent?
- Do recent sales data support this trend?
- Can you identify a percentage figure that will reflect the sales trends you have observed?

Analyze Changes in Economic Conditions

You may need to adjust the trend percentage figure you have identified after reviewing economic trends and examining published national and local economic forecasts.

Analyze Changes in Sales Potential

Your next step will be to relate demographic changes in the market to your store or the products for which you are responsible. Such information may be difficult to obtain, but here are sources that you can use. The *Census of Population* (published every ten years) can supply some data, but they will be dated, and you may face problems using the data. Merchandise line categories may be too broad for your forecast, or sales data may not be current enough for short-term forecasting purposes. You may want to modify your sales trend percentage figure at this point to reflect changes in market conditions.

Analyze Changes in Marketing Strategies

Next, you need to consider any changes in marketing strategies planned by your store as well as by the competition. For example, a decision to remodel a store, the addition of new lines of merchandise, or a new promotional event will attract customers and can increase sales. There is little information that can be used to predict what the competition will do in the future; however, you can gain information through comparison shopping trips, studying competitors' ads, and listening to customers. Your trend percentage figure will need to be adjusted again based on any changes in marketing strategies by your store or the competition.

Forecast Sales

Now it is time to make your sales forecast. Assume that after analyzing past sales records, you determined that there was an average 6 percent increase in sales for the previous six-month period. You determine that economic growth will increase sales by 2 percent and the size of your market will grow by 5 percent. In addition, you have learned that a competitor will be opening a new store this year, causing an estimated 5 percent decrease in your sales. From this information, you decide to forecast an 8 percent (6 percent + 2 percent + 5 percent − 5 percent) increase in sales for the next period.

Sales forecasting is not a precise process, but ultimately it provides the best starting point available from which to plan future sales. The only other alternative—no planning—is not acceptable to professional buyers.

Because sales forecasts have such a critical impact on your store, they need to be simultaneously challenging and attainable. If they are not, it spells disaster. If your sales forecasts are dramatically increased over previous periods, the cost of doing business will also have to rise to accommodate the projected sales increase. For example, advertising expenditures may need to be increased or additional sales associates may be needed.

If your sales forecasts are set too high and cannot be attained, your resulting expenses-to-sales ratio will be too high, causing profits to fall below expectations. Or if you dramatically underestimate your sales forecast and purchase an inadequate amount of inventory, you will not be able to sufficiently meet consumer demand, which may translate into loss of loyal customers who turn to your competitors.

Once you have developed a sales forecast, your merchandise manager's approval will be needed. You will want to include a brief rationale that should summarize the assumptions that you made and the factors that you considered in developing the forecast. Input from your manager should also have been requested while you were gathering data to use in your sales forecast.

Once your forecast is approved, your next step will be to develop a merchandise buying plan. That process will be described in Chapter 8.

Making Adjustments

Actual sales should be periodically monitored to determine the accuracy of your sales forecasts; however, the forecast should not become a goal that must be met regardless of unforeseen competitive changes or changes in general economic or business conditions. That would cause inefficient use of store resources. During the selling season, you may uncover greater-than-expected sales. You may determine that your store does not have the capital to purchase the required inventory, greater competition than expected may occur, or consumer demand may be less than anticipated. Adjustments in your plan may be required.

For some products, reorders can be made quickly if you underestimated consumer demand; however, manufacturers may be out of stock, and customer dissatisfaction has already occurred. Overestimating sales will require changes in marketing strategies. First, examine activities that might be accomplished at little expense. Consider moving the merchandise location or retraining sales associates. Additional advertising expenditures may be required, or markdowns may be needed.

FORECASTING DECISIONS

Two of the most important forecasts that buyers make are of sales and stock levels. Let's examine how these two important calculations are made.

Forecasting Sales

Sales forecasting is a subjective part of the planning process, but it involves much more than guessing. Your forecasting abilities can be improved with practice and experience that will enable you to make more precise and reliable forecasts (Figure 7.2).

Most retailers will develop a sales forecast, then plan the amount of inventory required to generate that amount of sales. If basic merchandise is carried year-round, planning will be less complicated; however, where fashion changes are frequent, keeping inventories and sales balanced will be more difficult.

Past sales figures are important to a buyer when making sales forecasts, but they should be used only as a guide. In addition to past store records, your planning and forecasting activities must also consider other internal and external factors that are likely to affect sales. Following are some of these factors:

- Storewide or departmental promotions and sales.
- Holidays.
- Current storewide and departmental sales trends.
- Population shifts.
- Shifts in demographic characteristics of the population.
- New competition moving into the area.
- Economic conditions.

Figure 7.2

Today, buyers have many more tools available to them to improve the accuracy of their sales forecasts.

- Changes in store hours.
- Changes in the amount of selling space.

The accuracy of your forecasts will depend on the accuracy of your past records and your ability to interpret that information in relation to current trends and make projections about future possibilities. Forecasting also requires a certain amount of judgment and experience.

Buyers begin developing sales forecasts by reviewing past sales figures. Last year's sales figures are important, but you will also want to review the figures for the past two or three years. Then, determine the reasons for any sales increases or decreases.

By analyzing sales trends for several years, you get a more realistic picture of past sales to guide your forecasting efforts. Accurate forecasting also involves making adjustments for differences in the number of selling days in a month during different years. For instance, September may have five Saturdays one year, but only four may appear in the following year's calendar, therefore making it difficult to compare sales from one year to the next. A month with five Saturdays would tend to generate more sales than a month with only four Saturdays.

To compensate for these monthly changes occurring year-to-year, most retailers have adapted the **4-5-4 calendar**, which ensures sales comparability between different time periods in a year by dividing the year into a four weeks, five weeks, four weeks format. The layout of the calendar ensures that the same number of Saturdays and Sundays occur in comparable periods, making sales comparisons from one year to another more accurate. Table 7.1 illustrates an example of this calendar.

You must also realize that there may be a variation in monthly sales because some holidays occur at different times in different years. When Easter is in March, for example, the possibility of cold weather tends to reduce spring apparel sales.

Business conditions will also affect future sales. When business is good, sales may increase or remain at the usual level. Sales frequently decline, however, when business conditions become unfavorable.

TABLE 7.1

EXAMPLE OF 4-5-4 RETAIL CALENDAR

RETAIL 4-5-4 CALENDAR (52 WEEKS)											
Spring Season: February–July						Fall Season: August–January					
First Quarter			Second Quarter			Third Quarter			Fourth Quarter		
Mo. #1	Mo. #2	Mo. #3	Mo. #4	Mo. #5	Mo. #6	Mo. #7	Mo. #8	Mo. #9	Mo. #10	Mo. #11	Mo. #12
4 Weeks	5 Weeks	4 Weeks	4 Weeks	5 Weeks	4 Weeks	4 Weeks	5 Weeks	4 Weeks	4 Weeks	5 Weeks	4 Weeks
1 2 3 4	5 6 7 8 9	10 11 12 13	14 15 16 17	18 19 20 21 22	23 24 25 26	27 28 29 30	31 32 33 34 35	36 37 38 39	40 41 42 43	44 45 46 47 48	49 50 51 52

Sales cannot be forecast with absolute accuracy; yet buyers must make educated guesses. One helpful guide is the average rate of increase or decrease in sales. Although a trend may be evident, you will need to study the reasons for the changes and the conditions that may affect future sales before making any adjustments in plans.

A buyer has the following sales data available and wants to forecast sales for July. The discussion that follows shows how a sales forecast is developed.

Illustrative Problem

Based on the information in the table that follows, forecast sales for July, this year.

Month	Sales Last Year	Sales This Year
April	$50,000	$55,000
May	$55,000	$61,000
June	$59,000	$64,000
July	$60,000	?

Solution

First, you would need to determine the percentage of sales increase or decrease for the first three months from the previous year by using the following formula:

Percent increase or decrease in sales = Difference in sales from last year to this year / Previous year

Your calculations for each month would be as follows:

April = ($55,000 − $50,000) / $50,000 = 10% increase
May = ($61,000 − $55,000) / $55,000 = 10.9% increase
June = ($64,000 − $59,000) / $59,000 = 8.5% increase

Although sales are currently ahead of last year for each month, the percentage decreased from May to June. You would then want to consider the direction of monthly sales during the current year. For example:

April to May = ($61,000 − $55,000) / $55,000 = 10.9%
May to June = ($64,000 − $61,000) / $61,000 = 4.9%

Sales growth has been declining. You would also want to consider the direction of sales growth last year during the same period by completing the following calculation:

Stock-to-sales ratio = Value of stock / Actual sales

You could then conclude that the sales increase for July should be planned between 1.7 and 4.9 percent. At this point, you would want to consider other internal and external factors that might affect sales. If you feel that nothing drastically different will occur during the month, you might arbitrarily select a 3.3 percent increase because it is approximately midway between the two figures. Other conditions, such as more promotions from the competition or changes in your target market, could cause you to forecast the sales fluctuation at a higher or lower level.

Every effort should be made to ensure that your forecast is as accurate as possible because all other merchandising decisions are planned in relation to sales. Bad forecasts wreak havoc on any firm. If your sales forecast is in error, other decisions will be in error, too. Only by doing your homework, by researching your particular market segment, and by talking to customers will you improve the accuracy of your sales forecasts. Of course, you will never completely eliminate the uncertainty in forecasts, but you can reduce it to a manageable level. Once sales are forecast, you will need to plan inventory levels that will support the sales you have predicted.

Planning Inventory Levels

After you forecast sales for a specific period, you must then plan required inventory levels, another key quantitative performance measurement used to evaluate retail buyers. Merchandise in stock must be sufficient to meet sales expectations while allowing for unanticipated demand. As a buyer, your goal will be to maintain an inventory assortment that will be sufficient to meet customer demand and yet be small enough to ensure a reasonable return on the store's investment in inventory.

There are several methods of inventory planning; however, the one most often used is the stock-to-sales ratio method. The **stock-to-sales ratio** method involves maintaining inventory at a specific ratio to sales. Stock-to-sales ratios are calculated by dividing the dollar value of stock on hand by actual sales in dollars. For example, if a department had merchandise valued at $40,000 to begin the month of April and sales amounted to $20,000, the resulting stock-to-sales ratio would be 2. The stock-to-sales ratio is calculated using the following formula:

Stock-to-sales ratio = Value of stock / Actual sales

For this example, the calculation would be made as follows:

Stock-to-sales ratio = $40,000 / $20,000 = 2

The stock-to-sales ratio indicates the relationship between planned sales and the amount of inventory required to support those sales and is used to calculate planned **BOM stock levels**—the amount of stock required to begin the month. By multiplying the stock-to-sales ratio for the month by the planned sales for that month, you can determine the inventory level needed at the beginning of the month (BOM). Planned BOM inventory can be calculated using the following formula:

Planned BOM inventory = Stock-to-sales × Planned sales

Industry-wide stock-to-sales ratios are available from sources such as the National Retail Federation and Dun & Bradstreet. Buyers can also calculate stock-to-sales ratios for their store or department based on previous stock and sales levels.

Illustrative Problem

Using the stock-to-sales ratio method, calculate planned BOM inventory for November given the following information:

Stock-to-sales ratio = 1.2
Planned sales for November = $19,000

Solution

Planned BOM inventory = Stock-to-sales × Planned sales
Planned BOM inventory = 1.2 × $19,000 = $22,800

Therefore, using the stock-to-sales method of planning inventory, you would want to start the month of November with $22,800 worth of inventory.

Determining Stock Turnover

Decisions you make in relation to sales forecasting and stock planning must yield a profit for your store. One measure of how accurately you balance sales to inventory levels is the **stock turnover rate**. How fast merchandise is sold, replenished, and sold determines the stock turnover for a store or department. The stock turnover rate is the number of times the average stock is sold during a given period and is calculated using the following formula:

Stock turnover rate = Sales / Average stock

The **average stock** for any period of time is the value of inventory at the beginning of the period, plus the value of inventory at predetermined periods during the period (such as end of the month), plus the value of inventory at the end of the period divided by the total number of stock listings.

Buyers and management can determine a great deal about how well a store, department, or product classification is doing by knowing stock turnover rates. Like stock-to-sales ratios, turnover rates of comparable retailers can be determined from trade journals. Buyers can also use past sales data for their stores to calculate turnover. Turnover may be determined for any period of time; however, it usually refers to a one-year period.

The type of merchandise carried and store policies have an impact on stock turnover; however, almost every decision a retailer makes affects turnover. Less frequently purchased items, such as furniture and jewelry, have much lower turnover rates than items found in a grocery store.

Store policies in regard to carrying wide assortments of merchandise in many sizes and colors will tend to cause low turnovers because some colors and sizes may not sell as well as others. For that reason, some stores carry only fast-selling colors and sizes to generate higher turnover rates.

Higher stock turnover rates are usually an advantage to the store or department because rapid turnover of stock reduces the number and amount of markdowns required to move dated merchandise. Merchandise that is being replaced frequently always looks fresh and has much greater appeal to the customer. However, when attempting to increase turnover, you must also be concerned with increased expenses, such as advertising or more salaries for additional salespeople. Both might be required to generate more sales. In these situations, increased turnover may not result in increased profits.

How can buyers improve stock turnover? You will need to examine sales and inventory information from your store or department. Slow-turning merchandise may be due to several reasons.

Illustrative Problem

Calculate stock turnover given the following information:
Total sales = $60,000

Month	Stock Level
Jan 31	$8,000
Feb 28	$12,000
Mar 31	$14,000
Apr 30	$12,000
May 31	$10,000
June 30	$8,000
July 31	$10,000
Aug 31	$16,000
Sept 30	$18,000
Oct 31	$20,000
Nov 30	$30,000
Dec 31	$16,000
Jan 31	$6,000
Total Inventory = $180,000	

Solution

First, determine the average monthly inventory by dividing the total inventory in dollars by the number of inventory listings. Average stock would be $13,846 ($180,000/13).

Next, calculate the stock turnover rate using the following formula:

Stock turnover rate = Sales / Average stock
Stock turnover rate = $60,000 / $13,486
Stock turnover rate = 4.3

Therefore, the average stock for this department is sold and replenished 4.3 times during the year.

Stock turnover figures can also be used to plan both sales and stock levels using the following formula:

Sales = Stock turnover rate × Average inventory

For example, if your goal is a 3.1 turnover rate and your average stock is $25,000, planned sales to reach this goal would be $77,500.

- You may be attempting to carry too wide an assortment of merchandise. Offering a wide selection of styles, colors, and sizes often causes slow turnover rates. Merchandise may be remaining on your shelves for long periods of time to satisfy a few customers.
- You may have selected the wrong merchandise. The goods that have been purchased may not be the ones that your customers want or need. Learn from such situations to improve your buying decisions the next time.
- The merchandise may have been placed into stock too late. Delayed deliveries or late purchases may cause merchandise to arrive at your store after your customers have purchased the goods elsewhere.
- The merchandise may be priced too high. Prices may have to be reduced to generate sales.
- The store may not be conducting an effective sales promotion campaign for the product.

There are other reasons for low turnover rates, but these five should be examined first. Once you have developed a sales forecast and determined required inventory levels for your store or department, you are ready to develop your buying plan, a step that is examined in detail in the next chapter.

RETAIL ANALYTICS: THE FUTURE DIRECTION OF FORECASTING

Quantitative skills of buyers must continue to improve. The increased use of technology and retail analytics will affect sales forecasting in the years ahead. Software packages will become more versatile and easier to use. Large amounts of internal and external data will become available and accessible quickly through computerized information systems, and better techniques should improve the overall accuracy of forecasts. But, more competitive conditions and more volatile markets will increase the difficulty of making accurate forecasts. The successful buyer will be the individual who can best merge forecasts based on retail analytics with his or her experiences and personal insights about the marketplace.

Retail analytics is the process of providing analytical data on information (such as inventory levels, supply chain movement, consumer demand, and sales) that is crucial for making merchandising and marketing decisions. As illustrated in Figure 7.3, retail analytics can be defined as the process of analyzing and making sense of the flood of data that is accumulating everyday at a retail store, especially data collected from every possible customer touchpoint with the company.

Some people see data as only facts and figures, but they are more than that. Data are the lifeblood of any retail organization, and they are trying to tell decision makers something.

Many times it will take the assistance of business consultants and their specialized software to help retailers make sense of the data. Companies such as JDA, SAS, Intelligence Node, and others can transform data into insights that can give the retailer a fresh perspective on their business. They can identify what is working, help fix what is not working, and possibly discover new opportunities. Essentially, they can help turn large amounts of data into knowledge a retailer can use. Read the Snapshot

Figure 7.3

Retail analytics can be defined as the process of analyzing and making sense of the flood of data that is accumulating every day at a retail store.

"SAS: Providing Retail Analytic Solutions" to learn more about retail analytic software available from one company.

Analytics have become one of the most powerful tools available to retailers, and are being used to enable fact-based, insight-driven decision making by providing detailed customer insights. Some retail analysts suggest that companies that use retail analytics are 6.5 times more likely to retain customers and 7.4 times more likely to outperform their competitors on making sales to existing customers. By implementing retail analytics, companies greatly increase their potential to reach the right customers, in the right place, at the right time, and in the most effective way.

Even though implementing retail analytic solutions is a great idea, it is not as easy as it sounds. Data are easy to collect, but what really makes a difference is how well retailers can turn the data into usable information. Gathering and analyzing data is both costly and time-consuming; yet, it is a necessary investment. However, a majority of retailers either do not have data, or they have out-of-date data that are essentially useless. Moreover, retail analytics involves more than making the financial investment. To operate a retail analytics program successfully requires a combination of the right people, processes, and technologies to get the most out of the data. From the onset, however, retailers must realize that implementing a successful retail analytics program does not happen overnight. The challenge is turning data into something that helps drive a retail organization toward successful decision making.

For retailers, information is power and a game-changer. Retail analytics can help retailers stay ahead of trends by providing them ways of uncovering, interpreting, and acting on meaningful data insights—including the shopping patterns of both in-store and online customers. Retail analytics can be used to anticipate shopper needs and provide the ability to personalize marketing and promotions based on shopper data. Retail analytics can also help buyers and suppliers monitor online and store-level demand in real time to ensure best-selling items remain in stock. Delivering a good shopping experience improves customer satisfaction, repeat purchases, customer loyalty, customer referrals, revenues, and customer engagement.

Using software programs or suites, retail analytics analyzes large volumes of data and helps retailers gain a deeper understanding of customer demand. For example, Kroger, a grocery retailer, has used retail analytical programs to determine which products an individual customer actually wants to buy, then sends them customized digital coupons for many of these products. For Kroger, these coupon redemptions have greatly increased sales revenues. Amazon and other e-commerce giants have used retail analytics to uncover consumer insights on which they make purchasing decisions that provide the highest revenue returns.

There literally are hundreds of business consultants who provide data analytical solutions for retailers. Management, as well as retail buyers, must carefully evaluate the companies and solutions that are best for their organization. These solutions include existing software for the entire retail organization or stand-alone tools for specific functions such as merchandise management. Or, retailers may need to consider software solutions designed specifically for their unique needs. The breadth and complexity of the solution or solutions selected will depend on factors such as the retailer's size, number of storefronts, and number of stock-keeping units (SKUs).

Some of the solutions that retail buyers might want to examine include software dealing with merchandising, warehousing, and transportation management. Merchandise management software enables buyers to create the optimal balance of SKUs by providing the tools to plan merchandise purchases based on sales histories, trends, and forecasts. Warehouse management software can be used to automate inventory control within the warehouse, providing functions that include picking, packing, and pulling merchandise. Transportation management software helps retailers efficiently transport inventory from distribution centers to store locations and customers, which is extremely beneficial for omnichannel retailers.

Properly implemented, retail analytics should help retailers increase sales, increase inventory turns, minimize unsold inventory, and manage the company more efficiently. Today, retailers need to make and act on decisions with speed and agility; retail analytics provides a path to making the best decisions possible.

Summary Points

- Forecasting involves predicting what customers are likely to do in the future.

- Buyers use forecasting to predict what products customers will buy and how much they will purchase.

- Buyers can make short- or long-term forecasts for specific products, customer groups, time periods, or store locations.

- Long-term forecasts in volatile market conditions may be meaningless.

- Developing forecasts stimulates planning by forcing the buyer to have a thorough understanding of market conditions and customers, promotes coordination with other members of the merchandising team, and provides a control mechanism by which to evaluate a buyer's performance.

- When developing sales forecasts, buyers must examine all internal and external forces that may affect sales. They collect both primary and secondary data.

- Two of the most important forecasts that buyers make are sales and inventory levels.

- The key component of most sales forecasting is past sales records.

- Buyers can also use stock-to-sales ratios and inventory turnover to estimate sales.

- All other merchandising decisions are planned in relation to sales forecasts; therefore, if a sales forecast is in error, other decisions will be inaccurate, too.

- Decisions based on data analytics will be the future of retail forecasting.

- Retail analytics should help retailers increase sales, increase inventory turns, minimize unsold inventory, and manage the company more efficiently.

Review Activities

Developing Your Retail Buying Vocabulary

Consult the glossary if you did not add the following terms to your vocabulary.

4-5-4 calendar	external forces	long-term forecast	short-term forecast
average stock	forecasting	retail analytics	stock-to-sales ratio
BOM stock level	internal forces	sales forecast	stock turnover rate

Understanding What You Read

1. Identify the most important source of information when buyers develop sales forecasts.

2. Describe factors that will affect the accuracy of a sales forecast.

3. List and describe three benefits of forecasting sales.

4. Describe how buyers can increase their confidence in sales forecasting.

5. Identify economic conditions that would cause a buyer to project a decrease in sales.

6. Describe competitive conditions that would cause a buyer to project a decrease in sales.

7. Why do most buyers use secondary data before using primary data?

8. Describe the information provided in *Consumer Buying Indicators*.

9. List the steps needed to develop a sales forecast.

10. Describe the impact of a forecast that underestimates sales.

11. Describe the impact of a forecast that overestimates sales.

12. List several internal and external factors that should be considered along with past sales records when forecasting sales.

13. What will the accuracy of a sales forecast depend on?

14. How will holidays affect monthly sales forecasts from one year to the next?

15. What would be one source for industry-wide stock-to-sales ratios?

16. What are the advantages of forecasting an increase in stock turnover rates?

17. How can computers be used to make sales forecasts?

18. Why is the 4-5-4 calendar used by retail buyers?

19. How can retail analytics help retail buyers?

Analyzing and Applying What You Read

1. As a buyer, you must constantly make forecasts about consumer demand. What factors would cause the sale of men's ties, cigarettes, disposable diapers, and US flags to increase or decrease?

2. You have developed a sales forecast for men's suits that predicts a 20 percent increase in sales. Identify marketing strategies that could be utilized to reach that goal.

3. Sales last year during June were $20,000. Sales this June were $21,500. What percentage increase or decrease in sales has occurred? If this trend continues, what sales should be forecast for next June?

4. A firm wants to maintain an average stock of $25,000 every year. Last year, the firm had a 4.3 stock turnover rate. This year, management forecasts that stock turnover should increase to 4.5. By what dollar volume must sales increase for this forecasted turnover to occur?

Retail Buying Math Practice

1. Sales last year for a department were $124,560. This year planned sales are forecast to increase by 4.2 percent. What are planned sales for this year?

2. Sales last year for a department were $98,600. This year planned sales are forecast to decrease by 1.5 percent. What are planned sales for this year?

3. A department has the following sales data available. Forecast sales for May.

Month	Sales Last Year	Sales This Year
February	$24,000	$26,000
March	$26,000	$27,000
April	$29,000	$29,000
May	$33,000	?

4. Calculate the stock-sales ratio for each of the three months that follow.

Month	Monthly Sales	Retail Stock
January	$10,560	$19,655
February	$12,500	$17,850
March	$15,500	$22,800

5. Calculate the planned BOM inventory for each of the three months that follow. The stock-sales ratio for January is 2.0 and 2.3 for the other two months.

Month	Planned Sales
January	$11,600
February	$12,500
March	$26,000

6. Calculate the average inventory for the three-month season that follows.

Month	Ending Stock Level
January	$10,500
February	$11,600
March	$9,900

7. Planned sales for the three-month season in problem #6 are $10,000. Calculate the stock turnover.

8. Use the following information to answer the questions below.

Month	Last Year Monthly Sales	BOM Stock
January	$10,000	$20,000
February	$12,000	$25,000
March	$14,000	$30,000
April	$18,000	$38,000
May	$19,000	$40,000
June	$18,000	$39,000
July	$19,000	$41,000
August	$21,000	$43,000
September	$23,000	$47,000
October	$26,000	$52,000
November	$31,000	$60,000
December	$30,000	$58,000
Ending Inventory	December 31	$28,000

a. For the time period presented, what were total sales?

b. What was the average inventory for the period?

c. What was the annual stock turnover rate?

d. Calculate last year's stock-to-sales ratio for each of the months given.

e. Next December, the buyer wants to maintain the current stock-to-sales ratio but reduce the BOM stock to $55,000. What sales must occur next year for this to occur?

Spreadsheet Skills

Visit this book's STUDIO product at www.BloomsburyFashionCentral.com and open and print Assignment D. Follow the instructions to open a spreadsheet and answer the problems presented.

Internet Connection

1. Go to www.weather.com and record the weather forecast (highs, lows, and weather conditions) for the next three days for your town or nearest city. Each day record the actual conditions. Also, locate weather forecasts appearing in your local newspaper, on TV, or on the radio. Compare the forecasts and discuss their accuracy. Which source made the most accurate forecasts? Compare weather forecasting to retail buyers making short-term sales forecasts.

2. Visit the book's STUDIO to watch videos about Pantone color forecasts and retail data analytics.

TRENDWATCH

DATA MINING USING SOCIAL MEDIA

When fashion buyers make the right purchase decisions for their stores or departments, they can score fast inventory turns and large profit margins, but when they get it wrong, their stores end up with unsold inventory, requiring huge markdowns to be taken, and profits decline. Predicting what the fashion-conscious consumer will purchase has never been an exact science, but one new trend in this area to assist fashion buyers is the use of data mining of social media, such as Facebook, Instagram, and Twitter.

What can retailers learn by data mining social media? First, they can obtain behavioral data that will allow them to more appropriately target segments for better marketing results, and second, they can obtain data on personal preferences and interests to move closer to a true one-to-one relationship with their customers. Moreover, the use of social media data has the potential to increase the effectiveness of a retailer's marketing campaign—it enables them to take targeting to the next level.

How are data from social media mined? Several companies are now providing trend forecasting services based on analysis of social media. They constantly survey social media, blogs, forums, the press, and other places where consumers offer opinions. EDITD, headquartered in London, is a major player in this field and runs the world's biggest apparel data warehouse. The company's goal is to provide a tool for fashion buyers, merchandisers, and designers to quantify commercial trends. To analyze the data, the firm uses various tools, from linguistics (natural language processing) to computer science (quantitative analysis of variables such as reputation, persuasiveness, and influence). The goal of the analyses is to give retailers a deeper insight into market sentiment so they can align their product assortments to better meet consumer needs.

How are findings presented to retailers? Usually, the findings that have been mined by analyzing social media data are presented graphically in easy-to-understand charts or a "Top 20" list. Trends can also be broken down by geographic region, type of clothing, patterns, and colors. Popularity of a specific trend can also be measured over time, and users of such software can search for words or phrases to determine whether opinion is currently favorable or unfavorable.

Knowing what trends are slowing down and which ones are taking off can assist retail buyers in avoiding huge markdowns and, thus, in maximizing profits. For example, using such data mining techniques, retail buyers can fine-tune their ordering process as once-positive consumer sentiments for a product begin to wane.

BASED ON:

Chase Small Business Ad Academy. (2017, March 17). 10 digital marketing tips for small business owners. *Forbes.com*.

Dick, John. (2016, March 21). Being there: In-store apparel retailers put advantages to good use. *ChainStoreAge.com*.

Pincus, Walter. (2013, August 7). Mining social media: The new way of life. *Washingtonpost.com*.

Smith, Steve. (2014, July 9). Mining the aisles: In-store experiences will render troves of data, and better relationships. *Mediapost.com*.

Urbanski, Al. (2017, January 5). Be it in stores or on sites, the dollars are in the data. *ChainStoreAge.com*.

USING WEATHER FORECASTS TO IMPROVE RETAIL FORECASTS

When retailers mention the weather, it is usually as a way to explain sales, particularly poor sales. All retailers know from experience that store traffic and sales are definitely related to weather, but very few retailers keep any weather records at all. Although most retailers realize how dependent they are on weather, they also know how little they understand it.

The idea that weather can be forecast early enough to affect buying plans and promotional calendars is an entirely new concept for many retailers. Yet weather forecasting has tremendous implications for them, especially in areas that are subject to weather extremes, such as snowstorms, hurricanes, or seasonal temperatures that vary greatly. For instance, if buyers know that the weather is going to be unseasonably hot or cold, they can plan their purchases accordingly.

Most retailers, however, do not consciously factor future weather into their merchandising decisions. Typically, their actions merely assume the weather's effect on their business will repeat from last year to the current year. In fact, weather is similar one year to the next only about one-third of the time—causing most retailers to have too much or too little seasonal merchandise on hand. Moreover, having a better idea of when and where inclement weather is going to strike can help retailers move inventory to where more consumers will be willing to buy them.

Currently, there are a number of firms that use weather data to assist retailers in predicting consumer behavior and managing weather risk. One of those companies, Planalytics, includes among its customers Gillette's Duracell batteries, Home Depot, and Walmart. Planalytics makes forecasts twelve to fifteen months in advance, but their clients never see weather forecasts. What they see is the impact that weather has on specific businesses and product categories. Planalytics helps their retail clients understand how weather events change shopping patterns and how to better prepare for major weather disasters. Retailers can then use this information to adjust their merchandising plans.

Companies like Planalytics compare millions of data points about retail purchasing habits of consumers against specific weather events. Such research gives their clients more accurate predictions about what unexpected items might go out of stock and how to optimize product assortments. Suggestions are also given on how to increase sales for high-demand items.

One very important finding from such research has been that when storms were predicted but did not actually occur, consumers still purchased essential supplies for their homes. And, this emergency shopping tended to occur at the last minute—even when there were storm warnings given a week in advance. This information allows retailers time to create promotional campaigns and in-store displays for products that customers may need during and after a storm. They may also have the time to transfer additional products from stores in areas not being impacted by the storm.

Planalytics's forecasts have been correct about 70 percent of the time. Predicting the weather will never be perfect; however, some retailers are beginning to realize that such forecasts can help them fine-tune their merchandising decisions, so they are willing to spend the money to gain a competitive edge. Yet, not all retailers have been convinced that weather forecasting services are needed. At one time, Sears employed two meteorologists to assist with long-range planning, but discontinued the practice because of budget cuts.

For retailers, the challenge of how to use the data still remains. Knowing that more snow is forecast is great information. Determining how many additional pairs of skis to have in inventory is quite another matter. More understanding is needed on how to apply this information to various decision-making processes, including merchandise allocation and planning, merchandise delivery, markdown timing, and promotional scheduling.

Weather influences consumer behavior, affecting store traffic and demand for specific products. Weather determines the beginning and ending points of a merchandise season; yet, weather is a huge unknown. Retailers cannot control the weather, but they can control how it affects their businesses. Better planning based on weather forecasts can increase revenues and profits on weather-sensitive products.

BASED ON:

Bertolucci, Jeff. (2013, June 17). Big data reveals weather-related shopping patterns. *Informationweek.com.*

Grannis, Kathy. (2014, March 10). Digging out of one of the longest winters ever: The good, the bad and the ugly. *NRF.com.*

Ungerleider, Neal. (2013, June 27). Why retailers are becoming meteorologists. *Fastcompany.com.*

Valenti, Catherine. (2014, March 17). More companies use weather to forecast sales. *ABCNews.com.*

Webster, Ross. (2013, July 22). Weather data is red hot for retailers. *Huffingtonpost.com.*

SNAPSHOT: SAS: Providing Retail Analytic Solutions

SAS, headquartered in North Carolina, is a world leader in data analytics. Through innovative analytics, business intelligence, and data management software and services, SAS offers technology solutions that help customers at more than 83,000 business sites make better decisions.

One of their programs, *SAS Integrated Merchandise Planning*, allows retail clients to more accurately anticipate customer demand and create integrated merchandise plans. The technology enables buyers to make quick responses as demand changes in order to deliver a consistent customer experience across all channels. During this process, plans can be reconciled to help ensure that financial and merchandise plans work hand-in-hand.

In general, *SAS Integrated Merchandise Planning* delivers merchandising solutions for retail buyers by delivering technology that enables the following:

- *Merchandise Assortment Optimization.* Analytics and advanced clustering are used to understand a customer's path to purchase and identify missed sales opportunities.
- *Merchandise Financial Planning.* Customer demand can be predicted by channel, and opportunities to improve performance can be identified to boost customer satisfaction and increase profitability.
- *Merchandise Location Planning.* An omnichannel approach to predict sales by location, optimize inventory, and support e-commerce fulfillment initiatives can be implemented.
- *Size/Pack Optimization.* Gross margins can be increased by forecasting quantities down to the store/size level, and pack configurations to meet supply chain and distribution.
- *Revenue Optimization.* Profitable price strategies can be optimized over the product life cycle and analytics can be used to understand competitor pricing and meet financial goals.

How have retailers implemented SAS technologies? DSW, a footwear and accessories retailer, is one client. The company operates more than 377 stores as well as 345 leased departments for other retailers in the United Sates along with its e-commerce and mobile sites. Shoe merchandising is faced with fashion cycles that are accelerating. Moreover, shoes are also not like clothing—they come in more sizes and fit tends to be quite individual. Before using SAS, some individual store managers felt they could predict which sizes would sell out quickly and which would land on the clearance rack. But, at most, they could only ask for extra packs of a certain style or size; there was no optimized, sustainable, automated system in place.

With SAS, DSW worked with all its data to provide a more customized approach to stocking stores and offering the "right" sizes by developing accurate size curves. It is now possible for DSW to develop a "size by store" model that optimizes their inventory. SAS analytical tools recommended size replenishment orders that sell through with fewer markdowns while also reducing stock-outs. The efforts have been so successful that DSW management has convinced buyers to reduce the amount of inventory they purchase. In the past, buyers did not want to be caught without enough of a hot seasonal style. Now they are ordering less, but gaining confidence that they will have the right shoes on hand.

Generally, what are the benefits of retail analytics provided to retailers by companies like SAS? Sales and gross margins can be improved because in-season re-forecasting adjusts to changing demand and inventory conditions. Effective assortment plans can be optimized to meet customer demand for style, color, or size, which gets the right products to the right stores at the right times. Merchandise plans can be created driven by demand forecasts to improve in-stock positions and maximize inventory turnover, which reduces costly markdowns. Most importantly, integrated analytics provide buyers and planners the ability to focus on the implementation of plans. Insights from retail analytics software can help buyers spot emerging trends before their competitors, giving them a big opportunity to boost sales and customer loyalty.

BASED ON:

Mitchell, Dan. (2017, January 13). Traditional stores get smarter and better connected. *ChainStoreAge.com.*

SAS.com (2017).

Standish, Jill. (2017, February 13). Profit hunting: How to use analytic insights to drive profitable growth. *ChainStoreAge.com.*

PREPARING BUYING PLANS

Performance Objectives

- **Distinguish between top-down and bottom-up planning.**
- **Identify the purposes of merchandise plans.**
- **Outline a process to forecast sales.**
- **List and describe the components of a merchandise plan.**
- **Calculate planned BOM (beginning-of-month) inventory levels.**
- **Identify the components of planned reductions.**
- **Calculate planned purchases at retail and at cost.**
- **Prepare a six-month merchandise plan.**
- **Describe basic stock planning.**
- **Describe the importance of open-to-buy.**
- **Calculate open-to-buy.**

Whether buyers are purchasing fashion or basic merchandise, they must plan and control merchandise purchases. Planning is essential to provide direction and serve as a basis of control for any store or department. As a buyer, you must provide the right merchandise, at the right place, at the right time, in the right quantities, and at the right price. To accomplish these goals, you must plan a deliberate course of action—planning merchandise budgets and merchandise assortments. As you will learn, the merchandise budget or merchandise plan is a forecast of specific merchandise purchases in dollars that typically covers a period of six months or a year. Assortment plans break down merchandise budgets into specific units of merchandise to be purchased, such as styles, colors, and sizes.

In this chapter, you will learn how to prepare a six-month merchandise plan. Inventory planning for basic merchandise and the concept of open-to-buy are also described. Chapter 9 explains how the merchandise plan is translated into an assortment plan for specific units of merchandise.

MERCHANDISING MANAGEMENT

Integrally related to planning is the necessity to control merchandising decisions. You must check your plans periodically to ensure they are being followed and are achieving the desired results. Your success as a buyer will be measured by how well you plan and control the amount of money spent for merchandise to yield the desired sales and profit.

Retailers need some type of planning and control device to guide their activities toward the achievement of their stated goals and objectives. Most retailers develop merchandise plans for the entire store as well as specific departments and product classifications. These merchandise plans provide for an effective control over purchases and tend to prevent the department or store from becoming overstocked or understocked.

The **merchandise plan** is a projection in dollars of the sales goals of the store or department over a specified period of time—usually six months, but it may be for shorter periods. With this information, a buyer can determine how much money can be used to purchase merchandise. In addition, information from the merchandise plan helps top management judge the effectiveness of merchandising decisions that were made.

Two methods of developing the merchandise plan are used today. They involve top-down and bottom-up planning (Figure 8.1). **Top-down planning** involves top-level management estimating total sales for the upcoming period. Then, expected sales are planned for each department according to its past contribution to the sales of the entire store. One advantage of top-down planning is that top management tends to have a better perspective of all economic and competitive conditions facing the business than would other employees.

Figure 8.1

Examples of top-down and bottom-up planning.

TOP-DOWN PLANNING

BOTTOM-UP PLANNING

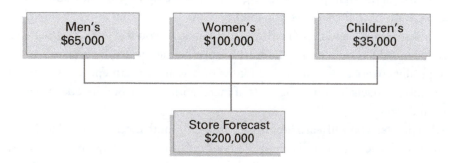

The other method used to develop a merchandise plan is **bottom-up planning**. The planned sales for the store are determined by adding together the planned sales figures that are developed by each department manager. Planned sales figures for all departments are then totaled to arrive at planned sales for the store. Many large retailers use both the top-down and bottom-up methods, and then arrive at the final planned sales figure for the store and each department through a process of discussion and compromise.

SIX-MONTH MERCHANDISE PLAN

Most retailers will use a **six-month merchandise plan** to represent planning efforts. Key components of every plan include sales forecasts and stock planning. In addition, the amount of merchandise to be purchased each period to generate the planned sales is calculated. The six-month merchandise plan is the tool that translates profit objectives into a framework for merchandise planning and control. Read the Trendwatch titled "Merchandise Planning: Taking the Holiday Pulse" to learn more about critical merchandise planning for most retailers during the fourth quarter.

The plan is normally established to conform to two distinct selling seasons: (1) spring–summer (February to July) and (2) fall–winter (August to January). Using these months allows the store the opportunity for clearance sales at the end of the summer and holiday seasons before making plans for new merchandise arrivals.

Purposes of the Plan

The merchandise plan regulates inventory levels in accordance with planned financial objectives. As with all merchandising activities, the essential goal of the merchandise plan is to minimize the use of capital and maximize profits. Key purposes of the merchandise plan are as follows:

- To provide an estimate of the amount of capital required to be invested in inventory for a specific period.
- To provide an estimate of planned sales for the period that translates into cash flow estimates for store management and accounting personnel.

If a merchandise plan is used successfully, the following outcomes should result:

- *Increased Turnover.* Merchandise that customers want should be more readily available at times when they want to make purchases.
- *Reduced Dollar Amount of Markdowns.* Because merchandise purchases in relation to planned sales and stock levels are anticipated, there is less likelihood of being in an overbought position and having to make markdowns.
- *Improved Ability to Maintain Markups.* Because fewer markdowns may have to be taken, an improved ability to maintain markups should result.
- *Maximized Profits.* A balanced assortment of merchandise leads to more sales and an increase in profits because items will not remain in stock too long and become shopworn and difficult to sell. Greater profits can result because the buyer is informed about both fast-selling items that should be reordered quickly and slow-selling items that should be dropped.

- *Minimized Inventory Investment.* A six-month merchandise plan helps determine how much money should be spent on merchandise. Ideally, a buyer makes the smallest investment possible in goods that will satisfy customer demands and sell well enough to build store profits.

Components of the Plan

Most retailers have different forms for developing a six-month merchandise plan, but generally they all contain the following components:

- *Initial Markup for the Period.* Goals will be indicated as to the desired markup that should be placed on merchandise when it enters the store.
- *Planned Net Sales.* Planned net sales represent gross sales minus customer returns and allowances. Last year's sales usually provide the basis for determining planned sales for the current year; however, you should also examine sales figures from previous years. Usually, you will be able to detect an upward or downward trend in sales, but what happens this year will depend on whether conditions are similar to past conditions.
- *Planned Beginning-of-Month Inventory.* There must be adequate stock to achieve planned sales. The relationship between the amount of stock in the store and planned sales is most frequently calculated using the stock-to-sales ratio method of stock planning.
- *Planned End-of-Month Inventory.* Planned **EOM inventory** represents the retail value of the ending inventory for each period. In merchandise plans, the **BOM inventory**, beginning inventory for a period (usually a month), must be the value of the ending inventory (EOM) for the preceding period.
- *Planned Reductions. Reductions* (the total of planned markdowns, shortages, and employee discounts) must also be entered into the merchandise plan. Dollar amounts for these items can be calculated using planned percentage-of-sales figures that are usually found in the seasonal data on the six-month merchandise plan.
- *Planned Purchases at Retail.* Planned purchases at retail represent the retail value of merchandise that is to be purchased during a given period. Planned purchases at retail are calculated by using the following formula:

Planned purchases at retail =
Planned sales + Planned reductions + Planned EOM — Planned BOM

- *Planned Purchases at Cost.* Planned purchases at cost represent the amount of money that the buyer expects to spend on merchandise purchases during a given period. (Note: Most retail buyers at corporate offices may not plan purchases at cost. All of their calculations would be at retail; however, buyers at independent retail stores will probably translate planned purchases at retail to planned purchases at cost.) Planned purchases at cost are calculated using the following formula:

Planned purchases at cost =
Planned purchases at retail × (100% — Initial markup %)

With the exception of planned purchases at cost, all amounts on the six-month merchandise plan are entered as retail values. Examine Figure 8.2 to view a merchandise plan based on these components. As you can see, each of these components is further subdivided into the following four categories.

- *Last Year (Actual).* This represents the actual amount last year for the month. This information would be found on the previous six-month merchandise plan from actual figures recorded.
- *Plan (This Year).* This represents the amount planned for the current year.
- *Revised (This Year).* This represents any revisions made in the current plan owing to unanticipated events. After you make your plans, you will need to check them periodically to determine if they are progressing as you thought they would. Sometimes everything goes as expected, but at other times, you have to adjust your plans. When a store or department does not meet its planned sales or exceeds its planned sales for a given month, adjustments will be required in future months.

Dept Name _____ Dept No. _____

SIX-MONTH MERCHANDISING PLAN

	PLAN (This Year)	ACTUAL (Last Year)
Workroom cost		
Cash discount %		
Season stock turnover		
Shortage %		
Average stock		
Markdown %		

SPRING 20____		FEB	MAR	APR	MAY	JUNE	JULY	SEASON TOTAL
FALL 20 ____		AUG	SEP	OCT	NOV	DEC	JAN	
SALES $	Last Year							
	Plan							
	% of Increase							
	Revised							
	Actual							
RETAIL STOCK (BOM)	Last Year							
	Plan							
	Revised							
	Actual							
RETAIL STOCK (EOM)	Last Year							
	Plan							
	Revised							
	Actual							
REDUCTIONS $	Last Year							
	Plan							
	Revised							
	Actual							
PURCHASES AT RETAIL	Last Year							
	Plan							
	Revised							
	Actual							
PURCHASES AT COST	Last Year							
	Plan							
	Revised							
	Actual							

Comments _____

Merchandise Manager _____ Buyer_____
Controller _____

Figure 8.2

Six-month merchandising plans involve making predictions about the components on this form.

- *Actual (This Year).* This represents the actual sales for the month. At the end of each month, you must record actual figures on the six-month merchandise plan form. A comparison of actual (this year) with planned (this year) sales determines whether you reached your goals.

The six-month merchandise plan is one of the buyer's most important planning and control tools. Because it shows the amount you should spend on new inventory purchases to achieve planned sales, the merchandise plan keeps you from overspending and not achieving planned profit for the store or department.

For a small store, the plan may be prepared for the entire store; however, for larger stores, the plan may be prepared on a departmental or product classification basis. Later, these individual plans are incorporated into a plan at the divisional or storewide level. Read the Snapshot titled "RMSA: Turning Numbers into Actions" to learn more about one firm that assists independent retailers in preparing, implementing, and monitoring merchandise plans.

PREPARATION OF A SIX-MONTH MERCHANDISE PLAN

In this section, you will be taken step-by-step through the process of preparing a six-month merchandise plan. Calculations for each component of the plan are described in detail.

Planned Sales

The first and most important part of the six-month merchandise plan is forecasting sales. All other merchandising decisions are planned in relation to sales or stated as a percentage of sales. Therefore, if the sales forecast is inaccurate, all the other parts of the plan will be in error, possibly causing disastrous results for the retailer.

From the previous year's merchandise plan, the following sales data were obtained:

Sales	February	March	April	May	June	July	Totals
Last Year Planned	$10,000	$12,000	$23,000	$18,000	$12,000	$12,000	$87,000
Revised							
Actual							

First, you will need to calculate last year's monthly sales figures as a percentage of last year's total sales. For each month, the calculations would be as follows:

	Sales Last Year	Total Sales Last Year	% of Sales Last Year
February	= $10,000	/ $87,000	= 11.5%
March	= $12,000	/ $87,000	= 13.8%
April	= $23,000	/ $87,000	= 26.4%
May	= $18,000	/ $87,000	= 20.7%
June	= $12,000	/ $87,000	= 13.8%
July	= $12,000	/ $87,000	= 13.8%

You may find that over several years, these percentage figures have remained stable. Therefore, you may forecast that a similar percentage of sales would occur each month of the current year. However, as previously explained, there may be both internal and external factors that would cause changes. For example, the Easter holiday occurs in either April or March, or your store may be planning on changes in marketing strategies during a specific month that did not occur in the past. In addition, most retailers track the busiest shopping days, particularly during holiday seasons. If you determine such factors will have an impact on the percentage of sales occurring each month, you must adjust the planned sales percentage for each month.

Let's assume that you detected no major changes during the current season. In addition, a sales analysis of previous years indicates that the percentage of total sales occurring during each month has remained fairly constant. Based on that information, you would plan for the following percentages of sales to occur each month:

Month	Percentage
February	11.5%
March	13.8%
April	26.4%
May	20.7%
June	13.8%
July	13.8%

Next, you would need to determine the total planned sales volume for the season. Using forecasting techniques described in Chapter 7, a 10 percent increase in sales is planned for the period. In some firms, top management may determine planned increases or decreases in planned sales and present them to you as a goal for your department or division.

Referring to last year's sales for the same period, you determine that total sales were $87,000. Therefore, planned sales for the current period would be $95,700 (10 percent of $87,000 = $8,700, the planned increase in sales that would be added to last year's sales; thus, $8,700 + $87,000 = $95,700).

Now, you must plan sales for each month of the current period. Using the planned percentage of total sales and the planned total sales figure ($95,700), you would make the following calculations:

	Planned % of Total	Planned Total	Planned Monthly Sales
February	11.5%	× $95,700	= $11,005
March	13.8%	× $95,700	= $13,207
April	26.4%	× $95,700	= $25,265
May	20.7%	× $95,700	= $19,810
June	13.8%	× $95,700	= $13,207
July	13.8%	× $95,700	= $13,206

These figures would then be entered on the six-month merchandise plan (on the Planned line) as follows:

Sales	February	March	April	May	June	July	Totals
Last Year	$10,000	$12,000	$23,000	$18,000	$12,000	$12,000	$87,000
Planned	$11,005	$13,207	$25,265	$19,810	$13,207	$13,206	$95,700
Revised							
Actual							

As you have learned, there is space to record any revisions in the plan as well as actual sales for the month. Keeping accurate records will improve your planning efforts in the future.

Planned BOM Inventory

Your next step in preparing a six-month merchandise plan is to determine the amount of stock required to meet the planned sales. You want to have sufficient stock on hand to meet customer demand. There must be an adequate opening merchandise assortment on hand that is in sufficient quantity to meet anticipated customer demand.

The stock-to-sales method of inventory planning requires that the buyer define a relationship between planned BOM inventory for a given month and the planned sales for that month. Using the stock-to-sales ratio method for planning stock levels, planned BOM inventory can be calculated using the following formula:

$$\textbf{Planned BOM inventory =}$$
$$\textbf{Planned sales} \times \textbf{Stock-to-sales ratio}$$

From trade sources and an examination of past years' sales and inventory data, you calculate the following stock-to-sales ratios:

February	3.1
March	2.8
April	2.0
May	1.8
June	1.8
July	1.8

Using these stock-to-sales ratios and planned sales for the current year, which were previously calculated, planned BOM inventory for each month can be calculated as follows:

	Stock-to-Sales Ratio	Planned Monthly Sales	Planned Monthly BOM Inventory
February	3.1	× $11,005	= $34,116
March	2.8	× $13,207	= $36,980
April	2.0	× $25,265	= $50,530
May	1.8	× $19,810	= $35,658
June	1.8	× $13,207	= $23,773
July	1.8	× $13,206	= $23,773

These figures would then be entered on the six-month merchandise plan (on the Planned line) as follows:

BOM	February	March	April	May	June	July	Totals
Last Year	$31,000	$33,600	$46,000	$32,400	$21,600	$21,600	$186,200
Planned	$34,116	$36,980	$50,530	$35,658	$23,773	$23,773	$204,830
Revised							
Actual							

Planned EOM Inventory

The EOM stock for any month is simply the planned BOM stock for the following month. On the sample six-month merchandise plan, planned EOM inventory levels would be as follows:

February EOM	= $36,980 (March BOM)
March EOM	= $50,530 (April BOM)
April EOM	= $35,658 (May BOM)
May EOM	= $23,773 (June BOM)
June EOM	= $23,773 (July BOM)
July EOM	= —

Because the BOM stock for August is unknown, you do not know the planned EOM for July. Therefore, you must plan an estimated EOM stock for the period. For our sample six-month merchandise plan, the EOM for the period is estimated to be $21,000.

These figures would then be entered on the six-month merchandise plan (on the Planned line) as follows:

COM	February	March	April	May	June	July	Totals
Last Year	$33,600	$46,000	$32,400	$21,600	$21,600	$20,000	$175,200
Planned	$36,980	$50,530	$35,658	$23,773	$23,773	$21,000	$191,714
Revised							
Actual							

Planned Reductions

The next component of the six-month merchandise plan to be planned is reductions. There are several types of reductions: markdowns, employee discounts, and shrinkage, usually inventory shortages from shoplifting or employee theft. Estimates for these reductions are based on past experience and are presented as a percentage of planned sales on the six-month merchandise plan. For the sample plan that you are completing, the planned reductions are as follows:

Planned markdown percentage	= 6.8%
Planned shortage percentage	= 2.1%
Planned employee discount percentage	= 1.1%

Therefore, total reductions are planned to be 10 percent of sales. Total reductions in dollars can be calculated by multiplying total planned sales by the reduction percent. Total reductions equal $9,570 ($95,700 ? 10%).

Based on past records, you have determined that reductions each month have occurred according to the following breakdown:

February	11.5%
March	7.0%
April	15.0%
May	18.5%
June	22.1%
July	25.9%

Again, internal or external conditions affecting the current year may cause you to make adjustments in these figures. You can calculate planned reductions for each month as follows:

	% Reductions Planned for the Month	Total Planned Reductions	Planned Monthly Reductions
February	11.5%	× $9,570	= $1,100
March	7.0%	× $9,570	= $670
April	15.0%	× $9,570	= $1,436
May	18.5%	× $9,570	= $1,770
June	22.1%	× $9,570	= $2,115
July	25.9%	× $9,570	= $2,479

These figures would then be entered on the six-month merchandise plan (on the Planned line) as follows:

Reductions	February	March	April	May	June	July	Totals
Last Year	$1,001	$609	$1,305	$1,609	$1,923	$2,253	$8,700
Planned	$1,100	$670	$1,436	$1,770	$2,115	$2,479	$9,570
Revised							
Actual							

Planned Purchases at Retail

Planned purchases each month should be adequate to implement the six-month merchandise plan. On the merchandise plan, purchases must be planned at retail first because all the other figures are based on retail. The following formula is used to calculate planned purchases at retail:

**Planned purchases =
Planned sales + Planned EOM + Planned reductions − Planned BOM**

Using this formula and the data that you have already entered on the merchandise plan, planned purchases at retail can be calculated as follows:

	Planned Sales	Planned EOM	Planned Reductions	Planned BOM at Retail	Planned Purchases
February	$11,005	+ $36,980	+ $1,100	− $34,116	= $14,969
March	$13,207	+ $50,530	+ $670	− $36,980	= $27,427
April	$25,265	+ $35,658	+ $1,436	− $50,530	= $11,829
May	$19,810	+ $23,773	+ $1,770	− $35,658	= $9,695
June	$13,207	+ $23,773	+ $2,115	− $23,773	= $15,322
July	$13,206	+ $21,000	+ $2,479	− $23,773	= $12,912

These figures would then be entered on the six-month merchandise plan (on the Planned line) as follows:

Planned Purchases at Retail	February	March	April	May	June	July	Totals
Last Year	$13,209	$25,705	$11,009	$9,123	$14,253	$19,100	$92,399
Planned	$14,969	$27,427	$11,829	$9,695	$15,322	$12,912	$92,154
Revised							
Actual							

Planned Purchases at Cost

From the seasonal data, initial markup for the period is planned at 46.3 percent. Planned purchases at cost can be calculated with the following formula:

$$\text{Planned purchases at cost} = (100\% - \text{Initial Markup \%}) \times \text{Planned purchases at retail}$$

The cost of planned purchases for each month can be calculated as follows:

	(100% – Initial Markup %)	Planned Purchases at Retail	Planned Purchases at Cost
February	(100% – .463)	× $14,969	= $8,038
March	(100% – .463)	× $27,427	= $14,728
April	(100% – .463)	× $11,829	= $6,352
May	(100% – .463)	× $9,695	= $5,206
June	(100% – .463)	× $15,322	= $8,228
July	(100% – .463)	× $12,912	= $6,934

These figures would then be entered on the six-month merchandise plan (on the Planned line) as follows:

Planned Purchases at Cost	February	March	April	May	June	July	Totals
Last Year	$7,093	$13,803	$5,912	$4,899	$7,654	$10,257	$49,618
Planned	$8,038	$14,728	$6,352	$5,206	$8,228	$6,934	$49,486
Revised							
Actual							

Figure 8.3
A completed six-month merchandising plan.

SIX-MONTH MERCHANDISING PLAN	Dept Name _____ Dept No. _____		
		PLAN (This Year)	ACTUAL (Last Year)
	Workroom cost		
	Cash discount %		
	Season stock turnover		
	Shortage %		
	Average stock		
	Markdown %		

SPRING 20___		FEB	MAR	APR	MAY	JUNE	JULY	SEASON TOTAL
FALL 20___		AUG	SEP	OCT	NOV	DEC	JAN	
SALES $	Last Year	10,000	12,000	23,000	18,000	12,000	12,000	$87,000
	Plan	11,005	13,207	25,265	19,810	13,207	13,206	$95,700
	% of Increase							
	Revised							
	Actual							
RETAIL STOCK (BOM)	Last Year	31,000	33,600	46,000	32,400	21,600	21,600	$186,200
	Plan	34,116	36,980	50,530	35,658	23,773	23,773	$204,830
	Revised							
	Actual							
RETAIL STOCK (EOM)	Last Year	33,600	46,000	32,400	21,600	21,600	20,000	$175,200
	Plan	36,980	50,530	35,658	23,773	23,773	21,000	$191,714
	Revised							
	Actual							
REDUCTIONS $	Last Year	1,001	609	1,305	1,609	1,923	2,253	$8,700
	Plan	1,100	670	1,436	1,770	2,115	2,479	$9,570
	Revised							
	Actual							
PURCHASES AT RETAIL	Last Year	13,209	25,705	11,009	9,123	14,253	19,100	$92,399
	Plan	14,969	27,427	11,829	9,695	15,322	12,912	$92,154
	Revised							
	Actual							
PURCHASES AT COST	Last Year	7,093	13,803	5,912	4,899	7,654	10,257	$49,618
	Plan	8,038	14,728	6,352	5,206	8,228	6,934	$49,486
	Revised							
	Actual							

Comments

Merchandise Manager_____ Buyer_____
Controller_____

The planned purchases at cost let buyers know how much money they will have to spend on merchandise for the season as well as individual months. Examine Figure 8.3 to view the entire six-month merchandise plan that you have just prepared.

Each month you must also enter actual figures to assist with future planning. Actual monthly figures can also aid you in making revisions to your plan if they are necessary. If sales are greater than planned, you will need to make larger purchases for the rest of the season to maintain the inventory level shown in the merchandise plan. However, if sales are less than planned, you must decrease the dollar amount of purchases. In Table 8.1 you can examine how planned sales and inventory levels compare with actual data for one product category.

TABLE 8.1

MISSES SPRING MERCHANDISING PLANS

Description	Actual Sales	Plan Sales	% of Dept/ St.	% Over Last Yr.	Plan BOM 2008	Planned Month Purchases	% Fresh	Stock to Sales Ratio
Dresses								
February	$56.4	$64.0	11.4%	13%	$241.5	$121.4	42%	3.8
March	$101.9	$106.2	18.9%	4%	$287.5	$117.1	41%	2.7
April	$105.1	$120.7	21.4%	15%	$287.5	$93.8	38%	2.4
May	$82.9	$90.0	16.0%	9%	$245.0	$98.7	41%	2.7
June	$88.7	$101.2	18.0%	14%	$238.1	$97.1	46%	2.4
July	$68.2	$80.7	14.3%	18%	$209.3	$106.5	51%	2.6
Dresses- Spring Season	$503.2	$562.8		12%	$1,508.9	$634.6	43%	2.8

Plan Turn = 2.30

		EOM Stock					Markdowns			
Description	Season 2014 Actual EOM	Season 2015 Plan EOM	% of Store	% Over Last Year	Season 2014	Season 2015	% of Store	% Over Last Year	Plan % of Sales
Dresses									
February	$113.8	$287.5	24.4%	153%	$11.9	$11.4	19.6%	25%	17.7%
March	$173.2	$287.5	28.3%	66%	$4.4	$10.9	23.1%	148%	10.3%
April	$241.9	$245.0	27.7%	1%	$7.1	$15.6	31.3%	120%	13.0%
May	$203.5	$238.1	27.8%	17%	$11.8	$15.6	26.5%	32%	17.3%
June	$151.7	$209.3	25.8%	38%	$31.6	$24.7	22.4%	222%	24.4%
July	$112.0	$207.0	22.9%	85%	$38.1	$28.1	22.5%	226%	34.8%
	$996.1	$1,474.4		48%	$104.9	$106.3		1%	18.9%

Note: This form illustrates a store's merchandising plans for misses dresses during a six-month period.

BASIC STOCK PLANNING

Some classifications of merchandise do not vary much from season to season in appearance, construction, or price. Such goods are known as basic merchandise. For basic merchandise, planned purchases can be calculated without using a six-month merchandise plan. A **basic stock plan** is a tool many retailers use in planning purchases of basic merchandise. The purpose of the plan is to determine the amount of merchandise a retailer must have on hand or on order to have a sufficient amount of merchandise available during the period. To make these calculations, you must gather information about the average sales volume each week, reorder period, delivery period, and reserve stock levels.

The following formula is used to calculate the maximum number of any basic merchandise item that should be on hand and on order at any given point:

Maximum =
Sales volume per week (Reorder period + Delivery period) + Reserve

Let us examine each of the elements of this formula:

- *Sales Volume per Week.* You must first determine the weekly unit sales of each item by analyzing past sales records.
- *Reorder Period.* The **reorder period** is the amount of time between orders for merchandise. Lengthy periods between reorder periods require ordering larger quantities of merchandise or keeping goods in storage.
- *Delivery Period.* The **delivery period** is the time between when the order is placed and when the merchandise is on the sales floor. Enough merchandise must be available in the store to cover the time the vendor must take to deliver merchandise once it has been ordered.
- *Reserve.* The **reserve** is the amount of merchandise necessary to meet unanticipated sales. Out-of-stock positions can cause your store to lose sales and profits; therefore, many buyers purchase additional merchandise to cover unanticipated sales to prevent customers from being lost to the competition.
- *Maximum.* The **maximum** is the amount of merchandise that must be on hand or on order at any reordering point. The maximum must be sufficient to provide merchandise for sale while goods are being delivered. The stock on hand never reaches the maximum because sales will occur during the time it takes for the new order to be received.

In using the basic stock plan, buyers will develop a basic stock list. The **basic stock list** provides information such as description of the item, the retail price, the cost to the store, the maximum, the rate of sale, and the minimum reorder quantity.

OPEN-TO-BUY PLANNING

In the six-month merchandise plan (Figure 8.3), you established the dollar amount of purchases that were to be made each month. However, not all the required monthly stock is purchased at the beginning of the month.

Definition of Open-to-Buy

Purchase decisions are distributed throughout the month in order to take advantage of new merchandise lines, to reorder fast-selling merchandise, or to acquire off-price merchandise to use in promotional sales. In addition, you may have outstanding orders—that is, commitments from vendors that have not been delivered. The value of these outstanding orders will reduce the planned purchases for the month. As a result, you must be able to calculate, on a specific date during the month, the amount of merchandise to be purchased during the remainder of the month. The remaining purchases are defined as open-to-buy. **Open-to-buy** is the amount the buyer has left to spend for a period, and it is reduced each time a purchase is made.

Open-to-Buy Calculations

Although the open-to-buy figures are not listed on the six-month merchandise plan, they are calculated using the planned purchases at cost.

Illustrative Problem

Based on the information in the table that follows, calculate open-to-buy.

Planned sales	$22,000
Planned BOM	$33,000
Planned reductions	$2,000
Planned EOM	$35,000
Stock on order at cost	$4,000
Initial markup percent	44.6%

Solution

Your first step is to calculate planned purchases at retail using the formula previously described:

**Planned purchases =
Planned sales + Planned EOM + Planned reductions – Planned BOM**

Thus:

$22,000 + $35,000 + $2,000 – $33,000 = $26,000

Then convert planned purchases at retail to planned purchases at cost as follows:

Planned purchases at cost = (100% Initial markup %) $\times$ Planned purchases at retail

Planned purchases at cost = (100% – 44.6%) $\times$ $26,000 Planned purchases at cost = $14,404

Next, determine open-to-buy:

$$\text{Open-to-buy} = \text{Planned purchases} - \text{Merchandise on order}$$
$$\text{Open-to-buy} = \$14{,}404 - \$4{,}000$$
$$\text{Open-to-buy} = \$10{,}404$$

Therefore, for the month given, the buyer would still have $10,404 to spend during the month.

Benefits and Uses of Open-to-Buy

The open-to-buy concept has two main goals. First, the buyer is assured that a specified relationship between stock on hand and planned sales is maintained. Second, buyers are able to determine how to adjust merchandise purchases to reflect changes in sales, reductions, and purchases. Open-to-buy allows you to determine if additional purchases during a period conform with the planned purchases for the period.

If effectively used, open-to-buy allows the buyer to:

- limit overbuying and underbuying;
- prevent loss of sales due to inadequate amount of stock;
- maintain purchases within budgeted limits;
- reduce markdowns;
- increase sales; and
- improve stock turnover.

Hold back purchase dollars to reorder fast-selling merchandise, to take advantage of off-price merchandise, or to sample new merchandise.

Open-to-buy can also be used to determine problem areas. The most common problem is the buyer being in an overbought position. For example, if the open-to-buy in dollars is less than what you need to offer an adequate assortment, you are **overbought** for that period. Being overbought usually results because you made inaccurate sales forecasts, which caused your planned purchases to be incorrect, or you failed to recognize sales or fashion trends and had the wrong merchandise in stock.

Being overbought usually increases markdowns, decreases maintained markups, decreases stock turnover, and decreases profit. If you find yourself in an overbought position, you may want to implement any of the following strategies:

- Analyze ways to increase sales through better training of salespeople, additional sales promotions, or moving merchandise on the sales floor.
- Increase the dollar amount of markdowns for the period, which should increase sales; however, keep in mind that changes in planned reductions will also cause other components of the merchandise plan to change.
- Cancel outstanding orders, if possible. However, you must realize that sometimes orders cannot be cancelled because of the sales contract the buyer has signed. Order cancellations also cause hard feelings to develop between the vendor and your store.
- Increase purchases because the original plan has proven to be inaccurate. Note that this might be a measure of last resort. New merchandise may be needed to generate sales.

Summary Points

- Buyers are responsible for providing the right merchandise, at the right place, at the right time, in the right quantities, and at the right price. To accomplish these goals, buyers must prepare merchandise plans (budgets) and assortment plans.

- Merchandise plans are developed using top-down planning, bottom-up planning, or a combination of both. Typically, merchandise plans are developed for a six-month period.

- Sales forecasting and stock planning are the key elements of merchandise plans. Sales forecasting involves examining past store records and current internal and external factors affecting sales. All other merchandising decisions are planned in relation to sales; therefore, if a sales forecast is in error, other decisions will be in error, too.

- Merchandise in stock must meet customer demand by offering customers variety. Yet stock levels must be small enough to ensure a reasonable return on the store's investment.

- The six-month merchandise plan is the tool used by buyers that translates profit objectives into a framework for merchandise planning and control.

- Successful merchandise planning should result in increased turnover, reduced dollar amount of markdowns, improved ability to maintain markups, maximized profits, and a minimum investment in inventory.

- Components of the six-month merchandise plan include sales, BOM inventory, EOM inventory, reductions, purchases at retail, and purchases at cost. The plan shows the buyer how much should be spent on new inventory purchases to achieve planned sales.

- Basic merchandise planning can be accomplished by developing a basic stock plan, which is used to determine the maximum amount of merchandise that must be on hand or on order at any reordering point.

- Buyers use merchandise plans and the amount of merchandise on order to determine open-to-buy, which is the amount of money the buyer has left to spend for a period, and is reduced each time a purchase is made.

Review Activities

Developing Your Retail Buying Vocabulary

Consult the glossary if you did not add the following terms to your vocabulary.

basic stock list	delivery period	open-to-buy	reserve
basic stock plan	EOM inventory	overbought	six-month merchandise plan
BOM inventory	maximum	reductions	top-down planning
bottom-up planning	merchandise plan	reorder period	

Understanding What You Read

1. What is the major benefit of top-down planning?

2. Why do many retailers use a combination of top-down and bottom-up planning?

3. List several internal and external factors that should be considered along with past sales records when you are forecasting sales.

4. On what will the accuracy of sales forecasts depend?

5. How will holidays affect merchandise planning from one year to the next?

6. For what two periods are six-month merchandise plans typically developed?

7. What is the purpose of "Revised (This Year)" on the six-month merchandise plan?

8. What is the first and most important calculation of the six-month merchandise plan?

9. How is planned EOM inventory on a six-month merchandise plan determined?

10. What are three types of reductions?

11. What is the drawback of lengthy periods between reorders of basic stock?

12. When would open-to-buy equal planned purchases at cost?

13. What would cause a buyer to be overbought?

Analyzing and Applying What You Read

1. Your store uses only top-down planning in developing merchandise plan goals. Outline arguments that you would use to convince top management to incorporate bottom-up planning in the process.

2. Your department is in an overbought position. What arguments could you use to make additional purchases?

Retail Buying Math Practice

1. Last quarter sales for a department were $78,000. Sales for each month in the quarter follow. Calculate the percentage of sales that occurred each month.

Month	Monthly Sales Last Year
January	$20,000
February	$23,000
March	$35,000

2. Your planned sales for the current quarter are $85,800. Using the monthly percentages of sales which follow, calculate the planned sales for each month of the current quarter.

Month	Monthly Percentage of Sales
January	30.5%
February	33.5%
March	36.0%

3. Your planned reductions for the current quarter are $8,000. Using the planned monthly reduction percentages that follow, calculate the dollar amount of planned reductions for each month of the current quarter.

Month	Monthly Reductions Percentage
January	50%
February	40%
March	10%

4. Your department uses an initial markup percentage of 47.2 percent. If your planned purchases at retail total $15,000, calculate your planned purchases at cost.

5. Your department uses an initial markup percentage of 50.0 percent. If your planned purchases at retail total $60,335, calculate your planned purchases at cost.

6. Prepare a six-month merchandise plan based on the information presented below. Planned sales are expected to be the same as last year.

Month	Last Year Monthly Sales	Last Year BOM Stock
February	$12,000	$25,000
March	$14,000	$30,000
April	$18,000	$38,000
May	$19,000	$40,000
June	$18,000	$39,000
July	$19,000	$41,000

a. Calculate last year's monthly stock-to-sales ratios and plan monthly BOM inventory levels.

b. Now, plan monthly reductions for the period. Reductions are planned at 8 percent and will be distributed as follows:

February	10%
March	5%
April	5%
May	15%
June	30%
July	35%

c. Next, plan monthly EOM stock for each month. Ending inventory for the season is planned at $43,000.

d. Now, plan purchases at retail. Then, convert this figure to cost. The initial markup percentage is planned at 46.4 percent.

7. A small business places reorders every two weeks. Once orders are placed, four weeks are typically required for delivery. The weekly sales rate of an item is 30. Calculate the maximum.

8. Planned purchases at cost for the month of February are $21,000. Two purchase orders are outstanding. The first is for $550, and the second is for $2,150. What is the open-to-buy?

9. Planned purchases for the month of March are $27,500. Three purchase orders are outstanding. The first is for $1,100, the second is for $20,000, and the third is for $6,600. What is the open-to-buy?

STUDiO

Spreadsheet Skills

Visit this book's STUDIO product at www.BloomsburyFashionCentral.com and open and print Assignment E. Then open file Spreadsheet E. Input formulas that will allow you to calculate planned sales, planned BOM, planned EOM, planned reductions, planned purchases at retail, and planned purchases at cost. Make the calculations requested and record your answers on the tables provided at the end of the assignment.

Internet Connection

1. Search the internet for sales predictions related to the upcoming holiday season. How do these predictions compare with previous forecasts?

2. Search the internet for recent retail sales by month (total retail sales or for a specific product category). Calculate the percentage increase or decrease from month to month.

3. Visit the book's STUDIO to watch videos about how retailers use planning to develop their strategies.

SNAPSHOT: RMSA: Turning Numbers into Actions

RMSA, a merchandising information consultant, provides sophisticated planning and management information services to independent retailers nationwide. The firm also develops and markets management information systems specifically designed for the retailing industry with the objective of solving problems, increasing the quality of merchandise inventory decisions, and improving the financial performance of its clients.

RMSA has developed highly automated and integrated systems to assist retailers in planning, monitoring, and making decisions related to merchandise management. To assist in making these forecasts, RMSA has created a retail database that combines more than sixty years of historical merchandising data with the intelligence necessary to offer planning services customized to the individual store location, type, and size.

RMSA has developed a strong reputation in the retailing industry and is an acknowledged industry leader in fashion merchandise planning and management information services, providing services to thousands of clients throughout the United States. Their client base also includes specialty and general merchandise stores.

The mission of RMSA is to help their clients get on the best path to maximum growth and profits. They promise their clients not to bury them with mind-numbing data. Rather, they provide merchandise action plans so that clients can make timely decisions.

To accomplish these goals, RMSA begins by learning all about a client's business—their brand, their markets, their customer profiles, and the product classifications being sold. Once that information is gathered and analyzed, actual sales, buying, and inventory information is collected monthly through the client's POS (point-of-sale) system.

Planning reports are then generated that turn these numbers into metrics that can be used for day-to-day management, such as open-to-buy, red-flag areas requiring more analysis, and mid-month planning updates. Forecasts are also generated for sales, inventories, recommended markdowns, and receipts. These reports alert clients as to where their attention needs to be focused in order to maximize cash flow, improve retail operations, and increase store profitability.

Forecasts are continuously refreshed based on monthly updates from the client's POS systems. They receive trending reports and mid-month updates that analyze performance against plan. Special alerts will identify exceptions that need management attention, such as overstocks, lost sales due to inventory shortages, cash flow issues, and underperforming classifications. Clients can also access software that allows them to ask "what if." They can test different planning scenarios that would impact their merchandising decisions.

Typically, RMSA clients have maintained higher margins compared with the industry. Using the system, retailers have been able to manage data more quickly and efficiently, allowing them to turn inventory at rates twice as fast as the industry average.

Buyers and merchandisers at independent retail stores may certainly want to consider RMSA or similar services before they begin merchandise planning. Small independents must constantly be alert to merchandising techniques that will allow them to successfully compete with larger retailers in their market.

BASED ON:

RMSA.com (2017).

MERCHANDISE PLANNING: TAKING THE HOLIDAY PULSE

Each year, one of the key components of merchandise planning for retailers is forecasting holiday sales during the fourth quarter; many retailers count on this quarter for as much as half the year's profit. Several factors influence holiday shopping, including gasoline prices, high debt, and slow income growth. Moreover, if household debt is high and real disposable income growth slows, some consumers will have less to spend. Consumer confidence in the economy is another factor that influences retail sales. However, even when faced with many of these problems, consumers have been fairly resilient. They have taken a number of economic challenges in their stride and have continued purchasing during the holidays, although at a reduced level.

Each year buyers and forecasters grapple with predictions about what shoppers will do during this critical period. They usually are faced with how to interpret mixed signals from consumers and the economy. Many years, indicators are all over the board. Job growth could be good, but retail sales could be only so-so during September and October. Consumer confidence could be high, but perhaps it has fallen slightly since the summer. The Dow Jones average could be diving and could shake consumer confidence. Often, buyers must build their merchandise plans based on murky conditions such as these.

Buyers can also examine consumer polls, and there are dozens during this time of the year. Often, even these poll results add to the uncertainty. For example, one year the International Mass Retail Association predicted spending would jump 7 percent from the previous year. At the same time, a *Money*/ABC poll reported that the majority of consumers would spend about the same as the previous year, but that a lack of confidence in the economy could cause them to scale back their purchasing. And, the National Retail Federation was predicting that consumer spending would follow the previous year's patterns.

Retail analyst firms, such as PricewaterhouseCoopers, also issue predictions each year. Many retail buyers closely monitor forecasts from Visa because that company processes $17 out of every $100 spent in the United States by the firm's 500 million credit card holders.

With such mixed messages, retail buyers must make their own predictions about holiday sales. In fact, some stores may experience much higher or lower growth than predicted for the entire industry. Predictions for better merchandise planning can be based on local consumer surveys. A question such as "Approximately how much will your household spend in total on gifts this holiday season?" can be followed by "Is this more, less, or about the same amount of money your household spent in total on gifts last holiday season?" Then with the amount of change, predictions can be made about local sales for the season. Similar questions can also be geared toward specific product categories.

Analyzing responses to questions such as these enables retail buyers to develop merchandise plans based on customer input. Along with national or regional predictions, buyers can then make better forecasts. Forecasting holiday sales either too high or too low can result in problems for the retailer. Merchandise planning that results in overbuying results in heavy markdowns and promotions to move excess inventories. If these plans result in underbuying, potential sales and profits will be lost. More than likely, it will be too late to place reorders for that season.

Buyers must use as many tools as possible in taking the pulse of consumers before the holiday season begins. Their decisions will have a critical impact on the store's profitability for the year.

BASED ON:

Farnham, Alan. (2013, September 18). Holiday sales forecasts: Black magic or science? *ABCnews.go.com*.

Mullaney, Tim. (2013, November 29). Will holiday sales herald better 2014 economy? *USAToday.com*.

NRF cuts retail sales growth forecast for 2014. (2014, July 23). *CNBC.com*.

Sherman, Erik. (2013, October 3). Holiday sales forecast: Lukewarm (unless you're Amazon). *Inc.com*.

DEVELOPING ASSORTMENT PLANS

Performance Objectives

- Identify the purposes of assortment planning.
- Describe how assortment planning differs by product categories.
- Describe how store policies affect assortment planning.
- Differentiate between stock breadth and stock depth.
- Explain how to determine when a product line should be expanded.
- Describe merchandise classification systems.
- Identify key merchandise selection factors used by consumers when purchasing merchandise.
- Explain how model stock plans are developed.
- Prepare an assortment plan.

The merchandising decisions related to product assortments that buyers make will have a strong impact on whether the store projects the desired image and attracts consumers in the identified target market. In fact, assortment planning decisions will have a strong impact on the store's overall performance.

Because no one retailer can provide all the product choices that are available in the marketplace to its customers, buyers must make decisions about which items to carry. In addition, most products will be available in a wide selection of options such as models, colors, and styles. Buyers will have to make those choices when deciding what to offer their customers. Merchandise selection should not be left to chance; it requires a careful analysis of (1) your store's goals and objectives, (2) types of products offered, (3) past sales records, (4) target market, and (5) other internal and external factors likely to affect sales.

In the previous chapter, you learned how a merchandise buying plan was developed. This dollar plan must be translated into a specific assortment plan of merchandise. In this chapter, you will learn how merchandise assortments are planned. Factors affecting merchandise assortments will be examined, and merchandise classification systems will be described.

PLANNING MERCHANDISE ASSORTMENTS

Buyers want to have enough products to meet customer demand without having to take markdowns because of having excess inventory. Maintaining such a balanced inventory requires skill and experience and takes considerable planning. As a buyer, you must prepare a detailed assortment plan for each item that you will be purchasing. You must also work within the framework established by your merchandise plan because quantity purchases for all items of merchandise must not exceed your dollar plan. Comprehensive and detailed assortment plans will also provide you with a merchandising control tool that can be used with the buying plan to help calculate your open-to-buy.

Assortment planning involves determining the specific quantities and characteristics of each product that you will be purchasing in relation to specific factors such as brands, colors, sizes, and materials. Figure 9.1 illustrates assortment planning for men's polo shirts. You must develop an assortment plan that best matches the needs of your customers without having an excess amount of inventory in stock. Assortment plans must be developed for all types of merchandise. For example, men's shirts can be purchased in many colors, sizes, sleeve lengths, materials, and styles.

The goal of assortment planning is to maintain a balanced assortment of merchandise that will meet the needs of as many customers as possible; therefore, an understanding of the various types of customers served by your store or department is essential to merchandise planning. Reliance on past sales records alone will be impractical for developing assortment plans for fashion merchandise because trends are volatile and

Figure 9.1
Assortment plans involve purchasing products of different brands, colors, sizes, and materials.

change quickly. Changing consumer interests and buying habits must be analyzed using trade papers, trade association information, reporting services, and consultations with fashion coordinators and manufacturers.

Assortment planning also forces you to make plans based on the floor or shelf space available for the merchandise. In most instances, you will not have the space to carry the entire assortment of every product available. For example, supermarkets used to carry only Coke, Pepsi, and several other flavors of soft drinks. Today, however, each of these brands is available in sugar-free, sweetened with cane sugar, and caffeine-free varieties, just to list a few. In addition, they are available in an assortment of many different sizes and containers. Most grocery store managers are not able to offer the entire assortment of all soft drinks available on the market.

Continuously increasing the number of items in a product assortment presents a major problem to retailers. Rarely will the product category be given more floor or shelf space when new varieties of the product are introduced; therefore, smaller quantities of each item must be purchased, which increases the likelihood of stockouts.

FACTORS AFFECTING MERCHANDISE ASSORTMENTS

When planning merchandise assortments, you will want to provide a variety of merchandise that is best suited to your customers' needs and is consistent with your store's image. As you develop the assortment plan, several key factors must be considered. They include (1) type of merchandise carried, (2) store policies, and (3) variety of merchandise available.

Type of Merchandise

The type of merchandise your store or department carries will affect your assortment planning. As you have learned, many methods are used to categorize merchandise, and each one requires the development of a different type of assortment plan.

Fashion or Basic Merchandise

Merchandise can be grouped into two broad classifications—fashion or basic. Fashion merchandise has high demand over a relatively short period of time, usually a season. Appeal for fashion merchandise is limited, which causes customer demand to end abruptly. To maximize sales, fashion buyers must quickly identify "best sellers" in their merchandise assortments and place reorders immediately. As the selling season progresses, few or no reorders should be placed. Customer demand could end quickly, leaving the store in an overstocked position, and then even substantial markdowns may not move unwanted merchandise. Read the Snapshot titled "Fashion Forecasting: Doneger Creative Services" to learn more about how buyers forecast new fashions.

Basic merchandise includes items that customers buy year in and year out and expect the store to have in stock at all times. For example, nails, hammers, stationery, men's white shirts, sheets, socks, and thousands of other items are considered basic merchandise items.

Buying basic merchandise is accomplished rather easily by checking past sales records and determining sales trends from previous years. Buyers know there is little danger of basic merchandise items not selling, so there is less likelihood of overbuying merchandise that will not sell, but if these items remain in stock too long, they will become shopworn. With basic merchandise items, the size of your assortment will be limited by the selling space and storage space that you have available.

Some basic merchandise items may be classified as **seasonal basics**—products desired by customers only during certain times of the year. Customer demand, however, is fairly consistent from one year to the next. Examples of seasonal staples would include Easter egg dye, Christmas ornaments, kites, overcoats, and swimwear (Figure 9.2). Planning for seasonal basics requires that you keep precise records for the period in which these items sell and clearly identify the length of the selling period. Without planning, you will probably become overstocked and not sell out of inventory when the season is over.

Planning and control are essential for both fashion and basic merchandise. However, fashion goods must be monitored more frequently than basic goods. Fashion merchandise is usually surveyed on a weekly basis, whereas basic merchandise does not require such frequent attention.

Convenience or Specialty Products

Convenience goods are items that customers expect the store to have readily available. These items are usually inexpensive and may include products such as candy, hardware, health and beauty aids, and stationery. For convenience goods, a large assortment is usually not required because most customers will make a purchase regardless of which brand is available.

Specialty goods are products that customers will usually accept only in well-known brands. Examples of specialty goods could include silverware, china, appliances, designer apparel, and cosmetics. You will want to identify the brand loyalty of your customers and determine which brands are demanded by the majority of your customers as well as which brands are substitutable for others in the customer's mind.

Figure 9.2
The selling season for some products is so short that buyers may not be able to place a reorder.

Store Policies

Store management is responsible for establishing and specifying merchandising policies that best serve the interests and preferences of your store's target customers. These policies will serve as guidelines as you develop and maintain merchandise assortment plans and will affect the quality, exclusivity, and brands of your purchases.

Quality and Price Range

Purchasing decisions throughout the store should be implemented to create the desired store image and attract the target customers that have been identified by management. If quality is a strong appeal to your target customers, store policies should be developed to bring into the store only products constructed from the best materials available. If your customers are more price conscious, the highest-quality materials may not be as important as providing products in the desired price ranges.

Price range and quality usually are related to each other; however, many times there is no specific correlation between the two. Because your store cannot offer merchandise at all price ranges, you must determine which price ranges will be demanded by the majority of your customers.

Exclusivity

Many buyers will add products to their assortments that will not be available at other stores in their trading area because many customers prefer shopping at stores that have the reputation for carrying exclusives. You may negotiate with suppliers to be the only outlet for an item, or you can ensure exclusivity by carrying private brands. Obviously, exclusivity is desired by most stores because their image tends to be enhanced.

Brands

Store policies will also determine the mix of national and private brand names from which you can select. Many stores today, such as Dillard's and Macy's, are offering a mix of national brands and private brands; other stores, such as Gap and H&M, offer only private-brand merchandise. In most product classifications, national brands dominate sales, and because of national advertising support, they are better known to customers. In fact, many customers are presold on nationally advertised merchandise before they enter the store. In addition, national brands represent quality to many customers.

On the other hand, private brands are usually more profitable to retailers because they have more control over merchandising decisions related to the products. Private brands are less expensive than national brands, and store loyalty is guaranteed because the competition will not have the product. Retailers, however, must create their own promotional plans for private brands.

Generics is another brand classification that may be found at some stores. **Generic brands** are usually unbranded items in plain packages that receive secondary shelf locations and obtain little or no advertising support. The advantage for the customer is that generics are priced well below other brands; however, for many customers a question remains about the quality of these brands. Most retailers, however, have moved away from generic brands in favor of private brands, which generate more customer loyalty.

Variety of Merchandise Available

Within the constraints of a specified dollar investment in inventory, you must offer a variety of merchandise by carrying a number of different product lines. A **product line** is a broad category of products having similar characteristics and similar uses. Liz Claiborne and Ralph Lauren are both well-known apparel lines that offer many different items, all carrying the same label. Over the past few years, there has been a rapid increase in the number of product lines as well as the number of products within existing product lines, making merchandise selection more complex. Rarely will any store be able to offer all the available choices within a product line, but in some instances, the manufacturer may require that your store carry a full product line if its merchandise is to be sold in your store.

In relation to the product lines carried, you must also make two decisions:

- What will be the stock breadth?
- What will be the stock depth?

Breadth

Breadth relates to the number of product lines carried or the number of brands carried within a product classification. The breadth of your stock can usually be described as narrow, broad, or somewhere in between. For example, one store may offer four brands of men's dress shirts (broad breadth), whereas another store may offer only one brand (narrow breadth). Broad stock breadth allows the retailer to appeal to a larger market, but a narrow stock breadth usually allows the store to offer fewer brands in a larger number of styles, colors, sizes, and materials.

Depth

The number of choices offered customers within each brand or product classification is known as **depth**. Many stores emphasize large stocks of a few product categories or brands. Stores find such assortment plans easier to stock, and customers are more likely to find what they want in the products offered for sale; however, customers are not offered a wide selection of brands, which may cause some of them to go to a competitor's store. Such an assortment would be described as a **narrow and deep** assortment plan (Figure 9.3).

On the other hand, stores may offer wide stock breadth and very little depth—a **broad and shallow** assortment plan. This would be the case for a men's clothing store that offers several brands of men's shirts, all of which are either blue or white.

A **balanced assortment** occurs when the breadth and depth meet the demands of your customers. Broad assortment plans are usually offered early in the season when new styles are being tested for customer acceptance. A broad and shallow assortment plan gives you the opportunity to experiment with several brands without making a heavy financial commitment. As customer demand becomes more clearly defined during the selling season, the assortment is likely to become narrow and deep.

Customers also vary in the amount of merchandise they want to examine before making a purchase. Some of them may know exactly what item they want, whereas other consumers may want to view many similar items before making a purchase.

Some types of merchandise, such as apparel, require that the store carry a wide variety. Customers who are more fashion conscious require a wide choice.

Unbalanced assortment plans must be corrected as soon as possible to improve the overall performance of your store or department. You must ensure that an adequate product assortment is stocked and inventory shortages are minimized. While furthering the goals of your store, your assortment plan must satisfy customers. Most retailers have the tendency to stock too many similar brands and classifications. When one item is a substitute for another, there usually is no need to stock both.

To satisfy your customers and remain ahead of your competition, new products must be continuously added to your assortment while others are deleted. As you add items to the assortment, some goods will probably have to be eliminated from your stock because of limited floor space. Product lines will also need to be eliminated before they become obsolete or outdated.

You can increase stock breadth by adding other product lines or additional items in an existing product line; however, new products may divert sales from your present assortment. **Cannibalization** occurs when potential sales of existing products are lost to new items. A careful evaluation of sales is required if product variety is increased to determine if total sales increased and if profits rose. For example, carrying five classifications of a product will not necessarily yield greater sales or profits than stocking three varieties. Carrying too many classifications would probably result in a shallow assortment offered for each product that could result in stockouts.

MERCHANDISE CLASSIFICATIONS

Every retail store is filled with a wide variety of merchandise in many different varieties. A merchandise classification system is needed to provide the means for better planning and control of this inventory.

Classifications and Subclassifications

Most retailers group the merchandise they carry into **classifications**, which refer to the particular kinds of goods in a store or department. For example, the shoe department could carry men's and women's shoes. Each of these broad product categories could be further divided into **subclassifications**. Table 9.1, for example, illustrates how men's shoes could be broken down into dress shoes, casual shoes, athletic shoes, work shoes, and boots, and subclassifications can also be developed for each of these categories. In the men's shoe category, athletic shoes could be classified as running shoes, court shoes, or cleated shoes. The type and size of your store or department, the image you

---

TABLE 9.1

EXAMPLES OF SHOE CLASSIFICATIONS

Men's Shoes	*Women's Shoes*
Dress Shoes	**Evening Shoes**
Oxfords	High Heels
Slip-ons	Medium Heels
Casual Shoes	Low Heels
Oxfords	**Dress Shoes**
Slip-ons	High Heels
Athletic Shoes	Medium Heels
Running Shoes	Low Heels
Court Shoes	**Tailored Shoes**
Cleated Shoes	High Heels
Work Shoes	Medium Heels
Regular Toe	Low Heels
Steel Toe	Wedge Heels
Boots	**Casual Shoes**
Dress Boots	Medium Heels
Casual Boots	Low Heels
Western Boots	Wedge Heels
Weather Boots	**Dress Sandals**
Work Boots	High Heels
	Medium Heels
	Casual Sandals
	Medium Heels
	Low Heels
	Fashion Flats
	Fashion Boots
	Weather Boots
	Duty Boots
	Athletic Shoes
	Slippers

---

want to project, your target market, and the financial resources available will all affect the number of classifications and subclassifications needed. For example, the variety and assortment of shoes would be much greater in a department that caters only to one specific group of customers. Departments carrying shoes for men, women, and children would not be able to offer a complete assortment in each category. As each classification is planned, it must be large enough to develop a separate assortment plan; otherwise, it should be labeled a subclassification of a broader merchandise classification.

For merchandising and control purposes, each classification and subclassification is usually assigned an identification number. The National Retail Federation has developed a **standard classification of merchandise** coding system that classifies merchandise using four-digit codes.

Each classification code is divided into subclassifications. For example, 1000 is the code for adult female apparel, which is subdivided into other areas, such as these:

1100	Cloth and All-Weather Coats
1200	Natural and Synthetic Leather and Fur Outerwear
1300	Women's, Misses, and Juniors' Dresses and Suits
1400	Formals
1500	Bridal, Maternity, and Uniforms
1600	Sportswear Tops

Each of these subclassifications can be further subdivided. For example, code 1600 (Sportswear Tops) can be broken down as follows:

1611	Skirts
1612	Blouses
1613	Cut and Sewn Knit Tops
1614	Sweaters

This coding system has not yet become universally accepted, but the concept has had great impact on the way retailers arrange inventory data and maintain inventory counts.

Closely associated with merchandise classifications is unit control, an inventory control system that tracks the movement of specific units of merchandise. Unit control information is essential to assortment planning. By using detailed inventory information, you can readily achieve a balance between sales and inventory in stock. Analysis of unit control records will also enable you to decide which items in the merchandise assortment to increase, eliminate, or reprice. Classifying merchandise and maintaining a unit control system also gives you the ability to make comparisons with other stores.

As a buyer, you should monitor the merchandise classification system used by your store to determine whether it continues to meet your needs and the needs of your customers. Frequently ask yourself, "Does the classification system reflect the way in which my customers buy merchandise?"

Selection Factors

Each subclassification of merchandise can also be broken down by various **selection factors**, which are product characteristics most important to your customers as they make their purchasing decisions. Usually, a customer's purchase is based on a combination of characteristics such as brand, price, size, color, and material. Characteristics important to the purchase of a product will differ depending on the product type and the target market. For example, when buying a tennis racquet, a customer may be interested only in brand and price; however, when buying a suit, the same customer may be interested in brand, price, size, color, and material. In addition, there may be other important product characteristics to consider. For example, when purchasing a new suit, styling may be important to the customer: "Is it double-breasted?" or "Is there a vented or nonvented back?"

You must identify the selection factors that are most important as customers purchase each item of merchandise that you stock. Your merchandise buying plan can also be used to determine the number of selection factors that can be represented in your assortment plan. For example, budgets may limit the number of brands you will be able to offer as well as the variety of each brand. Key selection factors that will be examined include (1) brand, (2) price, (3) size, (4) color, and (5) material.

Brand

You must determine if your customers exhibit brand loyalty when they purchase specific products. For example, do most of your customers ask to see lawn mowers or do they ask specifically to see John Deere mowers? If most of your customers are not brand loyal, you will not need to offer a broad selection of brands; you will be able to develop a wide assortment for one or two brands. In other words, you will be able to offer many more colors, sizes, models, or styles when only a few brands are offered. Stores carrying a large number of brands of each product type will probably have to limit the selection offered in each one.

Price

If one product classification has appeal to several income ranges, you will need to offer variations of that product at more than one price. Most retailers attempt to offer goods to customers in several different price ranges. The brands that you have selected to carry will also determine the price lines that would be available.

Some retailers offer several price lines at the beginning of a season and eliminate lines as the season progresses. Customers for higher-priced merchandise tend to buy in the early part of the season, and customers become less discriminating as the season advances. Customers at the end of the season are also more price conscious and are looking for lower-priced merchandise.

Size

For most products, size will also be an important selection factor. Size is not just important in apparel; size decisions must be made for home furnishings such as curtains and window treatments, appliances such as refrigerators, and even food packages. Product choices will confront you in almost all product categories. Table 9.2 illustrates

TABLE 9.2

ASSORTMENT PLAN BY SELECTION FACTORS FOR WINDOW BLINDS

Width	Lengths			
	42″	50″	64″	72″
17″	9.99			
23″	14.99		17.49	18.99
24″	14.99			17.99
25″			18.49	
26″	15.49		18.99	
27″			19.49	19.99
28″				19.99
29″	15.99		20.99	21.99
30″			21.49	22.99
31″	16.49		21.99	22.99
32″			21.99	23.99
33″			22.49	24.99
34″			22.99	25.49
35″	17.49	18.49	22.99	25.99
36″	18.99	19.99	25.49	27.99

size and price breakdowns for one brand of window blinds. Notice how the assortment is planned to include only the most popular sizes.

Size decisions for a product classification are based almost entirely on past records. Size requirements for customers remain fairly consistent from one period to another, and the size distribution of products sold during the past season is usually an indication of future demand. However, over a period of years, size requirements may change. For example, the average weight of women over age thirty has increased five pounds over the past ten years, which has affected the sizes required for many customers. Read the Trendwatch titled "All Shapes and Sizes: The Plus-Size Market Continues to Grow" to learn more about how the needs of this market are being met by retailers.

Color

You must also decide if color is an important consideration when your customers make purchases. You will need to decide which colors will be most important in the new season because you will be unable to offer all available colors. Nor can you simply buy colors that sold well in the past; fashion colors change from one season to the next. However, knowing past sales by color allows you to determine the degree to which your customers were fashion conscious when they accepted fashion colors in the past.

Before selecting colors, you will want to study current fashion trends, contact buying offices, and consult with your merchandise manager and the store's fashion coordinator. You must choose colors that complement the store's total "look" and that can be coordinated with other products offered for sale. You should never overstock fashion colors and neglect basic, more conventional colors. Even with fashion merchandise, basic colors usually account for a majority of sales.

Material

Knowledge of past sales will also help you determine the material in which products should be stocked. For example, handbags may be offered in leather or vinyl. Shirts may be 100 percent cotton or a polyester/cotton blend. Luggage is also constructed of many different materials. In fact, almost every product is available in a number of different materials; however, if you are offering a wide selection of brands, sizes, and colors, you may not be able to offer customers a selection of material.

Let us examine how one retailer has implemented a merchandise assortment plan. One national men's clothing store chain offers three broad classifications of merchandise—suits, sports coats and slacks, and accessories (underwear, hosiery, shirts, and ties). Suits account for about 55 percent of its business and are available in three fashion categories in sizes ranging from 36S to 50XL. Fashion categories include (1) traditional American styling, (2) the international collection (nonvented coats with lower gorge and button stance), and (3) the British collection, featuring squared-off, pitched shoulders with either center or side vents.

Each of the three looks is available in two levels of quality/price—the top-of-the-line premier edition and the private store label. The top-of-the-line premier edition suits are 100 percent wool, fully lined, with piping, cigarette pocket, passport pocket, shirt-hugger bands with brace buttons, and pants lined to the knees. The premier label also includes another tier with identical features except the fabric is a poly/wool blend. The private-label suits are primarily poly/wool blends, with piping, fully lined coats, and pants lined to the knee. Some basic suits in this category round out the line of suits available.

All retail stores must offer a balanced merchandise assortment that will meet the needs of the majority of their customers and that is based on a thorough understanding of customer needs. When customers enter a store or go online to shop and cannot find exactly the item they want in the right size, color, or material, they have made a frustrating and fruitless shopping trip. The retailer has also lost an almost-certain sale by not having a balanced merchandise assortment.

PREPARING AN ASSORTMENT PLAN

Because customers buy specific items of merchandise, dollar merchandise plans must be translated into some form of unit assortment plan. When you plan unit assortments, it is not a randomly selected collection of merchandise. Assortments of merchandise are balanced to customer needs while being bound by the financial constraints of the merchandise buying plan.

Assortment planning will result in establishing a **model stock**, the desired assortment of stock broken down according to factors important to your target market, such as brand, price, material, color, and size. When developing model stocks, you should be guided by current trends as well as by previous sales in order to purchase the goods that seem to best fit the needs of your store's customers. The objective of establishing a model stock is to maximize the sales and profits from your inventory investment.

Furthermore, a model stock does not have to be rigidly followed during the selling season. The plan should serve only as a guide because demand in regard to various selection factors will vary during the season. Adjustments are frequently made once the selling season is under way; reorders also change the nature of the model stock. Fashion buyers cannot be as specific as other buyers when developing model stocks. Dress buyers, for example, go to market knowing they can buy so many dozen dresses at the $59.99 range in assorted sizes. They do not determine other specifics, such as colors and styles, until they view the suppliers' offerings.

After you have determined the budget for merchandise purchases and examined store records, trends, and external factors affecting sales, you are ready to prepare an assortment plan; this can be achieved using the following steps.

Step 1

Decide what general classifications of products your store or department will carry. For example, you may decide to sell men's, women's, and children's apparel. You would then divide these classifications into subclassifications. For example, men's apparel could be broken down into suits, sports coats, blazers, neckwear, and so forth. By answering these questions, you will have determined the breadth of your product assortment. Examine Table 9.3 for a detailed list of other possible subclassifications for apparel.

TABLE 9.3

EXAMPLES OF APPAREL MERCHANDISE CLASSIFICATIONS

Men's Wear	Women's Wear	Children's Wear
Suits	Misses Dresses	Infant and Layette
Sports Coats	Junior Dresses	Toddler Boy
Blazers	Petite Dresses	Toddler Girl
Dress Slacks	After-Five Dresses	Girls Tops and Bottoms
Casual Slacks	Blouses	Girls Jeans
Top and Raincoats	Knit Tops	Boys Tops
Dress Shirts	Novelty Tops	Boys Pants and Jeans
Jackets	Sweaters	Boys Suits and Sports
Sweaters	Skirts	Coats
Sports Shirts and	Pants	Activewear
Knit Shirts	Shorts	Outerwear
Neckwear	Blazers	Swimwear
Underwear and	Swimwear	Sleepwear and
Hosiery	Activewear	Underwear
Belts	Suits	Accessories
Swimwear	Coats	
Shorts	Jackets	
	Lingerie	
	Sleepwear	
	Handbags	

Step 2

Determine the brands and price lines that you will carry for each of these subclassifications. Knowing characteristics of your target market is vital. You must know the brand preferences of your customers for each brand carried, and you will need to decide on the price lines that will be most appealing to your customers.

Step 3

Next, identify all the general characteristics of an item that customers may consider when purchasing it. For example, sweatshirts may be available in different colors, sizes, materials, and styles. Men's dress shirts have different colors, sizes, sleeve lengths, and collar styles and are made with different materials. The assortment plan that you develop should allow you to make purchases according to the most important of these characteristics in relation to the majority of your customers.

You cannot and do not need to plan for every possible customer; therefore, select major characteristics that present a balanced assortment. Your budget will also determine the breadth and depth of the assortment that you will be able to offer. For example, it would be possible to stock men's dress shirts from a size 14 neck to a size 27. However, the bulk of sales will be made at around size 151/2.

Step 4

Now you must decide on the proportion of one classification to another. In addition, you must determine the proportion in which each selection factor will be represented in your stock. For example, not all sizes or colors will have the same rate of sale. Nor will each color be equally popular in every size that is manufactured. For some selection factors, such as size, these proportions can be calculated by using past sales figures. For others, such as color, you will need to know how readily your customers accept new fashion colors as they are introduced.

Step 5

Calculate the specific number of units to purchase. Let's examine a problem that illustrates how an assortment plan is prepared.

Illustrative Problem

Assume that your department is selling sweatshirts. From market research you realize that most of your customers for this product are not brand loyal. They will substitute one brand for another if you have the right size, color, and style they are looking for. Past sales records indicate that Russell has been the most popular brand with your customers, and your merchandise buying plan indicates that you have $3,000 to spend on sweatshirts for the coming season. If you decide to stock only Russell sweatshirts costing $10 each, you will be able to purchase 300 sweatshirts. You must then calculate the specific unit breakdowns of these sweatshirts.

Russell has these sweatshirts in sizes from extra small to extra-extra large in twenty different colors. They also are available in 100 percent cotton or a polyester/cotton blend. Hooded and nonhooded sweatshirts are also available.

By examining past sales records, you determine that the size distribution of your customers has been as follows:

Small	15%
Medium	20%
Large	45%
X-Large	20%

Basic colors of white and gray have been your best sellers in the past, accounting for 20 percent and 35 percent of sales, respectively. Black has been a good seller too, with 15 percent of sales. You decide to supplement these three colors with two other colors (green and garnet) that are predicted to be very fashionable for the fall. Each of these will represent 15 percent of your assortment plan.

Solution

At this point, you decide to calculate the number of sweatshirts that you will purchase for each of the sizes and colors selected:

Size	Number	Color	Number
Small	45	White	9
		Gray	16
		Black	7
		Green	7
		Garnet	7
Medium	60	White	12
		Gray	21
		Black	9
		Green	9
		Garnet	9
Large	135	White	27
		Gray	47
		Black	20
		Green	20
		Garnet	20
X-Large	60	White	12
		Gray	21
		Black	9
		Green	9
		Garnet	9

Note: The number of sweatshirts purchased has been rounded. Forty-six small can be purchased, but only 134 large; however, the total order of 300 sweatshirts remains the same.

After reviewing these figures, you decide to offer only hooded, 100 percent cotton sweatshirts. If you had broken the assortment down by offering both hooded and nonhooded, and all cotton and cotton/polyester blends, you would not have been able to offer an adequate number of many of the sizes and colors. For example, if you had decided to offer each color in a breakdown of 80 percent nonhooded and 20 percent hooded, and 60 percent all cotton and 40 percent blends, you would be offering only one or two of some types, as the following chart illustrates:

Small Garnet	Material	Style
7	4 (all cotton)	3 (nonhooded)
	3 (poly/cotton blend)	1 (hooded)
		2 (nonhooded)
		1 (hooded)

As this example shows, you would be purchasing only one small, garnet, hooded sweatshirt made of 100 percent cotton and only one small, garnet, hooded sweatshirt made of a poly/cotton blend. Once these sweatshirts were sold, your assortment would be depleted in those areas. As you can see, offering too many selection factors makes buying much more complex. In addition, more frequent reordering would be necessary.

As you prepare your assortment plan, be sure to carry brands for which there is adequate customer demand and carry a complete assortment of these brands. Attempting to offer an assortment plan with too much depth in relation to your merchandise budget will result in stockouts and dissatisfied customers. Determining the assortment plan that best meets your customers' needs is not a simple matter; it will require exhaustive research and analysis of past records and current trends.

Summary Points

- Assortment planning requires working within the framework established by the merchandise buying plan.

- Assortment planning must be based on attracting a specific target market and projecting the desired store image. Floor or shelf space available in the store will also affect assortment planning.

- Assortment plans will vary by types of merchandise. Assortment plans for fashion merchandise must be monitored on a frequent basis, whereas assortments of basic merchandise can be surveyed less frequently.

- The variety of merchandise available will also affect assortment plans. Many manufacturers offer product lines with a wide variety of options, whereas others offer only limited choices.

- For each product category, buyers must determine the assortment's breadth and depth.

- Assortments may be offered in either a broad and shallow or a narrow and deep plan.

- For fashion merchandise, buyers test the market early in the selling season by offering a broad and shallow assortment. As customer demand becomes more clearly defined during the selling season, the assortment is likely to become narrow and deep.

- Merchandise offered by retailers can be grouped into classifications and further subdivided into subclassifications. These breakdowns assist the retailer in maintaining inventory control records and in making comparisons with other stores.

- Each item of merchandise can be described in terms of selection factors. The most common selection factors include brand, price, size, color, and material.

- Assortment planning involves developing a model stock for the store that serves as a guide to the buyer, who must monitor the market to detect changes in customer tastes and needs and make adjustments in the assortment plan as needed.

Review Activities

Developing Your Retail Buying Vocabulary

Consult the glossary if you did not add the following terms to your vocabulary.

assortment planning	cannibalization	model stock	selection factors
balanced assortment	classification	narrow and deep	standard classification of
breadth	depth	product line	merchandise
broad and shallow	generic brands	seasonal basic	subclassification

Understanding What You Read

1. What is the goal of assortment planning?

2. Why is relying on past sales records not practical for fashion merchandise?

3. How does assortment planning differ between convenience and specialty goods?

4. What are the benefits of offering national brands as part of a store's merchandise assortment?

5. What is the benefit of offering a wider stock breadth?

6. What are the benefits and drawbacks of offering a narrow stock breadth?

7. Why would a store selling trendy fashions probably offer a broad and shallow assortment at the beginning of a selling season?

8. When would increasing product lines not be practical for a store?

9. What are the benefits of implementing a merchandise classification system?

10. Describe the relationship of unit control and merchandise classification systems.

11. How does a buyer determine which selection factors to use when developing an assortment plan?

12. How does a store usually determine the size distribution of an assortment plan?

13. Describe how a fashion buyer would select the colors for a new assortment plan.

14. What are the objectives of establishing a model stock plan?

15. Why is more frequent reordering required as more selection factors are represented in an assortment plan?

Analyzing and Applying What You Read

1. For one of the apparel merchandise classifications presented in Table 9.3, develop a list of possible subclassifications. For each subclassification, identify the selection factors that would be important to a customer.

2. Select one item that can be found at a store that sells home furnishings or hardware. For that item, identify major brands and price ranges. Then, identify other selection factors that customers would consider before purchasing the item. Discuss whether most retailers would be able to offer a product assortment that would match all the selection factors for this product.

Retail Buying Math Practice

1. You have a budget to purchase 1,000 sweatshirts for your department. Based on last year's sales, you have compiled the percentage of planned sales that you will need to purchase for each color that follows. Calculate the number of sweatshirts in each color that you will purchase.

Color	Percentage of Total Purchases
Black	50%
White	20%
Gray	20%
Brown	10%

2. As part of your assortment plan, you have determined that you need to calculate how many of each size you will need for each color in your plan. You have enough funds budgeted to purchase 500 black sweatshirts. Based on the size distribution percentages that follow, calculate the number of black sweatshirts that you will purchase in each size category.

Size	Distribution Percentage
Small	10%
Medium	20%
Large	50%
X-Large	0%

3. You have the budget to purchase 100 sweatshirts for your store. All the sweatshirts will be purchased from Hanes for $12 each. The distribution of sizes will be as follows:

Small	12%
Medium	28%
Large	32%
X-Large	20%
XX-Large	8%

a. Four colors will be represented in the assortment as follows:

Red	25%
Blue	25%
White	25%
Black	25%

b. One-third of the assortment will be hooded, and the remainder will be nonhooded.

c. Develop an assortment plan based on this information. Then, analyze the completed assortment plan. Is this an appropriate distribution for the assortment plan? If not, how could the distribution be improved?

4. You are the buyer for men's shirts at a local department store. You want to purchase short-sleeve, solid-color, 100 percent cotton shirts from two vendors, Gant and Arrow. You have a $20,000 budget that will be divided according to the following distribution—Gant, 75 percent, and Arrow, 25 percent. Each Gant shirt will cost $15, while each Arrow shirt will cost $21.

a. Colors will be distributed in the following manner:

Gant	White	50%
	Blue	35%
	Yellow	10%
	Pink	5%
Arrow	White	70%
	Blue	30%

c. First, calculate how many shirts of each brand will be purchased. Then, determine how many of each color will be purchased for each brand. Finally, calculate the number of each size that will be purchased by color and brand.

b. All colors will be purchased in the following size distribution:

14	5%
14 $\frac{1}{2}$	5%
15	20%
15 $\frac{1}{2}$	30%
16	15%
16 $\frac{1}{2}$	15%
17	10%

STUDIO

Spreadsheet Skills

Visit this book's STUDIO product at www.BloomsburyFashion Central.com and open and print Assignment F. Then open file Spreadsheet F. Use the spreadsheet to answer the problems presented, and record your answers on the tables provided at the end of the assignment.

Internet Connection

1. Go to http://www.jcpenney.com and locate the company's offerings to the plus-size market. Describe the breadth and depth of the products offered for this market at this site. Select one other national retailer of women's apparel. Go to that site and locate that firm's offerings to the plus-size market. Compare the two retailers' plus-size product offerings.

2. For three products of your choice, identify two retailers on the internet from whom each product can be purchased. Visit those sites and identify the breadth and depth of each product offered by the retailers that you have identified. Discuss the breadth and depth of the assortments offered: How do the internet sites compare? How do the assortments offered on the internet compare to assortments that can be found in bricks-and-mortar retailers?

3. Visit the book's STUDIO to watch videos about the plus-size market and Lulelemon's localized assortment plans.

SNAPSHOT: Fashion Forecasting: Doneger Creative Services

Retail buyers must constantly be involved with forecasting: What will customers want tomorrow? What will they want to buy next year? Forecasting such trends is a challenging job, and many buyers seek assistance from forecasting and consulting services. One such consultant is Doneger Creative Services, a division of the Doneger Group—a merchandising consulting firm located in New York and Los Angeles. The company is a leading source of global trend intelligence that focuses on merchandising direction, retail business analysis, and comprehensive market information.

Doneger Creative Services primarily provides forecasting and analysis of lifestyles, trends, and colors. They report on the apparel, accessories, footwear, beauty, home, and lifestyle markets in women's, men's, and youth product categories through printed publications, exclusive online content, and live presentations. These sources predict the direction for future colors and trends as well as report up-to-the-minute news, on which clients can quickly act.

What are some of the specific services that fashion forecasters like Doneger Creative Services offer? Following are some examples:

- Forecasting colors for each season is a critical element of the service. Doneger provides color information eighteen months prior to the selling season. Yarn swatches, inspirational storyboards, and text overviews are made available that suggest color combinations and applications for specific areas of a business.
- Organizing important elements of the design process that will serve as a foundation for the season is critical.

Doneger typically addresses factors such as fabric, print and pattern, trim and detail, and shape and proportion.

- Analyzing important themes that will emerge in coming seasons is another part of the forecast. Material provided by Doneger conveys influences and styling direction through trend collages, original color sketches, and fabric swatches. Emphasis is also placed on the season's important merchandising issues.
- Covering European markets and haute couture collections is another aspect of forecasting. Doneger identifies important concepts to come down the runways and tracks the hottest looks on US, Asian, and European streets and in store windows. Core color messages, fabrics, prints and patterns, and motifs are highlighted in special reports.

Many fashion forecasters, like Doneger, provide seasonal live presentations on trends as well as supplemental presentations on lifestyle or industry topics. In addition, Doneger's clients can access information online at the company's website, which provides the most up-to-date information available.

Should you hire the services of a fashion forecaster? If you are making purchasing decisions in a dynamic, changing environment, the answer is probably yes. If the information provided helps you make better buying decisions, which translates into increased sales and customer satisfaction, it will be money well spent.

BASED ON:

Doneger.com (2017).

ALL SHAPES AND SIZES: THE PLUS-SIZE MARKET CONTINUES TO GROW

How big is the plus-size market? Plus-sized clothing for women, which constitutes sizes 14 and up, generates over $17 billion in sales annually. In terms of demographics, fifty-five- to sixty-four-year-old consumers represent the largest dollar share of sales out of all age groups for plus-size apparel; however, the largest growth has been in the eighteen to twenty-four age group. As Americans gain weight, the plus-size market continues to grow.

Despite much of the media's focus on razor-thin models, more than half of all Americans are overweight, with one in four people medically obese. Plus sizes are in more demand than ever before. While Lane Bryant and Catherine's have continued to expand their plus-size merchandise, department and specialty stores are also increasing their product offerings in this area. For example, Kohl's has extended two of its private-label lines to include plus sizes, and now even Forever 21 and Lord & Taylor have plus-size departments. Lane Bryant also seems to be trying to shed its staid image. The store now carries an exclusive, sophisticated line from designer Isabel Toledo, and markets an intimate apparel line with an ad campaign called "I'm No Angel." Neiman Marcus is trying out plus-size departments in five of its discount stores, and online personal styling giant Stitch Fix launched Stitch Fix Plus in 2017 and already has a waiting list.

Celebrities have also lent their hands in championing the growth of the plus-size market. Queen Latifah and Oprah Winfrey have both presented positive images of full-figured fashion in the media. Melissa McCarthy, star of the TV program *Mike and Molly*, has also presented a positive image for this market and has even launched her own fashion line. In addition, more advertisers, such as Dove, are featuring plus-size models in their ads, and a recent winner of *Project Runway* was a plus-size designer.

Yet some manufacturers continue to overlook the plus-size market. In the past, the plus-size market had been an afterthought for many retail buyers. For example, many department stores placed their larger-size offerings in the basement or back of the store, and even limited the floor space targeted to this group. Moreover, when plus-size apparel was offered, there was a very limited selection offered to customers. Customers in this market are no different from the regular-size shopper—they want style and selection among a number of brand names available to them. Today, both manufacturers and retailers seem to be approaching this market with a new, more positive attitude. The plus-size market is telling them that they would buy more clothing if more trendy options were available to them. Buyers must purchase stylish and alluring apparel for the plus-size market that fits not only the body shape but also these consumers' expectations of feeling and looking good in the apparel they purchase.

To successfully market to this segment, retailers must also determine how to best promote product offerings. Retailers have used labels like "woman" or "the forgotten woman" to say "plus size" without using those exact words. Are these the best terms to use in promotional messages?

Retail buyers must understand that even though the plus-size market retains the image of older shoppers, it is well represented across all age groups, with young people increasingly wearing plus sizes. Once these customers find a brand that works well for them, they keep purchasing that brand!

BASED ON:

Bellstrom, Kristen. (2016, October 26). How social media is driving the plus-size fashion revolution. *Fortune.com.*

Bolling, Cristina. (2017, February 24). 75,000 women are waiting: Stitch Fix Plus launches in a plus-sized market that's still catching up. *CharlotteObserver.com.*

Fenn, Donna. (2015, August 7). Melissa McCarthy joins the plus-size fashion "revolution." *Fortune.com.*

Morell, John. (2014, January 31). Bigger (and better). *Stores.org.*

O'Connor, Clare. (2016, June 23). Eloquii aims to fill gap in $18 billion plus-size market for on-trend fashions. *Forbes.com.*

Thau, Barbara. (2014, January 10). Retailers wake up to plus-size market with trendier, tonier fare. *Forbes.com.*

Wahba, Phil. (2017, February 14). Neiman Marcus is testing plus-size departments at its outlet stores. *Fortune.com.*

CHAPTER 10

CONTROLLING INVENTORIES

Performance Objectives

- List the benefits of inventory control systems.
- Describe perpetual inventory control.
- Describe periodic inventory control.
- Differentiate between manual and computerized inventory control.
- Identify the basic information required for inventory control systems.
- Explain how buyers use inventory control systems.
- Differentiate between retail and cost methods of inventory valuation.
- Illustrate how FIFO and LIFO inventory valuations differ.
- Calculate GMROI.
- Describe Quick Response inventory management and its benefits.
- Outline a plan for implementing Quick Response.
- Describe methods for improving inventory management.

Merchandise planning requires a good control system that provides a way to determine if a store or department is functioning according to a plan. Moreover, controls provide a basis to correct problems before they become disastrous for the store.

As a buyer, you must constantly be aware of the amount of inventory in your store or department. Excessive inventory indicates there is a buying, selling, or pricing problem. For example, you may not have purchased the merchandise customers wanted to buy, or salespeople may not have provided an adequate selling effort, or the merchandise may not have been priced correctly in relationship to the product's quality. You will also need inventory information when calculating how much money is available for purchasing additional merchandise.

In this chapter you will learn about two types of inventory control systems—perpetual and periodic. Dollar control and unit control will be explained, and current trends in inventory management will be described.

INVENTORY CONTROL SYSTEMS

After deciding on the merchandise assortment that is to be carried, **inventory control systems** must be established. These controls involve the maintenance of stock levels in relation to changing consumer demand. The type of inventory control system used by a retailer will vary by type and size of the business and the kind and amount of information required. Inventory control for a department, such as hardware with thousands of different items, will probably be quite different from that for a product category such as apparel.

A good inventory control system offers the following benefits:

- The proper relationship between sales and inventory can be maintained more effectively. Without inventory control procedures in place, the store or department can become overstocked or understocked.
- Inventory control systems provide you with information needed to take markdowns by identifying slow-selling merchandise. Discovering such items early in the season will allow you to reduce prices or make a change in marketing strategy before consumer demand completely disappears.
- Merchandise control systems allow buyers to identify best sellers early enough in the season so that reorders can be placed to increase total sales for the store or department.
- Merchandise shortages, or **shrinkage**, can be identified using inventory control systems. Excessive shrinkage will indicate that more effective merchandise controls need to be implemented to reduce employee theft or shoplifting.

Buyers must establish a control process that allows them to analyze the current situation in relation to merchandise plans and correct any deviations. For example, you may compare actual inventory counts against planned inventory levels and determine that the store or department is overstocked. You must then decide what corrective actions are needed. Future merchandise orders may need to be reduced, prices may need to be decreased to increase sales, or salespeople may need additional training. Your job as a buyer is to decide on the most appropriate remedy. Read the Trendwatch titled "Why Are Customers Finding Empty Shelves at Many Discount Stores?" to learn more about how some retailers are dealing with inventory control problems.

The control system allows you to determine mistakes that have been made or identify areas that need your immediate attention. To be most effective, the inventory control system must also provide information in a timely manner to allow you to make decisions while problems can still be corrected. There are two basic types of inventory control systems—perpetual and periodic.

Perpetual Control

Retailers using a **perpetual control system** are recording business transactions such as sales, purchases, returns, and transfers on a continuous basis. At any point in time, stock levels can be calculated. Stores using perpetual control systems do not have to take actual counts of their stock except for regularly scheduled physical inventories. Two types of perpetual control systems include manual and computerized.

Manual

Although many retailers today have computerized their inventory control systems, some stores still maintain perpetual inventory control by manually recording transactions on inventory control forms. Inventory records are updated as transactions occur or on a daily or weekly basis, by designated employees. Manual systems are slow, and many times employees responsible for updating inventory control forms are so late in completing them that the information is of little use to the buyer. Because data entries are made manually, they can be incorrect—providing inaccurate and misleading information to the buyer.

Computerized

Store computers can be programmed to maintain the same type of inventory information that manual systems provide. With such a system, merchandise information is automatically collected and processed for every transaction occurring at the POS (point-of-sale) register, providing the buyer or manager with up-to-date sales and inventory data. The computer has improved inventory control systems by improving speed, accuracy, and efficiency of record keeping.

Computerized systems require that each item of merchandise be coded to identify specific information about it, such as department, classification, vendor, style, color, size, or price. Identifying merchandise by such specific characteristics involves **unit control**. Most buyers need to know more about inventory than simply broad merchandise classifications. Maintaining a unit control system requires coding each item. SKU (stock-keeping unit) numbers identify a single item of merchandise within a merchandise classification. For example, an SKU number such as 95621 could identify the vendor (95), classification (6), size (2), and color (1). Today, many stores use the **UPC (universal product code)** already found on merchandise when it arrives from the supplier. Some retailers print their own bar codes once the merchandise arrives at the store.

At the cash register, the code is "read" by a scanner like the one illustrated in Figure 10.1, and the information updates the store's inventory records. There is less danger of salespeople making errors when merchandise is coded and scanners are used to record transactions. Problems can result from using computerized systems, however, if incorrect data are entered. For example, if price changes are inaccurately recorded, incorrect records and reports will result.

Today, some computerized systems include automatic reorder capabilities. The computer automatically signals when merchandise on hand and on order drops below a required level. Some systems can even send the purchase order electronically to the supplier.

Periodic Control

Periodic control systems are used by those retailers who take a physical inventory on a regular basis, which involves the actual counting and recording of information about the merchandise on hand at a specified time. Retailers take physical inventories for several reasons. The value of actual stock is needed in preparing a firm's financial

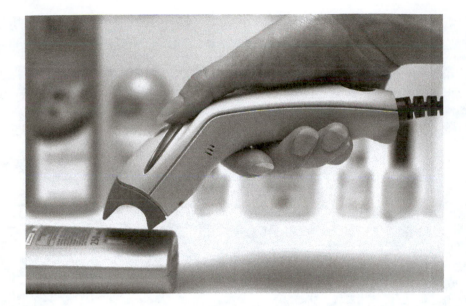

statements, such as profit and loss, and comparing physical inventory counts with store records allows the retailer to determine the amount of shrinkage that has occurred.

Methods of taking physical inventories vary among various types of retailers. Some retailers, such as large department stores, close while the inventory is being conducted. Most retailers take physical stock counts on an annual basis; however, others conduct stock counts every six months. Small stores may even conduct monthly counts. Most stores conducting annual physical inventories do so at the end of January—the end of a major selling season.

Careful preparation must be made to conduct physical inventories. Personnel conducting the inventory must completely understand inventory-taking procedures and the importance of their task. The importance of accuracy and thoroughness when counting and recording information must be emphasized to all employees. Some retailers even hire outside firms to conduct physical inventories.

Before taking a physical inventory, merchandise will need to be grouped by specific categories or classifications. Inventory takers must be supplied with inventory forms that allow them to record information such as product description, quantity, price, style, or vendor. Employees usually work in pairs, with one person calling out information and one recording the data. Spot checks are normally taken by supervisors to ensure the accuracy of inventory counts.

ESTABLISHING AND USING INVENTORY CONTROL SYSTEMS

One of the primary responsibilities of a buyer will be to maintain inventory control systems that require the selection of categories by which data are gathered (Figure 10.2). Control categories must be narrow enough to determine opportunities and problems with specific lines of merchandise; yet they should also make comparisons with industry data easy. When establishing control categories, many retailers use standard

Figure 10.2
Inventory control systems must
be in place on the selling floor
and behind the scenes.

merchandise classifications that have been developed by the National Retail Federation. Merchandising and operating statistics of department and specialty stores for various classifications are also provided by this trade organization.

Information Required

Maintenance of inventory control requires information about purchases, sales, transfers, and returns. Single independent retail stores will not be maintaining information on transfers.

Purchases

Records must be kept of each unit of merchandise ordered and received by the store. Information from the store's receiving report can be used to update perpetual inventory control records either manually or by inputting the data into the store's computer.

Sales

If a manual inventory control system is being used, a sales check or a price-ticket stub identifying the item sold must be collected and the information recorded on the appropriate form. In stores with computerized POS registers, sales are automatically recorded and inventory records updated as each sales transaction is completed.

Transfers

At chain stores, merchandise is frequently transferred from one store to another. Stores using manual inventory control systems must record these merchandise **transfers**. Stores sending merchandise to another store will delete the items from their inventory records, whereas stores receiving the merchandise will add the items to their inventory records.

Returns

Inventory control systems must also maintain records of **returns**, which include merchandise returned to vendors as well as merchandise that customers return to the store. Customers making returns to the store are usually issued a refund slip, as shown in Figure 10.3. A copy of this form is used to add merchandise back into stock when the store is updating inventory records. When merchandise is returned to the vendor, a return form is also completed. Again, information from a copy of this form is used to delete merchandise from inventory records. Stores using computerized inventory control systems must enter data related to these returns in order to update inventory records.

Using Inventory Control Information

The accuracy of an inventory control system requires the careful recording of every item that enters or leaves the store or department. Mistakes result in inaccurate inventory records that decrease their usefulness to the buyer. The following are reasons for inaccuracies:

- Inaccurate beginning inventory counts.
- Improperly coded merchandise.
- Failure to record markdowns.
- Incorrect recording of sales, purchases, returns, or transfers.
- Dishonesty of customers or employees.

Inventory control systems provide information on sales and merchandise in stock that will help you prepare for market trips. Facts, not guesses, are essential for you to determine sales trends and meet the wants and needs of your customers. These systems allow you to regularly check actual sales against planned stock and sales projections.

Figure 10.3
Refund slips help retailers know why products were sent back.

PART B – Return Goods Form

Within 60 days of original purchase: **Our Company** gladly accepts returns of unworn, unwashed, or defective merchandise for full refund. Refunds must be accompanied by the original receipt and will be made in the form of the original payment. If the original receipt is unavailable, we'll make an exchange or issue a merchandise credit based on the current selling price. After 60 days of original purchase: **Our Company** will gladly make an exchange or issue a merchandise credit for the price at the time of sale (with original receipt) or for the current selling price (without original receipt). For your convenience, catalog and internet purchases may be returned to any **Our Company** retail store for immediate credit. For retail store returns, a government issued photo ID will be required for cash and check returns and returns without an original receipt. **Our Company** Factory stores can only accept returns of items that were purchased at a **Our Company** factory location. Retail stores can only accept returns of items that were purchased at a **Our Company** Retail location or through the Catalog or Internet. Monogrammed or personalized items are not returnable or exchangeable. For our full return policy, please visit us at www.ourcompany.com.
To return goods: Please detach Part B and follow instructions on the reverse side of Part A. If an item is damaged in shipment, save item(s) and packaging and phone us at 800 555 0258.

For an exchange, use Part D on the reverse side of Part B, or phone 800 555 0258.
Return reason code: Please fill in appropriate letter in the left-hand column below.

B. changed mind	C. just didn't like	G. too small	
M. too large	D. wrong item shipped	V. arrived too late	E. defective, for our benefit please describe

Customer No. 12345678   Date 11/01/15   Order No. 10730405147

Reason Code	Item No.	Color	Size	Description	
	86221 pro	9h-m		shoe, printed peep-toe w/heel	
	85791 rpe	m		shirt, blue	
	86182 rpu	9h-m		shoe, printed ballet flat	

0123456789101112131415

You cannot rely on inventory records alone when determining purchases. Sales records do not show the requests made by customers for merchandise that was not in stock. For example, more sales might have been made if stock levels had not been depleted when customers came into the store to make a purchase.

If your store is using a computerized inventory control system, a number of reports can be generated on a weekly, daily, or even hourly basis to assist you in making merchandising decisions. Sales reports will show how rapidly or slowly inventory is being converted to sales, indicating whether adjustments need to be made in stock levels. Changes in consumer demand can also be detected. Reports can be generated to show unit sales for the current week, each of the past several weeks, month-to-date, or season-to-date. You may even receive reports that summarize sales for all styles of each vendor. An example of a computerized report is shown in Figure 10.4.

Exception reports may also be obtained that show areas where sales or stock levels do not meet predetermined levels. You should carefully review these reports to determine why sales are higher or lower than planned. Immediate action must be planned to correct problem areas.

Figure 10.4

Buyers use computer reports like this one to track inventory and sales.

```
FORM SI203     1-14                          PREPARED 03/17 15:55            PAGE   2
CLASS 00002 DRESSSES

= = = = = = VENDOR 000020       = = = = = = = = = = = = ************SALES UNITS****************** = = = = = =
STYLE DESCRIPTION                UNIT    UNIT  ON   ON                                      LAST
            COLOR    SIZE  ST   RETAIL   COST ORDER HAND  MTD 1-AGO 2-AGO 3-AGO 4-AGO  MTD  STD  RECEIPT STAT

80415 LIN BF SS JWLNK
                           01  120.00   59.00   0    1    0    2    2    0    0    4
                           TL  120.00   59.00   0    1    0    2    2    0    0    4
81035 DRESS
                           01   47.00   59.25   0    0    0    0    0    0    0    0
                           TL   47.00   59.25   0    0    0    0    0    0    0    0
81220 SS CHEX SHAPE DRS
                           01  132.00   65.00   0    1    0    2    1    1    0    3
                           TL  132.00   65.00   0    1    0    2    1    1    0    3
81235 DRESS
                           01   50.00   63.00   0    0    0    0    0    0    0    0
                           02   50.00   63.00   0    0    0    0    0    0    0    0
                           TL   50.00   63.00   0    0    0    0    0    0    0    0
81705 RAY/LIN BF COAT
                           01  150.00   74.00   0    4    0    1    0    0    0    1
                           02  150.00   74.00   0    3    0    0    0    0    0    0
                           TL  150.00   74.00   0    7    0    1    0    0    0    1
82402 SS RAYON SKT BF DOTS
                           01  150.00   74.00   0    2    0   1-    2    0    1    1
                           02  150.00   74.00   0    2    0    1    0    0    0    1
                           TL  150.00   74.00   0    4    0    0    2    0    1    2
84408 SS BASIC SKT COT/LIN
                           01  112.00   55.00   0    1    0    0    0    1    2    0
                           02    0.00   55.00   4    0    0    0    0    0    0    0
                           TL  112.00   55.00   4    1    0    0    0    1    2    0
84412 DRESS
                           01   47.00   59.25   0    0    0    0    0    0    0    0
                           02   47.00   59.25   0    0    0    0    0    0    0    0
                           TL   47.00   59.25   0    0    0    0    0    0    0    0

VENDOR TOTAL               01                  0    9    0    4    5    2    3    9
                           02                  4    5    0    1    0    0    0    1
                           TL                  4   14    0    5    5    2    3   10
= = = = = = = VENDOR 000038     = = = = = = = = = = = = = = = = = = = = = = = = = = = = = = = = = = = = = =
2015  REO COATDRESS L/S
                           01  136.00   99.00   0    0    0    0    0    0    0    0
                           02  136.00   99.00   0    2    0    0    0    0    0    0
                           TL  136.00   99.00   0    2    0    0    0    0    0    0
2023  REO SB CREPE GLD BTN
                           01  111.00   81.00   0    0    0    0    0    0    1    0
                           02  111.00   81.00   0    0    0    0    0    0    0    0
                           TL  111.00   81.00   0    0    0    0    0    0    1    0
D2015 CREPE DB COATDRESS
                           01  228.00   99.00   0    0    0    0    0    0    0    0
                           TL  228.00   99.00   0    0    0    0    0    0    0    0
D2023 CREPE GOLD BTN FRT
                           01  111.00   81.00   0    0    0    0    0    0    1    0
                           02  111.00   81.00   0    0    0    0    0    0    0    0
                           TL  111.00   81.00   0    0    0    0    0    0    1    0
```

To be effective, inventory control systems require frequent reviews by the buyer; however, they should not be used as a substitute for experience. Merchandise control systems provide input into the decision-making process, but a buyer cannot rely solely on information from computer printouts. Used properly, inventory control systems will allow you to make more effective merchandising decisions. Read the Snapshot titled "Zumiez: Creating Online Fulfillment Centers at Their Retail Stores" to learn more about how and why this company eliminated its distribution center for online sales.

INVENTORY CALCULATIONS

As you learned in previous chapters, most buyers develop a merchandise plan in advance of the selling season. The merchandise plan becomes the means by which actual results are evaluated. Once the selling season is under way, actual stock records can be used to control the amount of inventory on hand. Two types of inventory calculations that retailers often use are (1) dollar control systems and (2) GMROI, which measures the gross margin return on inventory.

Dollar Control Systems

Dollar control involves comparing the planned value of stock on hand with the value of stock on hand. These comparisons require that retailers place a value on inventory. Two methods are typically used for inventory valuation: the cost method and the retail method.

Cost Method

The **cost method** of inventory valuation requires that inventory records be maintained using cost figures—exactly what the retailer paid for the merchandise. Stores using this method usually include the cost of the merchandise using codes on the price ticket that customers and most employees cannot readily decipher. If costs remain constant, the cost method presents no problem; however, prices that retailers are charged for many products are continually changing. Because these prices change, stores using the cost method of inventory valuation have a choice in placing a value on the inventory. They can use either the LIFO or the FIFO method.

The **FIFO** (first in, first out) method assumes that the merchandise that was received first sold first. This may not always occur. Many retailers use the **LIFO** (last in, first out) method, which assumes that the merchandise that was received last was sold first. Such a situation does not likely occur, but in periods of rising wholesale prices, a lower inventory valuation results when this method is used because it is valued at lower prices.

Illustrative Problem

Let's examine a situation to better understand the differences in these two methods. Assume a department purchased 100 ties for $10 each on January 1 and purchased another 200 ties at $11 each on February 1. On March 1, inventory records revealed that fifty ties remained in stock. Dollar control requires that a value be placed on ending inventory.

Solution

Using FIFO, the ending inventory would be valued at the cost of the last ties purchased. In this instance, that would be $11. Therefore, the inventory would be valued at $550 ($11 × 50)

Using LIFO, the ending inventory would be valued at the cost of the first ties purchased. In this instance, that would be $10. Therefore, the inventory would be valued at $500 ($10 × 50).

For a buyer wanting to place the lowest value on ending inventory, the LIFO method would be best. Remember that when buyers develop six-month plans, they enter the value of beginning and ending inventories. Lower inventory values provide the buyer with opportunities to buy more merchandise. For this reason, the LIFO method is generally used by most retailers who use the cost method because of continually spiraling wholesale prices.

Retail Method

Today, most retail stores value inventory using the retail method. Stores using this method do not have to be concerned with changing wholesale prices, which may be difficult to determine and track. The **retail method** values the inventory using the current retail price. The retail value of all purchases, sales, transfers, and returns is recorded either manually or input into the computer system. Each change lowers or increases the value of current stock levels when the retail method is used.

Markdown, the reduction in the retail price of merchandise already in stock, is the key price change that must be recorded. Markdowns decrease the value of the inventory. **Markdown cancellations**, increases in retail price to offset all or any part of previously taken markdowns, usually occur when the retail price of merchandise has been reduced only temporarily for promotional purposes. Recording markdown cancellations increases the value of inventory. In some instances, the value of inventory may be increased by taking **additional markups**, increases in retail prices above those at which the goods were marked when they were first received into stock. Accuracy is vital when you are recording any of these changes in retail prices because mistakes could result in inventory overages or shortages.

GMROI—Measuring Profitability of Sales

Another inventory calculation that retail buyers examine is **GMROI** (gross margin return on inventory), which measures the profitability of a retailer's sales. It is a quick and easy way to measure how much cash a business is producing and how well it is using its investment in inventory. GMROI gives retailers a way to relate sales and the cash those sales are generating. In other words, GMROI integrates two performance measurements, gross margin and turnover, to create a single measure of performance.

On a daily basis, retailers plan and measure their business in terms of sales, but the ultimate measure of success for any business is profitable sales volume and the cash flow those sales produce. Profitable sales growth provides the cash a business needs to survive and grow. If it does not produce enough cash, it will fail and cease to exist. GMROI, stated in simple terms, attempts to answer a very basic business problem: "If I spend a dollar for merchandise to sell in my store, how much money do I need to get back if I wish to remain a viable business?" The objective is that a minimum dollar amount invested produces a maximum amount of gross margin.

Retailers calculate GMROI using the following formula:

$$\text{GMROI} = \frac{(\text{Gross margin percentage} \times \text{Turnover})}{(1 - \text{Markup percentage})}$$

Again, in simple terms retailers are measuring the following:

$$\frac{(\text{How much they made on the sale} \times \text{How long it takes to sell})}{\text{How much they had to pay for it}}$$

Illustrative Problem

A business has a gross margin of 40 percent combined with a turnover rate of 2.5. It has a markup percentage of 50 percent. Calculate GMROI.

Solution

$$\text{GMROI} = \frac{(\text{Gross margin percentage} \times \text{Turnover})}{(1 - \text{Markup percentage})}$$
$$\text{GMROI} = (0.40 \times 2.5) / (1 - 0.50)$$
$$\text{GMROI} = 1 / 0.50$$
$$\text{GMROI} = 2$$

GMROI should be viewed as more than a statistic; it is a driving force in the day-to-day management of inventories. In this formula, turnover measures the relationship between sales and stock levels. Both higher sales and managed inventories will boost turnover. The key is to increase sales without a corresponding increase in average inventory. It is important to realize that turnover represents the freshest, newest, and most wanted assortments to customers. In general, high turnover and high gross margin yield high GMROI, and low turnover and low gross margin yield low GMROI. Because high turnover and high gross margin are very desirable merchandising objectives, maximizing GMROI is an important goal for most buyers.

INVENTORY MANAGEMENT: QUICK RESPONSE

More than ever before, retailers are seeking a competitive advantage by streamlining the flow of goods from suppliers. Many retailers are implementing an inventory management system that allows them to keep their shelves stocked with the fastest-selling items while reducing the cost of placing orders. The time between ordering and receiving merchandise is reduced, and the system allows the store to increase customer service by always having the right items in stock. This system is known as **Quick Response**.

By using POS computerized registers that are capable of automatically reordering specific items as they are sold, retailers can lower their inventory levels, and suppliers can increase their sales with a greater number of small shipments. Quick Response, however, is more than the use of technology to manage inventories—it is also a cooperative effort between retailers and their suppliers.

Ideally, Quick Response is a strategy whereby retailers can forecast today what they will sell tomorrow and have the merchandise in the store on time and in the right quantities, colors, sizes, and styles. The concept is quite simple: get the right merchandise in the store with a minimum amount of inventory. For retailers, Quick Response means monitoring sales down to the item level, spotting trends as they occur, and then quickly relaying this information to the supplier.

In today's intensely competitive marketplace, "quick" is important. Longer forecasting periods may result in merchandise being ordered that does not meet customer demand. Longer order periods and delivery periods also make it more difficult to keep merchandise in stock that customers want to purchase. Getting the quick results that Quick Response promises requires a partnership between supplier and retailer, as well as the implementation of new business practices.

To start, retailers must share sales information with suppliers to help them better plan production, and suppliers must be willing to meet new, stringent delivery demands. Using Quick Response strategies, a supplier would receive an electronic purchase order from a retailer. Almost immediately, the supplier would prepare a shipment attaching a bar-code label to each carton. As cartons are loaded onto trucks, bar codes are scanned to develop a shipping manifest that is sent to the retailer electronically. Retailers scan the bar codes of cartons as they arrive to ensure that the correct ones are received. The entire process is completed in the time required to move the goods to the retailer—usually a few days. Using traditional purchase orders and invoices would require weeks to complete the same process.

Requirements for Quick Response

Quick Response requires an alliance between the retailer and the supplier that is built on mutual trust and teamwork. The use and implementation of technology is also required, specifically the use of model stocks, bar coding/scanning, and electronic data interchange.

Model Stock Development

After the technology is in place to implement Quick Response, **model stocks** for each product classification are developed. Model stocks are based on the ideal number of any item that should be on hand. Lower inventory levels are required in the store because more frequent and smaller reorders will be placed using Quick Response. Model stocks are adjusted periodically as indicated by the most current sales trends. Every item in the model stock is maintained in specific quantities by SKUs. Each product must also have a standard identification number, usually in the form of a bar code that is scanned at the POS register.

Bar Coding/Scanning

Implementing Quick Response also requires the use of **bar coding** and scanning. UPCs have become standardized in almost every part of the retail industry. A pattern of variable-width bars and spaces, representing a code of letters and numbers, is on most products when they arrive from the supplier. Some retailers, however, generate their own bar codes using a bar-code printer once the merchandise arrives from the supplier. The bar codes are scanned at the POS register, which enters the sale in the store's computer system. The retailer is then able to track merchandise on the item or SKU level.

Bar coding and scanning provide several benefits to the store and its customers, as well as the buyers:

- Faster customer checkout because manual entry of the item information is eliminated.
- Ability to track merchandise down to the SKU level, which reduces stockouts.
- Elimination of the need to remark merchandise.
- Increased employee productivity because manual checking and marking procedures are eliminated.

Both bar coding and scanning are continuing to make major gains in the retail industry; however, instances of pricing errors remain high at some retail stores.

Electronic Data Interchange

The final requirement for Quick Response is **electronic data interchange** (EDI). EDI supports the communication of sales data and business documents, such as invoices and purchase orders, between retailers and suppliers. In fact, the computer systems can electronically send purchase orders that are triggered when specific items of merchandise are sold. Delays due to paper handling are kept to a minimum. In addition to accelerating the ordering process, the major benefits of EDI are derived through reductions in clerical and administrative costs associated with data entry and tracking huge volumes of business documents.

Management cannot make all the changes required by Quick Response at once, and it should not even try. Usually, retailers develop a pilot program for only several product categories. Doing so allows them to identify everything that can go wrong. Most retailers have implemented Quick Response in basic merchandise areas first. Demand for basics is easier to forecast because of year-round demand; however, Quick Response promises significant benefits for fashion merchandise, too. In the fashion area, the approach most retailers take is to place smaller preseason orders and closely monitor initial sales. They quickly reorder fast sellers. Required changes in manufacturing processes are obvious, but Quick Response leads to increased sales for both the retailer and the supplier because retailers are more often in stock with merchandise desired by the customer. For the retailer, fewer markdowns result because only those styles for which significant demand has been demonstrated are reordered.

Implementing Quick Response

Management cannot make all the changes required by Quick Response at once, and it should not even try. Usually, retailers develop a pilot program for only several product categories. Doing so allows them to identify everything that can go wrong. Most retailers have implemented Quick Response in basic merchandise areas first. Demand for basics is easier to forecast because of year-round demand; however, Quick Response promises significant benefits for fashion merchandise, too. In the fashion area, the approach most retailers take is to place smaller preseason orders and closely monitor initial sales. They quickly reorder fast sellers. Required changes in manufacturing processes are obvious, but Quick Response leads to increased sales for both the retailer and the supplier because retailers are more often in stock with merchandise desired by the customer. For the retailer, fewer markdowns result because only those styles for which significant demand has been demonstrated are reordered.

Implementation of Quick Response requires the following strategies:

- Inventory and sales must be tracked at the SKU level.
- Automatic replenishment systems must be used to constantly monitor inventory levels; therefore, smaller and more frequent deliveries are made.
- Suppliers must commit to a higher level of service through improved shipping accuracy and on-time deliveries.
- Retailers must cooperate more closely with suppliers by sharing sales data to improve production planning.

Implementing Quick Response requires defining new relationships with vendors, which is central to the concept. Without the right vendor relationships, Quick Response would not exist. This new relationship requires give-and-take by both the vendor and the retailer. Vendors cannot underproduce and short-ship to the retailer; nor can retailers make last-minute substitutions or requests for special ticketing or handling. The best Quick Response strategies are jointly developed by retailers and vendors.

Quick Response requires a change in how buyers and suppliers work and think, but all studies conducted in the area point to dramatic improvements in operating results. Not all retailers, however, have readily adopted such merchandise management strategies. Two key barriers have kept some retailers from implementing Quick Response:

- Lack of knowledge of how to implement Quick Response or a basic fear of technology.
- Perceived beliefs that suppliers will not uphold their end of the agreement.

Measuring the Impact of Quick Response

Results of numerous studies indicate the potential for incredible industry-wide savings with the implementation of Quick Response. The impact of Quick Response can be seen not only above the gross margin line (through increased sales and decreased markdowns), but also below the line, with significant reductions in operating expenses. The following are some of the areas where benefits have been achieved by retailers implementing Quick Response.

Sales

Sales are up in basic, seasonal, and fashion merchandise. By tracking merchandise on an item level, buyers can quickly react to actual customer demand. Industry leaders are increasing their in-stock positions from the 70 to 80 percent range to more than 95 percent.

Markdowns

By stocking more of what customers want and less of what they do not want, markdowns decrease—an average of 30 percent in basic merchandise and 40 percent in fashion merchandise.

Administrative Expenses

EDI significantly reduces the amount of data entry for both retailers and vendors. At the same time, clerical costs for the retailer can be cut by as much as two-thirds.

Interest on Inventory

Perhaps the easiest-to-measure bottom-line benefit of Quick Response is reduced inventory. Traditionally, retailers have kept large amounts of inventory throughout the pipeline—in transit, on hand, and in storage. By increasing inventory turns, there are significant savings in inventory carrying costs.

These benefits come at a cost, however. Purchasing hardware and software can be expensive. In addition, implementing Quick Response requires that management provide education and training for store employees.

IMPROVING INVENTORY MANAGEMENT

Retailers today are under pressure to adapt quickly to changing conditions, resulting in inventory management playing a far more strategic role in merchandising decisions. Getting merchandise from one point to another as quickly and inexpensively as possible is certainly a goal of most retailers. Moreover, inventory management is not just a logistical problem; it is also a concern of buyers and merchandisers, who are responsible for getting the right product to the right place, and at the right time.

As retailers seek ways to improve inventory management, some of them are implementing **RFID** technology to replace UPC bar codes and anti-shoplifting devices on merchandise (Figure 10.5). RFID (radio frequency identification) technology is already being used in many stockrooms and warehouses. With RFID-equipped merchandise, retailers can follow a tagged item from place to place.

Once buyers purchase merchandise and it enters the supply chain, they must be able to track their purchases from the beginning of the process until the goods are placed on store shelves. Having an efficient inventory control system in place gives a firm a competitive advantage; to make the best decisions, buyers must have an understanding of what inventory they have positioned at every point in the supply chain. Data from RFID tags allow these centers to know which goods are on which pallets, when goods should be arriving at the facility, and when they need to be shipped.

RFID technology uses radio frequency identification tags on individual products that are read by a receiver anywhere along the supply chain. These RFID tags are basically microchips and antennae from which electronic readers can communicate with the tag from a range of approximately thirty feet. Implementing RFID allows retailers to locate inventory from the time it is shipped until it is sold to individual customers. Those retailers already implementing item-level RFID are reporting improved inventory accuracy and fewer out-of-stock situations. Viewing inventory anywhere in the supply

Figure 10.5
Small RFID tags can replace bulky anti-shoplifting devices like these.

chain allows suppliers and retailers to better provide the right products in the right stores and at the right time.

At the store level, buyers and managers must also utilize inventory control software that allows them better serve their customers. Too often, data being collected are not used in a timely manner, resulting in missed sales opportunities. For example, good inventory data should provide the buyer with details on stockouts, allowing them to accelerate a replacement order or move inventory to a location where it is needed. Ideally, using good inventory control software increases stock turns, reduces inventory requirements, and improves profit margins. Retailers are able to sell more items at full retail prices and are left with fewer items to mark down.

Macy's and Bloomingdales are using RFID technology nationwide in their stores for size-intensive "replenishment goods"—those items regularly stocked and automatically resupplied as sales occur. These items represent about 30 percent of the company's sales. RFID allows Macy's to more frequently count item-level inventory and to have that count made with greater accuracy.

Some retailers are also testing RFID technology inside the store, not just the warehouse. For years, advertisements have appeared, presenting scenarios of customers pushing shopping carts through a checkout lane and an electronic reader being able to scan the price of every item in the cart as it rolls by—without the shopper having to unload the cart and individually scan each item. This is not a dream; technologies are already available with which to accomplish this feat, and Amazon is testing them at a grocery store the company has opened. However, customers should not expect this technology to be implemented widely at the store level tomorrow. Initially, it took years for consumers to accept product scanning, and it took years to fully equip the majority of retailers with scanners and to develop policies and practices that would help alleviate consumer fears of pricing mistakes. Implementation of this technology will not occur overnight; yet retail analysts feel it will occur. The pace of acceptance is the unknown variable.

Some retail analysts project that RFID will ultimately have more value at the item level on the store floor than it does in the warehouse, but most retailers are not yet ready to make that transition. Costs are the primary concern. However, as a critical mass is reached, costs will drop.

Improved inventory control systems often result in a retailer reducing the amount of inventory that it carries. Reduced inventory is an important part of more efficiently managing working capital and building a better inventory control system. Above all, better inventory management should allow retailers to better predict potential inventory problems and identify possible solutions.

All retailers must examine methods on how to do business differently, not just how to install the newest technologies. Resistance to change is best overcome by a systematic process. For many companies, this means converting the buyers. Buyers must realize that the system frees them to do what they do best—determining what is going to sell in the coming months. The primary mission of buyers does not change. They are still responsible for understanding customer demand, analyzing sales trends, merchandising products, and maintaining the correct image for the store in the marketplace. Buyers are also increasingly responsible for managing bottom-line profitability—that means responsibility for inventory turns and related costs.

Summary Points

- **Inventory control involves the maintenance of stock levels in relation to changing consumer demand.**

- **Buyers must establish controls that allow them to analyze current inventories in relation to merchandise plans and take corrective action if needed.**

- **Buyers use either perpetual or periodic methods when establishing inventory controls.**

- **Maintaining inventory control systems requires the selection of categories by which data are gathered. Maintenance of inventory control requires information about purchases, sales, transfers, and returns.**

- **Inventory control systems provide buyers with information about sales and merchandise in stock as they prepare for market trips.**

- **Two inventory calculations used by retailers include stock-on-hand valuations and GMROI. Stock on hand can be valued using FIFO, LIFO, or retail methods. GMROI measures the profitability of a retailer's sales.**

- **Quick Response is an inventory control system that many retailers and vendors are implementing to shorten the time between ordering and receiving merchandise.**

- **Implementation of Quick Response requires the use of bar coding and EDI.**

- **As retailers seek ways to improve inventory management, some of them are implementing RFID technology to replace UPC bar codes.**

Review Activities

Developing Your Retail Buying Vocabulary

Consult the glossary if you did not add the following terms to your vocabulary.

additional markup	exception report	markdown cancellation	return
bar coding	FIFO	model stock	RFID
cost method	GMROI	periodic control system	shrinkage
dollar control	inventory control system	perpetual control system	transfer
electronic data interchange (EDI)	LIFO	Quick Response	unit control
	markdown	retail method	UPC (universal product code)

Understanding What You Read

1. How are perpetual inventory systems maintained manually?

2. When can information from perpetual inventory systems provide misleading information to buyers?

3. What are the key advantages that computerized inventory systems provide when compared with manual systems?

4. How can errors occur in computerized inventory systems?

5. When do most retailers conduct physical inventories?

6. Explain how returns affect inventory counts.

7. Why do most retailers use the retail method of inventory valuation?

8. Describe how shrinkage is determined using inventory control records.

9. Using a retail method of inventory, what type of price changes would increase the value of inventory?

10. Using a retail method of inventory, what type of price changes would decrease the value of inventory?

11. Why is a "quick" response by suppliers so important to buyers?

12. What are the benefits of scanning to both retailers and their customers?

13. What steps are required to implement EDI?

14. What are the benefits of using EDI?

15. Describe specific benefits enjoyed by businesses using Quick Response.

Analyzing and Applying What You Read

1. After analyzing inventory control records, a buyer determines she is overstocked in 80 percent of the merchandise categories carried. Explain possible causes of this problem. Present a plan that could improve future inventory levels.

2. The owner of a small sporting goods store is considering changing from periodic inventory control to perpetual control. Outline the benefits and drawbacks of each plan. Present your decision as if you were a consultant and the rationale for your recommendation.

3. Outline the arguments you would use to convince your store manager to implement Quick Response.

Retail Buying Math Practice

1. One hundred scarves were purchased for your department for $20 each at the beginning of the season. Two months later, fifty more scarves were purchased for $21 each (due to a price increase by the vendor). At the end of the season, ten scarves remained in stock. Calculate the value of the ten scarves in ending inventory based on the FIFO method. Then, calculate the value of the ten scarves based on the LIFO method.

2. The children's department made the following purchases:

   January 1: 20 pants purchased at $20 each

   February 1: 20 pants purchased at $20 each

   March 1: 50 pants purchased at $20 each

   April 1: 20 pants purchased at $23 each

   On April 30, fifteen pants remained in stock. What is the inventory value of these pants based on both LIFO and FIFO?

3. At the end of the fall season, your department had a gross margin of 45 percent combined with a turnover rate of 2.3. It has a markup percentage of 47 percent. Calculate the GMROI.

4. At the end of the fall season, Department 58 had a gross margin of 41 percent combined with a turnover rate of 2.2. It has a markup percentage of 49 percent. At the end of the spring season, Department 58 had a gross margin of 41 percent combined with a turnover rate of 2.3. It has a markup percentage of 48 percent. Which season produced the highest GMROI?

STUDIO

Spreadsheet Skills

Visit this book's STUDIO product at www.BloomsburyFashionCentral.com and open and print Assignment G. Then open file Spreadsheet G. Input formulas for GMROI calculations. Record your answers on the tables provided at the end of the assignment.

Internet Connection

1. Use the internet to develop a list of three firms that are currently using RFID technology. Describe how the technology is being used in each firm. Provide the URL for each source.

2. Visit the book's STUDIO to watch videos about inventory management at Amazon.

WHY ARE CUSTOMERS FINDING EMPTY SHELVES AT MANY DISCOUNT STORES?

Out-of-stocks disappoint customers and deprive stores of sales. Such stockouts have long been seen as inevitable due to the complexity of a national retailer's supply chain and its desire to offer a wide assortment of sizes and formats. But, two national discount chains, Walmart and Target, are experimenting with solutions to this problem, which can be costly in terms of lost sales and lost profits. During one year, for example, store executives at Walmart reported the company was leaving almost $3 billion on the table as a result of out-of-stock situations. That is $3 billion in sales that could have been generated if the product shoppers wanted had been on the shelves.

In reaction to the problem, management at both chains implemented similar approaches. First, the number of store employees restocking shelves was increased, and secondly, both companies cut back on their total inventory. In recent years, inventory had been growing faster than sales at both retailers. In fact, unproductive inventories and out-of-stocks have been listed by some retail analysts as two of the top three challenges facing retailers today.

Both Walmart and Target have carefully examined the many categories of products they sell to see how many different formats and pack sizes of products like bottled water or soap they really need to stock. This has led to shrinking the variety of sizes, flavors, and even brands on store shelves to reduce inventory. For instance, Walmart has eliminated 15 percent of its assortment by doing things like offering a brand of ranch dressing in one size rather than six. Similar efforts at Target have resulted in out-of-stocks being down 40 percent.

Such actions have eased some of the inventory shortage problems, but one retail analyst feels that these chains face a more important problem—they may be trapped by stock turnover goals that are based on the "law of averages." For example, retailers are examining sales and inventory levels for not just one brand of gum, but more probably for all brands of gum in the store, and, in all likelihood, data are being studied for gum as part of the overall category of "candy." Moreover, it is usually that broad product category for which the retailer has established a specific inventory turnover goal.

Improved turnover can be generated by increasing sales or decreasing average inventory. Therefore, if in the product category of "candy," cinnamon gum is selling well but sales are extremely slow for a chocolate candy bar, the inventory turnover goal for the category is not being met. The retailer has two choices: try to increase sales of the chocolate bar or other products in the category or reduce the amount of inventory carried in the entire category. So, to improve inventory turnover for "candy," buyers may end up purchasing less cinnamon gum, resulting in that product selling out faster and causing empty space on the shelf. That is the trap of the "law of averages." And, it is this process that may be causing an increase of out-of-stocks, which is an especially difficult problem to solve for companies like Walmart and Target that carry over a hundred thousand different items.

Delivery problems may also be contributing to the empty shelf problems. When products that the company is selling are being produced half a world away, it takes weeks and even months to begin correcting the problem.

On a positive note, Walmart and Target have recognized that they have a problem and realize that inventory shortage problems cannot be solved overnight. But, how much time will customers give the companies before they shop elsewhere for the products they could not find in stock?

BASED ON:

Anderson, George. (2013, March 1). Does Walmart have restocking problems? *Retailwire.com*.

Dudley, Renee. (2013, February 28). Walmart struggles to restock store shelves as U.S. sales slump. *Bloomberg.com*.

Is there a solution to Walmart's restocking troubles? (2013, March 2). *Itasca-retail.com*.

Rosenblum, Paula. (2014, April 14). Walmart's out of stock problem: Only half the story? *Forbes.com*.

Rosenblum, Paula. (2014, May 22). How Walmart could solve its inventory problem and improve earnings. *Forbes.com*.

Wahba, Phil. (2016, March 13). This is how Target is solving its out-of-stock problems. *Fortune.com*.

SNAPSHOT: Zumiez: Creating Online Fulfillment Centers at Their Retail Stores

Are you a part of Zumiez's target market? The company was founded in 1978 in the Seattle, Washington, area and now has over 600 stores in the United Sates and over forty in Canada. Most of you may never have heard of this niche retailer. But, some of you may already be a customer of this apparel, footwear, equipment, and accessories store that caters to a tech-savvy millennial shopper base who participates in action sports. Products carried by the retailer center on action activities, including skateboarding, surfing, snowboarding, and motocross. The company's apparel offerings include tops, bottoms, outerwear, and accessories (such as caps, bags and backpacks, belts, jewelry, and sunglasses). Footwear consists of action sports–related athletic shoes and sandals, and equipment offerings include skateboards, snowboards, and ancillary gear such as boots and bindings. With an appeal to such action-oriented customers, the retailer realized that the shopping experience offered by the company had to be unique.

For years the heart of that customer experience at Zumiez has been interacting with employees in-store. People who work there know what they are doing. If fact, it is not just a job for most of them; they are brand evangelists. They knew their merchandise, and they lived and breathed the Zumiez brand. In fact, most of their employees were probably already Zumiez customers before they started working for the retailer. This gave store associates at Zumiez the ability to relate on a personal level with the store's customers and provide a special shopping experience.

With the growth of online sales, store management sought technology that would provide a seamless and integrated customer experience with its stores. Primarily, they wanted the ability to sell and deliver inventory from each store, and be able to show all in-store inventory on its e-commerce site. Previously, only a limited number of items that were sold in the stores were available at a single online fulfillment warehouse. At the same time, Zumiez wanted the software to be intuitive for easy use and implementation by their store associates.

To those ends, Zumiez partnered with Sales Warp, a supply chain software provider, to enhance the performance of order management, customer service, warehouse management, and in-store fulfillment. The role of the new technology implemented at Zumiez was to ensure a seamless experience for its customers while being an invisible, nonintrusive part of the transaction.

Store management believed that most customers have never thought about shopping from an omnichannel perspective although they interacted with Zumiez using a variety of methods—the store's website, sales associates in the store, the company catalog, or whatever mix they chose. Most importantly, Zumiez customers expected a certain experience, and they expected that experience to be the same regardless of how they interacted with the company in the shopping process.

The company conducted extensive testing to ensure that Sales Warp software could handle demand, especially during peak season volume. The new platform supported flexible paths for shoppers to make a purchase, including reserve/buy online, same-day pick-up in the store, ship from any store to any location, and order online from the store. In addition, store associates were provided with the tools to access comprehensive information on all products the company sold. In addition, the software gave them chain-wide visibility of all inventory on hand, and the ability to process transactions anywhere on the sales floor. Eventually, the new technology gave Zumiez the ability to essentially turn its store base into an omnichannel retailing experience, making each store a mini online fulfillment center, which allowed the company to close its web fulfillment center.

From a customer experience perspective, using the stores as mini fulfillment centers has allowed the company to meet shoppers' specific product needs more often and speed up the order delivery process by shipping products directly from the store nearest the customer. Moreover, Zumiez has implemented an omnichannel approach that keeps their bricks-and-mortar stores viable as customer shopping behavior continues to change!

BASED ON:

Berthiaume, Dan. (2016, January 12). Zumiez has seamless customer experience in store. *ChainStoreAge.com*.

Berthiaume, Dan. (2016, March 23). Zumiez turns stores into mini-fulfillment centers. *ChainStoreAge.com*.

Soltes, Fiona. (2016, May 16). What do they want? *Stores.org*.

PART IV

PURCHASING AND PRICING MERCHANDISE

CHAPTER
11

SELECTING VENDORS AND BUILDING PARTNERSHIPS

Performance Objectives

- Identify how buyers locate new vendors.
- List and describe different types of vendors.
- Explain criteria that buyers use to select vendors.
- Describe methods that buyers use to evaluate vendors.
- Outline procedures for developing buyer–vendor partnerships.
- Recognize that strong buyer–vendor partnerships are needed for retailers to be successful.

After you have developed your merchandise plan, you will need to locate sources of supply, or **vendors**, to provide the merchandise that will satisfy the wants and needs of your customers. Manufacturers, wholesalers, jobbers, and manufacturers' representatives are just some of the vendors from which you can choose. There are numerous types of vendors for each category of merchandise that you will be purchasing for your store, and it will be an important part of your job to select the right ones. As you will learn, profitable buying decisions are based on choosing both the right merchandise and the right vendor. In addition, much of your success as a buyer will hinge on your ability to deal with vendors and develop a strong partnership relationship with them.

In this chapter, you will learn about the different types of vendors with which buyers will conduct business, as well as the criteria used to select those vendors. Emphasis is also placed on developing and maintaining strong buyer–vendor partnerships.

TYPES OF VENDORS

For some product categories, you must not only choose from many different vendors, but you must also decide whether to purchase directly from the producer or from a **middleman**, an **intermediary** between the buyer and seller. Again, careful analysis should allow you to choose the one that best meets your needs. Vendors are typically classified as (1) manufacturers, (2) wholesalers, (3) manufacturers' representatives/brokers, and (4) rack jobbers.

Manufacturers

Selecting a manufacturer as your source of supply may not be your decision to make. The minimum order required by many manufacturers is so large that your store may be unable to make a purchase directly. If so, you will be forced to make your purchases from some type of intermediary.

Buyers of fashion goods typically make purchases directly from manufacturers or their representatives in the market. Because of the rapidity of the change in most fashion goods, styles could change if the merchandise had to go through other middlemen. Also, most fashion goods are produced just before the selling season, which requires that they reach the market with a minimum of handling and delay.

Those retailers who want to establish their own private brands also place their orders directly with manufacturers who are willing to make minor changes in their products if a large enough order is being placed. Thus, purchasing private brands directly from the manufacturer allows the retailer to secure merchandise that will not be available in other retail stores. In addition to purchase quotas, some manufacturers may also establish both promotion and pricing requirements for goods they sell directly to the retailer. You will need to analyze such policies before making the purchase agreement. The chief benefit of purchasing direct is that costs are lower because intermediaries are eliminated from the distribution process.

Wholesalers

You may choose a wholesaler as the source of merchandise that you are unable to purchase directly from a manufacturer. A **wholesaler** is an organization that purchases merchandise from a manufacturer in large quantities and resells the goods in smaller amounts to retailers. Wholesalers are also known as **merchant middlemen** because they take possession of the goods they purchase from manufacturers.

A local wholesaler may be an ideal choice for your merchandise purchases if it maintains a broad assortment of merchandise that is ready for quick delivery. Also, most wholesalers will accept small orders, which allows you to experiment with new merchandise at a minimal risk because less of the store's capital is tied up in inventory. The store may also realize an improved stock turnover due to the smaller amounts of merchandise needed in stock because it can be quickly replenished from a nearby wholesaler.

Although most large retailers make purchases directly from the manufacturer, there are times when they need to purchase some merchandise from a wholesaler. For example, products with limited customer demand cannot be ordered directly from the manufacturer because the order would not be large enough. Quick shipments for emergency stock fill-ins also require that purchases be made at a nearby wholesaler.

In recent years, wholesalers are increasingly providing merchandising assistance to retailers in addition to just selling them merchandise. Such practices improve the working relationship between the retailer and the vendor, further developing a mutual partnership. The primary disadvantage of using a wholesaler, rather than buying direct from the manufacturer, is that merchandise will cost more because a middleman is involved in the buying process.

Manufacturers' Representatives/Brokers

You may also place an order through a **manufacturer's representative** or **broker**, who acts as an agent for the manufacturer. These brokers are also known as **nonmerchant middlemen** because they do not take possession of the merchandise before selling it to the retailer. The manufacturer pays a fee to the representative or broker for bringing the producer and buyer together. The fee is usually a percentage of net sales that varies by product category, sales volume, and the number of services provided.

You can visit these vendors at showrooms in regional markets or trade shows, and most of them make personal calls on client stores. They typically represent several noncompeting lines from manufacturers across the country, thus saving you time and travel expenses by giving you the opportunity to view merchandise samples in a nearby showroom or your own store.

Rack Jobbers

Rack jobbers are a special type of vendor who service client stores themselves. They are chiefly found in the food industry, but some department stores use them in areas where special merchandising techniques are needed. As supermarkets extended their operations to nonfood lines such as cosmetics, toiletries, and housewares, they needed special assistance in purchasing and other merchandising decisions. They turned to rack jobbers.

Retail stores that use rack jobbers assign them rack or shelf space that they are responsible for keeping stocked with quick-turning merchandise. The store is visited by the rack jobber once or more a week to restock shelves and make any needed changes in the merchandise assortment being offered. Jobbers usually make better use of the space than would the store manager because they have had more experience in anticipating consumer demand, pricing the merchandise, and displaying it.

Although using a rack jobber may cost more than making purchases from a wholesaler, the retailer usually realizes a cost saving because of the benefits gained from the jobber's services. In most cases, these costs are only slightly higher because the rack jobber is a volume purchaser and is entitled to quantity discounts.

MAKING CONTACT WITH POTENTIAL VENDORS

One of the first questions new buyers will need to answer is, "Where can I locate vendors?" In some instances, you may have to initiate contact with potential vendors. In other situations, they may initiate contact with you.

Buyer-Initiated Contacts

A primary source of vendors will be found by visiting markets and trade shows, as illustrated in Figure 11.1; however, not all vendors have showrooms at regional markets or exhibit at trade shows. You may have to schedule appointments to personally visit some vendors. Read the Snapshot titled "IKEA: Selling a Lifestyle" to learn more about how IKEA products are produced internationally yet still retain their identity with Scandinavia.

If you are a client of a buying office, its representatives will be able to locate resources for you. In fact, buying offices are constantly scouting the market for new vendors that could be of special interest to their client stores.

Reading current magazines and trade journals and subscribing to a retail reporting service are other ways to learn about potential new vendors in the market or learn more about established vendors. Many trade directories are also available that list and describe vendors.

Phone calls or emails to other buyers and conversations with them during market visits can also provide you with information that others have found to be beneficial. Shopping the competition's store can also help identify possible new suppliers.

Vendor-Initiated Contacts

Some vendors send sales representatives on frequent visits to retailers, whereas others rely on catalogs and bulletins for such contact. Many buyers for independent small stores tend to purchase from those vendors that assume the cost of the contact because of the expense and time involved in making market visits. They also prefer representatives who call at regular intervals, follow up on their requests, and help maintain stock assortments in the store.

Most manufacturers' representatives contact their retail clients on a periodic basis to ensure there is an adequate supply of merchandise in the store. However, relying solely on representatives who visit your store does not allow you to compare merchandise offerings, prices, and services with those of other vendors.

Figure 11.1
Buyers can locate new vendors by visiting markets and trade shows.

Having the broadest possible market contacts with potential vendors will be most advantageous to you and your store. Changes are continuously occurring in the market, so it is essential that you maintain contact with other vendors even though you may not be making purchases from them. This practice allows you to determine if the quality and price of the merchandise you are purchasing is equal to or better than that of the competition.

Although broad market coverage is important, most stores select a few vendors to handle a large part of their purchases. These selected vendors are known as **key resources**. Concentrating your purchases ensures your importance to these vendors because of the size of your order. In addition, larger orders more easily qualify for quantity discounts. Because a mutual feeling of partnership develops when purchases are made repeatedly from the same vendor, your store will usually receive better service from the vendor. You always want to be open to new, exciting products from new vendors, so do not overdo the concept of key resources.

After selecting key resources, most buyers distribute a certain amount of their purchases to other vendors in order to broaden their market contacts and to experiment with new merchandise or new vendors. This practice provides them with an alternative source of supply if the key resource is unable to meet an order. Having broader market coverage also allows the buyer to keep a close eye on what other vendors are offering.

CRITERIA FOR SELECTING VENDORS

Once you have identified the potential vendors from whom you can make your purchases, you will need to screen each of them. The following criteria should be considered as you select the vendors that are right for your customers and your store: (1) merchandise and prices offered, (2) vendors' distribution policies, (3) vendors' reputation and reliability, (4) terms offered, and (5) services offered.

Merchandise and Prices Offered

Your primary consideration should be whether the merchandise carried by the vendor is compatible with the needs and wants of your customers. If the merchandise is not right for your customers, the vendor should not be considered. You will also want to ensure that merchandise being offered meets the quality standards that both you and your customers expect. For example, when purchasing apparel, you will also be responsible for checking the quality of merchandise delivered to your store to make sure that it meets the quality of the samples you saw when the order was placed.

A wide assortment of merchandise offered by the vendor would be a key consideration for many retailers. Probably, you will also be looking for unique or distinctive merchandise. Having distinctive merchandise for your customers is a necessity if your store image is one of providing fashion leadership in the community. In this case, you must have new merchandise that has not yet gained acceptance from the masses. You may also look for vendors who distinguish their products in some way. Differences may occur in construction or styling or simply in the packaging provided by the vendor.

Another decision you need to make is whether to purchase national brands or develop private brands for your store. If you are looking for a particular brand of merchandise, selection of a vendor may be automatic. National brands have immediate recognition and usually ensure that a large number of customers already know about the product and want to purchase it. Private brands will offer your customers merchandise they cannot obtain at other stores, but there has been no national advertising campaign to presell your customers. For that reason, your costs are lower, allowing you higher markups.

Vendors' Distribution Policies

Choosing a vendor will also be affected by the distribution policies of the vendor. **Exclusive distribution** is a practice of some vendors whereby they sell the product to only one retailer in a trading area. Vendors benefit from an exclusive image that is created for the product. With exclusive distribution, the vendor usually retains some control over how the product is merchandised and promoted in the store.

Designer lines are frequently marketed through exclusive distribution, as illustrated in Figure 11.2. Also, owners of clothing stores in small communities frequently request exclusive distribution from vendors. They want to be able to offer their customers unique merchandise that cannot be found in competing stores in the town. Receiving exclusive distribution may be the factor that determines from which vendor you decide to make your purchases.

Some vendors use a similar practice known as **selective distribution** whereby they sell the product to one or more selected retailers in the same trading area. The number of stores selected is usually determined by the potential sales volume in the area. Again, because the number of stores is controlled, the vendor will usually place certain restrictions on retailers selling the product. For example, Ralph Lauren has established specific merchandising and display criteria for stores carrying the Polo line.

The price of the merchandise being offered by the vendor must also be a consideration as you decide from which vendor to make your purchases. The image and target

Figure 11.2
Many vendors have established specific merchandising and display criteria for their merchandise.

customer of your store will dictate the price range of merchandise that you will be able to consider.

Vendors' Reputation and Reliability

Vendors vary in dependability with respect to the way they conduct business. Prompt delivery of the complete order will be an essential criterion by which to judge vendors. In addition, you will also want to determine a vendor's reputation for such areas as quality control and speed in handling complaints and adjustments. Talking with other buyers or consulting with your resident buying office will allow you to determine if a vendor with whom you are considering doing business is having major problems.

Terms Offered

Some retailers may want substantial cash discounts from vendors, whereas stores with limited financial resources may want more time in which to pay. Discounts offered by vendors you are considering should be at least equal to those prevailing in the industry. Some retailers choose vendors who are located near their store or near shipping routes to speed delivery. In addition to credit terms, most retailers are also interested in having shipping charges paid for by the vendor. Both credit and shipping terms are described in detail in Chapter 14.

Services Provided

Services provided by the vendor can be a deciding factor in determining from whom you will make your purchases. Services provided by vendors that may be valued by your store could include any or all of the following:

- *Cooperative Advertising Arrangements.* Many vendors will share the cost of local advertising with the retailer if their products are featured in ads, as shown in Figure 11.3.
- *Advertising Aids.* Vendors may provide copy suggestions, mats, and broadcast scripts for products your store purchases from them. Small stores may prefer vendors that provide signs, counter and window display units, fixtures, and other point-of-sale aids. Larger stores prefer the uniformity of their own fixtures.
- *Return and Exchange Privileges.* When choosing vendors, many buyers look for liberal return policies.
- *Participation in Store Promotions.* Retailers want vendors who will participate in promotions planned by the store. For example, vendors may be asked to provide prizes for contests or clothing to be used in fashion shows.
- *Sales Training.* Some vendors will provide training for store salespeople when their products are purchased by the store. They may even establish awards programs for salespeople who sell above a specified quota of their products.
- *Assistance in Stock Control.* Bar coding of merchandise and improved computer technology are allowing many vendors to help retailers conduct stock counts and develop model stocks.
- *Preticketing of Merchandise.* Some vendors will mark merchandise ordered by the retailer before it arrives at the store. Such a service saves the store money and allows shipments to move quickly to the sales floor.

Figure 11.3
Example of cooperative advertising between Saks Fifth Avenue and Vera Wang.

ANALYZING VENDOR PERFORMANCE

A common error that some new buyers make is to eliminate many of the vendors used by the store in the past and start fresh. You do not want to dismiss a well-established vendor haphazardly, but there are reasons to seek out new vendors. For example, a vendor's standards may have slipped or its prices may have increased too rapidly. Also, your store may move toward a different target customer and a new vendor may be required, or a new and better resource may enter the field.

Relationships with vendors should not be disrupted arbitrarily. As a buyer, before deciding to drop a vendor and select a new one, you will need to carefully analyze the situation. In addition, you may also be required to check with your merchandise manager before making such a decision. Before disrupting your store's partnership relationship with a vendor, a systematic analysis needs to be conducted. Such a practice will strengthen your store's buyer–vendor relationships.

If several vendors offer you comparable merchandise, you have to decide which offer is best. If you have not previously purchased from a vendor, you may have to rely on what others have to say about the vendor's reputation. As a buyer, you will value your vendors, both in terms of the merchandise they provide and the profit potential of that merchandise.

If you are ordering from vendors with whom you have had prior experience, vendor profiles can be developed based on information you, or the store, have accumulated. You will want to develop a systematic method of evaluating the vendors that you use. One way to do this is by keeping a **vendor diary**—brief summaries of your dealings with each vendor with whom you do business. Even though the amount and type of information collected will vary from one buyer to another, certain basic data are essential. For each vendor you might want to record the following information:

- Total purchases for the year or season, at cost and original retail.
- Returns to the vendor, if any.
- Initial markup percentage.
- Advertising allowances granted, if any.
- Markdowns taken, by dollar value and as a percentage of sales.
- Cash discounts as a percentage.
- Transportation expense as a percentage of purchases.

This information provides you with a good indication of how much a vendor has contributed to your store's or department's sales volume and profit. In addition, you might want to consider other subjective factors such as these:

- Customer opinions about the vendor's merchandise.
- Reliability of the vendor's deliveries, including delivery of reorders.
- Reliability of merchandise quality.
- Promptness of the vendor in adjusting complaints.
- Services provided to your store or department in such areas as conducting stock counts, preticketing of merchandise, and sales training.

You can use the information that you have collected in several ways to evaluate each vendor:

- Each vendor can be measured against its own performance when compared with prior years or seasons.
- Vendors can be measured against the performance of other vendors. For this reason, it is extremely important to record much of your data as a percentage.
- Vendors can be measured against their percentage of the store's or department's total orders. For example, if a vendor accounts for 25 percent of the merchandise purchased by your store, did it also account for 25 percent of the profits earned?

A sample vendor analysis report is detailed in Table 11.1. You must set standards about what is considered acceptable or unacceptable performance. As a buyer, you would analyze the information found on reports like this one before making a final judgment about making future purchases from this vendor or seeking a new vendor.

Remember that as you rate your vendors, they are also analyzing the profitability of doing business with your store. They rate your store or department on how you merchandise and sell their products, as well as how fairly they have been treated.

TABLE 11.1

A SAMPLE ANALYSIS REPORT OF ALL PRODUCTS PURCHASED FROM VENDOR #125

Form SI-248 — VENDOR TRAK (R)

Style	Class	Imu pct	First recvd stat	Beg qty	Sls qty	Markdowns pct	Markdowns qty	On order pct	On order qty	Rec qty	End qty	Sales retail	Gross profit	Gp pct	Proj gp pct	Sell thru	On order rank
							VENDOR 000125										
3410 POLY/L A LAW L/S	00200	60.4%	10/16	0	31	0.0%	1	13.9%	5	62	31	1602.	1013.	63.2%	61.9%	50.0%	01H
5700 ASST PR/S-S JWL NCK	00200	56.5%	05/14	0	48	14.9%	34	0.0%	0	48	0	1588.	796.	50.1%	50.1%	100.0%	02H
7370 HARLEQUIN/FLANGE JWL	00200	55.3%	11/01	0	9	0.0%	0	0.0%	0	12	3	594.	328.	55.3%	55.3%	75.0%	03H
9506 CHIFFON/ELAS WST SKT	00262	55.1%	11/13	0	10	23.0%	8	16.7%	2	15	5	626.	321.	51.3%	44.6%	66.7%	04H
7347 PLAID/FL JWL NK L/S	00200	55.3%	10/16	0	7	17.1%	9	0.0%	0	8	1	434.	227.	52.4%	49.4%	87.5%	05H
6508 ABSTR SPLSH/PLT COL	00200	52.2%	06/26	0	10	36.7%	19	0.0%	0	10	0	518.	193.	37.3%	37.3%	100.0%	06H
7369 PUZZLE/FLANGE JWLNK	00200	55.3%	11/01	0	5	0.0%	0	0.0%	0	11	6	330.	182.	55.3%	55.3%	45.5%	07H
2502 ABSTR FL/V-CRSH DRAP	00200	53.7%	08/02	0	5	5.1%	1	0.0%	0	5	0	314.	161.	51.4%	51.4%	100.0%	08H
7367 ABSTR HNDTH/FL JWL	00200	55.3%	12/05	0	4	0.0%	0	0.0%	0	10	6	264.	146.	55.3%	55.3%	40.0%	09H
6501U POLY/D B DRAPE FICHU	00200	62.5%	11/13	0	3	0.0%	0	0.0%	0	12	9	180.	112.	62.5%	62.5%	25.0%	10H
7372U MULTI TRI/FLNG JWLNK	00200	55.3%	11/01	0	3	0.0%	0	0.0%	0	10	7	198.	109.	55.3%	44.8%	30.0%	11H
1302V POLY/S/S SHELL	00200	64.2%	12/10	0	1	0.0%	0	0.0%	0	3	2	38.	24.	64.2%	64.2%	33.3%	12H
VENDOR TOTAL				0	136	9.9%	72	4.9%	7	206	70	6686.	3615.	54.1%	54.4%	66.0%	
FINAL TOTAL				0	136	9.9%	72	4.9%	7	206	70	6686.	3615.	54.1%	54.4%	66.0%	

DEVELOPING STRONG BUYER–VENDOR PARTNERSHIPS

Respect and cooperation between buyer and seller are necessary to ensure long-term profitability for both parties. Once you decide to place orders with a vendor, you both will need to work to build a strong partnership.

Vendors want to do business with buyers who pay bills promptly, accept goods they order, and do not return merchandise unless it has been authorized. Buyers seek to do business with vendors who ship the merchandise that was ordered in the right quantities and at the time specified. To achieve these goals, buyers and sellers need to act as partners, not adversaries.

Basis for Strong Partnerships with Vendors

You can build strong partnerships with your vendors by following simple courtesies such as the following:

- Being prompt in keeping appointments with vendors.
- Visiting with manufacturers' representatives who call on your store. There is probably always something new to learn about the market.
- Giving your full attention to their presentations.
- Promptly confirming or cancelling any tentative orders you have placed. You should confirm in writing all agreements with vendors to avoid misunderstandings.
- Keeping the promises that you make. Orders should not be cancelled before their cancellation date.
- Providing feedback to the vendor on how the merchandise has done in your store or department.
- Not making snap judgments when deciding to eliminate or change vendors. Changes should occur only after careful analysis on your part. Long-term performance by the vendor, not a temporary setback, should be the most important consideration.

Your success as a buyer will be based, in part, on your ability to establish good working relationships with your store's vendors.

Buyers' Expectations of Vendors

What do experienced buyers expect from their vendors? What makes an ideal relationship between a retailer and its vendors? Most buyers probably want the following.

Merchandising Help through Technology

Most buyers need assistance in developing an assortment plan that would be specific to each store. Electronic data interchange (EDI) is really revolutionizing the business. It is vital that manufacturers have UPCs (universal product codes) on their packages. Automatic reordering benefits the store because retailers using the system can carry less inventory and make quicker reorders than with manual counts. Automatic reorder systems also allow retailers to get a quicker handle on which sales trends are up or down.

Many buyers also want assistance in managing inventory and creating model stocks. The best way vendors can help most stores is by helping to eliminate the nonperformers and keeping retailers in stock on the items that perform well. Vendors can help buyers by analyzing sales reports and model stocks on a frequent basis. What is needed are vendors who continually service the stores, filling in stock based on sales.

Sales Training

Many buyers want vendors to provide in-store training and retraining of salespeople. Other buyers feel vendor-supplied sales training is not as helpful because of the high turnover of salespeople.

Fixtures and Visuals

Some buyers believe that vendors could do a much better job in providing store fixtures at a reasonable and minimal cost. However, the higher the class of store, the less likely it is to use vendor-supplied fixtures. Many buyers want fixtures that do not have any vendor identification, whereas others have asked for funds from vendors to improve fixtures displaying the vendor's merchandise.

Packaging

Most buyers want packaging that is clear and self-explanatory. Packaging needs to be distinguished so that customers can say, "I know what I'm looking for—it's the one in the blue package." Some buyers feel that vendors need to reexamine the way they package products. For example, some products that are only shipped by the dozen might provide a better assortment to customers if packaged by fewer units.

Timely Delivery

All buyers want "faster delivery" from vendors. Prompt shipment of orders and timely delivery are crucial. Timely delivery and merchandise quality and consistency should be givens that buyers can expect from any vendor.

Future Trends

The changes in retailing over the past few years have also contributed to changes in the relationships between retailers and vendors. Business troubles have forced the closing of hundreds of specialty stores, and mergers have consolidated many department stores. The move by Sears and other retailers to shift toward national brands has also had an impact on vendors.

Closer Buyer–Vendor Relationships

Most vendors and retailers are forming closer relationships. As retailers consolidate and merge, there is a tendency to develop stronger relationships with large vendors who can provide the quantities and service level that most small vendors would not be able to match. Yet some vendors complain that consolidation in retailing may have given too much power to a handful of very large firms. Some of these large retailers have placed demands on vendors that they feel cannot be refused for fear of losing such a large account.

Closer relations between retailers and vendors are also a result of better communications. The vendor and the retailer must know each other's problems. Vendors must discuss with buyers the markups they need, the markdowns with which they can live, and the speed of inventory turns. Technological advances have also aided improved communication. Bar coding and computerized systems now allow vendors to give retailers accurate and up-to-date information on the status of their orders.

Consolidation of Vendors

Many small and medium-sized vendors could also be in trouble. Just as in retailing, those vendors in the middle with little to distinguish themselves will face stiff competition from other vendors who appeal to specific retailing niches. Smaller vendors will need to increase their efforts to compete with the larger vendors. They will have to learn how to offset technological advantages of size by being more flexible and by customizing their approach to stores. The small vendor will have to find a way to do things for the retailer that the larger vendors, due to their size, are not going to be able to do.

Vendor-Owned Stores

Some vendors are using another approach—doing their own retailing with **vendor-owned stores**. Manufacturers that open vendor-owned stores feel they can do a better job of selling their products than traditional retailers. For example, many fashion designers do not feel that department stores do justice to their lines. A designer may have fifty styles in a line, but a buyer may select only eleven of the fifty. The designers feel that because department stores are not displaying their lines correctly, sales are not what they should be.

Vendor-owned stores offer three key benefits: (1) the ability to display the entire line, (2) the ability to create an environment for the line according to the designer's concept, and (3) the ability to obtain feedback from customers on the entire line, not just pieces of the line. Rather than starting their own stores, other vendors are asking for an area specifically dedicated to their merchandise within a retail store. They also increase designer identification by not being thrown in with the rest of the store's assortments. For retailers, such a concept is acceptable only if they can justify a return in terms of sales per square foot. They will not give the space to any vendor who simply asks for it.

Vendor-owned stores must be viewed with more than mixed feelings by retailers. Retailers will need to keep a watchful eye on sales to determine the long-range effect of competition coming from these stores; they may erode sales. If vendor-owned stores are successful, many products may no longer be available to traditional retailers. These stores also mean more competition for retailers, and retailers are also providing more competition for vendor-owned stores as they open outlets next to some of them. Read the Trendwatch titled "Changing Perceptions: Outlet Stores for Luxury Retailers" to learn more about many high-end retailers opening outlet stores.

Vendor-owned stores also face certain problems. Products being sold in vendor-owned stores are being dropped by some traditional retailers. Vendor-owned stores relying on a single manufacturer may experience a poor product mix, and buyers may become lazy in their search for new ideas and styles because their choices are limited. Many manufacturers have learned that retailing is a very different business from manufacturing—there have been failures as well as successes.

Today, there is a conscious effort by buyers to treat their vendors as valuable company assets. They are working to lessen past adversarial relationships and replace them with partnerships based on trust. Vendors continue to offer new products and use sales pitches to enhance their brands. Buyers continue to ask for better terms and deals, and the relationships between the two continue to change.

Summary Points

- Once they have made their merchandise buying plans, buyers must select vendors to supply needed merchandise.

- Vendors are typically classified as manufacturers, wholesalers, manufacturers' representatives, and rack jobbers. For many purchases, buyers must use middlemen to supply their needs.

- Buyers can initiate contacts with vendors through market visits or personal calls, or by contacting their buying office. Vendors initiate contacts with buyers through bulletins, catalogs, and personal visits by manufacturers' representatives.

- Most buyers rely on key resources for the majority of their purchases in order to qualify for quantity discounts and receive better service; however, purchases are made with other vendors to broaden market contacts, keep key resources competitive, and experiment with new merchandise.

- Buyers select vendors based on the following criteria: merchandise and prices offered, vendor's distribution policies, vendor's reputation and reliability, terms offered, and services offered.

- Buyers should develop vendor diaries to evaluate each vendor in relation to predetermined goals in areas such as sales, returns, markups, and markdowns.

- After selecting vendors, buyers should work to develop strong buyer–vendor relationships. Buyers and vendors need to be partners, not adversaries.

- Many buyers want vendors to provide them with merchandising help through technology, sales training, special fixtures, visuals, packaging, and timely delivery.

- Closer relationships between buyers and vendors will likely occur in the future.

Review Activities

Developing Your Retail Buying Vocabulary

Consult the glossary if you did not add the following terms to your vocabulary.

broker	manufacturer's representative	rack jobber	vendor-owned store
exclusive distribution	merchant middleman	selective distribution	wholesaler
key resource	middleman	vendor	
intermediary	nonmerchant middleman	vendor diary	

Understanding What You Read

1. Describe why a retailer might require a buyer to get approval from top management before changing vendors.

2. What procedures should a buyer follow to locate new vendors?

3. Describe why retailers should not rely solely on vendors who have made the effort to contact them.

4. Describe why many buyers rely on key resources.

5. Can a buyer put too much reliance on key resources? Explain.

6. Identify types of retailers who would buy directly from a manufacturer.

7. Describe why fashion goods do not typically go through a wholesaler.

8. Identify types of retailers who would buy from a wholesaler.

9. Describe how manufacturers' representatives are paid.

10. What benefits do rack jobbers provide retailers?

11. What is the drawback to using a rack jobber?

12. Describe how identifying store image and target customers will allow buyers to narrow the choice of vendors from which they can choose.

13. Describe why clothing stores in small towns want exclusive distribution from vendors.

14. What are the drawbacks to exclusive and selective distribution?

15. Describe why many large retailers do not accept vendor-supplied fixtures.

16. What will small vendors have to do in the future to successfully compete with larger vendors?

17. What factors should be considered by the buyer when evaluating a vendor?

18. Describe why buyers should periodically evaluate all vendors.

19. Identify benefits that vendor-owned stores offer designers.

20. What can vendors do to strengthen their partnerships with buyers?

Analyzing and Applying What You Read

1. Describe why a newly hired buyer would want to change many of the vendors used by a store in the past. Describe the procedures you would follow before dismissing a vendor.

2. Describe why some buyers go to central markets often, whereas others go infrequently. What are the drawbacks of each practice?

3. You have recently signed a contract with a new vendor that you expect will develop into one of your store's key resources. Describe what you would do to ensure that the relationship develops into a strong partnership.

4. When would it be better to compare a vendor's performance with its own past performance rather than the performance of other vendors? Explain.

5. Describe why a strong buyer–vendor partnership is important to the vendor as well as the retailer.

6. Even though owners of vendor-owned stores say retailers have nothing to fear from them, why might retailers worry?

Internet Connection

1. Visit the book's STUDIO to watch videos about how venders negotiate with buyers and software to help buyers and vendors communicate better.

SNAPSHOT: IKEA: Selling a Lifestyle

IKEA, the world's largest home furnishings chain, has developed a successful global strategy. In fact, the company and its products have now become the norm for consumers who are furnishing their first apartments or homes. IKEA continues to demonstrate the standard of always putting customers first and subsequently impressing them. In fact, the company's vision statement, which was crafted in 1943, continues to be "to create a better everyday life for the many people." IKEA's key marketing strategy has remained focused on improving customer loyalty by selling a unique lifestyle by offering a wide range of well-designed, functional home furnishing products at prices so low that as many people as possible will be able to afford them.

IKEA, which is targeting 50 billion euros in sales for 2020, does most of its business in Europe and the United States but is entering China, India, and other emerging markets. Germany remains the company's biggest single market, and Poland is its fastest growing market.

Although China accounts for 20 percent of the products manufactured for IKEA, the firm uses a network of 1,300 suppliers located in fifty-three different countries, and operates trading offices in twenty-six of those countries in order to be close to its suppliers. This closeness to the manufacturing process allows IKEA to enhance the firm's ability to monitor production, test new ideas quickly, better negotiate prices, and monitor working conditions at vendor plants. Although IKEA products are produced internationally, products still retain their identity with Scandinavia.

Customer loyalty at IKEA is built on more than the chain being a home furnishings merchant. The company sells a lifestyle that customers around the world have embraced. The success in the global marketplace has been based on a simple philosophy: offering a wide range of home furnishings that have good design and function at a price that the majority of consumers can afford. Function has always guided IKEA design, which started out with light woods, birch and pine, combined with natural materials, such as cotton and linen. Virtually all IKEA furniture falls into the knocked-down category, requiring some work on the part of the customer.

IKEA continues to experiment to keep one step ahead of the competition. Fifteen to twenty in-house designers are employed, plus other outside design resources, to help keep IKEA on the forefront of furniture design. However, no design, no matter how inspired, finds its way into the showroom if it cannot be made affordable to customers.

What enthralls customers and keeps them returning to the store is the store visit. Shopping at IKEA is meant to be a family outing—from the gigantic parking lots to the supervised playroom filled with multicolored balls, slides, and other fun things just inside the entrance. An inexpensive self-service restaurant specializing in Scandinavian fare is usually placed about midway through most stores. Globally, IKEA customers tend to think of a store visit as an outing rather than a chore.

As the store plans for future expansion, management at IKEA realizes that the firm has stumbled before. A foray into Japan more than thirty-five years ago was a disaster. In China, there are reports that profits remain elusive—with more "lookers" than "shoppers," but the stores there have experienced growth.

Even IKEA's first store in the United States was too quirky for many customers' tastes—for example, its European bed sizes did not match American mattress and sheet sizes, beds were measured in centimeters, sofas were not deep enough, and curtains were too short. Although the first store was profitable, a quick expansion to seven US stores put the chain in the red. Financial experts even suggest that if IKEA had been a public company, shareholders would have demanded it close operations in the United States. By 1997, however, with new product lines, IKEA was in the black.

Who is the customer that IKEA wants to attract and remain loyal to the store? In terms of life stage, they run the gamut from college students to first-time home owners to families with children. The retailer also looks for areas with more than 1.5 million people within a thirty-mile radius.

Experts agree that one factor primarily accounts for IKEA's success and keeps customers returning to the stores—the company has stayed consistent over time. The stores always occupy large spaces, offer modern furniture and home goods, provide outstanding service, and are kid-friendly, leading rivals to continually reinvent themselves to compete. IKEA has found a formula, perfected it, and leveraged it to the hilt. The firm's best marketing investment has been in satisfied customers who help sell IKEA to others. Management knows what has made IKEA successful, and it has delivered that concept successfully around the globe.

BASED ON:

Brautlecht, Nicholas. (2014, June 30). IKEA goes urban with first high street store in Hamburg. *Finance.yahoo.com/news.*

Chew, Jonathan. (2016, February 24). IKEA is facing huge problems in this important country. *Fortune.com.*

D'Innocenzio, Anne. (2014, June 26). IKEA raises hourly pay for US retail workers. *Finance.yahoo.com/news.*

IKEA eyes higher quality to fend off new rivals. (2016, July 8). *Fortune.com.*

IKEA sets sights on making sustainable cotton affordable for all. (2014, July 24). *Edie.net.*

IKEA submits plans to open a Las Vegas store in summer 2016 as Swedish retailer continues to expand U.S. presence. (2014, July 14). *Finance.yahoo.com/news.*

Jordan, Karen. (2017, January 13). The biggest IKEA in the U.S. opens next month in LA. *Forbes.com.*

Kowitt, Beth. (2016, March 15). At IKEA: No ranks, no rancor. *Fortune.com.*

Lavin, Frank. (2016, July 12). How IKEA got China wrong. *Forbes.com.*

Pontefract, Dan. (2016, June 8). How IKEA delights its customers. *Forbes.com.*

CHANGING PERCEPTIONS: OUTLET STORES FOR LUXURY RETAILERS

At the beginning of the decade, most retailers in the United States were faced with a precipitous decline in demand and sales due to a slowdown in the economy, forcing them to make heavy markdowns that damaged the cachet of many retailers and significantly hurt profit margins. Additionally, it placed customers in a "discounting" mind-set. Since that time, retailers have begun experimenting with ways to return sales to previous price levels. Customer expectations and priorities changed during that time, and any stigma associated with outlet stores nearly evaporated.

During the economic downturn, a strong outlet business helped insulate some retailers from the volatility of economic fluctuations. For example, sales per square foot at Simon Property's forty-one outlet centers slipped 1.8 percent, which was far less than the 7.9 percent decline seen at the developer's regional malls.

In recent years, consumer spending has rebounded somewhat, but not to previous levels. Similar patterns exist for luxury retailers also. To combat these economic fluctuations in the marketplace, numerous luxury retailers have expanding their presence with outlet stores while expansion of their full-priced stores has remained limited. Outlet stores allow them to appeal to a wider range of customers without having to offer big discounts at traditional stores. Moreover, many of these outlets sell more outlet-only products, not just marked-down leftovers that did not sell in the stores.

In fact, several luxury department stores have followed the lead of many high-end manufacturers, who for years have used outlet stores as a way to liquidate excess products in a controlled environment. For example, Polo Ralph Lauren Corp. and Coach have both expanded their outlets without diluting their brands.

How have luxury retailers expanded into outlet stores during recent years? Nordstrom has been opening many more of its off-price stores, Nordstrom Rack, than its full-line department stores. By the end of 2016, Nordstrom had 123 full-line stores and 215 Nordstrom Rack stores. Moreover, Nordstrom Rack stores have fared better than their bigger sibling, with comparable sales either rising, or falling less sharply than at the full-line stores. As Nordstrom Rack expands, however, there's the question of whether its sales are cannibalizing from the full-line stores.

Neiman Marcus Group has tested a new outlet concept called Last Call Studio, and Saks has also increased the number of its Off 5th outlet stores. Originally conceived as a clearinghouse for Saks Fifth Avenue merchandise, Off 5th today has reinvented itself as a major national retailer. An engaging environment, exclusive savings, and wide product assortments allow customers to discover deals and find high-quality products that are on-trend.

Bloomingdale's and Lord & Taylor have both opened outlet stores too. After a six-month study, the management at Bloomingdale's concluded they were missing out on a big sales opportunity without outlet stores. At the Bloomingdale's outlets, overstock from the full-price stores will be limited to no more than 20 percent of the inventory. The rest of the stock will be from vendors' previous seasons and products made exclusively for the outlet stores.

With more luxury retailers opening outlet stores, many outlet centers have changed. Outlet stores for luxury retailers are not garishly lit spaces, filled with boxes heaped with clothing. In fact, "upscale" became the new buzzword for developers, as outlet centers have taken the form of upscale "villages" with a strong emphasis on brand names.

Outlet stores also present new challenges for buyers at these luxury stores. They must now try to appeal to a broader customer base with different product offerings. At the same time, they must ensure that products available at the firm's outlet stores do not cannibalize sales from the regular stores. They may have to walk a precarious tightrope as they stock both regular stores and the outlet stores and establish prices that will be appealing to both types of customers.

BASED ON:

Baker, Jason, & Cheatham, Dave. (2014, May 2). Changing perceptions. *ChainStoreAge.com.*

Berthiaume, Dan. (2014, January 31). Report: Saks to add luxury items, outlet stores. *ChainStoreAge.com.*

Fickes, Michael. (2014, April 30). Outlets are in. *ChainStoreAge.com.*

Wahba, Phil. (2016, March 18). Low oil prices hit luxury retailers hard. *Fortune.com.*

MAKING MARKET VISITS AND NEGOTIATING WITH VENDORS

Performance Objectives

- Identify the purposes of buying trips.
- Describe the planning steps required before making a buying trip.
- Identify a buyer's typical activities during a buying trip.
- Recognize that buyers can prepare for negotiations before face-to-face meetings occur with vendors.
- Develop objectives for negotiations.
- List and describe frequently used negotiation tactics.
- Recognize that the outcome of negotiations should be to develop a long-term partnership with the vendor.

Once buyers have identified potential suppliers, their next step is to prepare to visit the market, which can be located locally or in some other country, and today, markets can even be found online. Before you arrive at the market, you must begin developing your negotiation skills. Successful negotiations with vendors begin with adequate preparations while you are in the office.

In this chapter you will learn about the planning steps required for making a market visit and how to prepare for negotiations. Development of negotiating strategies and tactics are described, and the desired outcomes of negotiation are presented.

PREPARING FOR A MARKET VISIT

Most buyers begin searching for merchandise in domestic markets because of their closeness and accessibility. However, lower costs are the primary reason that buyers seek out appropriate foreign markets today. As they prepare for trips to either foreign or domestic markets, buyers will typically find central markets, merchandise/apparel marts, and expositions/trade shows. After deciding which type of market they will be visiting, buyers must clearly define their purpose and thoroughly plan any trip that will take place outside their offices.

Types of Markets

A **central market** is a city where a large number of key suppliers are located. New York and Hong Kong are key supply cities for many types of merchandise, particularly apparel. As pictured in Figure 12.1, the Garment District in New York City is home to thousands of showrooms that display apparel, textiles, fabrics, and many other apparel accessories. That city is still considered the major apparel market in the United States. Central markets also exist for other products. For example, key US furniture markets are

Figure 12.1
The Garment District in New York is home to showrooms with many types of merchandise, particularly apparel.

located in High Point, North Carolina, and Las Vegas, Nevada; there are also furniture market locations in Germany and China.

In some cities, buyers will find a single complex (a **merchandise/apparel mart**) like the one shown in Figure 12.2. At these marts, it is easy for buyers to view all merchandise lines available and make comparisons. Because manufacturers or their representatives lease showroom space, the marts function as a one-stop shop so that buyers do not have to go to different sections of a city to locate suppliers. Marts located near buyers also allow them the opportunity to make quicker and more frequent buying trips. Marts present several market weeks during the year, and registered buyers are sent guides detailing vendors available, lines carried, and their location in the mart. Large marts can be found in Atlanta, Chicago, Dallas, Los Angeles, and Miami.

For other product categories, buyers can locate **trade shows** or **expositions**. These shows are typically held at convention centers or exhibition halls in large cities to showcase the latest merchandise in a particular product category. For example, yearly shows are held in areas such as toys, electronics, groceries, automobiles, and computers. Buyers are able to easily compare vendor offerings while attending these shows and have the opportunity to identify new trends and resources in the market. Trade shows and expositions are usually held for only a few days each year, so your calendar must be left open for this time. Read the Snapshot titled "The North American International Toy Fair" to learn more about the toy industry's annual show.

Purposes of Buying Trips

Buyers make market visits for a number of reasons:

- To obtain merchandise for the upcoming season.
- To gain knowledge about trends and new merchandise.
- To evaluate new resources and merchandise offerings from vendors.

Figure 12.2
All vendors are located under one roof at various merchandise marts around the country.

- To seek out special values for an upcoming promotion—special deals that could be featured in new promotional events or sales.
- To replenish stock in order to fill in sections of stock that have been selling well.
- To attend previews of new vendor lines. Fashion designers and manufacturers of such products as automobiles, electronics, and computers typically have special shows for buyers to preview changes in styles and models.

Frequency of Market Trips

The purposes of your buying trip will determine the frequency of your market visits. Most buyers usually visit foreign or central markets only once or twice a year and make other trips to regional markets to supplement their assortments. If they are not located a great distance from a market, buyers may make more frequent buying trips. When and how often you make market visits will also depend on a number of other factors, as follows.

Season of the Year

Most buyers will make market visits depending on the season of the year. Market weeks, like the ones held in Atlanta at AmericasMart, are planned around a particular season such as fall–winter or spring–summer (Figure 12.3). Each product category has a specific number of major selling seasons, depending on changes in styles and models. If new styles develop for each season, frequent trips may be required.

Figure 12.3

An advertisement for AmericasMart in Atlanta for the Fall market.

Type of Merchandise

Buyers of all types of products make market visits. Fashion buyers will need to make more frequent visits because of the rapidity with which fashion changes, but even with fashion merchandise there are more shows for some product lines and fewer for others. For example, there might be five shows annually for women's wear and only two for menswear.

Size of Store or Department

Large firms will require more market visits than would smaller stores in order to keep the merchandise assortments fully stocked. Larger stores tend to have a higher merchandise turnover, which requires more frequent market visits.

Stores' Merchandise Policies

Stores that want to maintain a fashion leadership position will certainly need to make frequent market visits.

Proximity to a Market

Being located a distance from the market city may necessitate fewer market trips because of the time and expenses involved. Some buyers substitute trips to regional merchandise/apparel marts rather than going to foreign or central markets for all their needs.

Business Conditions

Business slowdowns may negatively affect sales to such an extent that some market trips may not be needed. On the other hand, slowdowns may be an opportune time to make market trips to locate new and exciting merchandise that might spur sales.

Planning the Market Trip

Like any business activity, your buying trip should be thoroughly planned. As many details of the trip as possible should be arranged before you leave so that your time in the market can be spent on merchandise-related decisions. Planning should involve the following steps.

Step 1

You should have prepared a merchandise buying plan. If you go to market with facts about your inventory, sales, and customer preferences, your decisions will be based on facts and not feelings. Also, your vendors can provide you with more concrete assistance when they are provided with such information. Have a vendor analysis form completed for any firm you plan to visit if you have carried their products previously. Even with a buying plan, you will still have decisions to make on specific selections, particularly if you are making fashion purchases. Large stores may have a fashion coordinator to advise you on any trends in styles, colors, or silhouettes; otherwise, you need to have researched these trends yourself.

Step 2

Make certain that you have obtained all approvals that you need for your buying plan. At many stores, both the merchandise manager and the finance officer will be required to approve of plans before buyers go on market visits.

Step 3

If you have one, notify your buying office of your upcoming visit, and inform people there about your specific merchandising needs and vendors you would like to visit. Without a buying office, you will need to schedule visits with vendors yourself. Make sure that key resources are notified early so you will be assured of an appointment time that best fits your schedule. You may also want to examine market reports, trade journals, and other publications to identify new manufacturers or designers that you may want to visit. When you call for appointments, ask about the length of time the sales representative feels is adequate to review the merchandise line.

Step 4

Determine how many days will be needed for your buying trip, and then arrange your hotel and travel reservations. These arrangements may be made for you if your store is a client of a buying office.

Step 5

Establish a work schedule for your staff members while you are away. Prepare an itinerary of your market visits so you can be reached by your staff or management. While in the market, keep them informed of any changes in your plans. A good practice is to establish a regular call-in time so that any messages can be easily relayed to you.

Planning will make your buying trip more enjoyable and more profitable. In the market, you will find that you have the time needed to visit vendors and evaluate merchandise.

VISITING THE MARKET

Now that your trip has been thoroughly planned, you need to consider the activities in which you will participate while in the market. Most market trips are generally planned for a week or less, but on occasion you may need more time. While in the market, you will want to talk with representatives of your buying office, visit vendors and showrooms, tour factories, attend seminars or fashion shows, talk with other buyers, and tour outstanding retail stores in the market. Use your time wisely during market week; it is likely to be a hectic period. A sample week at the Denver market is shown in Figure 12.4. An exciting and stimulating atmosphere prevails; vendors are there to sell, and they will use a maximum of showmanship.

Working with a Buying Office

As you learned in previous chapters, buying offices perform many advisory and consultant services for client stores. Before your trip, people at the buying office can

Figure 12.4
A sample week at the Denver Mart.

THURSDAY
Show Hours: 9:00 a.m.–5:00 p.m. Mart Building Only

FRIDAY
Show Hours: 9:00 a.m.–6:30 p.m. Mart Building Only

Buyer Information Session
8:30 a.m.–9:00 a.m. Forum Meeting Room #2

"Moving Your Business onto the Web"
3:30 p.m.–4:30 p.m.

Buyer Appreciation Reception
6:30 p.m.–8:00 p.m.

This special evening is to say "thank you" to buyers for attending the Denver Show.

Complimentary hors d'oeuvres and cocktails with live background music set the scene for a comfortable, relaxing evening.

SATURDAY
Show Hours: 9:00 a.m.–6:00 p.m. All Buildings Open

"50 Great Visual Marketing Ideas in 50 Minutes"
8:30 a.m.–9:30 a.m

Buyer Information Session
10:30 a.m.–11:00 a.m.

"Merchandising the Misfits"
2:30 p.m.–3:30 p.m.

SUNDAY
Show Hours: 9:00 a.m.–6:00 p.m. All Buildings Open

"It's More than Just Price"
8:30 a.m.–9:30 a.m.

"Ways to WOW Your Customers and Keep Them Coming Back"
3:30 p.m.–4:30 p.m.

Sunday Night Extravaganza
6:00 p.m.–8:00 p.m. Plaza at the Mart

An evening of music and dancing, with a complimentary bar and buffet dinner for buyers and exhibitors!

MONDAY
Show Hours: 9:00 a.m.–6:00 p.m. All Buildings Open

"Your Employees: Hiring, Firing, Retaining, Training"
9:00 a.m.–10:30 a.m.

"Vendor Partnerships"
3:30 p.m.–4:30 p.m.

Monday Night Party
6:00 p.m.–8:00 p.m. Plaza at the Mart

Enjoy a night of music, a complimentary buffet dinner, beer and cash bar.

TUESDAY
Show Hours: 9:00 a.m.–4:00 p.m. All Buildings Open

WEDNESDAY
Many of the Mart's permanent showrooms will be open for late buying opportunities. A list of participating showrooms will be available at the show.

assist you with travel and hotel arrangements, and if you have informed them of your merchandising needs, they will have scouted the market and previewed merchandise lines for you. They can save you valuable time by eliminating visits to vendors whose lines are inappropriate for your needs.

Before visiting vendors or participating in other market activities, you will want to talk with the representatives of your buying office. You should make an effort to build a strong relationship with these individuals. The better you get to know them, the more assistance they can be to you. By having a better understanding of your needs, buying offices can provide much more valuable assistance. You will want to review your merchandise buying plan with them and discuss the general market outlook. In addition, they will likely inform you of any new resources in the market. Some buying offices provide a room in which store buyers can view samples of merchandise from vendors. Again, valuable time can be saved by eliminating visits to vendors whose merchandise lines are inappropriate for your needs.

Representatives of buying offices may also present some ideas concerning resources, styles, colors, or fabrics, as shown in Table 12.1. Many buying offices also hold fashion shows or seminars for buyers from stores similar to yours. Take the time to participate in these activities. They offer you the opportunity to exchange ideas and opinions with other buyers who may be experiencing similar buying situations. They do not represent the competition, so you will not be giving away trade secrets.

Visiting Vendors

Whether the vendors to be visited are in a central market, regional merchandise mart, or trade show, there are certain procedures you should follow to make the visits successful:

1. Establish a tentative itinerary each day. Do not be too rigid, because delays may occur.
2. Visit resources in a planned sequence. Determine which classifications of merchandise you will be viewing on the market trip. Then make a list of vendors that you will visit for each classification. Many buyers examine merchandise for

---

TABLE 12.1

EXAMPLES OF HOME FASHIONS INFORMATION BUYERS WOULD LEARN IN THE MARKET

Concepts	Colors	Fabrics & Textures	Key Items
High Tech	Peacock	Stainless Steel	Frosted Glass
Balanced	Daffodil	Platinum/Chrome	Embossed Woods and Leathers
Contemporary	Cantaloupe	Polypropylene	Etched Metals
Pure and Simple	Squash	Leather	Alternative Metals
Sleek	Coral	Shearing	Leather Furniture
Linear	Aqua	Scoring	Plastic Dinnerware,
Interlocking	Black	Overlays	Drinkware, and Furniture
Modular	Grey	Embossing	
Tubular	Off Whites	Stamping	
Curves		Transparent Wax	

each classification separately, which helps them sort through their thoughts better at the end of the day. If you use such an approach, you would complete viewing one merchandise classification before moving to the next one; however, in central markets the location of resources may prevent using this approach. For example, several vendors that you wish to visit may be located in the same building; however, they may deal with different classifications of merchandise. During a visit in one showroom complex, it would be an unwise use of your time not to visit all the vendors there. Viewing one classification at a time works well in merchandise/apparel marts, because similar vendors are located near each other—many times on the same floor. Many buyers also like to view the most expensive lines before lower-priced lines in order to better understand the components of a quality product.

3. Be on time for appointments. If you must cancel an appointment, call as early as possible. Do not rush through your market visits. Rushing through showrooms usually causes buyers to miss important items or overlook significant product features. Carefully viewing merchandise from a few carefully selected vendors is better than rushing through twenty to thirty vendors.

4. View all merchandise before placing orders. During your first viewing of the merchandise, take careful notes and make tentative choices, as illustrated in Figure 12.5. A second viewing of some lines may be required, but you will be able to reject many lines during the initial viewing.

5. Price the merchandise while viewing. Do not ask the price of merchandise you are viewing until you have thoroughly examined it. While viewing the merchandise, mentally attach a price to it. If the price quoted by the vendor is lower than you judged, it possibly is a good buy or you may have overlooked weaknesses in the item. If the price quoted is higher than you judged, you may have overlooked some features or the item may be overpriced.

6. Make careful notes. Your notes should include specific details about the merchandise, such as prices and size ranges; allowances and discounts permitted; and

Figure 12.5
Buyers must carefully record information that they learn when visiting each resource.

the name, address, and phone number of the vendor. Weigh all your intended purchases against your buying plan before placing any orders. Purchase orders need to be analyzed against your plan to ensure proper coverage of classifications, price lines, colors, sizes, and required areas. Make your selections in the quiet of your hotel room or back in your office at the store. Use your own order sheets when placing orders, because you will know that the required information is contained on the form.

Visiting Factories

While in the market you may want to visit the manufacturers of products carried in your store. Many times these factories are located near the central market, and such visits give you more detailed knowledge of the products your store is selling. Also, you are able to obtain a better idea of how the manufacturer operates. Such visits are especially useful if you plan to obtain any minor alterations in the merchandise.

You may also want to visit factories from which you are considering making purchases. These visits will allow you to determine if the manufacturer can handle the amount of work that would be required to produce the products you need. You would also be able to determine evidence of quality control steps taken by the manufacturer. Visit small manufacturers, too. From them you may be able to locate unusual and unique items. Read the Trendwatch titled "Made in the USA: On the Rebound?" to learn more about the growth of some domestic manufacturing in the United States.

Other Market Activities

While in the market, talk with other buyers to learn about their views of the current market and even the selections they have made for their stores. Much valuable information can be learned from informal conversations with fellow buyers.

Also allow time for nonmarket activities. Watch people in the streets or at group functions to detect any new fashion trends. Visit retail stores and window shop throughout your visit. You may even want to tour outstanding stores in the market city.

Visiting Online Showrooms

Today, buyers are able to visit some markets without ever leaving their offices. Retail business-to-business online showrooms are sprouting up at a dizzying pace these days on the internet. These marketplaces bring multiple buyers and sellers together at a central hub, where they can collaborate and negotiate at a fraction of the cost and time previously needed for complex transactions. In addition, online showrooms provide easy reach for international and geographical areas without easy access to traditional markets. Read the Snapshot titled "Alibaba: China's Answer to Amazon?" to learn more about how this online giant conducts business-to-business sales as well as business-to-consumer sales.

Today, there are a number of online showrooms available to fashion buyers. Showroom New York (fashionsourceny.com) provides a home for emerging designers. Designers pay a $250 monthly fee and a 5 percent commission on all sales. Bel Esprit (belesprit .net) is another online showroom that promotes new and emerging designers. They also provide assistance to designers in the areas of marketing sales and distribution. The LA Showroom (lashowroom.com) promotes itself as the online wholesale fashion marketplace with styles from top manufacturers.

In general, online showrooms make money by charging a percentage of the value of the transactions carried across their hubs. Often the transaction fee is the responsibility of the seller, who can be charged from less than 1 percent to as much as 15 percent of the purchase price, depending on the products being sold.

For retailers, online marketplaces open the door to more variety and more partners without having to compromise efficiency. Most experts predict, however, that online showrooms will probably hold greater appeal for small and midsized retail firms and suppliers. All they need to do is use their computer to start interacting in the internet's dynamic, real-time environment. Today, most retail analysts believe there is little doubt that the business-to-business segment of the internet will continue to grow rapidly.

PREPARING TO NEGOTIATE

Before you arrive at the market, you should develop a negotiation plan in addition to your merchandise buying plan. The actual starting point of negotiation always precedes the face-to-face meeting by weeks or even months. **Negotiation** is more than an event; it is a process that involves gathering and using information to your advantage.

What images come to mind when the word "negotiation" is mentioned? For many people, the images they have are "dirty tricks" and endless haggling sessions in which only one side can emerge as the winner. As you will learn, negotiation involves much more. Most Americans do not seem to enjoy negotiating, but in many other countries, negotiation is a part of daily life. If you have ever traveled abroad and visited any of the many public markets, you know that everyone haggles over price; however, in the United States, many people tend to view haggling as an approach used by those who are cheap, petty, and noncooperative. Yet there are many occasions when you have to negotiate.

Did you ever have to convince your parents to buy you a car? What arguments did you use? Did you stress to them what they would gain by purchasing the car for you? If they decided to purchase the car, who negotiated with the car dealer? Did you pay the sticker price? Probably not, if you negotiated.

In fact, almost every activity involving other people probably involves some form of negotiation. Rarely do two people agree on everything. If you are married, you probably have to negotiate such activities as who is going to shower first in the morning, what kind of new car will be purchased, where to go for dinner on weekends, when to purchase a new appliance, or where to spend your summer vacation. We all use negotiation every day.

Like most people, you learned to negotiate as a child when you first had to share your toys with your brothers and sisters or other children in the neighborhood. You had to negotiate who would get to play with them and for how long. Negotiation in business involves that same kind of give-and-take between two people. In other words, negotiation is the process of reaching a mutually satisfying agreement. Negotiation is also based on the premise that people are willing to give up something in order to get something else.

As a buyer, you will be involved with negotiation every time you deal with a vendor. Your goals are to lower costs and improve terms and allowances, whereas the vendor's goals are to obtain your business with you paying the highest possible price. Each of you must be willing to give up something if agreements are to be reached during negotiations.

Before entering into any negotiations, you need to thoroughly understand the market, and the larger impending purchases will mean a greater need for research. You need to understand your customers' needs, competitive and economic conditions, and technical aspects of the products you are planning to purchase. You will want to frequently visit various types of vendors to make comparisons. You will also want to keep abreast of current trends by reading newspapers, magazines, and trade journals. In addition, an understanding of the manufacturing costs involved will enhance your ability to negotiate price concessions. Time spent on research is seldom wasted.

Analyze Your Position

Prepare yourself for negotiations with relevant facts. Have information such as your inventory position, desired profit margins, and current market trends for products that you are purchasing. Before negotiating, conduct a vendor analysis of every vendor with whom you plan to do business. Be sure you are able to justify your offers to vendors, and be ready to offer reasons that explain any concessions for which you are asking.

Determine the Vendor's Position

You will also need to research the vendor's position. Your buying office may be helpful in providing you with information about vendors with whom you will be dealing. Talking with buyers from noncompeting stores is another way to learn about vendors. Obtain as much information as possible from those buyers who have negotiated with the vendor in the past.

Knowing information about the vendor's firm will also be helpful as you plan your negotiations. For example, if manufacturers are doing well, vendors may be more generous in their negotiations with buyers. Or if the firm is experiencing difficulties, the vendor may need to get rid of goods by offering special prices.

Develop Negotiation Skills

Negotiations require that you develop a variety of skills. Successful negotiation techniques come down to essentially one thing—understanding people. Good negotiators consider both their own firm's needs and those of the other party. Some characteristics of good negotiators include creativity, good listening skills, good organizational skills, and self-confidence. Good negotiators force themselves to exert diplomacy and tact. The best negotiators are good listeners who ask questions to get information or to stimulate and direct the other person's thinking.

A knowledge of human behavior is essential to anyone involved with negotiation. You must study people, because they—not terms or conditions—are the key to negotiations. Successful negotiators are sensitive to the needs of others. You need to study psychology, but more importantly, you need to listen and observe. Determine how people have previously reacted in similar situations. Elements of human behavior are predictable, but understanding those elements requires research and analysis.

You must be flexible, too. You will need to keep an open mind and always be ready to make changes in your appraisal of a situation. Above all, you must keep on friendly terms with the vendor. Alienation of the vendor, as a result of a negotiation, will only create additional problems for you in future business dealings.

Determine Objectives of Negotiations

Before entering negotiations, you should carefully develop your objectives. Know exactly what you want to achieve for each point on which you will be negotiating. In your preparation, you should answer the following questions:

- "What is the minimum that I can accept?"
- "What is the maximum I can ask for?"
- "What is the maximum I can give up?"
- "What is the least I can offer?"

Set your minimums and maximums in advance. Do not reveal them during your initial negotiations with the vendor, and stick to them. Once you have determined the minimum you can accept and the maximum you can give away, you will need to assess the maximums and minimums of the vendor. Never assume that vendors with whom you will be negotiating will be reasonable; their objectives might make sense only to them. Also, points that are important to you may be unimportant to the vendor.

SETTING THE STAGE FOR NEGOTIATING

Skillful negotiators know that the other person is not the enemy. Instead, the enemy is whatever will keep both sides from arriving at a positive outcome. Realize that people and circumstances change, so you must be prepared for change. As a buyer, you will be involved in thousands of negotiations, and it is doubtful if any two are ever alike.

Build Rapport

Communicating with friends is much easier than with strangers, so try to build a rapport with the vendor before you start negotiating. Even if you have met the vendor before, you will need to reestablish rapport. Establishing an open, warm atmosphere will help immeasurably when you get to tough issues.

Open your negotiations by focusing on small issues—the points that seem easiest to resolve. Exuding confidence plays a big part in negotiations, too. Be confident and enthusiastic. One way of gaining confidence and maintaining it throughout the negotiation is to ensure that your position is based on sound research. Do not come into negotiations unprepared.

Ask Questions

During negotiations you will also want to determine the vendor's needs. Ask questions, listen carefully, and give the vendor the opportunity to talk. Specifically, you should seek answers to two questions about the vendor:

- "What is the least the vendor can accept?"
- "What is the most the vendor can offer?"

Ask probing, open-ended questions, and keep asking questions until you learn everything you want to know. Be persistent. Listen carefully to the answers, because you may identify hidden messages. Your questions should be relevant and not offend the vendor, and you should make sure to let the vendor know why you want the particular information.

Ask questions to clarify what the vendor has said. You might say something like, "Let me make sure I understand you." Then paraphrase what the vendor has said.

Listen and Watch for Nonverbal Clues

Effective negotiations depend on effective listening. Vendors may reveal clues about their minimums and maximums as they talk with you (Figure 12.6). By listening more and talking less in negotiations, you will increase your chances of gaining more information

Figure 12.6
Nonverbal clues may reveal a lot about the negotiation.

about the vendor's position. With enough information, you are more likely to get the results you want without giving up too much. Listening can be as persuasive as speaking.

Experienced negotiators also look for certain body signals and gestures. For example, vendors leaning back in their chairs and folding their arms may mean they object to something you have said. Be aware of the nonverbal clues you give to the vendor, too. Remain still during negotiations, sit with your shoulders squared, and look the vendor in the eye. You may need to practice these techniques, but they work.

DEVELOPING A NEGOTIATING STRATEGY

Achieving a common understanding is the nature and purpose of negotiations. In a successful negotiation, everybody wins. Unless both parties to an agreement come away feeling that they have made the best deal they could under the circumstances, there has been no real negotiation. There can be no losers when negotiations are successfully completed.

Negotiation is a competitive activity that should be carried on assertively, yet professionally. As you develop a negotiation strategy, you should analyze your personality traits and the traits of vendors with whom you will be negotiating. Then develop tactics or techniques to use in order to reach your objectives. Keep in mind, however, that the vendor will also be developing strategy and tactics.

Personality Styles in Negotiations

Ask people like Donald Trump or Bill Gates about their negotiation style, and they may brag about their toughness. But keep in mind that if you use "tough guy" tactics and bully vendors, they probably will not want to do business with you again, and neither will anyone else who hears about your tactics. Before negotiating, analyze your personality traits, and during negotiations, analyze the traits of the vendor. For successful negotiations to occur, both you and the vendor must be interested in collaboration.

Do you approach negotiations as if you are entering combat? If your only concern is winning, you may not be a successful negotiator for the long term. Some negotiators are not concerned with the relationship or its longevity; their goal is victory through power, threats, or even deception.

Do you concede easily when negotiating? Some people concede too easily on every issue; they try to maintain a low profile and avoid confrontation. Buyers or vendors who display this personality trait will not last long in their jobs.

Either of these traits are extreme examples of negotiation styles. You will want to develop traits that will allow you to become a **collaborator**. That is, you want to view concerns as mutual problems and seek to arrive at solutions that allow both you and the vendor to win.

Negotiation Tactics

Individuals should be aware of their objectives before selecting **tactics** for negotiations. Tactics should be based on becoming acquainted with negotiators and their organizations. The strategy and tactics that you select will be based to some extent on the power that you, or the vendor, possess. You both possess a certain level of power; however, neither side possesses complete power. Your store needs to purchase products from a vendor, but there are many other vendors. Vendors need to sell products to you, but there are other retailers who will make purchases from them. At times, economic and market conditions may give either you or the vendor more power. For example, during recessions, vendors may not be selling large quantities of merchandise, which gives you more power in the negotiation process. Conversely, when economic times are good and a large demand exists for the product that the vendor is selling, power lies with the vendor, who will be unlikely to make concessions. You need to understand the limits of your own power and recognize the limits of the vendor's power. Never intimidate vendors with your store's clout. You may face lean times and will need them later.

Learn to recognize and react to negotiation tactics. Following are some of the more frequently used negotiation tactics:

- *Take It or Leave It.* This tactic is used when there is a deadlock or no time for further negotiation. Obviously, there is a risk that no agreement will be reached, and the other side may leave it. This tactic produces resentment if not handled carefully.
- *Limited Authority.* This tactic requires the buyer to say that he or she is authorized to pay up to $20 for a particular item, and higher prices would require the approval of the merchandising manager or controller.
- *But You Can Do a Little Better.* This tactic challenges the vendor to do a little better to finalize the deal.
- *But I Can't Make Up My Mind.* This tactic places the burden of convincing the buyer on the vendor. Often the vendor will assume the buyer's role, summarize the issues, and point out the relative strengths and weaknesses. Ultimately, the vendor may be put into the position of assisting the buyer to make up his or her mind by improving the offer.
- *Facts and Data.* This tactic may determine the outcome of a negotiation. The individual with the most data can build the best case for his or her position.
- *What If?* This tactic uses questions such as the following:
  - "What if I increase the purchase quantity?"
  - "What if we combine similar items?"

- "What if I pay the invoice in ten days instead of thirty?"
- "What if we offer to extend the warranty period an additional six months?"
- "What if we offer an option to buy an additional unit at 20 percent discount?"
- *Let's Split the Difference.* This tactic requires that both the buyer and vendor relinquish an equal amount of a disputed difference. Usually this tactic is used when the difference is small and the end of the negotiation is near.
- *Time Pressure.* This tactic is also frequently used by both vendors and buyers. It is designed to make the other person give up something. The vendor may attempt to force you into an immediate decision with any of the following statements:
  - "The price will increase next month."
  - "The offer is good for only ten days."
  - "Delivery is four weeks after the receipt of the order."
  - "There is only limited inventory available."

As a buyer, you may use time-pressure tactics, too. For example, you may say, "I'm returning home tomorrow, and I will need your final offer by the end of the day." Time-pressure tactics work for the person who has time, but an actual lack of time may work against you in negotiating.

Negotiation involves bargaining and compromise. A person entering negotiations should concentrate on tactics and only use compromise at the end. Being prepared to negotiate and taking the initiative are important for leverage during negotiating. Moreover, negotiating can be learned, and practice is the most effective way to sharpen negotiating skills.

Bargaining

The negotiation process involves bargaining and agreement between you and the vendor in relation to the business transaction. Try to see vendors' proposals from their point of view so that you can learn what is important to them.

One of the more formidable tools in negotiating is silence. People dislike silence and usually try to fill it with information. For example, suppose a vendor says to you, "I cannot guarantee this price will be available at the end of the month." If you remain silent and let the vendor talk, he or she may reveal that this is not the real position.

Compromise is usually arrived at during the normal course of negotiating; however, the sole intent of negotiation should not be compromise. The real skill in negotiating is to work out a settlement that gives the other side just enough to make them willing to agree—but no more.

It is not wise to accept the first offer in a negotiation, because doing so does not test the other person's position. Avoid quick concessions. You risk giving up something unnecessarily if you hurry to expedite negotiations. Negotiations require a full discussion, not shortcuts.

The last 20 percent of negotiating time is believed to be when most concessions are made. If you have to make trade-offs during negotiations, which you inevitably will, make sure you do not give up something that will derail your long-range strategy.

Negotiators often answer affirmatively too quickly when they could have bargained for a better deal. Learn to "flinch" as a standard reaction to any proposal made, then play the role of the reluctant buyer.

If you think negotiations are near an end but have not arrived at a decision, ask the vendor for a solution. Build on the partnership concept. In fact, the vendor may offer an acceptable alternative that you may not have even considered. At that stage of the negotiations, avoid **ultimatums**, one of the most common but least effective negotiating tactics. Even if the vendor gives in, he or she will resent you. If you ever plan to do business with the vendor again, and the chances are that you will, you cannot win if the other side loses. Your winning and the vendor losing cannot be good for future business. When you both win, you are likely to walk away from negotiations with more than a deal; you have acquired a relationship based on mutual respect. Negotiations should not be "winner takes all." When you realize that, you are on your way to becoming a successful negotiator.

Negotiation Checklist

Before entering negotiations, make a list of areas to guide your negotiations. Be assertive, and ask for what you want in a straightforward manner. Following are some of the most important topics that you may negotiate:

- Price
- Discounts
- Transportation terms
- Allowances

- Return privileges
- Exclusives
- Off-price
- Specification buying

- Private brands
- Vendor-supported promotions
- Delivery

These areas are more fully explored in Chapter 14. As a buyer, your responsibility is to negotiate every allowance or service for which your store is eligible. You therefore must know what vendors have available.

Outcomes of Negotiation

Negotiating is a business relationship in action. It involves more than merely setting out to win some concessions from the other person. Although such an attitude may work in a single transaction, in an ongoing business relationship, the outcome must hold benefits for all parties. Furthermore, mutually beneficial solutions should convey the perception of benefits. Great negotiators are outstanding problem solvers.

Negotiation is an essential business skill that involves the attitude you convey, the tactics you use, and the concern you show for the other person's feelings and needs. The objective is for both sides to win—to develop a long-term partnership. Understanding, acceptance, respect, trust, and a lasting business relationship will be the outcome of successful negotiations.

Summary Points

- **Central markets offer buyers access to a large number of key resources in close proximity to one another. Regional markets have developed to serve specific areas of the country by offering one-stop shopping to buyers at merchandise/apparel marts. Buyers can also locate sources at trade shows or expositions held yearly in many areas.**

- **Before planning a buying trip, buyers need to determine the purpose of the trip and develop a merchandise buying plan as well as a negotiation plan.**

- **The season, type of merchandise, size of store, its merchandise policies, proximity to markets, and business conditions will determine the frequency of a buyer's visits to market.**

- **In the market, buyers will want to talk with buying offices, visit vendors and showrooms, tour factories, attend seminars and fashion shows, talk with other buyers, and tour outstanding retail stores.**

- **When viewing lines, buyers must be systematic and take careful notes. Some buyers prefer to view** all of one classification before moving to the next classification.

- Buyers must negotiate every time they deal with vendors.

- Negotiation is a process that begins before the face-to-face meeting between the vendor and buyer occurs. Before negotiating, buyers must gather and use information about their customers, competitive and economic conditions, and facts about products they will be purchasing.

- Before negotiating, buyers should learn about their vendors from buying offices and other buyers who have dealt with them in the past.

- Negotiation requires that buyers understand people and have good listening skills. Successful negotiators are self-confident and exhibit tact and diplomacy.

- Before negotiating, buyers should establish the minimum they can accept and the maximum they can give away. During negotiations, buyers must also assess the minimums and maximums of the vendor.

- Questions help the buyer determine the vendor's position during negotiations. Asking questions requires that buyers listen carefully in order to obtain more information about the vendor's position.

- The intent of negotiation should not be compromise. The real skill in negotiating is to work out a settlement that gives the other person's side just enough to make it willing to agree—but no more.

- Successful negotiators are collaborators. Their goal is for both sides in negotiations to "win."

- Various negotiation tactics are available for both the vendor and the buyer to use. The same tactics are frequently used by both sides to make the other side give up something.

- The end result of negotiation should be a mutually beneficial solution for both the buyer and the vendor.

Review Activities

Developing Your Retail Buying Vocabulary
Consult the glossary if you did not add the following terms to your vocabulary.

central market	exposition	negotiation	trade show
collaborator	merchandise/apparel mart	tactics	ultimatum
compromise			

Understanding What You Read

1. Describe what a buyer would typically find in a central market.

2. List and describe three purposes for making a buying trip.

3. For what reasons would a buyer make shorter and more frequent buying trips?

4. What should be developed first as a buying trip is planned?

5. Who may be required to approve a buyer's merchandise buying plan?

6. What services can a buying office provide buyers before they reach the market?

7. Why would buyers want to attend seminars sponsored by their buying office?

8. Describe the benefits of viewing an entire classification of merchandise before viewing other classifications.

9. Why do most Americans not enjoy negotiating?

10. Where does the starting point of any negotiation begin?

11. Why is knowing the vendor's position important to the negotiation process?

12. What four questions should buyers answer as they prepare for negotiations?

13. Describe ways to build rapport with vendors during negotiations.

14. While negotiating, what two questions about the vendor's position should the buyer attempt to answer?

15. Why is listening so important to the negotiation process?

16. Why should buyers not approach negotiations as if they are entering combat?

17. When should the "let's split the difference" tactic be used in negotiations?

18. Describe how both the buyer and the vendor can use time-pressure tactics.

19. Why should buyers never intimidate vendors by using their store's clout?

20. Why should buyers avoid quick concessions during negotiations?

21. Why should buyers ask the vendor for an alternative when the negotiation process seems to be stalled?

22. What should be the outcome of any negotiation?

Analyzing and Applying What You Read

1. What problems might result from buyers rushing through the viewing of a vendor's lines?

2. Why should buyers "price" a vendor's line of merchandise before inquiring about the cost?

3. Explain why the sole intention of negotiations should not be compromise.

4. Your research has revealed that the vendor with whom you will be negotiating has the reputation for heavy use of facts and statistical support. As a buyer, what should you do before meeting with the vendor? How should you respond when the vendor begins pouring out all these data?

5. The vendor with whom you are negotiating has just hit you with a take-it-or-leave-it stand. He will sell dress shirts to you at $15.50 each and not a penny less. What should be your response? Explain.

6. Outline a plan that any new buyer could follow to practice the skills needed for successful negotiation.

Internet Connection

1. Access the websites for both major US furniture markets at http://www.highpointmarket.org and http://www.las vegasmarket.com. Locate information on the process a buyer must follow in order to attend both markets. Identify attendance figures at the most recent market. Compare and contrast these attendance figures to those in the past. Finally, identify current furniture trends.

2. Access http://www.magiconline.com to learn more about the MAGIC market held in Las Vegas. Identify fashion trends that are predicted on the site for the coming season.

3. Visit the book's STUDIO to watch videos about markets all over the world.

Which toy will be the Tickle Me Elmo or Silly Bandz hit of this year? Every toy maker hopes the answer to that question will be found in its new product lines revealed in February each year at the North American International Toy Fair held in New York City. The event, the largest toy trade show in the Western Hemisphere, is hosted by the Toy Industry Association and attracts more than 1,100 exhibitors who showcase over 100,000 toys, games, and entertainment products. In addition, over 10,000 buyers from 100 countries usually attend. In fact, retail buyers from nearly all of the top twenty-five toy retailers in the United States, such as Amazon, Build-A-Bear, Costco, CVS, Disney Stores, Target, Toys "R" Us, and Walmart, attend. During the show, they explore a vast array of skill-building toys and games, ranging from cutting-edge robotics, drones, and active toys as well as classic playthings like dolls, plush toys, and board games.

At this annual trade show, the buzz is always about which toy will be this year's hit. But it is impossible to know. Tickle Me Elmo was the surprise hit of 1996—selling out of stores nationwide well before the holidays. Moreover, thanks to the Elmo craze that year, sales of all plush dolls climbed 12 percent. An Elmo phenomenon, however, is not planned, and even the largest toy companies usually cannot predict what the hits are going to be. And, who would have ever predicted that Silly Bandz, colorful silicone rubber bands in different shapes, would fly off retailers' shelves in 2010?

A lot is riding on this event. Each year as the toy fair opens, manufacturers will show their new lines, and retailers will be scouting around for what will be the year's next big hit. This annual market mixes business with outright silliness. Firms construct elaborate sets and hire teams of actors to push the products they hope will be big sellers for the year, especially during the holiday season. Men in suits lick lollipops and executives discuss the merits of various dolls. Actresses sit in bedroom sets built just for the show and tickle the feet of toy infants. Public relations people blow bubbles. But by the end of the show, millions of dollars in orders have been placed, and toy manufacturers have a strong idea what the big hits of the year will be.

Most years, manufacturers depend heavily on licensed toys, linking their products to new movies from Hollywood. Today, it seems that every movie has products tied to it. Toy makers like movie-related products because they are identified with a heavily advertised entertainment package. But each year manufacturers and retailers have to wait to see if kids respond to the new movies. They know these toys can be highly profitable. With the rerelease of the *Star Wars* trilogy in the late 1990s, Hasbro and Galoob Toys reissued their full line of action figures associated with the movies. They sold $425 million worth of toys based on twenty-year-old characters.

Technology also has played a part in many of the new toys hitting the market in recent years. Perhaps the most surprising new category that reflects the influence of technology has been in the infant and preschool segments. A substantial part of the growth came from the creative use of computer chips in musical instrument toys such as Barney's Magical Banjo and preschool learning toys such as VTech's AlphaBert. Additionally, many toys today have an online component. From stuffed animals to board games, toy companies give kids a reason to go online to continue the fun, and there they are encouraged to visit regularly.

Each year, retail buyers also place orders for classic toys; they know many parents purchase toys for their kids similar to the ones with which they played as children. Many manufacturers even update these classics with new interactive technology. For example, construction toy maker Lego went high-tech with the release of a CD-ROM game, *Adventures on Lego Island*, which mixed technology with traditional Lego building.

At the most recent toy fair, gender inclusivity for toys was a major theme, and was embraced by Mattel, Hasbro, and Lego, who have created and marketed toys with both genders in mind, rather than dividing the toy aisles in stores into pink and blue. Hollywood has also produced more movies with female characters in lead roles, which has led to more gender-inclusive toys.

Personal customization, the ability to make toys unique to the child, is clearly another big trend here to stay. Whether it is with stickers and markers or choosing the color, many toys today have components that kids need to create something that is one-of-a-kind. And, many new toys have been developed with Mom in mind. For art supplies, science kits, and craft sets, the message is that they are "mess-free" or that "clean-up is easy."

For retail toy buyers, the toy fair represents the most important show they will attend each year. Yet they must cut through the hype and make selections based on what they think will be hits with their customers. There is lots of pressure associated with those decisions—no retailer wants to be stuck with the toy no one wants during the holidays.

BASED ON:

Karol, Gabrielle. (2014, February 20). 3 hot toy trends at the 2014 international toy fair. *Newyork.cbslocal.com.*

Kell, John. (2017, February 23). How tech and gender inclusivity are propelling the toy industry. *Fortune.com.*

Sandler, Anna. (2014, March 4). Trends and top picks from the 111th American International Toy Fair. *Kids.baristanet.com.*

SNAPSHOT: Alibaba: China's Answer to Amazon?

Who or what is Alibaba? It's one of the world's largest retailers, as well as being one of the largest internet companies. Alibaba is a Chinese e-commerce company that provides consumer-to-consumer, business-to-consumer, and business-to-business sales services via the internet—a fusion of eBay and Amazon. It is one of the hottest e-commerce companies of the last five years, with six times the sales volume of its biggest Chinese competitor. Moreover, Alibaba's Singles Day promotion doubled the e-commerce sales totals in the United States from Thanksgiving, Black Friday, and Cyber Monday combined.

Aiding in this rapid growth was the fact that Alibaba arrived on the retail scene to serve a generation of Chinese consumers who were just attaining middle-class prosperity. These customers have tended to adopt new retail formats and online shopping much faster than their counterparts around the world. Alibaba reports that there are approximately 430 million buyers across its internet platforms each year, with one-third of them located in China. Company forecasts predict that number will rise to over 2 billion consumers around the world in the next twenty years.

When the company was founded in 1999, it was basically a business-to-business web portal designed to connect Chinese manufacturers with overseas buyers. That role has drastically changed today with the emergence of two portals at Alibaba—Taobao and Tmall. Taobao is essentially China's eBay and is dominated by small businesses and individuals selling to one another. At the site, customers can find small retailers and individuals selling such things as collectibles, phone cases, selfie sticks, and even live scorpions. In its early years, Taobao also become a market for counterfeit Western brands—a problem that persists today even though Alibaba has taken steps to curb it.

Tmall is distinctly different; it is positioned as a marketplace for higher-quality clothing, food, and electronics, with a focus on luxury brands. On the site, customers can purchase such items as Olay face creams, sheets and towels from Macy's, and Burberry coats. It is also the site on which Alibaba has staked its future growth.

With recent slowdowns in the Chinese economy, Alibaba wants to feature more U.S. companies whose brands often have stronger appeal and better reputation in China than their Chinese equivalents. Recent crises involving harmful chemicals in Chinese-produced food and cosmetics have fueled that sentiment.

To woo firms such as P&G, Estee Lauder, and Macy's, Alibaba has promoted itself as a shortcut to the world's most populous market by allowing foreign companies to sidestep many of the taxes, regulatory hurdles, and logistics hassles that have caused major problems for companies expanding to China. Foreign companies that sell through Alibaba can start selling to customers almost immediately. Moreover, Alibaba is providing foreign companies with marketing, data analytics, and shipping. Such partnerships can be beneficial for both parties—new markets for foreign companies and increased income for Alibaba, which charges these companies fees of 2 to 5 percent of sales on its site. For additional fees Alibaba will also handle transaction processing with the foreign companies' home banks and provide inventory control and shipping as well. Above all, Alibaba provides foreign companies the ability to learn the Chinese market and its consumers without a massive investment. For example, the company helped Macy's focus its product offerings on accessories, shoes, towels, and sheets—a selection of "touch the skin" categories where China's shoppers covet foreign brands.

Alibaba has been successful in attracting some US companies to sell on its site. Costco has used Alibaba to make an impressive debut on the Chinese market, and Macy's also has a "storefront" on the site. Even some companies, such as P&G, which already had a wide presence in China, is using Alibaba because it lets them bring new products to market faster. While U.S. companies are generally positive about their exposure on Alibaba, almost everyone remains silent on exactly how much they are selling. And, Alibaba does not disclose sales for international products.

Highly publicized promotions on Alibaba create a lot of buzz and sales. For example, in one six-day promotion Estee Lauder generated 1.3 million dollars in sales. Even though products are sold at steep discounts during such promotions, it is beneficial to a foreign company if it helps their brand get a foothold in the China market, with its 1.3 billion potential customers. Such partnerships should provide a boost for both sides.

BASED ON:

Alibaba tops Singles' Day record despite sales growth slowdown. (2016, November 11). *BloombergNews.com*.

Cendrowski, Scott. (2016, October 13). Alibaba's Jack Ma just predicted the next 30 years of technological change. *Fortune.com*.

Rao, Leena. (2015, December 29). Why Alibaba wants Chinese shoppers to buy American. *Fortune.com*.

MADE IN THE USA: ON THE REBOUND?

In the United States, approximately 12 million Americans are employed directly in manufacturing, representing about 10 percent of the workforce, but that is dramatically down from a peak of 19.6 million manufacturing workers in 1979. However, even as some companies have outsourced their manufacturing, others have continued to make their products in the United States and boast about that fact to their customers. Moreover, since the recession at the beginning of the decade, manufacturing growth in the United States has outpaced that of other advanced nations.

American workers are making more products that customers around the world want to purchase. Apple is now producing one of its Mac computer lines in the United States, and Walmart announced that it would increase spending with American suppliers by $50 billion over the next decade. Ashley Furniture is also investing $80 million to build a new plant in North Carolina, a state that in recent years has lost over 70,000 jobs to sites offshore.

Manufacturing costs in Europe can be 15 to 20 percent higher than in the United States—one of the reasons that both Rolls-Royce and Volkswagen are also expanding in the United States. Rolls-Royce has announced a $136 million addition to its plant in Virginia, and Volkswagen's new plant in Tennessee has added a third shift and boosted its employment in that state to 3,300—a big commitment from a company that stopped all production in the United States in the 1980s.

However, manufacturing jobs have not increased in all areas. Apparel manufacturing is a prime example. Although, some companies, such as Brooks Brothers and Saks, have increased their purchasing from domestic manufacturers, the national picture is gloomier. Apparel manufacturing jobs in the United States continue to decline—decreasing by 50 percent during the last decade.

What is causing this increase in US manufacturing? The economics of outsourcing is beginning to change. Some low costs evaporate when goods have to be shipped thousands of miles to stores in the United States. For example, shipping costs from China to the West Coast of the United States have nearly doubled in the last ten years. Additionally, workers in China, India, and other third-world countries are demanding and getting bigger paychecks. In 2000, for example, the average wage of Chinese workers was $0.50, but today it is over $4.50. In addition, some US companies have won massive wage concessions from labor unions over

the past decade, keeping wages from spiraling. However, American workers still are no bargain when compared with workers of emerging economies, and American workers still make 7.4 times as much per hour, on average, as their Chinese counterparts.

What can be done to increase more manufacturing jobs in the United States? The key is for companies to develop new manufacturing techniques ahead of their competitors around the world and then use those techniques to produce goods more efficiently. In fact, labor productivity in the United States has already risen sharply over the past decade. Much of that increase can be attributed to better technology.

Even though manufacturing in the United States is increasing, those jobs will look very different than in the past. Factories that have more machines and fewer workers are evolving. Moreover, those factory workers must have better training than in the past; they must be technologically advanced to be able to master the machines on the factory floor.

Getting and keeping well-paying jobs are still primary concerns for most Americans, and keeping jobs in the United States is a message that resonates with many consumers here when promoting "Made in the USA" products. But, the question remains whether or not "Made in the USA" will become a core value for shoppers or whether it will be just another passing fad.

Some analysts predict that there will be a steady increase in manufacturing jobs in the United States, but China will remain the dominant manufacturer for the world. They also stress that such gains will not be distributed evenly across the United States by geography or by industry. The question that remains is, "Will this rebound continue?"

BASED ON:

Coy, Peter. (2014, April 23). An apparel-making revival? This "made in USA" story doesn't hold up. *BusinessWeek.com*.

D'innocenzio, Anne, & Schneider, Mike. (2013, August 22). Walmart pushes "made in America" at summit. *BusinessWeek.com*.

Foroohar, Rana, & Saporito, Bill. (2013, April 22). Made in the USA. *Time*, 22–29.

Harnish, Verne. (2014, February 3). Five ways to make it in the U.S.A. *Fortune*, 28.

Roberts, Andrew, & Lin, Liza. (2014, February 27). Made-in-USA luxury brands win fans in China. *BusinessWeek.com*.

Searching for what's still made in the USA. (2013, July 18). *CNN.com*.

St. John, Oliver. (2013, January 21). Made in USA makes comeback as a marketing tool. *USAToday.com*.

LOCATING SOURCES IN FOREIGN MARKETS

Performance Objectives

- **Identify reasons buyers purchase goods in foreign markets.**
- **Identify drawbacks buyers face when purchasing goods in foreign markets.**
- **Outline the factors to consider when determining the feasibility of purchasing goods in foreign markets.**
- **List and explain methods of locating foreign sources.**
- **Identify the components of calculating the landed cost of foreign merchandise.**
- **Identify special considerations buyers face when their stores expand into foreign markets.**
- **Recognize that a continual globalization of the marketplace is occurring.**
- **Cite examples of "Buy American" efforts.**

You have spent days or even weeks researching the market and preparing your merchandise buying plan. Now you have to make purchases that will put your plan into action, and that involves selecting the right merchandise for your customers. Merchandise selection is a continuous process that can take place at your desk, in a manufacturer's showroom, at a merchandise mart, or in foreign markets. Wherever you decide to make your purchases, you must ensure that the merchandise is what your customers will purchase once it is in your store. In addition, the amount of money that you have to spend will probably affect where you make your purchases.

In this chapter, the focus will be on selecting and importing purchases from foreign sources. You will also examine the opportunities and drawbacks that these sources offer. Methods of locating and identifying the right foreign sources will be explained, and the impact of "Buy American" programs and the globalization of retailing will be described.

PURCHASING AND IMPORTING PRODUCTS FROM THE GLOBAL MARKETPLACE

Making the decision to import purchases from foreign sources requires that you prepare yourself for entering the global marketplace. Learn as much as you can about the people, the culture, and the retailing practices of any country that you are considering as a foreign source. Possibly even learn a new language or at least a few key phrases.

Making the Decision to Buy from Foreign Sources

Buyers in the United States who are considering foreign sourcing can locate exciting alternatives in the global marketplace; however, before making the decision to import products from these sources, the following guidelines should be considered:

- Ensure that products from a foreign source are a logical extension of the store's current product assortment.
- Consider foreign sourcing only when the cost of a product has made it uncompetitive for it to be purchased in domestic markets.
- Recognize that communications may be more difficult when foreign sourcing is used.
- Analyze shipping costs and delivery times for merchandise purchased from foreign sources.
- In addition to shipping, be aware of all other costs involved with foreign sourcing.
- Start small and slowly. Test some products from foreign sources before making large merchandise commitments.
- Initially, keep alternative sources of supply.

Identifying Reasons to Buy from Foreign Sources

A multitude of products are already produced in the United States, yet buyers seek out and purchase from foreign sources. Automobiles, furniture, and clothing are just some of the product categories that are being imported from foreign markets in large quantities to compete with products manufactured in the United States. Why do buyers purchase from foreign sources? Key reasons follow.

Unavailability of Merchandise

For some products, the only available sources may be in foreign markets. For example, almost no cameras or CD players are produced in the United States today. Some specialty food items must also be imported, as well as many wines and liquors. In addition, handmade products that cannot be replicated in this country are imported. When merchandise that customers want is unavailable from domestic sources, buyers must turn to foreign markets for those purchases.

Low Cost

Imports from foreign markets are often less expensive than similar merchandise purchased from domestic sources. Contributing to this low cost are typically much lower wages paid to factory workers in many underdeveloped countries; however, the wages in many countries, such as Japan, China, and Korea, are escalating.

Quality

Merchandise produced in the United States is of high quality; however, some countries are producing products of superior quality. The finest linen in the world is from Belgium and Ireland. Italy has some of the finest leather for clothing and accessories,

Figure 13.1
Italy has some of the finest leather for clothing and accessories, such as handbags, shoes, and belts.

such as handbags, shoes, and belts (Figure 13.1). Silks from China and cottons from India are world renowned. Many US consumers also perceive foreign products to be of higher quality. Ask consumers to name top-performing automobiles, and they probably will mention BMW and Mercedes from Germany and Sweden's Volvo. However, for some products, problems with product quality has begun to surface. Read the Trendwatch titled "Recalled Products: What Went Wrong?" to learn more about recent product recalls of products imported from other countries.

Uniqueness

Customers are always looking for something different. Foreign markets are one source of unique merchandise. Special handmade items with distinctive styling are not readily available from domestic sources. In the United States, customers seem to always be searching for new, different, unique products. Keep in mind that many unique brands continue to be manufactured in the United States. A list of some of these brands is presented in Table 13.1.

TABLE 13.1

PRODUCTS STILL BEING MANUFACTURED IN THE UNITED STATES

Product	Manufactured in the US Since	Product	Manufactured in the US Since
Stanley tools	1843	New Balance sneakers	1938
Stetson hats	1865	Slinky toys	1945
Tabasco hot sauces	1868	Weber grills	1952
Louisville Slugger bats	1894	Sharpie pens	1964
Crayola crayons	1903	Kettle potato chips	1982
Red Wing shoes	1905	Mrs. Meyer's Clean Day products	2000
Pyrex kitchen products	1915		

Source: Time, April 22, 2013.

Fashion Trends

Globally, Europe is still a great influencer of fashion apparel. Buyers from all over the world attend fashion shows in Paris and Milan to discover new trends. Making foreign purchases allows buyers the opportunity to offer their customers what is new and exciting and keep their store in a fashion leadership position. Read the Snapshot titled "Zara: Providing Style and Rapid Response" to learn more about how one international retailer from Spain has dramatically changed the fashion cycle with "fast fashion."

Identifying Drawbacks to Buying from Foreign Sources

If you choose to import products from foreign sources, you must realize that there are some drawbacks. These problems should not scare you away from foreign sources but should simply make you cautious. Some typical drawbacks follow.

Early Purchase Commitment Required

Because of the long lead time needed to guarantee delivery of imports, purchases from foreign sources must be made much earlier than with domestic sources, and that makes sales forecasting more difficult. Trends are much more difficult to forecast over longer periods of time; however, trade journals, fashion forecasters, buying offices, and reporting services can all be helpful to buyers in predicting long-range trends.

Delivery Problems

Delivery of merchandise purchased from foreign sources is also subject to unforeseen shipping delays caused by events such as dock strikes and weather problems. Because of the delivery distances involved with foreign sourcing, there may be an inability to check on the location of shipments in transit. In addition, the delivery of reorders is nearly impossible for fashion merchandise. The season would probably be over before the reorder arrives. Completion dates for delivery of merchandise should be a part of any contract that a buyer signs. Penalties should be negotiated in case the merchandise arrives late.

Size Discrepancies

easurements vary in the global marketplace. Products purchased from many foreign markets may not be compatible with sizes found in the United States. As shown in Table 13.2, S, M, and L mean different sizes in different countries. Providing specific dimensions to the manufacturer is the most effective way to overcome this drawback.

Added Expense and Time Involved

Foreign markets are not as convenient as domestic markets when you need to make personal buying trips. Much more time is needed to visit many foreign markets because of the difficulty in moving from one vendor to another. You may have to go to different parts of a city or even to different cities to see lines and compare product offerings.

Clothing sizes in the United States are different than those found in the rest of the world. Therefore, it is important to know what your size is in US measurements before you shop in foreign markets. Here is a clothing guide to help you find your size. All sizes are approximate.

TABLE 13.2

CLOTHES SIZE GUIDE

Women

Dresses and Suits

European	34	36	38	40	42	44	46	48
UK	6	8	10	12	14	16	18	20
USA	4	6	8	10	12	14	16	18

Shoes

European	38	38	39	39	40	41
UK	$4\frac{1}{2}$	5	$5\frac{1}{2}$	6	$6\frac{1}{2}$	7
USA	6	$6\frac{1}{2}$	7	$7\frac{1}{2}$	8	$8\frac{1}{2}$

Men

Suits and Overcoats

European	46	48	50	52	54	56	58
UK	36	38	40	42	44	46	48
USA	36	38	40	42	44	46	48

Shirts

European	36	37	38	39	41	42	43
UK	14	$14\frac{1}{2}$	15	$15\frac{1}{2}$	16	$16\frac{1}{2}$	17
USA	14	$14\frac{1}{2}$	15	$15\frac{1}{2}$	16	$16\frac{1}{2}$	17

Shoes

European	41	42	43	44	45	46
UK	7	$7\frac{1}{2}$	$8\frac{1}{2}$	$9\frac{1}{2}$	$10\frac{1}{2}$	11
USA	8	$8\frac{1}{2}$	$9\frac{1}{2}$	$10\frac{1}{2}$	$11\frac{1}{2}$	12

Socks

European	39	40	41	42	43	44
UK	$9\frac{1}{2}$	10	$10\frac{1}{2}$	11	$11\frac{1}{2}$	12
USA	$9\frac{1}{2}$	10	$10\frac{1}{2}$	11	$11\frac{1}{2}$	12

Children

European	125	135	150	155	160
UK (cm)	43	48	55	58	60
USA (ins)	4	6	8	10	12

Funds Tied Up

When making foreign purchases, the retailer's capital funds have to be tied up for longer periods of time than when purchasing domestically. Factories in foreign countries usually require payment before the goods leave the country. Most domestic manufacturers, however, will extend credit terms, allowing the retailer to wait a period of time after goods have been delivered before having to remit payment.

Locating Foreign Sources

Once buyers have analyzed the marketplace and decided that foreign sourcing is the best option for their company, the next step is to locate foreign sources or suppliers. Retail buyers can (1) make personal buying trips to foreign markets or (2) use intermediaries.

Making Personal Buying Trips

Many buyers have developed their own programs that will provide their stores with unique merchandise brands from foreign sources. One way to develop such programs is to make personal contacts in foreign markets. Because direct negotiation is needed, fashion merchandise is typically purchased in this manner; however, only large retail organizations can afford the significant expense of sending buyers directly into foreign markets.

In addition to visiting foreign factories, buyers' market trips should also include visits to expositions and trade shows in foreign markets. These shows are similar to ones held in the United States; they run for a few days or a week and attract buyers and retailers from around the world.

Buyers considering personal buying trips should realize there are problems to overcome, among them, language and social/cultural differences.

Buyers must have a knowledge of the language of the country where they are negotiating purchases. Being able to communicate without an interpreter has tremendous value when negotiating and will make misunderstandings less likely to occur. Although English is becoming the international language of trade, many small countries may not enjoy the luxury of having a large number of English-speaking representatives.

Buyers must be aware that cultures vary around the world. A sign or gesture may destroy a deal that a buyer has been negotiating. Removing your shoes in someone's home is considered proper etiquette in Japan, but it would likely be frowned on in the United States. Data presented in Table 13.3 provide etiquette tips for visiting other countries.

Using Intermediaries

For most buyers, making personal buying trips to foreign markets may not be an option. Expenses and time involved would be too great for their store. In addition, some buyers who make trips to foreign markets may not be comfortable with the language and customs. In such situations, buyers could use **intermediaries**, or middlemen. Several kinds of intermediaries are available:

- *Foreign Buying Offices.* **Commissionaires,** or foreign buying offices, operate in foreign markets and function similarly to domestic buying offices. Staff members of these firms live in the local area, so they can provide the retail buyer with an understanding of the language and customs of the foreign market. They are also much more familiar with markets than a buyer who is spending only a week or two there. In addition, representatives from these buying offices can reorder merchandise for the buyer and make arrangements for merchandise storage. Above all, they are constantly scouting foreign markets for the best available merchandise. Their fee is typically charged based on a percentage of total purchases.
- *Domestic Buying Offices.* Many US buying offices are represented in major foreign markets and bring imported merchandise to client stores. Buying offices are providing such services as more retailers have developed import programs.

TABLE 13.3

ETIQUETTE TIPS FOR VISITING OTHER COUNTRIES

Cambodia	Never touch or pass something over the head of a Cambodian because the head is considered sacred.
China	As in most Asian cultures, avoid waving or pointing chopsticks, putting them vertically in a rice bowl, or tapping them on the bowl. These actions are considered extremely rude.
India	Avoid giving gifts made from leather because many Hindus are vegetarian and consider cows sacred. Keep this in mind when taking Indian clients to restaurants. Do not wink because it is seen as a sexual gesture.
Japan	Never write on a business card or shove the card into your back pocket when you are with the giver. This is considered disrespectful. Hold the card with both hands and read it carefully.
Malaysia	If you receive an invitation from a business associate from Malaysia, always respond in writing. Avoid using your left hand because it is considered unclean.
Philippines	Never refer to a female hosting an event as the "hostess," which translates to "prostitute."
Singapore	If you plan to give a gift, always give it to the company. A gift to one person is considered a bribe.
Vietnam	Shake hands only with someone of the same sex who initiates it. Physical contact between men and women in public is frowned upon.
France	Always remain calm, polite, and courteous during business meetings. Never appear overly friendly because this could be construed as suspicious. Never ask personal questions.
Greece	If you need to signal a taxi, holding up five fingers is considered an offensive gesture if the palm faces outward. Face your palm inward with closed fingers.
Mexico	If visiting a business associate's home, do not bring up business unless the associate does.
Spain	Always request your check when dining out in Spain. It is considered rude for wait staff to bring your bill beforehand.

- *Importers.* Buyers may find that merchandise costs only a little more from **importers** located in the United States when compared with making a foreign market trip themselves. Importers may be able to qualify for quantity discounts and pass the savings along to the buyer. Many import wholesalers take the initial risk by making purchases in foreign markets and import merchandise to store in their warehouses in the United States. Buyers are then better able to compare the cost of foreign merchandise to that of merchandise available from domestic sources.

Choosing the Right Foreign Sources

Once buyers have identified foreign sources for products that they wish to purchase, their next step will be to find the best sources. Initially, they will look for some of the same benefits that are available in any domestic source—reliability, attractive prices, credit terms, assured quality, and timely delivery. However, problems can more easily develop since buyers are making purchases from companies in other countries that are located thousands of miles away from their stores.

Before signing any contracts with foreign sources, always conduct a credit check on any potential supplier. References should routinely be requested, and is an important step in weeding out any unreliable sources. If possible, visit factories where your products will be manufactured. Determine if the supplier can meet your quality standards as well as complying with any government regulations. You may also want to observe employee working conditions and other safety issues.

For items such as apparel, the manufacturing process does not begin until the order is placed. Therefore, it is imperative to request samples to analyze. However, keep in mind that even sources that provide excellent samples may send a shoddy shipment.

Buyers from the United States may also be able to contact some foreign sources without making a trip to a foreign country. Some foreign manufacturers have opened offices in the United States.

The importance of carefully identifying and evaluating all potential foreign sources cannot be overestimated. Buyers selecting the wrong source can create insurmountable problems for a selling season.

Analyzing Other Factors Affecting Purchase Decisions

Once appropriate foreign sources have been identified that meet buyers' standards and specifications, the next step would be identifying governmental regulations or restrictions affecting their purchases. Most of the goods imported into the United States are subject to a tax, known as a **duty** or **tariff** (Figure 13.2). The key reason for these taxes is to lower the number of imports by making them cost more than goods produced domestically. Duties are charged as a percentage of a product's value and vary according to the type of merchandise and the country of origin.

Figure 13.2
Most goods imported into the United States are subject to duties or tariffs.

Many US retailers pay higher tariffs than necessary because of many bureaucratic rules governing imports. Retail buyers may be able to realize considerable savings on tariffs by carefully detailing product descriptions on purchase orders and invoices. For example, a home center retailer importing tiles could save 33 percent on certain tariffs by precisely describing the merchandise purchased. The duty rate on tile varies from 20 percent on glazed mosaic floor tile to 13.5 percent for roofing tile, while the tariff on non-mosaic floor tile is 19 percent. Simply writing the word "tiles" on an invoice would result in a higher tariff. Purchasing apparel requires the same precise descriptions; tariff rates vary for a "blouse" and a "top."

For the United States, two agreements related to tariffs and duties have dramatically affected trade with foreign markets. The General Agreement on Tariffs and Trade (GATT) and the North American Free Trade Agreement (NAFTA) have had far-reaching effects on what and how buyers purchase from foreign sources.

GATT (1994) reduced tariffs by about 40 percent on a large number of products and included new trading rules between the United States and 123 other countries. NAFTA (1994) also gradually eliminated the trade barriers between the United States, Mexico, and Canada. Mexico has also become an important country to US buyers for sourcing products, especially apparel and textiles. With Mexico's close proximity to the United States, buyers can also get their orders faster.

Properly noting a product's country of origin can also reduce tariffs. Rates vary depending on where the product is purchased. At one time, the same ceramic tile on which you would pay a 13.5 percent duty from Italy would have a duty of 4.3 percent if from Israel, would be duty-free if from Brazil, and would have a 55 percent duty if from the Czech Republic. As retailers compete in an increasingly global market, monitoring tariffs will become more important as a means of bolstering profit margins.

In addition, buyers will need to identify countries that have been granted normal trade relations status. A similar classification, **most-favored-nation status**, still remains in widespread use. Such status allows imports from these countries to be taxed at a lower level. To illustrate the impact of most-favored-nation status, consider the following example. Before receiving this special status, tariffs added $1.07 to the cost of a 750-milliliter bottle of Stolichnaya Russian vodka sold in the United States. That tariff was lowered to eight cents a bottle under a different trade agreement.

Quotas also have an impact on the number of imports coming into this country and on the price consumers pay. A **quota** is a predetermined amount of merchandise that a country's government allows to be imported for a specific product category. Quotas are another means of protecting US manufacturers from underdeveloped countries that can produce products much less expensively than in the United States because wage rates are far less. When imports are restricted, price tends to rise for the goods if demand is high while supply is limited. In the past, quotas have been used to protect some industries in this country, especially the automobile and apparel industries.

Imports must also comply with governmental regulations regarding product safety. For example, when purchasing children's pajamas from foreign sources, they must be flame retardant. Buyers must ensure that the fiber content and any textile treatment are indeed inflammable. Some retailers even conduct their own testing for products with special restrictions.

Pricing Merchandise from Foreign Sources

At this point in the process, buyers have already made a lot of decisions about foreign sources from which they will be making purchases. However, before signing the contract, all costs associated with purchasing the goods from a foreign source need to be examined carefully. Constant monitoring of such factors as US trade regulations, insurance, shipping costs, fees for intermediaries, and storage costs will be required. Only by knowing such information can you make informed comparisons with similar products that are manufactured in the United States or other countries.

Buyers must identify all possible expenses associated with purchases being made from foreign sources. They must be able to calculate the landed cost of any import being purchased. **Landed cost** is the final cost of merchandise purchased from foreign sources, which includes the following expenses: (1) merchandise cost, (2) duties and tariffs, (3) commissions, (4) insurance, (5) storage expenses, and (6) transportation charges.

Financing Purchases from Foreign Sources

Once the contract to purchase goods from a foreign source has been signed, the next step would involve deciding upon a method of payment. One unique feature of planning for the foreign buying trip is that buyers may have to present a letter of credit to foreign suppliers. A **letter of credit** is a promise from the purchaser's bank to the seller that money is available to purchase the goods ordered. Retail buyers must realize that the letter of credit guarantees only that a bill will be paid. It does not guarantee product quality or timely delivery. A letter of credit is good only for one specific shipment.

UNDERSTANDING THE GLOBAL MARKETPLACE

As you begin sourcing product purchases from foreign sources, it becomes imperative that you understand how globalization is impacting retailing around the world and especially in the United States. The globalization of retailing is proceeding in many ways, including the transfer of retail techniques, ideas, and practices, and an increasing number of retailers are emerging as truly global firms. Most visible is the rising number of retailers trading outside their home markets, which has primarily been caused by constrained growth in mature, domestic markets.

Globalization of Retailing

Today, buyers can choose suppliers from around the world. Trade barriers between countries have been falling, and virtually every retailer in the United States buys some foreign-produced products. Most retailers in the United States are also facing competition from businesses headquartered in other countries. To thrive in the twenty-first century, retailers must realize that a global marketplace exists. Not only will US retailers continue to expand globally, but local markets will also be more open to foreign competition.

Domestically, the automobile and apparel industries have already been affected by the global expansion of markets. For both industries, foreign competition from the Far East has become a dominant force in the US market, and many domestic factories have closed because of the influx of foreign competition. Foreign manufacturers, however, cannot take their market share for granted; they must continually monitor the marketplace and keep an eye on competition—from both the United States and other countries.

A closer examination of the apparel industry illustrates some of the changes that are occurring. The Far East–Southeast Asia region has become the leading importer of apparel and textile products to both the United States and Europe. Apparel factories in China, Taiwan, Korea, and Hong Kong have prospered; however, their continued prosperity may be threatened. Wage rates in these countries have also increased substantially, causing prices of exports to increase dramatically. And new competition is entering the world marketplace for apparel from countries such as Bangladesh, the Philippines, Sri Lanka, Vietnam, and Turkey, where wage rates remain low. See Table 13.4 for a list of some of the manufacturing labor costs around the world. In addition, many apparel importers in the United States are looking to the Caribbean Basin as a sourcing alternative. The proximity of the region to the US mainland would give them a much greater degree of control. Although this area offers a large labor supply, it is not yet able to produce the quality and quantity of the higher-end goods currently produced in the Far East.

NAFTA is a trade agreement that the United States signed with Mexico and Canada. All tariffs between these three countries are scheduled to be eliminated. Opinions about whether or not initial steps have been successful vary, depending on the source contacted. The trade agreement has produced both winners and losers, with most firms likely finding themselves somewhere in between. US consumers have benefited from less expensive retail prices, but many jobs have been lost in the United States.

Buyers will need to constantly monitor the global marketplace for the right merchandise at the right price because changes in the market may occur virtually overnight. Foreign sources will also have to monitor the American marketplace if they are to supply the products that consumers want and need. Buyers and retailers must be alert to the evolving role that different countries play in the global marketplace. The growth or decline of a country can have a great impact on where buyers make purchases. At the beginning of the decade, the global economy has decelerated in many of the world's leading markets. Across Europe, some economies were weakened and customer confidence was undermined. Even China faced a slowdown in growth.

In 2015, Walmart remained the undisputed leader on the list of Top 250 Global Retailers. Six of the retailers in the Top 10 were from the United States and four were from Europe. The Top 10 Global Retailers are presented in Table 13.5. It is interesting to note that nearly one-third of the Top 10's total retail revenue came from foreign operations—another sign of the globalization of the world marketplace.

US Expansion to Foreign Markets

Globalization of retailing presents several issues for buyers. When US firms expand into foreign markets, decisions must be made about the merchandise mix. "Should it remain largely American?" or "Should products reflect local tastes?" are two key questions buyers must answer as they move into foreign markets. Expansion also presents problems involving the logistics of supplying stores.

Expansion into international retail markets is both appealing and challenging for many US retailers (Figure 13.3). Interested retailers must decide if they want to expand by purchasing an existing foreign firm or exporting a store format that

TABLE 13.4

HOURLY COMPENSATION COSTS IN MANUFACTURING (U.S. DOLLARS)

Country	1997	2014
Norway	25.88	62.88
Belgium	28.95	55.60
Denmark	23.72	52.45
Sweden	25.05	50.15
Germany	28.86	49.47
Australia	19.29	46.07
Austria	24.91	45.71
Finland	22.36	45.03
France	24.87	44.18
Ireland	17.42	43.38
Netherlands	22.71	42.21
Italy	19.77	37.37
United States	23.04	37.04
Canada	18.50	34.56
United Kingdom	19.30	33.01
Spain	13.96	28.19
Japan	22.00	26.94
New Zealand	12.04	26.93
Singapore	12.16	26.82
South Korea	9.24	23.77
Israel	11.62	23.04
Greece	11.61	19.21
Argentina	7.55	17.68
Slovakia	2.84	12.92
Portugal	6.44	12.68
Estonia	NA	12.41
Czech Republic	3.25	11.74
Brazil	7.03	10.54
Poland	3.29	9.83
Hungary	3.05	9.49
Taiwan	7.07	9.49
Mexico	3.47	6.76
Turkey	NA	6.25
Philippines	1.24	2.11

Source: Conference-board.com, 2016.

has an identity unfamiliar to customers there. Another dilemma facing US buyers whose stores have added foreign units is whether or not to use the same merchandise sources as for their domestic stores. Talbots, for example, has expanded to Japan and has decided not to change its merchandise sources. Buyers from Japanese stores come to the United States four times a year to review merchandise samples. One difference between merchandising policies in Talbots' Japanese and US stores is that even more

Figure 13.3
Many US retailers, like Walmart, have expanded into the Chinese market.

TABLE 13.5

TOP 10 GLOBAL RETAILERS

Retail Sales Rank	Company	Country of Origin	Net Revenue (US $mil)	Dominant Operational Format	Countries of Operation
1	Walmart	USA	$482,130	Hypermarket/Supercenter/Superstore	30
2	Costco	USA	$116,199	Cash & Carry/Warehouse Club	10
3	Kroger	USA	$109,830	Supermarket	1
4	Schwarz Unternehmenstreuhand KG	Germany	$94,448	Discount Store	26
5	Walgreens	USA	$89,631	Drug Store/Pharmacy	10
6	Home Depot	USA	$88,519	Home Improvement	4
7	Carrefour	France	$84,856	Hypermarket/Supercenter/Superstore	35
8	Aldi Einkauf GmbH	Germany	$82,164	Discount Store	17
9	Tesco	UK	$81,019	Hypermarket/Supercenter/Superstore	10
10	Amazon.com	USA	$79,268	Non-store	14

Source: Stores, January 2016.

of Talbots' private-brand labels are offered in Japan in an attempt to establish the name as an important retailer.

Retail buyers also face key differences in planning product assortments for stores in foreign markets. For example, Talbots in Japan operates in 2,100-square-foot stores that are about half the size of a Talbots store in the United States. One reason is that retail space is expensive, but less inventory is also required to stock the stores there. A wide assortment of sizes is not necessary. Whereas sizes in US stores range from petite size 0 to 18, Japanese stores usually need to stock only three or four sizes.

Before expanding to foreign markets, US retailers must evaluate all aspects of the market to determine if their retail concept will travel well to other markets. There are also some foreign companies exporting their retail concepts to the United States. H&M and Zara (specialty clothing stores) and IKEA, a Swedish furniture retailer, are examples of foreign retailers who have expanded successfully to the United States. Read the Snapshot titled "Uniqlo: Japan's Entry into Fast Retailing Stumbles in the United States" to learn more about the difficulties Uniqlo faced as the company expanded into the U.S. market.

A Reaction to Globalization: Buy American Campaigns

As a reaction to the domestic job losses caused by the increasing number of imports, many businesses and organizations in the United States have undertaken "Buy American" promotional campaigns, as illustrated in Figure 13.4. The most ambitious advertising "Buy American" campaigns come from the apparel and automobile industries—market segments that have been most hurt by imports.

US textile, apparel, and home furnishings industries have re-energized a promotional campaign called "Crafted with Pride in the USA." Some retailers are also picking up the theme by stocking and promoting American-made products, whenever possible. For example, Walmart became one of the first major retailers to launch an ongoing "Buy American" campaign. This campaign was also one way to communicate the chain's support for US manufacturing. Walmart offered US manufacturers the chance to replicate items that the chain acquired from foreign sources. If they could do so on a cost-effective basis, Walmart purchased from the firm.

In the United States, "Buy American" campaigns generally have more appeal to certain segments of the population than others. For example, the campaigns have strong appeal to blue-collar workers, who have been most seriously affected by unemployment

Figure 13.4
Many manufacturers prominently display "Made in the USA" tags on their products.

caused by imports. They blame foreign competitors for plant shutdowns. Women and older Americans have also been targets of these campaigns.

One controversy caused by "Buy American" campaigns is trying to define what qualifies as an American-made product. For example, are these two examples American-made products—a TV made by US-based Zenith at a plant in Mexico, or a General Motors car assembled at a California factory co-owned by Toyota? Increasingly, there may be no such thing as an "American-made" product. US brands are often foreign owned, and foreign brands are often manufactured in the United States.

In the final analysis, American consumers may never fully embrace "Buy American" campaigns. Consumers want low prices. Suppliers want to produce a quality product with the greatest efficiency and cost savings. And, retailers want to get the best product at the lowest possible cost.

Future Trends in the Global Marketplace

What does the future hold in the global marketplace? Consider the following developments that may have an impact on buying:

- Four large trading blocs have emerged. They include (1) the Western Hemisphere, (2) the European Union, (3) Russia and some of its former satellite countries, and (4) China, Japan, and the western Pacific Rim. Trade within these blocs will probably flourish, while trade may grow more difficult between these blocs.
- Free trade agreements are coming under tighter scrutiny in many countries, including the United States. Such agreements are likely to result in lower consumer prices for many products and provide a larger market for all goods; however, some domestic industries will suffer as products are produced more efficiently in other countries. In addition, loss of those industries increases unemployment.
- American cultural dominance will continue to expand throughout the world. Sales of branded goods that are associated with American culture will continue to grow in the global market.

Summary Points

- Buyers have a choice of domestic or foreign sources for most products that they purchase.
- Buyers purchase foreign merchandise because of (1) unavailability of some merchandise in the United States, (2) low cost, (3) quality, (4) uniqueness, and (5) fashion trends.
- Drawbacks to purchasing foreign merchandise include (1) early purchase commitment required, (2) delivery problems, (3) size discrepancies, (4) added expenses and time involved, and (5) funds tied up for longer periods of time.
- Foreign sources can be located by making personal buying trips; however, personal buying trips require that buyers have familiarity with both the language and the customs of the country they are visiting.
- Buyers can also obtain merchandise from foreign markets by using intermediaries such as foreign buying offices, domestic buying offices, or importers.
- The landed cost of merchandise must be calculated by buyers in order to compare foreign merchandise costs with domestic merchandise costs.
- Today, buyers can select goods from a global marketplace rather than just domestic sources. US retailers are also facing competition from foreign sources.

Review Activities

Developing Your Retail Buying Vocabulary

Consult the glossary if you did not add the following terms to your vocabulary.

commissionaire	importer	letter of credit	tariff
duty	intermediary	most-favored-nation status	
free trade agreement	landed cost	quota	

Understanding What You Read

1. Which countries are the sources of most apparel and textile imports in the United States?

2. Which countries are providing competition to Far East apparel manufacturers?

3. Identify foreign products that are unavailable for buyers to purchase in the US market.

4. List reasons buyers have for purchasing foreign products.

5. Why could delivery problems be more severe for foreign merchandise than for domestic merchandise?

6. After deciding to make purchases from foreign sources, why should retailers keep contact with alternative sources of supply?

7. Why would most buyers who consider purchasing foreign products go through intermediaries?

8. List the components of landed cost of foreign merchandise.

9. What is the primary purpose of most tariffs and quotas?

10. How could buyers save money on tariffs when merchandise is described on purchase orders and invoices?

11. Give examples of US retailers who have expanded into foreign markets.

12. Give examples of foreign retailers who have expanded into the US market.

Analyzing and Applying What You Read

1. You are the buyer for several lines of footballs that have been purchased from domestic sources. Market research has revealed that your customers make an effort to purchase American-made products. Describe plans that your store could initiate to make your customers aware of where your footballs were manufactured.

2. Research reveals that only 17 percent of Americans strictly avoid purchasing imports. Does this indicate that "Buy American" campaigns have not been successful? Explain.

3. Should the United States tighten quotas against apparel manufacturers? After listing the pros and cons, present arguments to support your final decision.

4. You are a retailer interested in expanding into foreign markets. Would you expand with your existing store or purchase an existing retailer there? Support your decision.

Internet Connection

1. Access the Social Accountability International website at http://www.sa-intl.org. Report on the goals and activities of this organization in relation to the human rights of workers around the world.

2. Visit the book's STUDIO to watch videos about fast fashion and manufacturing in Bangladesh.

SNAPSHOT: Zara: Providing Style and Rapid Response

Zara is a trendy Spanish clothing chain that produces "fashions for the masses" for young, hip, urban consumers. Today, the company's over 2,000 stores have reached $14.5 in global sales. In fact, Inditex, Zara's parent company, has become the world's largest clothing retailer. Moreover, China now ranks second in the chain next to Spain in terms of number of stores.

Growth continues to occur for a variety of reasons. The firm has pioneered the concept of "live collections," which are designed, manufactured, distributed, and sold almost as quickly as their customers' fleeting enthusiasm. Traditionally, fashion collections are designed only four times a year, and major retailers outsource most of their production to low-cost subcontractors in far-off developing countries. Zara, however, ignores this old logic. For quick turnaround, some two-thirds of its clothes are made at a company-owned facility in Spain, and stores around the globe are restocked twice a week with an astounding 12,000 different designs a year.

Zara creates fashion ideas that resonate with customers. Recognizing that what is "in" today may be "out" next month, Zara has organized a design and fulfillment network capable of moving ideas from the drawing board to store shelves in ten to fifteen days—a lightning pace by industry standards. Zara meets this objective by getting its designers and store personnel out of their offices and into the plazas, discos, and universities where consumers congregate. That information then gets fed back to Zara's headquarters—often using handheld computers that transmit images as well as data.

Other data also help Zara provide the answers to what consumers want. Guided by daily data feeds from each store showing what is selling and what is stalling, merchandising teams at headquarters develop fashions for the coming weeks. In addition to sales figures, they monitor thousands of comments from customers, store managers, and country directors. The designs that emerge from these data then enter a fast-paced production and logistical system.

Customers love the results—they stand in lines outside stores on designated delivery days. They understand that if they like something in Zara, they must buy it then because it will probably not be there the following week.

Several other factors have contributed to the success of Zara. The firm does not have to carry the cost of high inventory levels, and it gets a big revenue boost by putting fresh fashion on shelves so rapidly. In fact, because of the fast sales, Zara gets nearly 85 percent of the full retail price on its clothes, while the industry average is 60 to 70 percent. In fact, Zara is roughly four times more profitable than the average retailer due mainly to these higher margins. Most apparel retailers also depend on advertising. Zara shuns the medium altogether except for social media marketing, preferring to invest in prime locations.

Zara is building its growth on speed, customization, supply chain management, well-managed inventories, lower markdowns, and higher gross margins, which have transformed the retailer into a global powerhouse. Some analysts predict that unless other apparel retailers can duplicate this approach, they may not be in business in the next decade.

BASED ON:

Baker, Stephanie. (2016, November 23). Zara's recipe for success: More data, fewer bosses. *Bloomberg.com*.

Berfield, Susan, & Baigorri, Manuel. (2013, November 14). Zara's fast-fashion edge. *BusinessWeek.com*.

Hernandez, Carlos. (2014, March 31). Inditex still heads the field. *Stores.org*.

Loeb, Walter. (2013, October 14). Zara's secret to success: The new science of retailing. *Forbes.com*.

Petro, Greg. (2015, July 23). The future of fashion retailing, revisited: Part 2—Zara. *Forbes.com*.

Soltes, Fiona. (2016, December 5). Staying ahead of fast fashion. *Stores.org*.

RECALLED PRODUCTS: WHAT WENT WRONG?

- September 2016: Samsung recalls the Galaxy Note 7 worldwide over batteries that could explode and cause fires.

- November 2016: Samsung recalls top-load washing machines because the lid may detach from the chassis, posing an impact injury risk.

- January 2017: Toshiba expands a recall of Panasonic battery packs used in Toshiba laptop computers because the lithium-ion battery packs can overheat, posing burn and fire hazards.

- January 2017: IKEA recalls Mysingso beach chairs because the chairs can collapse, posing fall and fingertip amputation hazards.

- February 2017: Walt Disney recalls Happy Holidays! Mickey Mouse Nightlights because liquid from the nightlight can leak into the electrical outlet, posing a fire hazard.

- February 2017: Restoration Hardware recalls eighteenth-century-style glass beveled mirrors because the mirrors were not properly glued to the backing and the mirror could fall, posing a laceration hazard.

- February 2017: Target recalls Threshold Aluminum Top/Steel X Base patio benches because they can collapse while in use, posing a fall hazard to consumers.

What has gone wrong? Are there more product recalls today than in the past? Product recalls have always existed, but today, with the arrival of social media formats, such as Facebook and Twitter, millions more consumers can be alerted to a recall in a single posting.

With these global alerts, the bad news for consumers is that most manufacturers are not set up to manage the logistics of a widespread recall, especially the multi-jurisdictional compliance requirements that govern recalls in multiple countries. Manufacturers, and retailers in some instances, facing recalls must be equipped to handle a greater incoming call volume of customer complaints, be able to provide requisite notifications to consumers, and repair or destroy the offending products. And, all these activities require additional time and money.

Many of the products listed above were manufactured in China, which has awakened both that country and the United States to the looming question as to who is legally responsible when a recalled product has caused consumers harm. For example, who faces liability when lead paint ends up on a toy sold in the United States and a customer is injured? Companies and consumers have found that US regulators generally have held US importers responsible for ensuring that foreign-made products meet American safety standards.

Some companies will not be able to withstand the repercussions. For example, one family-owned tire business hurtled toward bankruptcy when it faced a $90 million recall. The company sued the Chinese supplier, which denied any defect. However, even if US plaintiffs win default judgments against foreign firms, it is unclear whether they will be able to enforce them. Moreover, in Chinese courts, tiny awards and frequently hostile local judges often make litigation pointless.

Recalls are not always the result of shoddy production monitoring. In 2007, Mattel Inc. recalled eighty-three Fisher-Price products, 1.5 million units made in China, because they were finished with lead paint. Mattel goes to great lengths to try to ensure that the companies with whom it does business operate properly and ethically, even subjecting them to outside audits from the International Center for Corporate Accountability. Mattel's crisis illustrates just how difficult it is for US companies purchasing foreign products to keep tabs on all their suppliers around the world.

What extent of an effect will these recalls have on sales? It is still unclear, but for many toys, manufacturers and retailers have already begun advertising the fact that their toys are made in the United States. Retail buyers must be alert and carefully select suppliers for the products they sell. Repeated product recalls will undermine consumer confidence and reduce sales—something no retail buyer wants to occur.

On the other hand, if foreign exporters want to stay in business, they will have to become accountable for injuries to consumers and businesses around the world. To stay in the global market, countries will have to stand behind the products manufactured there, and that means stronger regulation and more accountability.

BASED ON:

Koenig. Bill. (2014, May 20). General Motors recalls another 2.42 million vehicles. *Forbes.com*.

Levick, Richard. (2014, March 5). The "beast" that's driving product recalls. *Forbes.com*.

Mullen, Jethro, & Kwon, K.J. (2016, September 2). Samsung is recalling the Galaxy Note 7 worldwide over battery problems. *CNNTech.com*.

SNAPSHOT: Uniqlo: Japan's Entry into Fast Retailing Stumbles in the United States

Uniqlo, headed by Tadashi Yanai, has become Japan's biggest clothing store and the first Japanese brand to make it big internationally in decades, and the company only sells basics such as T-shirts, socks, and jeans that combine a touch of style with enticingly low prices. Although the firm is not as big as its major competitors—Gap, H&M, and Zara—Uniqlo plans to catch up. For example, sales at Gap have remained almost unchanged over the past decade, yet Uniqlo's worldwide sales have nearly tripled.

What started as a tiny family clothing store has been transformed to an international presence, with stores from London's Oxford Street to Shanghai's West Nanjing Road to New York City's Fifth Avenue. Even after some major stumbles as the company entered the US market, management at Uniqlo have said they have not abandoned hopes of becoming the world's largest fashion retailer. The company has consistently lost money in the US market since expansion began there at the beginning of the decade, and they have scaled back the number of stores they had originally planned to open. Yet, the company's strategic plan still calls for 100 new stores to be built in the United States.

Yanai inherited his parents' menswear store in Ube, a small town in Japan's coal-mining region. In 1984, he followed the industrial boom by opening a store in Hiroshima, calling the new shop Unique Clothing Warehouse, which he renamed Uniqlo a year later, meaning "unique clothing." From those humble beginnings, Yanai has become Japan's richest man, worth over $9 billion dollars.

Uniqlo also employs a different business model than its competitors. For example, Zara and H&M bring the latest fashions to the masses quickly by adding new lines many times a year. In contrast, Uniqlo offers only about 1,000 items, far fewer than its rivals, and keeps them on the shelves longer. Offering fewer lines allows the company to negotiate lower-priced, higher-volume deals with competitors. Fewer lines also make managing inventory a much simpler and less expensive process. Uniqlo compensates for the narrowness of its product selection by selling the same item in many different colors. For example, at the flagship store in Tokyo, socks are available in fifty different colors.

Moreover, Uniqlo has also taken control of all processes from design to distribution, bringing down prices for the store's customers. Managing its own supply chain means that Uniqlo can control quality as carefully as it controls costs, which has resulted in a broad customer appeal beyond those just looking for a bargain. For many of Uniqlo's customers, it is not just about low prices and marquee store locations. For example, on either side of the Uniqlo store on Fifth Avenue in New York City, consumers can purchase an inexpensive T-shirt at either Gap or H&M.

Although price certainly is an appeal, many customers are also drawn to Uniqlo's reputation for innovative textile technology, which is stressed in the firm's advertising. Testimonials stress that the firm's shirts dry quicker and do not stain as much as ones from the competition. Moreover, one of the firm's top-selling items is a down coat thick enough to ward off cold temperatures but thin enough to crunch into a small bag.

Yanai attributes his company's success to a "nothing-to-lose" entrepreneurial zeal, which is difficult at Japanese firms, where the culture is so risk-averse that managers are ridiculed for their mistakes. Yanai also feels that traditional Japanese management practices are a bottleneck to growth and expansion. Yet, the company is not without its failures. Uniqlo initially stumbled in expansion to some foreign countries. For example, in the United States brand recognition for Uniqlo is high in major cities like New York, San Francisco, and Chicago, but there is poor name recognition in suburban areas. Uniqlo is also trying to catch a better known, and better established, rival in H&M. That chain recently opened twenty-five new stores in the United States during a one year period.

Even with problems the company faces in the US market, investors are not urging Uniqlo to exit the market. The company also faces shrinking population in Japan, and success in the United States would greatly boost Uniqlo's brand image worldwide. In fact, management has said their top priority is to turn around the struggling stores in the United States.

Some analysts believe that the firm's owner may also be a problem. Even though he is a brilliant strategist with uncanny fashion instincts, Yanai has been unable to successfully delegate responsibilities in the company. He controls all decisions, down to approving samples and colors. In addition, there have been several media reports claiming that some workers complain about long hours, exacting standards, and high stress.

Can Uniqlo meet its growth projections? Will the company need to add trendier lines to supplement the basics that have already proved so successful? The next few years will hold the answers to questions like these.

BASED ON:

Ando, Ritsuko. (2016, May 25). Uniqlo says top priority is to turn around "struggling" U.S. stores. *Fortune.com*.

Ando, Ritsuko. (2016, May 25). Uniqlo's Yanai says revamping U.S. operations a top priority. *Fortune.com*.

Biers, John. (2014, June 18). US is key to Uniqlo's global aspirations. *YahooNews.com*.

Fast retailing feels pain of price cuts at Uniqlo. (2016, April 7). *Fortune.com*.

Gil, Billy. (2014, June 19). UNIQLO pop-up shops bring cute yet cheap fashion to SoCal this summer. *YahooNews.com*.

Huang, Grace. (2016, November 20). How one fashion brand is beating Uniqlo at its own game. *Bloomberg.com*.

Petro, Greg. (2015, July 17). The future of fashion retailing, revisited part 1—Uniqlo. *Forbes.com*.

Schuman, Michael. (2013, May 13). What they'll wear to the revolution. *Time*, 40–44.

Wahba, Phil. (2015, October 8). Uniqlo's big American mistake? Betting on suburban malls. *Fortune.com*.

MAKING THE PURCHASE

Performance Objectives

- Describe techniques for price negotiations in the market.
- List and describe types of discounts for which buyers can negotiate.
- List and describe types of FOB (free on board) terms.
- Identify and describe allowances and return privileges that vendors may grant buyers.
- Recognize the impact of private brands on retailing.
- Describe special buying situations (e.g., job lots, off-price, seconds, and irregulars).
- List and describe types of orders placed by buyers.
- Identify key parts of a purchase order.

After you have decided what to order and have developed a clear understanding of the negotiation process, you and the vendor must agree on the price of the merchandise and terms of the order. In this chapter, you will learn about the terms for which buyers negotiate. Special buying situations are described, and how orders are placed with vendors is explained.

NEGOTIATING TERMS OF THE SALE

The most important terms that you will negotiate include (1) price, (2) discounts, (3) transportation, (4) allowances, and (5) return privileges.

Price

Price negotiation really starts before you go to market. You should learn as much as you can about market conditions and individual vendors with whom you will be negotiating. For example, economic slowdowns or internal troubles that a manufacturer may be facing are indications that the vendor may be willing to offer price concessions. If you know that the merchandise is already manufactured and subject to becoming outdated, you may have a better opportunity to negotiate price reductions. Also, by having an understanding of the manufacturing costs involved, you will have a better idea of how much the vendor may be willing to reduce prices.

While viewing a product in the market, you will want to estimate its retail value before inquiring about the cost. If the price quoted by the vendor is lower than you judged, it possibly is a good buy, or you may want to reexamine the merchandise to determine if you overlooked any shortcomings or weaknesses in the item. If the price quoted is higher than you estimated, reexamine the merchandise to determine if you have overlooked some important features before determining that the item is overpriced. You could practice this technique by predicting retail prices in stores where you shop.

In the market, compare price quotes offered by different vendors. Shop the market thoroughly; some vendors may be willing to reduce their price to meet the competition. Most buyers, however, do not simply select the vendor with the lowest price. You will also want to check other criteria such as the vendor's dependability, delivery times, discounts, or allowances offered.

Many price reductions that vendors offer are based on increasing the quantity of merchandise purchased. You may not be able to increase total purchases, but you may be able to consolidate orders with one resource to qualify for larger quantity discounts. Also, some price reductions may be offered in the form of free deals. For example, you may be offered two free cases of a product when 100 cases are purchased.

In all price negotiations, vendors must be concerned with not violating the Robinson–Patman Act of 1936, which outlawed price discrimination in interstate commerce. All price reductions must be offered on a "proportionally equal" basis to all buyers. The manufacturer must be able to justify any price reductions given a buyer that result from differences in the seller's manufacturing costs, selling costs, or delivery costs. For example, if the seller's cost to deliver a large shipment to Retailer A is actually less than making a small delivery to Retailer B, the vendor could pass on this difference in the form of a price reduction to Retailer A.

In relation to price, you may also negotiate a **price decline guarantee** that protects the store if market prices drop over a stated period of time. For example, a buyer may purchase computers for $1,000 each on March 1; the manufacturer may then drop the price to $950 on March 15. With a price decline guarantee, the buyer would be protected against such price reductions for a period of time after the order was signed. In this case, the vendor would credit or refund the buyer's store $50 for each computer purchased.

Discounts

Probably the most important terms that you will negotiate are discounts, a reduction in the price of the merchandise. You must determine the types of discounts offered by each vendor, and where possible, attempt to qualify for them. There are several types of discounts for which you may qualify.

Quantity Discounts

Often vendors will offer **quantity discounts** to buyers to entice them to order more merchandise. Some buyers place an order for the estimated quantity of merchandise they will need for the entire season, with a cancellation date approved by the vendor. The buyer is able to place an order for a larger quantity for discount purposes.

Vendors offer buyers quantity discounts because they save money in handling and processing orders in large quantities. By offering quantity discounts, manufacturers can benefit from lower production costs—they can order raw materials in larger quantities and plan their operating schedules more efficiently. Also, completing the order forms for a large order takes about the same amount of time as for a small order. An example of a quantity discount would be a vendor offering a 2 percent discount for orders of more than 125 dozen. The quota could be expressed in units or dollar amounts.

Seasonal Discounts

Some buyers may be offered **seasonal discounts** for making purchases in advance of a selling season. Seasonal discounts may be offered on such products as skis, air conditioners, or lawn mowers. Manufacturers benefit because they are able to plan their production schedules more efficiently and keep skilled employees working throughout the year. An example of a seasonal discount would be a vendor offering a 2 percent discount to buyers who place orders for next year's lawn mowers in October. Seasonal discounts are attractive; however, you must be certain that only the newest styles or models are shipped.

Trade Discounts

Many times buyers are offered **trade discounts** based on the manufacturer's list price. Manufacturers may quote trade discounts as a series of discounts. For example, an item with a list price of $1,000 may be offered with discounts of 40 percent and 10 percent—which is not a 50 percent discount. Instead, each discount is computed on the amount that remains after the preceding discount has been taken. With the example given, the 40 percent discount is calculated first, and is $400. That amount is subtracted from the list price, for a total of $600. Then, a 10 percent discount is taken on the $600, which equals $60. The cost to the buyer would be $540 ($600 – $60).

Cash Discounts

Manufacturers also grant **cash discounts** to retailers for early payment of invoices. Manufacturers want payments as quickly as possible, and most retail managers want buyers to negotiate for cash discounts because of the price advantages they offer the store in the marketplace. Discounts can turn a breakeven year into a profitable one, so a store cannot afford to ignore them. Typically, cash discount terms are expressed in a form such as "2/10 net 30," which means that a 2 percent discount will be granted if the buyer pays the invoice within ten days of the invoice date. If the invoice is not paid within that period, the total amount is due in thirty days.

Several dating terms are used to determine the amount of time given to the retailer to take advantage of the cash discount. The most commonly used are as follows:

- **Ordinary dating terms** are the most common type of cash discount. The amount of time to take advantage of a discount is calculated from the invoice date. The preceding example illustrated ordinary dating terms.

Illustrative Problem

A shipment was received on November 12 and carried an invoice date of November 10. Based on terms of 5/10 net 30, what is the discount date on this purchase? When is the entire bill due?

Solution

Because ordinary dating terms were used, all calculations are made from the invoice date—in this situation, November 10. Terms indicate that the retailer has ten days to pay the bill and take advantage of the discount. The discount date is November 20, which is ten days from the invoice date. The entire bill is due thirty days from the invoice date—December 10.

- **ROG (receipt of goods) dating terms** allow the buyer to calculate the discount period from the day the merchandise was received in the store rather than from the invoice date. These terms are written "2/10 net 30 ROG." In this situation, the buyer would have ten days from the delivery date to take advantage of the 2 percent discount offered.

Illustrative Problem

A shipment was received on November 12 and carried an invoice date of November 10. Based on terms of 5/10 net 30 ROG, what is the discount date on this purchase? When is the entire bill due?

Solution

Because ROG dating terms were used, all calculations are made from the delivery date—in this situation, November 12. Terms indicate that the retailer has ten days to pay the bill and take advantage of the discount. The discount date is November 22, which is ten days from the delivery date. The entire bill is due thirty days from the delivery date—December 12.

- **EOM (end-of-month) dating terms** allow the buyer to calculate the discount period from the end of the month. These terms are written "2/10 net 30 EOM." In this situation, the buyer would have ten days from the end of the month in which the invoice was written to take advantage of the 2 percent discount offered. There is one exception. If the invoice date falls on the twenty-fifth day of the month or later, the last day to take advantage of the discount is calculated from the end of the following month rather than from the month in which the invoice was written.

Illustrative Problem

A shipment was received on November 12 and carried an invoice date of November 10. Based on terms of 5/10 net 30 EOM, what is the discount date on this purchase? When is the entire bill due?

Solution

Because end-of-month dating terms were used, all calculations are made from the end of the month in which the invoice was written—in this situation, November. Terms indicate that the retailer has ten days to pay the bill and take advantage of the discount. The discount date is December 10, which is ten days from the end of November. The entire bill is due thirty days from the end of the month—December 30.

- **Extra dating terms** give the buyer a specified number of additional days in which to pay the invoice and earn the cash discount. The terms are usually written "2/10 net 30 60X." In this situation, the buyer would have ten days from the invoice plus an additional sixty days to take advantage of the 2 percent discount offered.

Illustrative Problem

A shipment was received on November 12 and carried an invoice date of November 10. Based on terms of 5/10 net 30 30X, what is the discount date on this purchase? When is the entire bill due?

Solution

Because extra dating terms were used, all calculations are made from the invoice date—in this situation, November 10—and include extra days that the vendor is granting the buyer. Terms indicate that the retailer has ten days to pay the bill and take advantage of the discount plus an additional thirty days—forty days in total. The discount date is December 20, which is forty days from the invoice date. The entire bill is due sixty days (the net payment is due in thirty days plus the additional thirty extra days) from the invoice date—January 10.

- **Advance dating terms** indicate that the invoice is dated for some specified time in the future. For example, an invoice for lawn mowers shipped on January 14 may have terms of "2/10 net 30 as of May 1." In this situation, the buyer would have ten days from the date given (May 1) to take advantage of the cash discount.

Illustrative Problem

A shipment was received on November 12 and carried an invoice date of November 10. Based on terms of 5/10 net 30 as of December 1, what is the discount date on this purchase? When is the entire bill due?

Solution

Because advance dating terms were used, all calculations are made from the date given in the terms—in this situation, December 1. Terms indicate that the retailer has ten days to pay the bill and take advantage of the discount. The discount date is December 11, which is ten days from the date given in the terms. The entire bill is due thirty days from the date given—December 31.

Anticipation is an extra discount that some manufacturers give buyers for paying an invoice in advance of the cash discount date. Anticipation is usually taken only if your store has ready cash available.

Buyers may not always be given discount terms. If a vendor is uncertain of a buyer's credit, merchandise is sent **COD** (collect on delivery), which means that the transportation company will collect the amount of the invoice when the goods are delivered.

Transportation

Transportation terms may also need to be negotiated. If your store is to pay the cost of shipment, you will want to specify how the merchandise is to be shipped. Time and cost are important considerations as you select methods of shipment (Figure 14.1). If the merchandise is needed quickly, you will want to select the fastest method of shipment possible; however, speed is usually associated with more expense.

Just as with discounts, there are a number of transportation terms available. Each transportation term indicates who is to pay the shipping charges and when the buyer takes

Figure 14.1

Delivery time and cost are important considerations as buyers negotiate methods of shipment with vendors.

title to the goods. Title of the goods is important because it indicates who is responsible for goods while they are in shipment. **FOB (free on board)** is the term associated with transportation charges. Commonly used transportation terms include the following:

- **FOB origin (factory)** is the most commonly used term under which merchandise is shipped. Title passes to the buyer when the seller delivers goods to the transportation carrier. Transportation charges as well as other expenses and risks are the responsibility of the buyer.
- **FOB destination (store)** is the term that indicates that the manufacturer pays the shipping charges, and title passes to the buyer when the merchandise is delivered to the retail store. For a buyer, FOB destination terms are ideal.
- **FOB destination, charges reversed** indicates that the buyer pays the shipping charges but the seller assumes responsibility for the goods while they are in transit.
- **FOB destination, freight prepaid** indicates that the seller will pay the freight charges but the buyer takes title to the goods as soon as they are shipped.
- **FOB shipping point** indicates that the manufacturer has title to the goods and will pay shipping costs until the merchandise reaches a distribution point. From that point, the buyer takes title to the goods and pays transportation charges until they reach the store.

Allowances

Many vendors may also grant special allowances to buyers. **Cooperative (co-op) advertising** is one of the most common. If the buyer runs an advertisement featuring the manufacturer's products, the manufacturer will agree to pay a percentage of the ad's cost. Usually the vendor will require proof that the ad ran before credit is issued. With co-op advertising, vendors may exercise some control on the kind of advertising that the store can use. Co-op advertising provides one way for the store to reduce its promotion budget; however, there are problems. The advertising may disrupt the store's current advertising program, and the retailer may be tempted to promote only those products for which co-op advertising is given. Some vendors may be willing to pay for preferred selling space at some stores. Research has determined the value of specific spaces in the store, so vendors are willing to pay for preferred space that could increase sales volume.

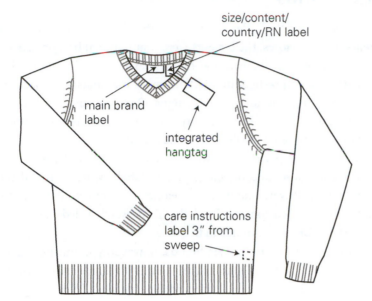

FOR LABELING/PACKAGING ONLY NOT FOR STYLE

size/content/
country/RN label

main brand
label

integrated
hangtag

care instructions
label 3″ from
sweep

Figure 14.2
Buyers indicate to manufacturers where tags should be placed before items arrive in the store.

Vendor-supported promotions are also frequently used for grocery items, automobiles, and cosmetics. In addition, vendors may be willing to provide advertising, in-store entertainment, free products, or public relations surrounding an in-store promotion.

Today, many buyers also negotiate for floor-ready merchandise shipped from the manufacturer that already includes price tags (Figure 14.2) and RFID (radio frequency identification) tags designed to make inventory control much more effective as well as curbing shoplifting.

Return Privileges

Some vendors may agree to accept returns of merchandise that did not sell. Return privileges are frequently used by vendors when they are selling new merchandise, which the retailer feels is quite risky since there are no past sales data for the product. Vendors may agree to accept the return of merchandise if it has not sold within a specified period of time. Vendors offering returns must realize that this practice may result in excessive returns of unsold merchandise at the end of the season. Two frequently used terms for returns are the following:

- **On memorandum** indicates that the merchandise coming into the store has a return privilege with it. The store pays for the merchandise but has the opportunity to return any unsold items at the end of a specified period.
- **On consignment** indicates the buyer will take merchandise into the store but will pay for it only when it sells. The buyer can then return any unsold merchandise. On consignment allows the store to increase inventory without increasing capital investment, but slow-selling merchandise may occupy valuable selling space.

NEGOTIATING SPECIAL BUYING SITUATIONS

Your negotiations with vendors may also involve special situations, some of which are described in this section. They include private brands, specification buying, promotional buying, job lots, off-price buying, and seconds and irregulars.

Private Brands

For many years, retailers offered only national brands as part of their product assortments. For the stores, the benefits were that national brands had already gained widespread customer acceptance, and being associated with national brands tended to increase the store's prestige. In addition, most manufacturers backed up national brands with extensive promotional campaigns. One problem, however, developed for retailers—the products lacked exclusivity. Sameness was created in the marketplace because competitors were all selling the same brands.

As retailers began experimenting with ways to distinguish themselves, some turned to **private brands** (also categorized as private label), which allowed them to avoid direct competition. Private brands are developed by retailers in order to offer unique merchandise to their customers. Read the Trendwatch titled "Private Brands Spell Profits" to learn more about trends in this area.

Before you decide to offer private brands, however, you must conduct research to determine their feasibility in your market. You need to identify buying motives that cause your customers to choose one brand over another. With an understanding of your customers' needs, you can provide the product mix that will best meet those needs.

Brands must mean something to your customer. In other words, they must add value. If your store decides to replace national brands with similar products under your store's private brand, quality must be controlled. Private brands must be of sufficiently high quality that they can be compared with national brands. Today, consumers are more sophisticated and look beyond low prices when purchasing products; they look at workmanship and quality.

If your store decides to offer private brands, several questions must be answered. You must determine the percentage of your total merchandise assortment that will be private brands, and you must decide what name should appear on the label—the store's name or some other "signature." Today, most stores are moving away from using the store's name as the private brand.

Instituting a private-brand program also requires capital. Manufacturers may require larger-quantity purchases because changes may be required before your label is placed on the product. In addition, your store must conduct promotional campaigns to make consumers aware of your new brand.

Advertising and visual merchandising play a crucial role in making private brands recognizable and meaningful to consumers. Most retailers advertise national brands alongside their private brands. Promotion also is needed to build customer preference, which requires that private brands be given treatment similar to national brands. J.C. Penney displays its private brands prominently alongside national brands, stressing their quality and features. Macy's has created such an effective private brand in Morgan Taylor that many people believe she is a real woman.

The quality of private brands is also critical. Before adding a private brand, buyers must take steps to guarantee customer satisfaction. Product testing ensures that colors stay true, that the fit is right, and that the fabric is long-wearing. As Figure 14.3 illustrates, product testing may occur while the buyer is in the market.

Many private brands outperform national brands, but they must be distinctive to be successful. Private brands cannot be simply knockoffs of a national brand. When your store decides to develop private brands, you may take your designs to a manufacturer or rely on the manufacturer for product development. Some merchandising consultants and buying offices will also help with private-brand development programs.

Figure 14.3
Buyers must test the quality of products that are shown in the market.

Your store might develop private brands because of the possibility of higher markups, but that will be a short-sighted reaction unless private brands meet the needs of your customers. Private brands also allow stores more control of merchandising decisions, such as price and promotion.

To be successful, your private brands must offer exclusivity at a special price, and be well made in order to compete effectively with national brands. In the past, too many retailers have regarded private brands as brands that should be cheap, low-priced products. Quality and consistency are the key today. There is even a trend toward upscaling private brands and packaging them to appeal to a specific market niche. Increasingly fragmented consumer markets present an opportunity for new brands, including private brands targeted to specific consumer segments.

What are the trends of private brands in today's marketplace? The debate continues over private brands versus national brands in many stores. Some retailers strongly support private brands, while others oppose them vehemently. Some retailers, such as Old Navy, Eddie Bauer, Benetton, and Gap, carry 100 percent private brands, whereas other retailers have few or no private brands.

Many retail executives feel that national brands benefit them in the long run. If a Claiborne blouse does not sell, it may have to be marked down only 15 percent, whereas a private-brand blouse may have to be discounted 30 to 40 percent in order to move it out of the store.

There have been highly publicized increases in the use of private brands at stores such as Kmart, which continues to build private brands associated with personalities. Its Jaclyn Smith apparel collection has been successful, as has Sofia by Sofia Vergara, a collection of fashion and accessories from one of the stars of *Modern Family*. In this way, Kmart is using private brands to develop a fashion image.

There have been equally publicized decreases in the use of private brands. Sears is the most notable, as it switched to Sears Brand Central. In previous decades, Sears had built its reputation on many of its private brands, such as Kenmore (appliances), Craftsman (tools and lawn and garden), Diehard (auto batteries), Road Handler (tires), and Toughskins (boy's jeans). Today, Sears carries over 1,000 national brands along with a mix of private brands.

After a period of decline, private brands have been growing in supermarkets. Today, most supermarket operators are reporting increases in the number of private brands being offered. For years, private brands for food were plagued by consumer concerns about product quality. Primarily this occurred because past emphasis had traditionally been placed on low prices. Store owners have now realized that it is not price alone that sells products; consistency and value must be there, too.

Improvements in packaging have also boosted private-brand business in supermarkets. For most stores, updated packages have translated into increased sales, and more emphasis on advertising and promotion has also improved the image of private brands. Many grocery store ads now feature nearly 30 percent private brands.

Retailers have also realized that price differences between private brands and national brands cannot be either too high or too low. They know that pricing too low can do more harm than good, because consumers will then question the quality of the product. Although consumers expect national brands to cost more, the private brand should typically be priced no less than 20 percent under the national brand—less than that and the consumer will gravitate to the national brand. On the other hand, if there is over a 30 percent difference, the consumer will be reluctant to purchase the private brand.

Most retailers are not likely to give up national brands entirely. They feel that national brands create energy and drive trends in the marketplace. Private brands, however, will continue to be presented as an alternative in the merchandise mix.

Specification Buying

Rather than developing private brands, some buyers may become involved in **specification buying**. In some situations, buyers may suggest specifications (Figure 14.4) or changes that upgrade the quality of the merchandise, its workmanship, or styling. Some specification buying involves no upgrades but simply making the merchandise different from similar goods carried by the competition.

If your store does specification buying, you may need product development personnel. In addition, specification buying requires a sales volume large enough to warrant the manufacturer making the suggested changes. You must also be concerned with quality control when conducting this type of buying.

Figure 14.4

An example of plans for specification buying.

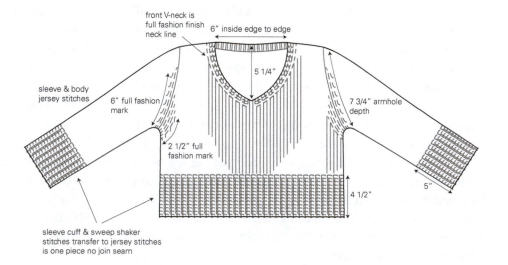

Promotional Buying

Promotional buying involves purchasing merchandise to be featured in the store's promotions, and it is usually a part of the buyer's overall merchandise plan. Because most retailers have frequent promotions during the year, buyers must scout the market for special promotional buys to feature in those promotions. Typically, you will be interested in locating merchandise that can be offered to your customers at a price lower than its regular selling price. You must carefully calculate your needs so that excess merchandise is not left after the promotion is completed. Also, before bringing new merchandise into the store, you should analyze your current stock to determine if the price of any items could be reduced as part of the promotion. Customers will more easily recognize value when the merchandise on sale had previously been sold in the store.

Job Lots

While in the market, you may also be offered a **job lot** by a vendor. A job lot is an assortment of merchandise that the vendor has been unable to sell at regular prices and therefore offers at a reduced price. The job lot will frequently contain merchandise of different value, so you should determine the retail price that could be realized for selling the goods quickly. If the estimated margin on the job lot does not reach the department's plan, you should consider other purchases.

There are other dangers in purchasing job lots. A poor assortment of sizes, colors, and styles may be offered. The quality may be excellent, but your customers may not want to purchase the items in the job lot. If your store already carries the items in the job lot, there is less danger involved because the merchandise can be added to your existing merchandise lines. Another danger occurs when job lots are offered to the buyer near the end of the selling season. Even though a bargain price is offered, the merchandise will arrive at your store so late in the season that you may not be able to sell it without taking more markdowns.

You must also determine the effect of any job lot purchases on your existing lines. Cannibalization of the line may occur. In other words, the sale merchandise from the job lot may take away sales from existing merchandise in the store. As a result, planned margins are not maintained because you may be forced to take heavy markdowns on merchandise already in the store.

Off-Price

Buyers for some stores may specialize in buying **off-price**, which occurs when retailers purchase manufacturers' overruns at deep discounts for the purpose of offering consumers low prices on name-brand merchandise. Stores such as Burlington Coat Factory, Marshalls, and T.J. Maxx are retailers that offer off-price merchandise. Some vendors have even established their own factory outlet stores to sell their own overruns. Prices at off-price stores are about 20 to 30 percent less than those at department stores selling the same merchandise. Read the Snapshot titled "TJX: One Retail Chain Doing Things Right" to learn more about what makes this off-price chain so successful.

Buying off-price requires that you wait longer into the selling season before making purchases. Customers of off-price stores are more concerned with price, rather than being the first to have a new fashion. By waiting into the selling season to make their purchases, buyers can usually find overruns in the market or vendors willing to sell products at a lower price.

Seconds and Irregulars

In the market, you may also be offered merchandise with slight imperfections or minor damage. For example, small pulls or snags may appear in apparel. The nature of the manufacturing process results in a certain amount of goods in this category. Manufacturers may inform buyers of the availability of these products through trade paper advertisements or through market representatives.

Imperfect or damaged merchandise is typically classified as **irregulars** or **seconds**. Irregulars have slight imperfections not visible to the naked eye. Seconds contain more obvious imperfections or damage. Because they are available at low prices, buyers purchase them to offer products to their customers at enormous savings. Some outlet stores stock seconds and irregulars exclusively.

There are dangers with purchasing seconds and irregulars. There must be a demand for these products by your customers that should coordinate with other products and fit into the merchandising policies of your store. Some buyers will not purchase irregulars or seconds because they may damage the quality image that the store has worked to develop.

Stores that offer seconds and irregulars usually sell them in an area set off from other first-quality merchandise. A special tag is usually attached to the item informing customers that the item is an irregular or a second. Large department stores usually put the merchandise in their budget departments.

PLACING THE ORDER

After you have made the decision to purchase merchandise and agreed to terms and conditions, you are ready to complete the purchase order. The purchase order is a contract between a buyer and a vendor and must be completed carefully to avoid any costly mistakes. The manufacturer's representative will provide order forms, but most buyers prefer to use their own. Because each form is different, there is a danger of some essential information being omitted.

Types of Orders

Buyers may place several types of orders, as follows:

- Regular orders are placed by the buyer directly with the vendor.
- Reorders are additional orders for merchandise previously purchased. Some fashion retailers are limiting reorders and placing orders for new merchandise to have continuously fresh and exciting stock moving into the store.
- Special orders are placed to satisfy the needs of individual customers.
- Advance orders are regular orders whose delivery is negotiated for some time in the future. Special discounts may be given to buyers who are willing to place orders early.
- Open orders are usually placed with the buying office. The buyer will select the vendor that is best suited to fill the requirements specified by the store.
- Back orders are placed by the buyer for shipments or parts of orders that the vendor had been unable to fill in the past.

Parts of the Purchase Order

Each purchase order, similar to the one illustrated in Figure 14.5, is usually marked with a serial number and includes the following information:

- name and address of the store
- date of the purchase order
- vendor's name and address
- where the goods are to be delivered, if not the store
- terms of sale (dating and FOB terms)
- cancellation date for the order
- department number
- classification number
- description of the merchandise, including quantity, stock number, unit price, and total price
- signature of the buyer or other authorized signatures
- special instructions

Typically, buyers will have a number of copies of the purchase order. The original is given to the vendor, and a copy remains with the buyer. In larger stores, additional copies may be sent to (1) receiving, which checks incoming merchandise on arrival at the store, and (2) the finance department, which pays for merchandise that has been ordered.

Sometimes it may be better to wait until you have returned from a market visit before completing purchase orders. You then have the opportunity for reconsideration, the ability to review your order without pressure from the vendor or other market activities.

Follow-Up of Orders

After the order is written, you still have certain responsibilities to ensure that the merchandise arrives at the store. For example, you may need to check with the manufacturers or transportation companies when merchandise does not arrive on time. Before special promotions, you may want to contact the manufacturer to ensure that the amount of merchandise needed will be arriving on time. You may also have to trace delayed or lost shipments.

Buyers also may be involved with **quality checks** to ensure that the quality of the merchandise shipped is identical to that of the merchandise seen in the market. Other store employees can be responsible for **quantity checks** that involve counting the number of items received as well as checking for correct sizes, colors, and models. These numbers are compared with both the purchase order and the invoice to determine that (1) merchandise received was actually ordered and (2) the store was billed correctly. If goods are to be returned to the vendor, proper forms must be completed. Different action may be required if other types of discrepancies are found.

Vendors should notify buyers if they are sending substitutions. On occasion, the vendor may be unable to complete the order exactly as requested but may be able to send merchandise that is nearly identical. Buyers should have the opportunity to decline substitutions before they are ever shipped. By accepting merchandise that was not ordered, you would be establishing a dangerous policy for your store.

Throughout the negotiation and ordering process, you will want to build a partnership with your vendors based on mutual respect, fair treatment, and honesty. Part of your success will depend on the cooperation and understanding that you develop with your vendors. And, in today's global marketplace, you may even want to assess how vendors have responded to human rights and environmental concerns. Read the Snapshot titled "Bangladesh: Will It Continue as a Hot Spot for Apparel Sourcing?" and learn more about safety concerns with factories in this country.

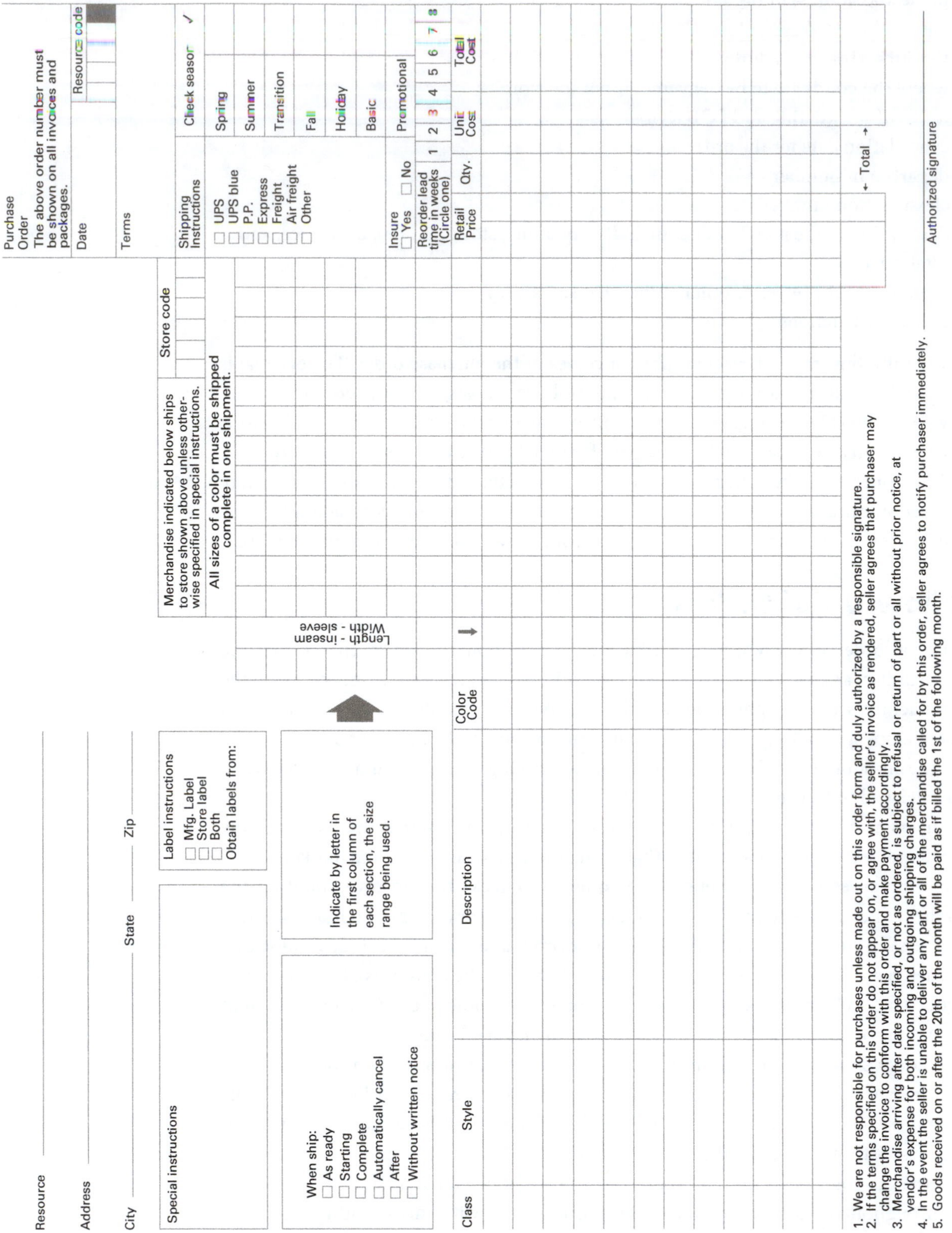
Resource ______

Address ______

City ______ State ______ Zip ______

Purchase Order

The above order number must be shown on all invoices and packages.

Date ______ Resource code ______

Terms ______

Special instructions

Label instructions
- ☐ Mfg. Label
- ☐ Store label
- ☐ Both
- ☐ Obtain labels from:

Merchandise indicated below ships to store shown above unless otherwise specified in special instructions.

Store code

Shipping Instructions
- ☐ UPS
- ☐ UPS blue
- ☐ P.P.
- ☐ Express
- ☐ Freight
- ☐ Air freight
- ☐ Other

Check season ✓
- Spring
- Summer
- Transition
- Fall
- Holiday
- Basic
- Promotional

When ship:
- ☐ As ready
- ☐ Starting
- ☐ Complete
- ☐ Automatically cancel
- ☐ After
- ☐ Without written notice

Indicate by letter in the first column of each section, the size range being used.

All sizes of a color must be shipped complete in one shipment.

Length - inseam

Width - sleeve

Insure ☐ Yes ☐ No

Reorder lead time in weeks (Circle one) 1 2 3 4 5 6 7 8

Class	Style	Description	Color Code	→	Retail Price	Qty.	Unit Cost	Total Cost
						← Total →		

1. We are not responsible for purchases unless made out on this order form and duly authorized by a responsible signature.
2. If the terms specified on this order do not appear on, or agree with, the seller's invoice as rendered, seller agrees that purchaser may change the invoice to conform with this order and make payment accordingly.
3. Merchandise arriving after date specified, or not as ordered, is subject to refusal or return of part or all without prior notice, at vendor's expense for both incoming and outgoing shipping charges.
4. In the event the seller is unable to deliver any part or all of the merchandise called for by this order, seller agrees to notify purchaser immediately.
5. Goods received on or after the 20th of the month will be paid as if billed the 1st of the following month.

Authorized signature ______

Figure 14.5

A sample purchase order used by retail buyers.

Summary Points

- Buyers must shop the market thoroughly to compare prices from vendors. Buyers may actually realize price reductions on merchandise through discounts, free deals, or other allowances granted the vendor.

- Buyers should be aggressive when seeking discounts from vendors. Discounts may turn a breakeven year into a profitable one. Types of discounts offered by vendors include quantity, seasonal, trade, and cash.

- When negotiating dating terms, buyers can negotiate discount percentages as well as the number of days in which the bill is to be paid. Types of dating terms include ordinary, EOM, ROG, extra, and advance.

- Buyers will also negotiate transportation terms. In addition, buyers may determine the method of shipment to be used. FOB destination terms are the most favorable for the buyer.

- Buyers may also negotiate for cooperative advertising and return privileges.

- Private brands allow buyers to establish exclusives for their store; however, advertising and visual merchandising are crucial to developing sales for private brands.

- When considering job lots, off-price buying, and seconds and irregulars, buyers must determine if the products will deliver the desired markup and how they will affect sales of other products.

- Buyers complete purchase orders, which become a legal contract between the store and the vendor.

- When merchandise arrives in the store, both quality checks and quantity checks should be conducted.

Review Activities

Developing Your Retail Buying Vocabulary

Consult the glossary if you did not add the following terms to your vocabulary.

advance dating terms	FOB (free on board)	off-price	quantity check
anticipation	FOB destination, charges reversed	on consignment	quantity discount
cash discount	FOB destination, freight prepaid	on memorandum	ROG (receipt of goods) dating
COD	FOB destination (store)	ordinary dating terms	terms
cooperative (co-op) advertising	FOB origin (factory)	price decline guarantee	seasonal discount
EOM (end-of-month) dating	FOB shipping point	private brand	seconds
terms	irregulars	promotional buying	specification buying
extra dating terms	job lot	quality check	trade discount

Understanding What You Read

1. Under the Robinson-Patman Act, how are manufacturers able to charge lower prices to large retailers?

2. Give examples of products for which price decline guarantees would be desired.

3. Why are manufacturers willing to offer seasonal discounts to buyers?

4. On merchandise with a list price totaling $2,520, a wholesale buyer is offered trade discounts of 40 percent and 15 percent. For what dollar amount will the buyer be billed?

5. Why are manufacturers willing to offer cash discounts to buyers?

6. In most cases, why would ROG terms be better for a buyer than ordinary dating terms?

7. The invoice date is January 5 and the delivery date is January 6. Terms of the order are 2/10 net 30 EOM. When is the last day the buyer can pay the bill and still receive a discount?

8. When could a buyer be in a position to take advantage of anticipation?

9. Goods are sent from the manufacturer with the following terms: 2/10 net 30 FOB factory. Who pays the shipping charges?

10. What are the dangers to the retailer of accepting cooperative advertising allowances?

11. When would a seller most often grant a buyer on-memorandum terms?

12. Why do retailers offer private brands?

13. How should a retailer promote private brands?

14. Why have Sears and other retailers reduced the number of private brands they carry?

15. Why did sales of private-brand products slow down in supermarkets for several years?

16. Describe how private brands should be priced in relation to national brands.

17. What are the dangers involved with purchasing job lots?

18. What are the dangers involved with purchasing seconds and irregulars?

19. When would a buyer issue an open order?

20. Why do some buyers return to their hotel rooms or their offices before completing purchase orders?

Analyzing and Applying What You Read

1. A vendor has offered you a choice of the following terms on a purchase that is under negotiation:

> 2/10 net 30
> 2/10 net 30 ROG
> 2/10 net 30 EOM

Which terms will be best for you? Explain.

2. Your store manager is considering offering some private brands in menswear. As the buyer for that department, you have been asked to prepare a proposal recommending the action to be taken. After listing the pros and cons of establishing private brands, present arguments to support your final decision.

3. Describe techniques that department stores and specialty stores could use to effectively compete with off-price retailers.

Retail Buying Math Practice

1. A shipment of books just arrived at your store with discounts of 40 percent and 20 percent. How much will this purchase, with a list price of $100, cost the retailer?

2. Merchandise from the vendor carries an invoice of July 1 and is received on July 4. Terms are 2/10 net 30 EOM, and the invoice is for $5,000. What amount should be remitted if the retailer pays the bill on July 13?

3. An invoice for $3,000 is dated April 27, and the merchandise was received on April 30. Terms were 4/10 net 30 EOM. Calculate the discount date.

4. Assume that the invoice date is April 2 and the delivery date is April 5. For each of the following dating terms calculate (a) the discount date and (b) the date when the net amount is due.

   a. 2/10 net 30   c. 2/10 net 30 ROG
   b. 2/10 net 30 EOM   d. 2/10 net 30 30X

5. A retail store in Charlotte, North Carolina, places an order with a factory in New York. The order is delivered to the store on August 10 with an invoice date of August 5. Terms were 3/15 net 30 FOB Charlotte. Including shipping charges if they owe any, how much would the retailer owe if it paid the bill on August 19?

STUDIO

Spreadsheet Skills

Visit this book's STUDIO product at www.BloomsburyFashionCentral.com and open and print Assignment H. Input formulas on the spreadsheet that will make the calculations requested. Complete the assigned problems, and record your answers on the tables provided at the end of the assignment.

Internet Connection

1. Access a website for a department store, such as www.jcpenney.com. Record information about private brands offered for sale. Report on such factors as the brands offered, their prices, and the types of promotion these private brands received.

2. Visit the book's STUDIO to watch a video about Amazon's plan to expand into private-label products.

SNAPSHOT: Bangladesh: Will It Continue as a Hot Spot for Apparel Sourcing?

After a building containing five garment factories collapsed outside Bangladesh's capital in 2013, factory owners in Bangladesh as well as Western apparel retailers have faced intense pressure from governments, consumers, and labor groups to improve workplace safety. As the death toll from the collapse soared past 1,000, it became the world's deadliest garment industry disaster and one of the worst industrial accidents. This disaster and others at factories in the country have raised alarms around the world about the often deadly working conditions in Bangladesh. Why have safety issues in this underdeveloped country garnered headlines around the world?

In the past, China has dominated both US and European markets for ready-made apparel—accounting for over 40 percent of the import volume in each region. But, as wages and other costs have increased in China, retail buyers have begun decreasing their levels of sourcing in China and have started sourcing products in less developed countries that provide lower prices. One of those new "hot spots" that has attracted buyers is Bangladesh. For example, in recent years, the country has exported nearly $24 billion annually in apparel around the world. In fact, 80 percent of that country's total exports are ready-made garments. How will this factory collapse and other safety issues impact the growth of Bangladesh as an exporter of apparel?

Walt Disney Co. has already stated that the company is ending apparel production in Bangladesh, which has caused widespread alarm among government and business leaders there that other Western corporations might soon follow. Such an exodus would likely devastate Bangladesh's economy and threaten the livelihood of millions of workers. In fact, 14 million families in Bangladesh are dependent on apparel production jobs.

The Bangladesh Parliament has implored Western apparel producers not to leave the country, stressing that many factories there do comply with all safety standards. Those pleas may be having some impact. Several Western retailers are developing new plans to ensure workplace safety. Such efforts would involve investing in, rather than abandoning, their operations in Bangladesh. However, there have not been widespread commitments to endorse tougher safety inspections.

Gap announced a $22 million fire and building safety plan with its suppliers in Bangladesh, and Walmart pledged $1.8 million to train 2,000 Bangladesh factory managers about fire safety. Some have called such efforts only a "drop in the bucket." Several analysts estimate that it would cost $3 billion to make the needed fire safety and building improvements to ensure that the more than 4,000 garment factories in Bangladesh were safe. In addition, there does not seem to be a push for a united strategy among the big players. Factories there vary greatly in their degree of compliance with safety standards.

Western brands and factories, as well as the Bangladesh government, will all have to work together to solve the problem. What is needed is a broad, comprehensive plan to ensure building safety for the workforce. However, in the past, factory owners in Bangladesh have been more likely to invest in equipment that improves productivity rather than in safety upgrades. One workers' group indicates that disasters such as this building collapse will continue to occur because of the pressure on factories to keep prices low, which has resulted in substandard safety conditions. In fact, low costs have propelled Bangladesh's apparel industry into one of the biggest in the world, on track to surpass China within the decade as the largest apparel manufacturer in the world.

Many questions remain. Will the factory collapse and resulting loss of lives serve as a turning point for the apparel industry in Bangladesh, or will safety issues persist? There also have been demands for consumers to consider the human cost behind the bargain-priced apparel that they purchase. Will consumers care about such issues? Will retail buyers actively pursue compliance efforts on safety issues from factories before they place their next orders?

BASED ON:

Associated Press. (2013, May 10). Bangladesh factory collapse death toll hits 1,034. *USAToday.com*.

Fox, Emily Jane. (2013, April 25). Bangladesh factory collapse kills at least 160, reviving safety questions. *CNN.com*.

Greenhouse, Steven. (2013, May 5). Bangladesh fears apparel exodus. *The Charlotte Observer*, 15A, ff.

Kennedy, Bruce. (2014, April 24). Is the Bangladesh factory collapse a turning point? *CBSNews.com*.

Neate, Rupert. (2014, February 24). Bangladesh factory collapse: Big brands urged to pay into help fund. *TheGuardian.com*.

SNAPSHOT: TJX: One Retail Chain Doing Things Right

As retailers like Macy's, Sears, and Kmart close stores, one retail chain, TJX, has experienced strong sales in apparel as well as accessories and home goods. While these retailers were closing stores, TJX was reporting a 4 percent increase in sales. Recently, in fact, sales across all divisions of TJX were above projections. Who is TJX? Currently, the company headquartered in Framingham, Massachusetts, operates over 3,700 stores under several banners. In the United States, it operates T.J. Maxx, Marshalls, Home Goods, and Sierra Trading Post. In Canada, the stores are called Winners, Home Sense, and Marshalls. In Europe they are called T.J. Maxx and Home Sense, and in Australia they have acquired Trade Secret.

How has TJX become so successful? Generally, the chain has been able to successfully leverage the off-retail concept of selling mostly name-brand merchandise at a discount. There are many retailers, such as Nordstrom Rack and Steinmart, who have the same approach but have not been nearly as successful. TJX recognizes that off-price is based on volume—selling a ton of merchandise and selling it fast. In fact, TJX turns over its average inventory every fifty-five days, compared to eighty-five days for similar retailers. Some employees even report that merchandise moves so rapidly that it is often sold out in the stores before vendors are paid. Most importantly, the quick turnover keeps the merchandise fresh in the stores. TJX customers have shown they would rather have new stuff than continuous sales in the stores, which erodes their beliefs they are getting the lowest price possible from the onset.

By design, the product assortment at TJX stores is broad—prom dresses alongside pots and pans—but not deep. For example, only a few shoes from a famous designer may be available in each size. The company philosophy is that customers will buy a product when they see it, or it may be gone by their next visit.

Much of the success of TJX can be attributed to its 1,000 buyers, who are considered some of the best in the business as they work with more than 18,000 vendors negotiating deals worth millions of dollars. These buyers have completed a rigorous training program and are provided an enormous amount of autonomy. In fact, at TJX stores, buyers are empowered to make decisions that would require approvals from higher-ups at other retailers. In addition, TJX buyers have a more narrow focus than their department store counterparts. For example, rather than being responsible for accessories, a TJX buyer might specialize in just handbags. One other major difference is that most department store buyers purchase inventory seasonally, while TJX buyers are in the market most weeks of the year. They tend to make purchases as close to when they are needed in the store as possible. Waiting longer to make purchases often results in better prices from the vendors, but it also gives the buyer more information about current fashion trends. Moreover, the buyer-supplier relationship with TJX has been based on building a strong partnership—they need each other.

Furthermore, much of the customer appeal at TJX is based on stores selling what is currently hot, not last season's leftovers. Department stores, for example, may return or cancel orders from manufacturers, and TJX buyers find deals there. But, the company buys a big share of its merchandise from suppliers upfront. In fact, it has been reported that many vendors produce excess inventory on purpose, hoping TJX will purchase it. Additionally, about 10 percent of its merchandise may be produced under in-house labels to offer customers some products in a hot fashion trend. Hardly any customer goes to a TJX store to purchase something specific; the lure is discovery. They are shopping as explorers—taking part in the experience of the "treasure hunt." Inventory shifts regularly, so no customer visit is the same.

As shoppers across generations and demographics become more focused on value than ever before, the excitement of finding something on sale has a broad appeal. Even customers who grew up relying on e-commerce, like millennials, are coming through the doors at TJX stores. That is one reason that management expects to have nearly 5,600 stores when its current expansion plans are complete. Such expansion clearly indicates that TJX is one retailer that is doing things right!

BASED ON:

Bhasin, Kim, & Rupp, Lindsey. (2016, January 21). How one huge American retailer ignored the internet and won. *BloombergNews.com.*

Isidore, Chris. (2016, May 18). T.J. Maxx, Marshalls and HomeGoods plan to open thousands of new stores. *CNN.com.*

Loeb, Walter. (2016, August 17). TJX gains market share around the world, leads in earnings and raises outlook. *Forbes.com.*

Loeb, Walter. (2016, November 16). TJX's blockbuster earnings show Americans are still shopping—but not at full-price chains. *Fobes.com.*

Spagnolo, Sarah. (2017, February 7). How Macy's and Kmart store closures will impact American retailers. *ChainStoreAge.com.*

PRIVATE BRANDS SPELL PROFITS

Private brands, also categorized as private labels, keep growing and creating more competition for national brands. This trend also means that some merchandisers are increasingly becoming brand managers by taking responsibility for such things as trend tracking, product innovation, creating and maintaining the brand's image and identity, and developing expertise in brand marketing, brand repositioning, and brand renewal.

Retailers of every type—Best Buy, Saks, Home Depot, Walgreens, Nordstrom, Macy's, Kroger, Kohl's, J.C. Penney, and Target among them—have created private brands to compete with traditional national brands. For example, Target's Archer Farms brand has established itself as an affordable luxury convenience brand, Walgreens has turned its Nice! brand into high-quality everyday products for much lower prices than national brands, and Home Depot has made the shift to private brands with such labels as Hampton Bay, Husky, and HDX. Bar III is an example of a private label that has flown off the shelves at Macy's. The line was not the creation of a new designer; it was designed, manufactured, and marketed in-house by Macy's merchandising team.

At J.C. Penney, private brands, like clothing labels St. John's Bay and Arizona and houseware labels like Cooks, generate over half the sales revenue at the chain. Even Amazon is increasingly creating its own product lines. For example, Amazon's line of batteries, AmazonBasics, accounted for about one-third of battery sales online. The health of private brands like these is critical to the success of these retailers.

Historically, private brands lacked the same trust that consumers have given national brands, but that is rapidly changing. One recent survey found that 80 percent of all shoppers believe that private brands are equal to or better than national brands in terms of quality. During the recession at the beginning of the decade, over 90 percent of Americans changed their shopping habits because of the economic downturn. To save money, many of them tried private brands for the first time and changed their opinions about many of the labels. As the recession has eased, many consumers have developed a strong loyalty to these private brands for reasons other than price. To fight this trend, many national brands have rolled out more discounts and coupons to defend their market share.

Private brands still cost an average of 29 percent less than their nationally branded counterparts, but they are rising faster in price, at a rate of 5.3 percent compared with the industry average of 1.9 percent. For retailers, private brands mean more profit; they also give customers more options and help retailers attract and retain customers by building brand loyalty. Since Amazon and other retailers cannot carry a competitor's private brand, these labels give stores another way to differentiate themselves from the competition.

But for private brands to be successful, they must be promoted so that customers get to know them. Promotional campaigns must be conducted by the retailer, not the manufacturer. For example, Macy's rolled out the Bar III private brand with carefully orchestrated in-store promotions. They also held events outside the stores. In conjunction with Fashion Week, they hosted a pop-up store in the Flatiron district of New York. Social media were used extensively, and several suggestions from influential fashion bloggers were incorporated into Bar III, which created even more buzz about the label. To promote their new private brands, Publix, a grocery store chain in the Southeast, offered a free private-brand item to customers who purchased a similar national brand.

Today's private brands are alive with innovation, from a greater emphasis on the quality of products to increased sophistication of packaging and marketing. Most retailers are seeing private brands as an integral part of their business operations and have even begun transforming the marketing of these brands.

Retailers must realize that when competing for customers with private brands, customers will not make future purchases of the products based on price alone. Private brands must be used again and again by customers to create an emotional bond with the products. For customers to repurchase private brands, they must satisfy their needs in terms of both quality and price. Private brands seem to be accomplishing both, and for retailers that means more profits.

BASED ON:

Davis, Scott. (2013, May 23). How Target, Walgreens and Home Depot have forever changed the private label game. Forbes.com.

Dishman, Lydia. (2013, June 12). Can private labels restore J.C.Penney's profits? Forbes.com.

Rao, Leena. (2016, November 4). Amazon's private label brands are on fire. Fortune.com.

Wahba, Phil. (2016, March 10). Kohl's stakes its turnaround on relaunch of top house brand. Fortune.com.

Wahba, Phil. (2016, August 17). J.C. Penney might be falling into the same private label trap that Kohl's did. Fortune.com.

CHAPTER 15

PRICING THE MERCHANDISE

Performance Objectives

- Identify the elements of retail price.
- Calculate initial markup percentage.
- Calculate retail price using markup based on retail.
- Identify factors affecting retail price.
- Describe the benefits and limitations of price lining.
- Describe the impact of store image on pricing decisions.
- Describe the methods used to evaluate pricing decisions.
- Identify types of adjustments to retail price.
- Distinguish between markdown percentage and off-retail percentage.
- Calculate markdown percentages and off-retail percentages.

Once merchandise has been purchased by the buyer, its retail price must be determined. This price must cover the cost of the merchandise and the expenses of doing business while providing a profit. Yet retail price must be attractive to consumers and priced competitively for market conditions. There is no formula for determining the best retail price, but through an analysis of customer buying behavior, past sales records, anticipated expenses, and economic and market conditions, you will be able to arrive at an appropriate price for the merchandise.

Price is the value placed on what is exchanged. In other words, price quantifies the value of products or services and is a major determinant of the amount of merchandise that will be sold by your store or department. Moreover, price is usually the element of retail strategy that can be changed quickly in response to changes in economic and market conditions.

In this chapter, you will learn about the mathematical calculations necessary for establishing retail prices. Factors affecting retail price are described, and adjustments to retail prices are explained.

ESTABLISHING RETAIL PRICES

Retail price includes (1) the cost of merchandise, plus (2) an additional amount known as markup. Markup must be large enough to cover the operating expenses of the retail organization while providing a profit.

Elements of Retail Price

Cost of goods sold includes the actual cost of the merchandise plus transportation charges involved in getting the merchandise from the vendor to the store. **Markup** is added to the cost of goods to determine retail price.

To plan the most appropriate markup, you will need to estimate both expenses and profit. These estimates also require that you have already made a sales forecast. When planning expenses, you must realize that some of them will not change, while others will increase or decrease in relation to sales. Typically, expenses are classified as fixed or variable. **Fixed expenses** do not vary regardless of how much merchandise the store sells. Examples of fixed expenses include mortgage and insurance payments. **Variable expenses** change in a direct relationship to sales. Such expenses normally increase or decrease as sales increase or decrease. Examples of variable expenses would be commissions, delivery expenses, supplies, and advertising. Past records and industry averages can be used to predict expenses required for estimated sales levels.

The profit goal must also be planned before merchandise is priced. Profit earned by retailers varies by type of business. Grocery stores that turn over merchandise quite rapidly may earn a profit of less than 2 percent of sales, whereas specialty stores with much slower turnover may have more than 5 percent profit. The National Retail Federation reports average profit percentages for many categories of retail business, and these figures can be used as one retail performance measurement.

If the amount of markup is not carefully planned, the resulting retail prices may be too high and the merchandise may not sell. Or, if markups are too low, not enough revenue will be generated to cover expenses and provide a profit for the store.

Determining Markup Percentage

Based on these elements, the following formula expresses the elements of retail price:

$$\textbf{Retail price} = \textbf{Cost} + \textbf{Markup}$$

This formula can also be rearranged to calculate cost or markup as follows:

$$\textbf{Cost} = \textbf{Retail price} - \textbf{Markup}$$
$$\textbf{Markup} = \textbf{Retail price} - \textbf{Cost}$$

All components in the formula can be expressed as a dollar figure or as a percentage. In most situations, you will probably be more interested in the markup percentage rather than the markup in dollars. Percentages provide a better performance measurement when you are comparing results with past store records, goals, or industry averages.

Typically, markup is expressed as a percentage of retail. The formula is expressed as follows:

$$\textbf{Markup percentage} = \textbf{Markup in dollars} \,/\, \textbf{Retail price}$$

Let's examine one situation to make this calculation. Assume that the cost of an item of merchandise is $40 and the markup is $35. Markup percentage based on retail would be 46.7 percent ($35/$75 the retail price).

Planning Initial Markup Percentage

As a buyer, how can you plan the most appropriate markup? You must make estimates about the elements affecting the retail price–sales, expenses, profit, reductions, and cash discounts. You can determine an initial markup percentage using the following formula:

Initial markup percentage =
(Expenses + Profit + Reductions — Cash discounts) / (Sales + Reductions)

Let's examine this formula more closely. First, you must realize that all these figures are "planned," or predictions based on an expected level of sales. Inaccurate predictions will lead to inaccurate pricing decisions.

Sales

The sales level should be planned first. As you have already learned, sales forecasts are based on past sales records as well as changes in internal and external conditions. For example, as the season nears an end for many products, customer demand lessens, causing retailers to lower the retail price of the products in order to sell the remaining inventory (Figure 15.1). All the other components of this calculation are impacted by the expected level of sales.

Expenses

You must plan both fixed and variable expenses associated with expected sales levels. Estimates of the impact of sales on variable expenses must be calculated.

Figure 15.1
Lower consumer demand can decrease sales and lower retail prices.

Profit

The amount of profit the store wishes to obtain from the sales volume must also be estimated. Again, past store records or industry averages could be used to make this prediction.

Reductions

When determining initial markup, you must also consider planned **reductions** that your store or department will experience. Reductions include markdowns, employee and special customer discounts, and shrinkage.

- **Markdowns** are reductions in the original retail price. Almost every business must plan for markdowns because customers may not buy the merchandise at its original price, it may become shopworn, or the price may need to be reduced to clear the merchandise from inventory at the end of the season. Markdowns will be explained more fully in the section of this chapter dealing with adjustments to retail price. Original retail prices must be high enough to allow for markdowns to be taken and still result in the planned sales volume and profit.
- Discounts also reduce the original retail price of some items that are sold. Discounts may be given to employees or special groups of consumers such as senior citizens. You must have some estimate of how many discounts will occur during the period for which you are planning.
- **Shrinkage** includes reductions in inventory not accounted for by sales. Employee theft and shoplifting are the major causes of shrinkage. When making your estimates, you must realize that shrinkage will occur and probably cannot be controlled entirely. Estimated shrinkage is included in the initial markup calculation and will raise the planned retail price.
- Cash discounts may be given by some vendors to retailers who pay for merchandise at an early date. When cash discounts are provided, retail price can be lowered, because these discounts reduce the expenses of doing business. In the initial markup formula, cash discounts are subtracted.

The components of the initial markup formula can be estimated either as a dollar amount or as a percentage of sales. Let's examine examples using both approaches.

Illustrative Problem

Assume that a store plans sales of $50,000 with a profit of $2,500. Markdowns are planned at $5,000 and shrinkage is planned at $500. No employee or consumer discounts are anticipated. Expenses are planned at $15,000. Using the initial markup formula, markup percentage can be calculated as follows.

Solution

Initial markup percent = $15,000 + $2,500 + $5,500 / $50,000 + $5,500
Initial markup percent = $23,000 / $55,500
Initial markup percent = 0.414
Initial markup percent = 41.4%

When planning markup, many stores make predictions based on estimated percentages of retail sales. The assumption is that even though the dollar figure will change based on different sales predictions, the percentage of sales will remain fairly constant.

Illustrative Problem

Expenses may be planned at 30 percent of sales, and the store desires a 5 percent profit. Reductions are estimated to be 10 percent of sales, and shrinkage is estimated to be 1 percent. With the same formula, initial markup can be calculated from these percentages as follows:

Solution

Initial markup percent = 0.30 + 0.05 + 0.11 / 1.00 + 0.11
Initial markup percent = 0.46 / 1.11
Initial markup percent = 0.414
Initial markup percent = 41.4%
(Note: When using percentages, the sales percent will always equal 100.)

Seldom will you apply the same markup to all products carried in the store. Markups below the planned initial markup may be necessary for some items, while substantially higher markups can be achieved on other items. Also, products having the same cost may differ greatly in customer appeal and consequently will require different markups. Some fashion apparel and perishable items may require large markups to offset drastic markdowns or high spoilage rates. Even though different markups are used, the overall goal is to achieve the planned markup goal for the store or department.

Once the initial markup percentage has been established, retail prices for individual items can be calculated. As you learned, retail price is the cost of merchandise plus the desired markup. Many times, the markup percentage for your store will already have been established by management. Your task will be to determine the retail price of an item when its cost and markup are known.

Because we are dealing with markup percentages based on retail, the retail percentage will always equal 100 percent. Let's use this information to establish a retail price. In the example that has been presented, a 41.4 percent markup is planned. Assuming the cost of an item is $50, what would be the retail price? First, supply the information you already know, as follows:

	$	%
Cost	$50	
+ Markup		41.4%
= Retail Price		100%

We also know that the cost percentage is 58.6 percent (100% − 41.4%). Remember that the formula can be rearranged to calculate cost as follows: Cost = Retail − Markup. The formula works for percentages as well as dollar amounts. Now, using simple algebra, you can determine the retail price. You know that 58.6% of retail price equals $50 (the cost). This information can be expressed as:

$$0.586 \times \text{Retail price} = \$50.00$$
$$\text{Retail price} = \$50.00 / 0.586$$
$$\text{Retail price} = \$85.32$$

Some businesses use **keystoning** to establish retail price. They simply double cost to determine the retail price. The resulting markup will always be 50 percent based on retail. In competitive market situations, keystoning may result in pricing the merchandise much higher than the competition, which would result in fewer sales. In some instances, keystoning may not cover operating expenses or provide a profit for the business.

FACTORS AFFECTING RETAIL PRICE

The preceding explanation of establishing retail prices is based on a cost orientation, whereby a calculated markup is added to the cost of the merchandise. Obviously, costs and operating expenses must be considered when you are establishing retail prices. A retailer cannot survive if prices do not cover these costs and expenses and yield a profit.

In most situations, these considerations are considered a minimum or **price floor** below which the product cannot be priced. However, such mathematical calculations do not consider other important factors before a retail price is established. They include (1) target market, (2) store policies, (3) competition, and (4) economic conditions.

Target Market

The overall objectives established by management determine the store's target market. As a buyer, you must understand how your store is positioned in the marketplace, and you must determine the image customers have of your store and how they view price (Figure 15.2). Some customers relate higher prices to higher quality for some products, such as apparel and electronics. Knowing your target market also establishes the price range in the store or department. Fashion-conscious customers are eager to purchase the most current styles and are willing to pay a higher price for them, whereas price-conscious customers will scour the market for the lowest prices available. In the final analysis, you must determine whether your customers will recognize the value they will receive based on the price you place on the merchandise. Read the Snapshot titled "Nordstrom Rack" to learn more about how Nordstrom is appealing to different types of markets with two types of stores.

Store Policies

Management will also determine both the store image and policies that will be implemented to create the desired image. Store policies must be used to guide pricing decisions. You should develop a strategy to implement store policies and create the desired image. Stores wanting to create a prestigious image may use price skimming as the cornerstone of their pricing policy. Stores using **skimming** charge the highest possible price that customers who most desire the product will pay. The policy is used by many stores when new products are introduced, and it can also be used as a tool to limit demand when there is a short supply of the product available.

Figure 15.2
What image does this store
present in the marketplace?
What types of customers will it
attract?

Discounters, on the other hand, use **penetration** policies. They are concerned with penetrating a market quickly with low prices to produce large unit sales volumes. A small amount of profit is made on each item, but many more units are sold, which can result in higher overall profits for the store. Stores use this policy when they want to gain market share quickly. Also, lower prices tend to discourage many competitors from entering the market.

Some retailers even use **loss leaders**, pricing specific products at a point that will not generate any profits. The purpose of loss leaders is to build store traffic. Once in the store, retailers hope that customers will make other purchases. Some retailers also believe that loss leaders give customers the impression that all the store's prices are low. However, using loss leaders requires considerable skill. Management must determine if customers are indeed making other purchases. Many customers buy the special items and then leave without making other purchases. Also, too large a reduction may suggest damaged or inferior goods to some customers.

Retailers also establish pricing strategy based on anticipated emotional responses of customers. They most commonly use odd or even pricing. **Odd-cent pricing** attempts to influence customers' perceptions of the retail price by ending it with certain numbers. Users of the technique assume more customers will purchase a product at $9.99 rather than $10.00. It is thought that they view the price as $9.00 plus a few pennies because they pay more attention to the dollar figure rather than the cents. Research studies, however, suggest that odd-cent pricing has little effect on sales. Discounters typically use odd-cent pricing, whereas prestigious stores use even pricing.

Stores attempting to create a prestigious or upscale image often price products using **even pricing**. For example, they would use a retail price of $32.00 rather than $31.95. Even prices tend to enhance the upscale image of many products, such as jewelry and fragrances.

Stores may also implement a policy known as **price lining**, which will dictate pricing decisions. Price lining consists of selecting certain prices and carrying assortments of merchandise only at those prices. For example, men's white shirts may be carried at $29.95, $39.95, and $49.95.

Price lining developed because customers desire a choice when purchasing most merchandise; however, buyers must ensure that customers can distinguish the difference among the items offered for sale. Fewer price lines reduce the consumer's confusion and allow sales associates to become more familiar with the merchandise and more aware of the differences that exist. Buyers can more easily select merchandise because their selections must be priced at preset price levels.

Price lines are usually established through a careful analysis of past sales, selecting those prices representing the bulk of sales. Many retailers establish three **price points** for many items of merchandise, which could be broadly classified as good, better, or best; however, such relative terms have specific meaning for only a particular category of merchandise.

Let's examine an illustration of how one price point may be developed. Assume that a buyer has purchased scarves from four vendors at the following unit costs:

> Scarves from Vendor 1 at $5.25 each.
> Scarves from Vendor 2 at $5.33 each.
> Scarves from Vendor 3 at $5.00 each.
> Scarves from Vendor 4 at $5.13 each.

If a predetermined markup percentage were applied to each of these scarves, four different, but similar, retail prices would be calculated. Confusion would result for both the customer and the sales associates. Most buyers would establish one price point, such as $10.99, thus reducing confusion resulting from customers attempting to determine slight differences that might exist among the scarves.

The major limitation of price lining is that the price point requirements sometimes hamper the buyer's efforts to obtain adequate assortments. There is also difficulty in maintaining uniform quality.

A storewide single price policy is an extreme example of price lining. Under this policy, everything in the store is sold for the same price. This approach is usually found in stores that carry only inexpensive merchandise. Read the Trendwatch titled "Dollar Tree: Will Growth Continue?" to learn more about how one retailer has adopted a growth strategy based on a one-price pricing strategy.

Competition

Retailers must also examine the competition's prices when establishing retail prices. You must decide to price at, below, or above the competition. A pricing strategy based on the competition's prices requires that you closely monitor price changes as they occur in the marketplace.

Pricing to Meet the Competition

Stores using this strategy deemphasize price as a merchandising tool. Factors such as service and location are stressed to customers.

Pricing Below the Competition

Some retailers attempt to establish retail prices below those of competitors. To do so, however, requires that the merchandise be purchased at a lower cost or that operating expenses be less than those of the competitors. Some retailers may stock private-brand merchandise, which cannot be as easily compared with similar products carried by competitors. Because private-brand merchandise usually costs the store less, higher profit margins are obtained.

Attempting to underprice the competition may bring disastrous results if the store becomes involved in a price war. A **price war** develops when several competing retailers try to undersell each other. The stores in such a war keep reducing their prices to attract each other's customers. Lowering prices to beat the competition strains profitability, and if price is the store's only competitive tool, it may not be able to attract customers who desire more service or larger product assortments.

Pricing Above the Competition

Some retailers attempt to create a prestigious image by pricing above competitors' prices for similar merchandise; however, customers must perceive extra value for the higher prices. Usually stores with higher prices are offering free services (such as delivery, product assembly, and alterations), exclusive merchandise, higher-quality merchandise, or more personalized sales attention.

Economic Conditions

Pricing decisions must also be made in relation to economic conditions. For example, during economic slowdowns, prices are lowered to generate more sales. Supply and demand also have an impact on retail prices. When demand for a product is greater than supply, retailers can charge higher prices. The reverse is also true; prices must be lowered when supply exceeds demand. For example, during the winter when snow is abundant at a ski resort, prices of ski apparel and equipment will be high, but during seasons of little or no snow, prices on those same products plummet.

ADJUSTMENTS TO RETAIL PRICE

Retail prices must be adjusted frequently to meet changing conditions. Three typical price adjustments are (1) markdowns, (2) markdown cancellations, and (3) additional markups.

Markdowns

It is probable that not every item of merchandise will sell at its original retail price; thus, markdowns are a critical element of merchandising decisions. Because markdowns have such a significant impact on the revenues of a store or department, they must be carefully planned and controlled.

Reasons for Markdowns

Buying, pricing, and selling errors can all result in markdowns. In addition, some markdowns occur as a sales promotion tool to attract customers. The reasons merchandise is marked down include the following:

- Overbuying occurs when the buyer has overestimated customer demand. In order to move the excess inventory, price reductions are used. Carefully maintaining sales records and analyzing current trends will help you avoid this problem.
- Sometimes merchandise is priced higher than customers are willing to pay. Overpricing most frequently occurs when new merchandise that the store has never carried is purchased.

- Faulty selling practices are another reason for markdowns. Sometimes sales associates do not give proper sales efforts to a product. They may not point out new merchandise to customers when it arrives; consequently, the merchandise remains in stock until it is too late to sell at original prices.
- Markdowns also occur at the end of the season when only odds and ends of a particular line are left in stock. For example, only a few small and extra large sweatshirts may be left. These items are marked down to clear them from stock so fresh stock can be added to inventory.
- Also, some merchandise may have been in stock so long that it has become soiled or damaged. Price reductions are needed to move these goods.

Timing of Markdowns

There is disagreement among retailers on the best time to take markdowns. Some retailers delay markdowns as long as possible, hoping to sell the merchandise at the original retail price. These retailers wait until late in the season before taking markdowns to establish in the customer's mind that "special sales" will occur at the same time each year. Some of these retailers are well known for their **automatic markdowns** at the end of the selling season. For example, goods that remain unsold after six days are repriced at 25 percent of their original price; after six more days, at 50 percent; and after another six days, at 75 percent. After a final six days, if they remain unsold, they are given to charity. Even though customers know a larger markdown will occur later, many of them make purchases early to ensure they can get the merchandise before it is sold.

Most retailers, however, believe markdowns should be taken throughout the season to keep a fresh supply of goods flowing into the store. Also, early markdowns tend to be smaller than markdowns taken later in the season. For fashion goods, markdowns should be taken as soon as sales begin to fall off. Basic or staple merchandise items should be marked down before the goods have been in stock too long and have become shopworn.

To be effective, a markdown must be large enough to induce customers to buy merchandise. For example, marking an item down from $15 to $14 is probably not adequate to generate new customer interest in the product.

Recording Markdowns

As a buyer, you will need to maintain information about the number and dollar amount of markdowns taken. Knowledge of past markdowns is essential for planning initial markup. Also, markdown information is needed as a check on shrinkage. Moreover, knowing about specific markdowns gives you information about which types of products may not need to be reordered in the future.

Buyers are also interested in the **markdown percentage** during a selling season. To calculate this figure, you must know the total dollar amount of markdowns and total dollar amount of sales. The markdown percentage can be calculated using the following formula:

Markdown percentage = Dollar markdown / Total sales

Illustrative Problem

Assume 100 ties were originally purchased at $10 each and are marked to sell at $20 each. At the end of the season, all the ties sold at that price except ten, which were marked down to $12 and finally sold. Total markdowns are $80 (ten ties, $8 markdown). Total sales were $1,920 ($1,800 for ninety ties at $20 each plus $120 for ten ties at $12 each). Substituting in the formula, markdown percentage is calculated as follows.

Solution

$$\text{Markdown percentage} = \text{Dollar markdown} / \text{Total sales}$$
$$\text{Markdown percentage} = \$80 / \$1,920$$
$$\text{Markdown percentage} = 0.04166$$
$$\text{Markdown percentage} = 4.2\%$$

For retail accounting procedures, you will calculate markdown percentage as described, but for advertising purposes, an **off-retail percentage** is calculated. Customers view the markdown as a reduction of the original retail price (Figure 15.3). Off-retail is calculated using the following formula:

$$\text{Off-retail percentage} = \text{Markdown} / \text{Original retail price}$$

For the previous example, each of the last ten ties was marked down $8 from an original retail price of $20. The off-retail percentage that would be advertised would be 40 percent ($8/$20).

Markdown Cancellations

For many promotions involving markdowns early in the selling season, all items in stock that were marked down probably will not sell at the reduced price. A promotion such as a Presidents' Day sale, for example, may last for only a few days. At the end of the sale, merchandise is repriced, usually at the original retail price. A **markdown cancellation** has occurred.

You would need to record such cancellations. Assume that 100 items that had an original retail price of $12 each were marked down $2 each for a special sale. Ninety of the items sold at the sale price, and the others were repriced at $12 when the sale was over. A $20 markdown cancellation would be recorded for this item ($2 price increase × ten remaining in stock).

Figure 15.3
Off-retail percentages are used to communicate with customers through advertising, in-store displays, or other promotions.

Additional Markups

During periods of rising prices, many retailers may find it necessary to increase original retail prices. **Additional markups**, or increases in retail prices, are most likely to occur for basic merchandise items as wholesale prices increase. Merchandise already on the sales floor may be re-marked to reflect price increases of new purchases. Fashion merchandise would less likely have additional markups during the season because the selling period is so short.

EVALUATING PRICING DECISIONS

Retailers must evaluate the effectiveness of pricing decisions once they have been made. Pricing decisions are usually evaluated against the pricing objectives the retail organization planned to achieve. Three key measures of the success of pricing decisions are (1) market share, (2) profit, and (3) markup achieved.

Market Share

Market share describes a store's sales in relation to total sales in the industry or one specific trading area. A store's objective may be to maintain or increase market share. However, the organization with the largest market share is not always the most profitable. Stores may have had to lower prices to build market share, and lower prices could have resulted in lower profits.

Profit

All stores want to maximize profits with the retail prices they establish. Management usually states profit objectives as a percentage of sales. Actual profits can be compared with industry averages or past records. You may also express your objective as a percentage increase in profits from one period to the next.

Markup Achieved

Buyers will be evaluated on how well they achieved their markup goals at a specified sales level. The markup formula included a profit estimate; therefore, if markup is achieved at the desired sales level, profits will result.

Summary Points

- Retail price must cover the cost of the merchandise as well as the expenses of doing business while providing a profit for the store.
- Markup is calculated by estimating store expenses and planned profit. Both can be planned using past store records and industry averages obtained from trade associations.
- Markup percentage is usually more significant to a buyer than markup in dollars.
- The initial markup percentage can be planned by first making a sales forecast, and then estimating expenses, profit, reductions, and cash discounts planned for that sales volume.

- Seldom will a store apply the same markup to all the products carried. Even though different markups are used, the overall objective will be to achieve the planned markup goal.

- In addition to mathematical calculations, other factors must be considered before establishing retail prices. They include the target market, store policies, the competition, and economic conditions.

- Price skimming and penetration pricing are the policies used most often when introducing a new product. Skimming yields fewer sales but at a higher markup, whereas the goal of penetration pricing is volume sales at a low markup.

- Price lining essentially dictates pricing decisions. Price points are established, and only merchandise to be priced at those levels is bought for the store.

- Adjustments are made to retail prices through markdowns, markdown cancellations, and additional markups.

- The success of pricing decisions will be measured against market share, profit, and markups achieved.

Review Activities

Developing Your Retail Buying Vocabulary

Consult the glossary if you did not add the following terms to your vocabulary.

additional markup	loss leader	off-retail percentage	reductions
automatic markdown	markdown	penetration	shrinkage
cost of goods sold	markdown cancellation	price floor	skimming
even pricing	markdown percentage	price lining	variable expenses
fixed expenses	markup	price point	
keystoning	odd-cent pricing	price war	

Understanding What You Read

1. What are the two elements of retail price?

2. Describe the difference between fixed and variable expenses.

3. List four types of reductions.

4. Why do most stores not apply a uniform markup percentage to all products they carry?

5. Why does fashion apparel typically require larger markups than basic merchandise?

6. Describe situations when price skimming would be most appropriate.

7. Describe situations when penetration pricing would be most appropriate.

8. Why are loss leaders used by some retailers?

9. What are the benefits of price lining?

10. What are the drawbacks of pricing lining?

11. What is the rationale for using odd-cent pricing?

12. What is the rationale for using even pricing?

13. When is pricing above the competition a feasible pricing strategy?

14. How can a retail store price the same product for less than the competition is charging?

15. Describe how supply and demand affect retail price.

16. How will a store determine if correct pricing decisions have been made?

17. List and explain three causes of markdowns.

18. What are the benefits of taking markdowns early?

19. Explain why some retail stores take markdowns only at the end of the season.

20. Why do stores use additional markups?

Retail Buying Math Practice

1. Calculate the initial markup percentage for the following situations:

   a. Sales = $60,000
      Expenses = $25,000
      Profit goal = $8,000

   b. Expenses = 38%
      Reductions = 10%
      Cash discounts = 1%
      Profit goal = 5%

   c. Sales = $185,000
      Reductions = $12,000
      Expenses = $53,000
      Cash discounts = $18,000
      Profit goal = $15,000

   d. Profit goal = 7%
      Reductions = 18%
      Cash discounts = 4%
      Expenses = 33%

2. Calculate the retail price for the following situations:

   a. Markup percentage = 45%
      Cost = $14

   b. Markup percentage = 60%
      Cost = $2

3. Calculate the (1) amount of markdown in dollars, (2) markdown cancellations, and (3) markdown percentage for the following situation:

Original Retail	Sale Price	On Hand Start of Sale	Units Sold	Retail Price After Sale
$50	$40	36	20	$50
$35	$27	36	20	$35
$30	$20	48	25	$30
$20	$15	52	15	$20

4. Calculate the off-retail percentage that can be advertised for the following situations:

   a. Original retail = $50
      Sales price = $35

   b. Cost = $25
      Initial markup = $25
      Markdown = $5

   c. Cost = $125
      Initial markup = $120
      Sales price = $230

STUDIO

Spreadsheet Skills

1. Visit this book's STUDIO product at www.BloomsburyFashionCentral.com and open and print Assignment I. Complete the assigned problems, and record your answers on the tables provided at the end of the assignment.

2. Visit this book's STUDIO product at www.BloomsburyFashionCentral.com and open and print Assignment J. Complete the assigned problems, and record your answers on the tables provided at the end of the assignment.

Internet Connection

1. Access a website for an outlet store near you. Record the prices for five products offered at the outlet store. Compare those prices to retail prices at nearby stores in traditional malls or shopping centers. Report your findings. Who delivered the lowest prices?

2. Visit the book's STUDIO to watch videos about pricing strategies.

DOLLAR TREE: WILL GROWTH CONTINUE?

The corner five-and-dime store was supposed to have been killed off by the superstores long ago, but that has not occurred. In fact, three strong players, Dollar Tree, Dollar General, and Family Dollar (now owned by Dollar Tree), emerged to take their places. And, as economic downturns squeezed the finances of the middle class, sales growth in this sector surged. In one year the three chains combined opened nearly 1,500 stores nationwide, and all three appear on the National Retail Federation's list of Top 100 Retailers in the United States. In addition, Dollar Tree has been named a "Star Performer" by *Retail Merchandiser*, a retail trade magazine.

Traditional discount stores, such as Walmart and Kmart, have been upscaling their merchandise and their presentation, as well as bringing in more celebrity labels like Ty Pennington and Sofia Vergara. As they have made these moves, there was an unfilled need, and companies like Dollar Tree have taken advantage of the opening.

Currently, Dollar Tree operates thousands of stores in all forty-eight contiguous states, and the majority of those stores were profitable within a year. Most of them are about the size of one department in a big-box superstore and have average net sales of $1 million yearly.

As Dollar Tree has grown, the stores' merchandise mix has also changed. Only about 12 percent is now closeout merchandise. Dollar Tree imports many of its products itself, made to specifications or specially packaged for the company. In addition, the stores are always filled with seasonal merchandise. Dollar Tree buyers understand overseas manufacturing and have been skilled at negotiating with vendors. As the company has grown, its leverage with vendors has also increased. Buyers are able to negotiate deals that translate into better value for the firm's customers. Dollar Tree buyers also look for trends in gift stores, such as Hallmark, and in souvenir shops and then have items based on those trends made for Dollar Tree. In addition, buyers develop relationships with first-run vendors, producers of parallel brands, so, instead of Fantastik, Dollar Tree sells Fabulous.

Dollar Tree continues to have success in generating merchandise excitement through an ever-changing mix of variety and seasonal merchandise. The addition of more basic consumable products that are frequently purchased has contributed to increases in both traffic and sales. Dollar Tree also sets itself apart from Family Dollar and Dollar General with one clear strategy—everything costs exactly $1. The competition offers items at many different price points.

Dollar Tree, like most low-priced, limited-assortment retailers, is already well entrenched among low-income households, but during economic downturns the chain experiences strong increases in penetration across other income groups. However, as recessions ease, so do sales at dollar stores. Projections are for slower growth, but that growth is still nearly 4 percent—a rate that many retailers would envy. To remain competitive, Dollar Tree has added additional national brands, spruced up existing stores, and has even opened some stores in higher-income areas. Dollar Tree also stresses convenience—a quick stop for shopping. That is something the big-box discounters cannot offer. It seems that for now, Dollar Tree has found a niche in the marketplace and has positioned itself to grow in good and bad times.

BASED ON:

Gustafson, Krystina. (2016, August 25). Price wars heat up as dollar store echoes Walmart's battle cry. *CNBC.com*.

Hawkins, Carole. (2014, July 8). New strategy fuels growth for dollar stores. *Jaxdailyrecord.com*.

Soltes, Fiona. (2016, June 1). Off-price, on point. *Stores.org*.

Tully, Shawn. (2015, April 24). How the dollar store war was won. *Fortune.com*.

Wahba, Phil. (2016, May 27). In new challenge to Walmart, Dollar General is winning over millennials. *Fortune.com*.

Zillman, Claire. (2014, April 11). Dollar stores face hard times. *Fortune.com*.

SNAPSHOT: Nordstrom Rack

Even in difficult economic times, most retailers are still bullish on Nordstrom, a high-end retailer that operates stores in thirty-five states. The chain operates two types of stores—high-end department stores and off-price stores known as Nordstrom Rack. Rack stores offer a wide selection of apparel, accessories, and shoes from Nordstrom department stores and Nordstrom.com at reduced prices, as well as special value items purchased just for the off-price outlet. In fact, Rack stores are driving much of Nordstrom's growth while siphoning off only a limited number of customers from the department stores. One report estimates that the customer overlap is less than 30 percent. In fact, one Nordstrom Rack store in North Carolina is right across the street from a Nordstrom Department Store.

Nordstrom Rack first opened in the basement of the downtown Seattle store in 1972 as a clearance department. Since that time, it has grown into its own division, and currently there are 216 Nordstrom Rack locations where price draws customers. The Rack stores carry merchandise from Nordstrom stores and Nordstrom.com at 50 to 60 percent off original Nordstrom prices.

Nordstrom Rack allows the chain to expand its customer base while clearing merchandise that did not sell from the department stores. Additionally, Rack stores are appealing to the chain because they cost about one-tenth the price to open compared to the full-line department stores. Full-service department stores require dazzling assortments of couture and designer apparel, hundreds of well-trained personnel, and top-flight customer service. Rack stores, on the other hand, need only a presentable store layout with cashiers near the front of the store. Consumers go to outlets for price; their other expectations are reduced. However, while Rack stores are not luxurious, they are not so minimal that customers feel like they are shopping in a warehouse. In addition, for a fee, the outlets even offer some services, like alterations. Moreover, the Rack stores get new deliveries weekly.

In a sluggish economy, consumer spending slackens, and even the most upscale shoppers are hunting for bargains. For example, during one recent quarter, sales at Nordstrom department stores fell 6 percent, but during the same period, same-store sales at Nordstrom Rack rose 6.3 percent. So luxury retailers like Nordstrom are aggressively expanding outlet operations. In fact, the outlet stores for these retailers are not just offering discontinued or leftover inventory; some items may also be available at the full-priced department stores.

Nordstrom Rack stores now outnumber traditional Nordstrom stores. More importantly, average sales are also higher at Rack stores, which earn $550 in sales per square foot compared with $400 at Nordstrom Department Stores. Currently, major growth for the company is built on opening more Rack stores.

Nordstrom, which has been on *Fortune's* World's Most Admired Companies list six years in a row, has positioned itself for future growth with Rack stores by appealing to a different market segment.

BASED ON:

Fairfield, Caroline. (2014, April 7). Service with a style. *Fortune*, 22.

Loeb, Walter. (2013, December 13). Why the Rack will lead to greater growth for Nordstrom. *Forbes.com*.

Nordstrom Rack announces first Canadian store in Toronto. (2016, February 16). *PRNewswire.com*.

Solomon, Micah. (2017, March 17). Modernize your customer service experience the (new) Nordstrom way. *Forbes.com*.

Stock, Kyle. (2013, July 16). Why outlet stores are the hottest thing in high-end retail. *Businessweek.com*.

APPENDIX A
BASIC RETAIL MATH FORMULAS

BASIC PRICING CALCULATIONS

$ Markup = $ Retail – $ Cost

$ Retail = $ Cost + $ Markup

$ Cost = $ Retail – $ Markup

Markup % = $ Markup / $ Retail or ($ Retail – $ Cost) / $ Retail

Initial markup % = Expenses + Profit + Reductions – Cash discounts / (Sales + Reductions)

$ Retail = Cost $ / (100% – Markup % based on retail)

Markdown $ = Original retail price – Final retail price

Markdown cancellation = (New retail price – Sale price) × Number of items repriced

Markdown % = Markdown $ / Sales $

Off-retail % = Markdown $ / Original retail price

CALCULATING PLANNED STOCK LEVELS

Stock-to-sales ratio = Value of inventory / Actual sales

BOM inventory = Stock-to-sales ratio × Planned sales

Maximum = Sales volume per week (Reorder period + Delivery period) + Reserve

Stock turnover rate = Sales / Average stock

MERCHANDISE PLANNING CALCULATIONS

Planned purchases at retail = Planned sales + Planned reductions + Planned EOM – Planned BOM

Planned purchases (Cost) = Planned purchases at retail × (100% – Markup %)

$ Open-to-buy = Planned purchases – Merchandise on order

Unit open-to-buy = Unit planned purchases – Units on order

PROFIT CALCULATIONS

Net sales = Gross sales – Customer returns and allowances

Profit (loss) = Net sales – Cost of goods sold – Expenses

Profit % = Profit $ / Net sales

APPENDIX B
DECISION MAKING

Buyers must constantly make decisions in their job; therefore, they must develop their ability to solve business problems using a logical framework. Decisions are a part of our day-to-day living. Some decisions will be easy to make, whereas other decisions will require much more thought. Although you will make some decisions alone, some will require you to get help from other people or to work with others to reach a decision.

Closely related to the number of decisions that you make each day is the number of alternatives from which you have to choose. More alternatives make it more difficult to make a decision. As the number of alternatives increases, information becomes vital to effective decision making.

Without being consciously aware of it, you use a decision-making process automatically. In fact, the steps you use to make decisions in your daily life are similar to ones used in business. One way to approach the decision-making process is by following these four steps:

1. Identify the problem.
2. List and evaluate alternatives.
3. Select the best alternative.
4. Implement the decision and follow up.

Identify the Problem. Too many individuals rarely show a great deal of interest in planning how to solve a problem; they want to immediately start working on a solution. They incorrectly believe that planning is not very important to the decision-making process; however, evidence indicates that people who spend time clearly identifying the problem make better decisions.

If you are working with a group (other buyers, sales associates, managers, etc.), you need to make sure that everyone has the same perceptions of the problem or the decision that has to be made. If you have three people in your group, you may have three different perceptions.

You also need to share with others in the group how the issue or problem will affect them. We all tend to become more personally involved in the solution if we can see a connection between ourselves and the problem.

Moreover, your group will also want to state an objective for the problem in measurable terms. For example, you may want to "Increase sales 10 percent by November 15." No matter what decisions you make to increase sales, you will know if you succeeded or failed. Once you have agreed on what the problem is and how you will evaluate results, you are ready to develop a strategy to solve the problem.

List and Evaluate Alternatives. There will be many alternative ways to achieve your objective, and you need to identify and evaluate each one. The more input you receive usually leads to more effective decision making.

Brainstorming is a process that many groups use to identify alternatives. All ideas presented have potential value to your organization and must be considered. Brainstorming is like sowing seeds. Some of these seeds, just like some ideas, will be good and bear fruit; others will not. The result may be that inappropriate ideas may be presented; however, many good ideas may be triggered by some suggestions that seem "offbeat."

No idea is too ridiculous to be written down. If you do not write ideas down, good ideas may get lost. During the brainstorming process, ideas should be listed but not evaluated.

Next, you will want to screen good ideas and eliminate bad ones. You should separate the frivolous from the serious and reduce the list to a workable number. In evaluating each alternative, use criteria such as these:

- Is the suggestion feasible? Can it be done?
- Can the suggestion be implemented during your allotted time frame?

- Do you have the resources available to implement the suggestion?
- Has the suggestion been tried before? With what results?
- Is the suggestion practical?

Once you have reduced alternatives to a manageable number, carefully review both the positive and negative consequences of each of the remaining alternatives. Consider all information that is available.

Select the Best Alternative. Now you are ready to choose a solution—you have got to make a decision. In most situations, this will be much easier for individuals than groups. Group decision making is a much slower process because more people must be consulted. Votes by members may be required to make a decision. If so, your group must decide on whether a decision will be based on a simple majority or require unanimous agreement, or something in between.

Implement the Decision and Follow Up. After deciding which alternative to use, an action plan needs to be developed to list what is going to be done by whom and when it is to be accomplished.

Decision making is worthless without follow-up and feedback. There is a need to monitor how the action went. Decision making does not end when the decision is implemented. You must examine and evaluate the results. You need to know what went right, as well as what went wrong. In this way, you can identify opportunities for improvement that will make future decision making easier in this area.

Using Group Decision Making. Many of the decisions your organization faces will have to be made by groups rather than individuals. However, group decision making can be frustrating as you try to achieve unanimity or consensus with group members. Keep in mind that not all decisions should be made by groups. There is a place for individual as well as group decision making in all organizations. Groups should be used for decision making when they can contribute to the solution of the problem. For example, some problems are so complex that they cannot be handled easily by a single individual. Also, if implementation of the decision requires group members, it is best to involve them in decision making. People tend to carry out decisions that they helped make.

Group decision making has both advantages and disadvantages over individual problem solving. Key advantages of group decision making include the following:

- There is more information in a group than any one of its members possesses. Therefore, if a problem situation requires using knowledge, groups have an advantage over individuals.
- Individuals get into ruts in their thinking. Because group members will not have identical approaches, each member can contribute by moving others out of their ruts.
- Many problems require solutions that depend on the support of others to be effective. When groups solve such problems, a greater number of members feel responsible for making the solution work.

However, group decision making also has drawbacks:

- People tend to conform. The desire to be a good group member causes some members to be silent and not voice their disagreement. This causes consensus to be reached without a complete examination of all alternatives.
- Some groups become controlled by a dominant individual. That individual may have a great persuasive ability or just stubborn persistence when dominating discussion. This individual may not be the best problem solver in the group. Also, the leader may exert a major influence on the outcome of any discussion because of the position he or she holds.
- In general, more time is required for a group to reach a decision than for a single individual to reach a decision. If the problem requires a quick decision, individual decisions are needed.

Use the previous criteria to determine if the problem that you or your organization is facing should be handled by one person or a group. Then proceed with the decision-making process.

GLOSSARY

4-5-4 calendar A planning calendar used by retailers to ensure sales comparability between different years by dividing the year into a four weeks, five weeks, four weeks format, ensuring the same number of Saturdays and Sundays are in each period compared.

additional markup An increase in the retail price of an item, above the price at which it was marked to sell on arrival at the store.

advance dating terms Dating an invoice for a specified time in the future; thus discount calculations are made from that date, rather than from the invoice or delivery dates.

anticipation An extra discount that some manufacturers allow buyers to take for paying an invoice in advance of the cash discount date.

assistant buyer An individual who aids buyers in performing their duties; may be a buyer in training.

assortment planning Involves determining the specific quantities and characteristics of each product being purchased, in relation to specific factors such as brands, colors, and sizes.

automatic markdown Placing a predetermined markdown on merchandise that remains unsold after a given period of time.

automatic reordering system Involves the use of computers and bar coding to generate weekly merchandise orders that are based on sales, in relation to model stock plans.

availability Refers to the amount of effort customers are willing to exert to obtain a particular product.

average stock Calculated by dividing the sum of the value of inventory at predetermined periods of time by the total number of those time periods.

balanced assortment An assortment of merchandise that meets the needs of as many customers as possible, with a minimum investment in inventory.

bar coding Using a pattern of variable-width bars and spaces on merchandise to identify a product being scanned.

basic merchandise Items that customers buy year in and year out and that they expect the retail store to have in stock at all times.

basic stock list A list that provides the buyer with information such as merchandise descriptions, retail price, cost, rate of sale, and the maximum and minimum reorder quantity.

basic stock plan A plan used to determine the amount of merchandise that a retailer must have on hand or on order to ensure a sufficient amount of merchandise being available during a given period of time.

behavioristic data Includes information about consumers' buying activities, such as the time they typically make purchases or the average amount of their purchases.

big-box retailer The largest retailer in a field, for example, Home Depot, Walmart, Office Depot.

BOM inventory The amount of stock on hand at the beginning of the month.

BOM stock level The amount of inventory at the beginning of the month.

bottom-up planning Involves estimating total sales for a store by adding together the planned sales figures that have been developed by each department manager.

bounce rate The portion of internet users who click away from a site while waiting for the page to load.

breadth Relates to the number of product lines or to the number of brands that is carried by a store or department within a product classification.

bricks-and-mortar Refers to traditional retail presence as a physical storefront.

broad and shallow Refers to offering a wide selection of brands with little depth.

broker An individual who acts as an agent for the manufacturer when dealing with retailers.

buyer An individual in a retail firm whose primary job is to purchase merchandise.

buying The business activity that involves selecting and purchasing products to satisfy the wants and needs of consumers.

buying office An organization that is located in a major market center with the purpose of providing buying advice and other market-related services to client stores.

cannibalization Occurs when potential sales of existing products are lost when new items are added to a store's inventory.

career ladder/path Diagrams that show job progressions for a specific career.

cash discount The discount granted to retailers for paying an invoice early.

central market A city in which a large number of key suppliers for a product line are located.

central merchandising plan Occurs when a central office representing a group of stores has complete responsibility for the selection and purchase of merchandise for all the stores.

centralized buying Occurs when all buying activities are performed from a retailer's central headquarters.

chain store Two or more retail stores under single ownership.

churn Relates to a retailer having to constantly replace lost customers with new ones.

classic A style that is in demand continuously even though minor changes may be made in the product.

classification Refers to the particular kinds of goods in a store or department.

clicks-and-mortar Refers to retailers developing an online presence in addition to their traditional storefronts.

COD Collect on delivery, which means that the transportation company will collect the amount of the invoice when goods are delivered to the retailer.

collaborator A negotiator who views concerns as mutual problems; one who seeks to arrive at solutions where both parties win.

commissionaire A buyer who operates in foreign markets and functions similarly to domestic buying offices.

comparison shopper Firm that shops competing stores to provide information on the merchandise assortments, prices, and promotion of other retailers in the area.

compromise An agreement based on both sides in a negotiation giving in on some of their demands.

concentrated target marketing Involves a retailer focusing on one market segment.

concessions Vendor partners who take over selling space at a retail store.

consumer advisory panels Consists of typical customers who make suggestions about policies, services, and merchandise assortments.

convenience product An item that customers expect the store to have readily available at all times.

cooperative (co-op) advertising Allowances offered by some vendors to retailers whereby they will share the cost of any advertising that features the vendor's products.

cost method A method of inventory valuation that requires stock records to be maintained using cost, not retail, prices.

cost of goods sold Includes the actual cost of the merchandise, plus transportation charges involved in getting the merchandise from the vendor to the store and any workroom costs.

cumulative markup The markup achieved on all merchandise available for sale in a given period.

data Information.

data analytics Collecting and analyzing huge volumes of different types of information, such as customer databases, sales records, and social media trend reports.

data mining Searching through warehoused data to find trends and patterns that might otherwise have gone unnoticed.

data warehousing Involves electronically storing customer and operations data.

database marketing Activities that provide retailers with ongoing intelligence based on tracking and analyzing customer behavior.

decline stage The last stage of the product life cycle, which occurs when the target market shrinks and price cutting minimizes profit margins.

delivery period The time between when an order is placed and when the merchandise is available on the sales floor.

demographic data Include characteristics of customers such as age, sex, family size, income, education, occupation, and race.

demographic trend The trend related to characteristics of consumers, such as marital status and birth rates.

department store A business that sells all kinds of merchandise for the individual and the home.

departmentalization Organizing different store activities into departments or divisions.

depth The number of choices offered to customers within each brand or product classification.

destination store A store that consumers make a planned effort to shop.

discount department store Retailers that emphasize one-stop shopping to meet the needs of all family members but appeal to consumers who value savings over service.

dollar control Inventory planning based on a planned dollar value of stock, rather than specific units of stock.

durability Refers to how long a product will last.

durables Products (such as cars, furniture, and appliances) that are capable of surviving many uses and typically last for years.

duty A tax on merchandise imported into a country.

early adopter A consumer who purchases fashion merchandise in the early stages of the product life cycle.

electronic data interchange (EDI) The use of technology to support the communication of sales data and business documents, such as invoices and purchase orders, between retailers and suppliers.

emotional buying motive A buying motive that involves customers' feelings, rather than logic.

EOM (end-of-month) dating terms Dating terms that allow the buyer to calculate cash discounts from the end of the month.

EOM inventory Stock available at the end of the month.

even pricing A strategy to create an upscale image for a product by pricing it with even numbers, such as $32.00.

exception report A computer-generated report that is produced when sales or stock levels do not meet planned levels.

exclusive distribution A practice of some vendors to sell a product to only one retailer in a trading area.

exposition A show held at a convention center or exhibition hall on a periodic basis to showcase the latest merchandise in a particular product category.

external forces Forces occurring outside a business, such as economic and competitive conditions.

extra dating terms Dating terms that give the buyer a specified number of additional days in which to pay an invoice and earn a cash discount.

fad A short-lived fashion.

fashion The prevailing style that is accepted and used by a particular group of people at a particular time in a particular place.

fashion forecaster A business consultant who predicts long-range fashion trends.

fashion merchandise Merchandise that has a high demand over a relatively short period of time, usually a season.

FIFO First in, first out method of inventory control that assumes that the merchandise that was received first sold first.

fixed expenses Expenses that do not vary regardless of how much merchandise is sold.

FOB (free on board) A term on a purchase order that indicates whether the vendor or the retailer will pay for delivery.

FOB destination (store) A transportation term that indicates the manufacturer pays the shipping charges, and title passes to the buyer when the merchandise is delivered.

FOB destination, charges reversed A transportation term that indicates the buyer pays the shipping charges, and the seller assumes responsibility for the goods while they are in shipment.

FOB destination, freight prepaid A transportation term that indicates the seller will pay the freight charges, but the buyer takes title to them as soon as they are shipped.

FOB origin (factory) A transportation term where title passes to the buyer when the seller delivers goods to the transportation carrier; freight charges are the responsibility of the buyer.

FOB shipping point A transportation term that indicates the manufacturer has title to the goods and is responsible for shipping costs until the merchandise reaches a distribution point where the buyer takes title to the goods and pays transportation charges until they reach the store.

forecasting Involves predicting what consumers will probably do under a given set of conditions.

free trade agreement An agreement between countries to eliminate tariffs on merchandise being traded.

functional departmentalization Refers to activities of a similar nature being grouped together into a major area of responsibility and headed by an individual who reports to the owner or chief executive of the store.

generic brand Unbranded merchandise.

geographic data Comprise information on where consumers live such as Zip codes, neighborhoods, cities, counties, states, or regions.

geographic departmentalization Refers to an organizational structure based on geographic areas (e.g., a retailer having a north, south, east, and west division, each headed by an executive).

GMROI A measurement of the profitability of a retailer's sales.

gross margin Sales revenue that remains after the cost of goods sold has been deducted.

growth stage The stage in the product life cycle where innovators have recommended the purchase of a new product to their friends, causing increased sales and product variations.

hard lines All merchandise carried by a store with the exception of apparel and accessories and fashions for the home (e.g., hardware, sporting goods, appliances, furniture, lawn and garden).

haute couture High fashion, or those styles first accepted by the fashion leaders.

hot item Merchandise that is difficult to keep in stock because of tremendous customer demand for it.

image The perceptions consumers have about a retail store.

importer A business that purchases merchandise from foreign sources and then sells it to domestic retailers.

impulse product A product that is purchased by a consumer often because of an irresistible urge.

income statement A business report that shows profit calculations.

independent buying office A buying office that is privately owned and operated.

individual markup percentage Quantitative performance measurement calculated by first determining the dollar markup on an item (which is found by subtracting the cost of the item from its retail price) and then dividing the dollar markup by the retail price.

innovator A consumer who is more likely to purchase a new style.

intermediary A middleman.

internal forces Those activities within a business that will probably affect sales, such as increasing or decreasing advertising expenditures.

introduction stage The stage in the product life cycle that occurs when products are usually accepted by only a few people.

inventory control system Involves the maintenance of stock levels in relation to changing consumer demand.

irregulars Merchandise that contains slight imperfections usually not visible to the naked eye.

IT Information technology.

job lot An assortment of merchandise that the vendor has been unable to sell at regular prices; therefore, the entire lot is offered to the buyer at a reduced price.

key resource A vendor with whom retailers concentrate a large percentage of their purchases.

keystoning A technique used by some small retailers to calculate retail price by doubling the cost of merchandise.

laggard A consumer who accepts a style when it is in the decline stage of the product life cycle.

landed cost The importer's final cost for foreign merchandise, which includes the merchandise cost, duties and tariffs, commissions, insurance, storage expenses, and transportation charges.

late adopter A consumer who accepts a fashion when it is past its peak.

letter of credit A promise from the purchaser's bank to the seller guaranteeing payment for shipments.

licensed product A product that is designed and sold through identification with a celebrity or corporate name, logo, slogan, or fictional character.

LIFO Last in, first out method of inventory control that assumes the merchandise that was received last was sold first.

long-term forecast Forecasting for more than a year.

loss leader A pricing technique that involves pricing a product below cost in order to generate store traffic.

management training program A program offered by retail stores to college graduates pursuing a management career in retailing.

manufacturer's representative An agent for a manufacturer who deals with retailers.

markdown Reduction in the retail price of merchandise already in stock.

markdown cancellation Increases in the retail price to offset all or part of previously taken markdowns.

markdown percentage A control tool used by buyers that is calculated by dividing total dollar markdowns by total sales.

market A group of people with the ability, desire, and willingness to buy—a store's potential customers.

market-basket analysis Describes data mining solutions that identify the correlation among items in a customer's shopping basket.

market segment A group of potential customers that has similar needs or other important characteristics.

market segmentation Dividing the total market into segments.

marketing research The systematic process of gathering, recording, and analyzing information about problems related to marketing.

markup The amount of money added to the cost of goods to calculate retail price.

mass customization Providing individual customers with products that have been mass-produced, yet still giving them "exactly what they want."

mass merchant A retailer who offers products with broad consumer appeal, trying to meet the needs of all family members.

maturity stage The stage of the product life cycle that occurs when sales reach maximum levels and all types of retailers carry the product.

maximum The amount of merchandise that must be on hand or on order at any reordering point.

merchandise-broker office A type of independent buying office that is paid by the manufacturers it represents, rather than by retail clients.

merchandise manager The individual in a retail store who is responsible for managing the buying function.

merchandise mix The types or mix of products that are available for customers to purchase.

merchandise plan A projection in dollars of the sales goals for the store or department, over a specified period of time.

merchandise/apparel mart A single building or complex of buildings located in many cities that offers retail buyers one-stop shopping.

merchant middleman The middleman who takes possession of goods that it purchases from manufacturers, before selling them to retailers.

middleman An intermediary between the buyer and seller.

model stock The desired merchandise assortment, broken down according to the selection factors that are important to a store's customers.

most-favored-nation status Status granted to certain countries that allows them to qualify for lower tariffs on their exports.

multisegment target marketing Involves a retailer focusing on several different market segments.

narrow and deep Refers to stocking large amounts of a few product categories or brands.

national brand A product sold almost everywhere in the country, such as Arrow shirts or Levi's jeans.

negotiation The process of reaching a mutually satisfying agreement.

net sales Calculated by subtracting customer returns and allowances from gross sales.

networking Involves identifying and communicating with individuals who can be helpful in a job search.

niche A segment of a larger consumer market.

nondurables Products that are used up in a few uses or simply become out-of-date when styles change.

nonmerchant middleman A middleman who does not take possession of merchandise from the manufacturer before selling it to the retailer.

obsolescence The outmoding of a product due to a change in fashion before its usefulness has been exhausted.

odd-cent pricing A pricing technique used by some retailers to create the perception of a lower price in the customer's mind by using odd cents such as $5.99.

off-price Occurs when retailers purchase manufacturers' overruns at deep discounts for the purpose of offering consumers low prices on name-brand merchandise.

off-retail percentage The percentage used for advertising purposes that is calculated by dividing the amount of markdown by the original retail price.

omnichannel retailing Concept focused on consumers being able to interact with the retailer from whatever touchpoint (i.e., laptop, smartphone, social media platform, or a bricks-and-mortar store) is appropriate to them wherever they are in the purchasing process—from learning about a product to making the final purchase to providing feedback on how the product performed.

on consignment The term that indicates that the buyer will take merchandise into a store but will pay for it only when it sells.

on memorandum The term that indicates the merchandise coming into the store has a return privilege with it.

online retailing Electronic retailing occurring over the internet.

open-to-buy The dollar amount that the buyer has left to spend for a period.

operating expenses All the expenses incurred in operating a business, both fixed and variable.

ordinary dating terms Terms that indicate that cash discounts are calculated from the invoice date; the most common type of cash discount.

organizational chart A diagram of a firm's internal structure, indicating all employees and their relationship to each other.

outlet store A retail store that has typically sold slow-moving and out-of-date merchandise at discount prices.

overbought A condition that exists when a buyer has purchased more than planned during a specific period of time.

patronage buying motive A buying motive that involves customers choosing one store over another.

penetration Using low profit margins to generate greater sales; usually used to quickly gain market share.

periodic control system Inventory control on a seasonal basis, such as monthly or yearly.

perpetual control system Inventory control on a continuous basis.

planner Works with buyer to monitor stock levels by store and track key items by sales. Deals primarily with location planning and distribution of merchandise.

positioning Identifying a group of consumers and developing retail activities to meet their needs.

price decline guarantee Terms that protect the store if market prices drop over a stated period of time; the vendor would credit or refund the buyer the amount of the price reduction that occurs.

price floor The minimum price below which a product should not be priced.

price lining Selecting certain prices that appeal to target customers and only carrying merchandise assortments at those price points.

price point A certain price range that has been established by the store, such as good, better, and best.

price war Develops when a number of retailers attempt to underprice each other; increased sales may result, but usually at the expense of profits.

primary data Data that originate with the specific research being undertaken.

private brand A brand of merchandise that is developed by retailers that allows them to offer unique merchandise to their customers.

private buying office A buying office that is owned and operated by the one retail store that it represents.

product life cycle A diagram that illustrates the expected behavior of a product over its life span.

product line A broad category of products that have similar characteristics and uses.

product line departmentalization Departmentalizing a retail store based on broad categories of merchandise such as furniture, appliances, children's wear, or jewelry.

profit The amount of money remaining after operating expenses have been subtracted from gross margin.

profit or loss statement A business report that shows profit calculations.

promotional buying Purchasing merchandise that will be featured in a store's promotion plans.

psychographic data Include information on the lifestyles, interests, and opinions of consumers.

psychographic trend A trend related to consumers' lifestyles, interests, and opinions, such as how they use their time.

publicity The free and voluntary mention of a company, product, or service by the media.

pure play retailers Retailers who only operate online.

quality check Checking the quality of merchandise that has been received in the store to ensure that it is identical to the quality of the merchandise ordered.

quantitative performance measurements Evaluative criteria that have been established in numerical terms to measure a buyer's job performance.

quantity check Checking the quantity of merchandise that has been received in the store to ensure that it is identical to the number ordered, as well as in correct sizes, colors, models, and so on.

quantity discount A discount offered to buyers as an enticement for them to order a larger quantity.

Quick Response An inventory management system based on a partnership between the retailer and the vendor that uses unit control and electronic data interchange to ensure a store will have the right items in stock.

quota A predetermined amount of merchandise that a country's government will allow to be imported for a specific product category.

rack jobber A special type of vendor that services client stores where the vendor is assigned shelf space and the responsibility for keeping it stocked with quick-turning merchandise.

rational buying motive A buying motive concerned with basic human needs such as food, clothing, and shelter.

reductions Includes markdowns, employee and consumer discounts, and inventory shortages.

reorder period The amount of time between merchandise orders.

reporting service An organization that reports on changing market trends that will probably affect buying decisions for a retail store.

reserve The amount of merchandise kept in stock to meet unanticipated sales.

retail analytics Process of providing analytical data on information (such as inventory levels, supply chain movement, consumer demand, and sales) that are crucial for making merchandising and marketing decisions.

retail method The method of inventory valuation based on the retail price of merchandise in stock.

retail strategy The overall framework or plan of action that guides a retailer.

retailing All the business activities involved in the selling of goods and services to the ultimate consumers.

return Merchandise that has been returned to the store by the customer, or merchandise that has been returned to the vendor by the retailer.

reverse showrooming Customers research products online before making an in-store purchase to avoid the wait to receive the merchandise and to avoid shipping charges.

RFID Technology that uses radio frequency identification tags on individual items of merchandise.

ROG (receipt of goods) dating terms Dating terms that allow the buyer to calculate discounts from the delivery date (receipt of goods) rather than the invoice date.

salaried (fixed-fee) buying office An independent buying office that is paid directly by the retail stores it represents.

sales forecast A prediction of future sales for a specified period under a proposed marketing plan.

seasonal basic A product that is desired by customers consistently during certain times of the year (e.g., Easter egg dye or kites).

seasonal discount A discount offered to buyers for making purchases in advance of a selling season.

secondary data Data that have been gathered for some other purpose but are applicable to solving the problem at hand.

seconds Merchandise that contains obvious imperfections or damages.

selection factors Product characteristics that are most important to a store's customers when they make their purchasing decisions.

selective distribution Occurs when vendors sell their products to only selected retailers within a trading area.

shopping product A product for which consumers will make price, quality, suitability, and style comparisons.

short-term forecast Forecasting for a period of one year or less.

showrooming Customers visiting local bricks-and-mortar retail stores before they go online to compare prices and make a purchase.

shrinkage Merchandise shortage, usually a result of shoplifting or employee theft.

six-month merchandise plan A tool used by retailers to translate profit objectives into a six-month framework for merchandise planning and control.

skimming A pricing policy that occurs when stores charge the highest price possible; lower sales will result, but the profit margin on each item is high.

social listening Tracking conversations about the retailer or products on social media to gain a better understanding of which issues and trends are gaining importance among consumers.

social media Internet sites, such as Facebook, Twitter, Pinterest, and LinkedIn, that are used for communication by individuals within groups. Today, it is part of the promotional mix for most retailers.

soft lines Apparel and accessory product categories, as well as fashions for the home—items such as linens, curtains, or bathroom items.

specialized superstore A superstore that offers one to three categories of merchandise in large assortments and at discount prices that are unmatched by any other retailer in the area.

specialty product A product for which customers' buying behavior is geared to obtaining a particular product without regard to time, effort, or expense.

specialty store A retailer that primarily sells one specific product line.

specification buying Buying merchandise that is offered by the vendor, if certain specifications or changes are made.

standard classification of merchandise A coding system that classifies merchandise using four-digit codes.

stock-to-sales ratio A figure that indicates the relationship between planned sales and the amount of inventory required to produce those sales.

stock turnover rate The number of times that the average stock is sold during a given period of time.

store brand A brand sold only at a specific store; also known as a private brand.

style A form of a product that is significantly different from other forms of that product.

subclassification Dividing merchandise classifications into other classifications (e.g., men's shoes could be broken down into dress shoes, casual shoes, athletic shoes, work shoes, and boots).

supercenter A mega-supermarket or general merchandise store.

superstore Any store that is bigger than what is normally found in an area selling a specific category of merchandise.

tactics Techniques used to reach an objective.

target market The specific group or groups of consumers on which a retailer focuses its marketing activities.

tariff The tax on goods coming into a country.

top-down planning Involves the top level of management estimating total sales for the upcoming period.

touchpoint Anywhere customers can interact with retailers and make purchases, that is, iPad, in store, social media platform, smartphone, etc.

trade association An organization of businesses that have similar characteristics for the purpose of providing various services to its members, such as updates on current trends and market conditions.

trade discount A discount offered to buyers based on the manufacturer's list price.

trade show A show held at convention centers or exhibition halls on a periodic basis to showcase the latest merchandise in a particular product category.

transfer Merchandise that is either sent to or received from another store in a chain.

trend A change or movement in a general direction.

ultimatum A final proposal or offer that, if not accepted, will end negotiations.

undifferentiated target marketing Involves an attempt by retailers to please all consumers.

unit control An inventory control system that tracks the movement of specific units of merchandise.

UPC (universal product code) Merchandise identification that is found in bar codes on the product.

variable expenses Store expenses that change in a direct relationship to sales.

velocity The speed with which products move through the product life cycle.

vendor An organization or individual who supplies merchandise to retail stores.

vendor diary Brief summaries of a store's dealings with each vendor with whom it does business.

vendor-owned store A retail store owned and operated by the manufacturer.

want slip system Involves keeping a record of customer requests for merchandise not in stock, in order to make future purchases for the store.

warehouse club Huge warehouses that offer a limited number of product lines to customers in large quantities, usually with no frills, little sales assistance, no décor, and no deliveries.

warehouse requisition plan A type of centralized buying that occurs when in-store buyers must make merchandise purchases from the chain's warehouse, which houses merchandise selections that have already been purchased by central buyers.

wholesaler An organization that purchases merchandise from a manufacturer in large quantities and resells the goods in smaller amounts to retailers.

CREDITS

Chapter 1: Today's Buying Environment
1.1 Fairchild Books
1.2 Antonio Guillem/shutterstock.com
1.3 NetPhotos2/Alamy
1.4 Fairchild Books
1.5 Zapp2Photo/shutterstock.com
1.6 Rawpixel.com/shutterstock.com
1.7 HstrongART/shutterstock.com
1.8 pio3/shutterstock.com
1.9 Roman Tiraspolsky/shutterstock.com

Chapter 2: The Buying Function in Retailing
2.1 Francis Dean/Corbis via Getty Images
2.2 Iakov Filimonov/shutterstock.com
2.3 Ditty_about_summer/shutterstock.com
2.4 Rawpixel.com/shutterstock.com

Chapter 3: Buying for Different Types of Stores
3.1 Fairchild Books
3.2 Jonathan Weiss/shutterstock.com
3.3 iStock.com/slobo
3.4 Fairchild Books
3.5 g-stockstudio/shutterstock.com

Chapter 4: Obtaining Assistance for Making Buying Decisions
4.1 EM Karuna/Shutterstock.com
4.2 Dmitry Kalinovsky/Shutterstock.com
4.3 Elnur/Shutterstock.com

Chapter 5: Understanding Your Customers
5.1 WWD/© Conde Nast
5.2 Green Decisions, Success (2010, February)
5.3 Iakov Filimonov/shutterstock.com
5.4 *USA Today*, 2001

5.5 iStock.com/wetcake
5.6 Fedor Korolevskiy/Shutterstock
5.7 Dmitry Kalinovsky/Shutterstock.com

Chapter 6: Understanding Product Trends: What Customers Buy
6.1 Dominique Maitre/WWD/© Conde Nast
6.2 Patti McConville/Alamy
6.3 maxbelchenko/Shutterstock.com
6.4 Fairchild Books
6.5 Fairchild Books
6.6a Giannoni/WWD/© Conde Nast
6.6b Giannoni/WWD/© Conde Nast
6.6c Giannoni/WWD/© Conde Nast
6.7 Zhang Peng/LightRocket via Getty Images

Chapter 7: Forecasting
7.1 Fairchild Books
7.2 garagestock/Shutterstock.com
7.3 Melpomene/Shutterstock.com

Chapter 8: Preparing Buying Plans
8.1 Fairchild Books
8.2 Fairchild Books
8.3 Fairchild Books

Chapter 9: Developing Assortment Plans
9.1 Tuzemka/Shutterstock.com
9.2 Bambax/Shutterstock.com
9.3 Vtmila/Shutterstock.com

Chapter 10: Controlling Inventories
10.1 iStock.com
10.2 ESB Professional/Shutterstock.com
10.3 Fairchild Books
10.4 Fairchild Books
10.5 think4photop/Shutterstock.com

Chapter 11: Selecting Vendors and Building Partnerships
11.1 WWD/© Conde Nast
11.2 maximages.com/Alamy
11.3 Saks Fifth Avenue/WWD/© Conde Nast

Chapter 12: Making Market Visits and Negotiating with Vendors
12.1 Iannaccone/WWD/© Conde Nast
12.2 WWD/© Conde Nast
12.3 Courtesy of AmericasMart
12.4a Fairchild Books
12.4b Fairchild Books
12.5 WWD/© Conde Nast
12.6 boonchoke/Shutterstock.com

Chapter 13: Locating Sources in Foreign Markets
13.1 Creative Lab/Shutterstock.com
13.2 Antonio Gravante/Shutterstock.com
13.3 pcruciatti/Shutterstock.com
13.4 Africa Studio/Shutterstock.com

Chapter 14: Making the Purchase
14.1 Travel mania/Shutterstock.com
14.2 Yelena Safronova
14.3 © Cultura RM/Alamy
14.4 Yelena Safronova
14.5 Fairchild Books

Chapter 15: Pricing the Merchandise
15.1 Bikeworldtravel/Shutterstock.com
15.2 fiphoto/Shutterstock.com
15.3 bokmok/Shutterstock.com

INDEX